Understanding Child Maltreatment

UNDERSTANDING CHILD MALTREATMENT

An Ecological and Developmental Perspective

Maria Scannapieco
Kelli Connell-Carrick

OXFORD
UNIVERSITY PRESS

2005

OXFORD
UNIVERSITY PRESS

Oxford   New York
Auckland   Bangkok   Buenos Aires   Cape Town   Chennai
Dar es Salaam   Delhi   Hong Kong   Istanbul   Karachi   Kolkata
Kuala Lumpur   Madrid   Melbourne   Mexico City   Mumbai   Nairobi
São Paulo   Shanghai   Taipei   Tokyo   Toronto

Copyright © 2005 by Oxford University Press, Inc.

Published by Oxford University Press, Inc.
198 Madison Avenue, New York, New York 10016

www.oup.com

Oxford is a registered trademark of Oxford University Press

Library of Congress Cataloging-in-Publication Data
Scannapieco, Maria.
Understanding child maltreatment : an ecological and developmental perspective /
Maria Scannapieco, Kelli Connell-Carrick.
   p. cm.
ISBN-13 978-0-19-515678-2
ISBN 0-19-515678-1
1. Child abuse.   2. Child development.   3. Family assessment.   4. Risk assessment.
5. Family social work.   I. Connell-Carrick, Kelli.   II. Title.
HV6626.5.S33 2005
362.76—dc22   2004012392

9 8 7 6 5 4 3 2 1

Printed in the United States of America
on acid-free paper

To our life partners
Jane Sumner & Matt Carrick

CONTENTS

Understanding Child Maltreatment

1

HISTORY AND DEFINITION OF CHILD MALTREATMENT

Today, too many children are beaten, seriously neglected, sexually abused, and murdered by their parents and caregivers. Every day there are media stories of children who have suffered severely at the hands of a parent, whether they are found in a closet starving to death, drowned in the bathtub at the hand of their mother, or tied to a pole in the basement, beaten, while their dead brother lies in a container. Although these atrocities are the exception to what most children experience in today's world and what child welfare deals with, too many children continue to be harmed at the hands of their caregivers. Unlike in the past, today there are systems in place to protect children, assist families in developing healthier parenting, and punish perpetrators of maltreatment when appropriate. To understand the current state of practice and policy, it is important to reflect on the history of child maltreatment.

The history of childhood prior to the late nineteenth century is littered with tales of murder, burnings, beatings, and sexual exploitation that by today's standards are atrocious. To understand the evolution of childhood—and by extension child maltreatment—it is important to put in perspective the social, political, economic, and religious challenges of the past.

BIBLICAL FOUNDATION

Throughout the centuries, biblical passages have been used to justify the abuse and murder of children by parents and society as reflected in early societal policy and treatment of children (Radbill, 1968; Shepard, 1965). For centuries the Bible has influenced the handling and the status of children in society. It is this Christian religious domination through the nineteenth century that influenced parenting beliefs. Even today the Bible is used as justification for beating children. Proverbs tells us, "He that spareth the rod hateth his son: but he that loveth him chasteneth him betimes," and, "Withhold not correction from the child; for if

3

thou beatest him with the rod, he shall not die. Thou shall beat him with a rod, and shall deliver his soul from Hell." These and many other biblical passages imply or are interpreted by some as support for parental harm to children.

The killing of infants and young children as sacrifice and as punishment is also found throughout the Bible. The book of Judges tells of Jephthah's promise to sacrifice the first person he met when he returned home, should he be victorious in battle. Unfortunately, the first person he saw turned out to be his only daughter. We read of Abraham's intention to sacrifice his first son to God. In Deuteronomy there is a story of parents who take a rebellious son to the elders of the city and tell them, "This our son is stubborn and rebellious, he will not obey our voice; he is a glutton and a drunkard. " The men of the city stone him to death.

This is not to say that the Bible sanctions the beating and killing of children by their parents, but to illustrate rather that the foundation for child rearing and the status of children has biblical roots for western culture. The use of religious beliefs and practices as justification for child maltreatment as a means of child rearing is seen throughout the history of childhood and child maltreatment.

THE HISTORY OF CHILDHOOD

Prior to the nineteenth century in the United States and Europe, childhood was not viewed as a separate phase of human development. It was not seen as qualitatively different from adulthood. Child-rearing experts of the day based their advice on religious, cultural, and societal influences. Social control of the child was paramount, and this was achieved through beating and whipping. Willfulness, defiance, and wickedness was to be driven out of the child as soon as it showed itself, which was during the first year of life. Scholars and religious leaders repeatedly reminded parents that it was impossible to begin teaching obedience too soon. John Wesley, a Methodist leader, urged parents to "break the will of your child, to bring his will into subjection to yours that it may be afterward subject to the will of God" (James & Prout, 1997). Sulzer (1748), as cited in Miller (1983), says that "if parents are fortunate enough to drive out willfulness from the very beginning by means of scolding and the rod, they will have obedient, docile, and good children." Children were viewed as possessions that had to be trained to become faithful servants to their parents.

During this time there was a great deal of immigration combined with swift industrial and urban growth, all of which contributed negatively to the well-being of children (Trattner, 1984). Low wages, especially for immigrants, forced families to place children in the workforce. As a means of economic survival parents treated their children as chattel and forced them into the labor force at very early ages. Wages contributed by children often made the difference between a family ending up in a poorhouse or being independent. Whether laboring in factories, mines, sweatshops, or farms, children worked long hours under horrific conditions, often becoming injured (Katz, 1986).

By the eighteenth century a new attitude toward children and child rearing was emerging. John Locke and other philosophers of the time asserted the innate goodness of the child. Locke attacked the idea of infant depravity and the belief that all children were the same (James & Prout, 1997). Earlier cruel doctrines were being challenged, and by the middle of the nineteenth century children were seen as innately good and corrupted only by an overbearing society (Trattner, 1984). Rousseau, author of the seminal *Emile* (1762) contributed to the notion of the natural goodness of children and the idea that children should be allowed to be children before they are adults. *Emile* directed educators to treat children from both physiological and the psychological perspectives as "little human animals destined for the spiritual and moral life who developed according to certain laws whose progression must be respected above all" (cited in James & Prout, 1997). Children were seen as needing nurturing educational experiences and families that provided affection and support instead of harsh discipline.

The new child psychology caused a shift in the perceived value of children. By the early to mid–nineteenth century, a new construction of childhood was emerging: now childhood was seen as constituting a separate set of characteristics requiring protection and education (James & Prout, 1997). Viviana Zelizer (as cited in Katz, 1986, p. 116) refers to the shift as "the profound transformation in the economic and sentimental value of children . . . that is the emergence of the economically worthless but emotionally priceless child."

By the early twentieth century, the influence of Darwin and evolutionary biology continued to reframe the way people thought about childhood. Darwinism presented a developmental view of human growth and behavior and the influence the environment has on both (Trattner, 1984). G. Stanley Hall (1904), an influential child psychologist, argued that each developmental stage has an integrity of its own, which should be understood by parents and educators. (cited in Katz, 1986). At this time Freud, the founder of psychoanalysis, stressed the importance of nurturance in infancy and childhood for the formation of healthy and productive adults. All of these developments raised the status of the child and influenced child rearing. Many no longer thought that parents needed to "break" their children's willfulness, nor was it seen as acceptable.

The concept of the child was further refined during the latter part of the twentieth century and has culminated in the understanding that childhood matters. Children have cognitive, social, and physical domains that need to be nurtured and encouraged to develop in safe, nonthreatening environments. Childhood is now seen as having an inner world, one that reaches into the unconscious and has significance on adult maturity, on the functioning of the family, and ultimately on the functioning of society (James & Prout, 1997).

Although the social construction of the child and childhood has changed significantly over the centuries and has directly influenced what are acceptable child-rearing practices, parents and caregivers continue to harm or neglect children. It is important that we have a clear understanding of what society today considers to be child abuse and neglect.

CHILD MALTREATMENT HISTORY

The early history of child maltreatment refers to physical abuse and severe physical neglect of children. It does not address sexual abuse or emotional neglect of children. These phenomena were not addressed in the United States until the early 1970s.

Western society did not always formally recognize that children could be maltreated or that they could need protection from their parents. With few exceptions, society's view of children was similar across cultures for two thousand years. Parents had proprietary interest in their children and full rights to raise them without interference. This position dates from the Hammurabi Code, written in ancient Babylon in approximately 2150 B.C.E. Roman law formalized the rights of parents in the Doctrine of *Patria Potestas*, which gave fathers complete and unlimited control of their children for life. This doctrine was in effect between 1753 and 560 B.C.E. (Radbill, 1968).

As covered in the history of childhood, a similar doctrine, law, and philosophy of children and their relationship to their parents continued into the nineteenth century. Children owed their parents respect. If children fulfilled this duty, they were entitled to receive care and be treated well by their parents. If children did not treat their parents with the respect due them, the parents had no responsibility to treat them well and had the duty to bring the child in line through beatings.

Many early "child welfare advocates" tried to help indigent and abandoned children by providing them with shelter and care. Children were housed in generally deplorable conditions in "alms" or poorhouses with other indigents, including the mentally ill, mentally retarded, sick, aged, and criminals. "Many almshouses were vile catchalls for victims of every sort of misery, misfortune, and misconduct who were herded together and badly mistreated. The tales of uneducated, half-starved, tear-stained young outcasts in these wretched institutions, where, due to inadequate diet and lack of proper sanitary facilities, the mortality rates were extremely high, were sorrowful ones" (Trattner, 1984, p. 112).

The doctrine of *parens patriae* (literally, the "state as the father") was introduced into English law to protect the rights of children. It allowed children to "emancipate" into adulthood at age 21 and protected the property rights of minors when the parent was abusing these rights. This doctrine provided justification for later interventions by the state when other abuses in the parent-child relationship occurred (Pfohl, 1977).

U.S. HISTORY

The first major movement in the United States to protect children began during the early 1800s with the House of Refuge movement. *Parens patriae* was the doctrine that drove this movement, which represented the first attempt to intervene on behalf of abused and neglected children. Concurrently, professionals began to recognize that the needs of children could be better met in family settings than in institutions. Although the child welfare philosophy at the time was *rescuing the child from the family*, the preference was to place the child in a family setting. As discussed earlier, this coincided with the industrialization of the United States and with developments in child psychology that emphasized the goodness of the child and the need for supportive families.

The concept of family rehabilitation became the underlying philosophy of child welfare and the foundation for the family-centered child-protection approach that is still the focus of today's practice. This philosophy also bolstered the notion that children would be better served in a family setting, and the foster family home began to replace the orphanage as the primary child placement resource. The rescue of children, however, was still the goal of care.

In 1853, Charles Loring Brace founded the New York Children's Aid Society, the first American children's organization to adopt the foster family home model, or "placing out." Brace was not only concerned about the suffering and needs of children but also about purging the city of what he called the "dangerous classes." He was alarmed over the increasing number of juvenile delinquents and the increased crime rate among young poor children in New York City. Although Brace felt that family life, preferably in the form of good Christian farm families, was the cure for destitute children, he did not support the natural family or family rehabilitation. By the early 1890s child-rescuing strategies were radically changing to favor family preservation.

In 1874, the tragic case of Mary Ellen Wilson brought abused and neglected children into the public eye. Mrs. Wheeler, a volunteer church worker from St. Luke's Methodist Mission, was visiting an elderly woman in the tenements of New York City, when she learned about an eight-year-old girl named Mary Ellen Wilson. Mary Ellen lived with Mary Connolly from the time she was two years old, when the New York City Department of Charities placed her with her alleged biological father, Thomas McCormack, without proper documentation. Mr. McCormack died shortly after and Mary married Francis Connolly and moved to a tenement on West 41st Street.

Neighbors, who could not bear the sounds of Mary Ellen's screams from being frequently beaten, reported their concerns to Mrs. Wheeler. Although New York City had a law that permitted the state to remove children who were maltreated by their caregiver, authorities told Mrs. Wheeler they would not intervene. Mrs. Wheeler, with nowhere else to turn, went to Henry Bergh of the New York Society for the Prevention of Cruelty to Animals for help. Mr. Bergh sent a NYSPCA investigator to verify the allegations. Acting as a private citizen, and not in his role as president of the NYSPCA, Mr. Bergh had Elbridge T. Gerry, an ASPCA attorney, prepare a petition to remove Mary Ellen from her home so she might testify to her treatment.

Mary Ellen testified that her "mamma has been in the habit of whipping and beating me almost every day. She used to whip me with a twisted whip—a raw hide. The whip always left a black and blue mark on my body. . . . I have never been taken on my mamma's lap . . . I do not want to go back to live with mamma, because she beats me so" (Watkins, 1990). The judge immediately brought Mary Ellen under court control, and the child's guardian was sentenced to one year in jail. Mary Ellen was eventually placed with Mrs. Wheeler's mother, Sally Angell, on a farm in upstate New York (Lazonitz, 1990; McDaniel & Lescher, 2004).

Mary Ellen Wilson's case set into motion an organized effort to battle child maltreatment. The effort was not simply the result of an awareness that children, like animals, merited protection from cruel treatment; rather, it was an evolutionary step in the movement to protect children from harm while establishing their rights (Costin, 1985).

In 1875, Henry Bergh helped to found the New York Society for the Prevention of Cruelty to Children (NYSPCC) under the leadership of Elbridge Gerry, and thus began a notable movement to protect children from abuse and neglect. By 1900, there were 250 protective agencies across the country. Private, nonprofit societies of prevention like the NYSPCC took responsibility for child-protection efforts through the early twentieth century (McDaniel & Lescher, 2004).

Child welfare services were first addressed by public policy in the early 1900s. In 1909, the first White House Conference on Dependent Children was held to share ideas about dependent children and recommend a general plan for their care (Costin, Karger, & Stoesz, 1996; Trattner, 1984). Great emphasis was placed on family and home life and a rejection by most of institutional care for children.

As a result of the support generated at the conference, the U.S. Children's Bureau was established in 1912 to represent the interests of children. This was the first recognition that the federal government had a role in children's protection and well-being. The bureau quickly became the authority on child protection, although it did not deal with individual cases of maltreatment. Many public and private child welfare agencies were established to investigate and treat maltreated children.

In 1935, the Social Security Act mandated that states strengthen their child welfare services and focused on dependent, neglected children. It emphasized and mandated intervention but did not address the identification and prevention of child maltreatment.

It was not until the mid–twentieth century that the medical profession entered the fight. One of the first physicians to speak out was John Caffey of Columbia University. In 1946, Caffey commented on children who had unexplained fractures and subdural hematomas, and speculated that they may have been inflicted by the parents. In the early 1960s, Dr. C. Henry Kempe and his associates identified the battered child syndrome and published their research findings (Kempe, 1962). The research described the scope of child abuse. The report shocked many medical and social service professionals. The identification of battered child syndrome drew significant attention to the problem.

Throughout the 1960s and 1970s, research continued to explore the extent and etiology of child abuse and neglect. By the early 1970s, the need for federal intervention was paramount. In 1974, the Child Abuse Prevention and Treatment Act (CAPTA, PL 93-247) was passed. The act specified that states would be required to adopt specific procedures to identify, treat, and prevent child abuse. It provided for demonstration projects to prevent, identify, and treat child abuse and neglect; and it established the National Center on Child Abuse and Neglect that would be responsible for research and for distribution of training materials, and that would serve as a clearinghouse.

As a result of the CAPTA legislation, a formal public child protection service Child Protection Services, was established in each state to protect children from abuse and neglect. There was a dramatic increase in the number of investigations and in the number of children and families served in the child welfare system after CAPTA's enactment.

Since then, significant progress has been made on bringing policy, research, and practice attention to child maltreatment. Child welfare legislation has addressed many critical issues in the delivery of services to children who have experienced abuse or neglect. Following are the key pieces of legislation that directly impact services to maltreated children and give states direction on intervening with families:

THE INDIAN CHILD WELFARE ACT (ICWA) OF 1978 (PL 95-608)

- Was meant to promote the stability of American Indian tribes and families and to strengthen American Indian sovereignty by restoring child placement decisions to the individual tribes.
- Recognized tribal courts as having jurisdiction in child welfare issues involving American Indians and mandated that case decisions be released to tribal courts or include involvement of tribal child welfare staff in decision making.
- Mandated an end to out-of culture placements of American Indian children by specifying placement preferences for members of child's extended family or child's tribe or other American Indians.
- Mandated that termination of parental rights and custody cases of American Indian children require the highest standards of proof, namely, "beyond a reasonable doubt" as opposed to "clear and convincing" evidence.
- Mandated that both parents and tribes have the right to be notified of any proceedings. In order to do this, child welfare agencies must spend time determining tribal affiliations.
- Authorized grants to Indian tribes and organizations must provide a mechanism for "Indian-delivered" preventive services.
- NOTE: American Indian children are exempted from later legislation: MEPA of 1994.

THE ADOPTION ASSISTANCE AND CHILD WELFARE ACT (AACWA) OF 1980 (PL 96-272)

- Through funding regulations, the act discouraged state use of custodial foster care while supporting permanency planning for children unable to remain with their own families.
- Promoted the goal of permanency for each child by providing supports to families in order to prevent separation of children from their families and prevent children from spending unnecessarily long periods in foster care with no real plan for reunification with their families.
- Mandated that child welfare agencies implement preplacement preventive services and family reunification programs to keep children with biological families.
- Emphasized providing children with continuity of care and a respected social status through time limits.

Implemented time-limited case plans where family preservation was not possible.

Established a deadline of 18 months for making a permanent plan for a child.

Required a periodic case review (every 6 months) and a dispositional hearing within 18 months.

Provided adoption subsidies for children with special needs or low-income, hard-to-place children.

THE MULTI-ETHNIC PLACEMENT ACT (MEPA) OF 1994 (PL103-382)

Intended to prevent discrimination on the basis of race, color, or national origin by eliminating policies that favored same-race placements and removing prior language in child welfare law that explicitly included race and ethnicity as factors used to determine the best interests of the child.

Prohibited agencies that receive federal funds from making foster care and adoption placement decisions routinely on the basis of race, culture, and ethnicity.

Prohibited the denial of an opportunity to become a foster or adoptive parent on the basis of the race of either parent or child.

Intended to decrease the length of time children wait for adoption or placement with a foster family.

Amended by the Interethnic Adoption Provisions of 1996 to remove potentially misleading language in the original provisions of the MEPA and clarify that discrimination will not be tolerated.

ADOPTION AND SAFE FAMILIES ACT (ASFA) OF 1997 (PL 105-89)

Placed child safety as a paramount concern by clarifying and updating the AACWA of 1980 through policies to improve the safety of children, promote adoption and other permanent homes, and support families.

Required a more timely achievement of a permanent living situation and parenting arrangement for children.

Set a new time frame for a permanency planning hearing to occur within 12 months of a child's entry into out-of-home care. Required that states file petitions to terminate parental rights at an earlier time.

Encouraged the use of concurrent planning: agencies were encouraged to engage in reunification and adoption planning at the same time.

Encouraged the use of time-limited reunification services, for children and families, such as temporary child care, crisis nurseries, and transportation for services.

Required states to provide health insurance coverage for any child with special needs for whom there is an adoption agreement.

Continued Adoption Assistance subsidies even if adoption is disrupted.

(Brooks et al., 1999; Karger & Stoesz, 1996; Pecora, Whittaker, Maluccio, & Barth, 2000; USDHHS, 2001)

The values and focus of the child maltreatment field have undergone significant changes during the past 100 years. The needs of families and children are complex, and the child maltreatment field has been given considerable responsibility for addressing the many social and environmental problems that contribute to the abuse and neglect of children. New problems, including an increase in drug use and abuse, children with AIDS, and a high percentage of "unruly" adolescents whose backgrounds include abuse, neglect, and sexual abuse, continue to challenge us.

DEFINITION OF CHILD MALTREATMENT

Definitions of child abuse and neglect are based on current reflections of society's values of appropriate child rearing. What we consider abuse today was not viewed as such prior to 1960 and may well change in future decades. Furthermore, cultural implications must be considered when determining if child maltreatment has occurred. Child maltreatment can be defined on a variety of levels: individual, family, community, and societal. A discussion can be found in the literature Pecora, et al. The scope of this work is to assess maltreatment from an individual and family perspective, although the ecological correlates—which include individual and family but also interaction with social systems and societal values—of maltreatment will be considered throughout.

One significant difficulty facing workers is a lack of commonly agreed-upon definitions of the various types of maltreatment. (Giovannoni, 1989). It is unlikely that a universally adequate definition will be constructed, (Ammerman, 1990). With this in mind, legislation is drawn upon to conceptualize a definition of maltreatment. The Federal Child Abuse Protection and Treatment Act (CAPTA, P.L. 93-23/47) provides general guidelines for defining abuse and neglect and is the basis for many state laws. CAPTA, which was amended by Public Law 104-235 in 1996, defines child maltreatment as:

> Any recent act or failure to act resulting in imminent risk of serious harm, death, serious physical or emotional harm, sexual abuse, or exploitation of a child (minor age as described by state statutes) by a parent or caretaker (including out-of-home care providers) who are responsible for the child's welfare." (as cited in F. F. Ferrara, 2002, p. 34)

Each state is responsible to more specifically define the parameters of abuse and neglect through state statutes.

Child maltreatment falls into four broad categories: (1) physical abuse, (2) sexual abuse, (3) neglect, and (4) emotional abuse. State child protection agencies or researchers have largely identified subcategories within each broad category. Each of these subtypes of child abuse will be discussed separately.

Physical Abuse

Although physical abuse is somewhat more straightforward than the other subtypes, there is still some ambiguity based on cultural, community, and societal factors. Generally, physical abuse is defined as the nonaccidental injury inflicted by a caregiver on a child 17 years old or younger. At times, accidental injury may be looked at to determine if neglect has occurred. The definition used in the *Third National Incidence Study of Child Abuse and Neglect* (NIS-3) (Sedlak & Broadhurst, 1996) defined physical abuse as present when a child younger than 18 years of age has experienced an injury or risk of an injury as a result of having been hit with a hand or other object or having been kicked, shaken, thrown, burned, stabbed, or choked by a parent or parent-surrogate (as cited in Kolko, 2002). Physical abuse also includes a rare form called Munchausen by proxy, in which a caregiver will pretend or induce illness in a child in order to attract medical attention.

Some cultural practices may be seen as physical abuse but are not, when viewed within the context of that culture. For example, some Asian cultures use the rubbing of hot coins on a child's back to alleviate an illness. This may leave marks but due to the context would not be considered abuse.

The injury alone is not enough to determine maltreatment. A number of factors need to be considered when determining if the injury is a result of physical abuse.

> *The child's level of development.* It takes a certain level of physical development for children to injure themselves. The developmental stage of the child must be considered when determining if an injury is a result of physical abuse.
>
> *The pattern and size of the injury.* From the pattern of a bruise injury, we can often determine what instrument/object was used to create it.
>
> *The location of the injury.* In looking at the location of the bruise/abrasion/mark, unintentional or accidental injuries of this nature generally occur to the front of the body because our bodies have defense mechanisms forward, and on areas of the skin over bony prominences, with the knees and shins being the most common areas. Trauma to the soft, unsupported tissues of the body such as the cheeks are more often due to intentional action, such as slapping or pinching, as well as face and head injuries to a young child. Symmetrical injuries might also be indicative of abuse.
>
> *Caregiver's explanation of the injury.* The parents' explanation of the injury should be assessed in the context of the actual circumstances. A 3-month-old child can not accidentially fall out of a crib on his own. If the parents' explanation does not logically meet the injury, it may be an indication of abuse.

Sexual Abuse

Definitions of child sexual abuse vary by what ages, acts, and types of relationships are included. They can also vary based on the purpose of the definition, whether it is for research, practice, or policy. Generally speaking, sexual abuse involves any sexual activity with a child where consent is not or cannot be given (Berliner & Elliott, 2002). A more specific definition given by Sgroi, Blick & Porter (1982, p. 9) is as follows:

Child sexual abuse is a sexual act imposed on a child who lacks emotional, maturational, and cognitive development. The ability to lure a child into a sexual relationship is based upon the all-powerful and dominant position of the adult or older adolescent perpetrator, which is in sharp contrast to the child's age, dependency, and subordinate position. Authority and power enable the perpetrator, implicitly or directly, to coerce the child into sexual compliance.

As in all definitions of child maltreatment, the federal government gives guidance to the states through CAPTA (as amended in 1996, PL 104-235), which has defined sexual abuse to include:

> Employment, use, persuasion, inducement, enticement or coercion of any child to engage in, or assist any other person to engage in, any sexually explicit conduct or any simulation of such conduct for the purpose of producing any visual depiction of such conduct; or rape, and in cases of caretaker or inter-familial relationships, statutory rape, molestation, prostitution, or other form of sexual exploitation of children or incest with children. (as cited in Ferrara, 2002, pp. 34–35)

Each state proscribes sexual abuse of children and defines criminal and prohibited activities individually. States will vary based on individual statutes, both for child protective and criminal purposes. This variation will take the form of differences in age of consent (14 to 18 years); the age difference between perpetrator and child (usually at least five years); type of relationship (some states only include acts committed by a caregiver); and type of activities (some will not include noncontact type of offenses).

There is also a distinction made between incest and sexual molestation. Incest is generally defined as sexual abuse that occurs between family members (parents, grandparents, siblings, aunts, or uncles) or surrogate parent figures (foster parents or paramours). Intrafamilial sexual abuse, another term for incest, is characterized by the psychosocial dynamic of the familial relationship, which should be extended to the kinship role, regardless of blood ties. A nonrelated stranger or nonfamily member to the child commits sexual molestation, or extrafamilial sexual abuse. Neighbors, family friends, clergy, older children, and other types of individuals commit sexual molestation.

There is a continuum of sexual activities between a perpetrator and a child that constitutes sexual abuse. The offending person can be an adult or older child. These activities range from noncontact abuse to contact and are as follows:

Noncontact sexual abuse may include:

Exhibitionism. These indicators must be considered in relation to the cultural norms of the family.

- Nudity: The offender parades nude around the house in front of all or some of the family members.
- Disrobing. The offender disrobes in front of the child.
- Genital exposure. The offender exposes his or her genitals to the child.

Voyeurism. The offender secretly or overtly watches the child undress, bath, excrete, and urinate for purposes of sexual gratification.

Contact sexual abuse includes:

Kissing. The offender kisses the child in a lingering and intimate way.

Fondling. The offender touches, caresses, or rubs the child's breasts, abdomen, genital area, inner thighs, or buttocks, or the child similarly touches the offender's body.

Masturbation. The offender masturbates while the child watches or vice versa. The offender masturbates the child or has the child masturbate him/her.

Fellatio. Requires the offender or child to take a male penis into his or her mouth.

Cunnilingus. Requires the offender or child to place mouth and tongue on the vulva or in the vaginal area.

Vaginal or anal intercourse. This involves penetration of the vagina or anus with a finger, object, or penis.

Dry intercourse or simulated. This is when an offender rubs his penis against the child's genital-rectal area or inner thighs or buttocks.

Child pornography. Considered sexual abuse when it involves the use of pictures, videotape, or film depicting graphically specific sexual acts between offenders and children, or children (Pecora et al., 2000; Sgroi et al., 1982).

Child Neglect

Although the federally legislated definitions of maltreatment represent overall conceptual guidance to practice, policy, and research, they lack precision, dimensionality, and operationalization. In two recent reviews of definitional issues related to child neglect that cover the literature from 1964 to 1996, Zuravin (1999) and Berrick (1997) set forth a number of critical domains that need to be considered in the explication of child neglect. Dubowitz (1999) discusses similar definitional issues as they relate to medical neglect.

Statutory Definitions or Independently Derived Definitions for Research Purposes

Zuravin (1999) reviews the debate that initially started in 1980 with Ross and Zigler's recommendation that separate standardized definitions be developed for legal, clinical, social service, and research purposes. Ross and Zigler thought that this would facilitate accurate communication about child abuse. Opponents of this position argued that research would have no relevance to existing social policy and that research should operate from universal operational definitions.

Broad or Narrow Definitions of Neglect

Should neglect be viewed only by whether harm to the child is evident, or should it represent threats to the long-term development of the child? (Zuravin, 1999). Throughout the literature, this concern arises. Many of the issues seem to focus on whether to allow child protection services (CPS) workers, judges, doctors, and others discretion in making decisions. Part of the issue is states have the discretion to determine whether the definition will be broad or narrow. The broader the definition, the more latitude there is in making judgment assessments. This is viewed as a concern when there is not an emphasis on professionalization of child welfare and workers rely more on personal discretion than professional decision making (Berrick, 1997).

Parental Behavior or Consequences to the Child, or Both

Focusing on parental behavior was seen as a way to get needed early intervention and prevention services to families and children. This approach allowed for a broader interpretation of neglect. It also assumed that parental behavior is predictive of future harm to the child. According to Berrick, there is much disagreement about this assumption. Some argue that, particularly with neglect, parental behavior must be used as an indicator, since the sequelae of neglect are not immediately apparent.

The effects of the acts of omission are difficult to measure empirically, and this has caused many authors to advocate for defining neglect in terms of harm to the child (Berrick, 1997) and whether the child's basic needs are met (Dubowitz, 1999). Definitions of harm to the child range from evidence of immediate harm to a child's psychological well-being (Berrick, 1997) to indicators of behavioral difficulties. The issues concerning intentions of the parent and placing blame are minimized.

For the purposes of this book, physical and emotional neglect will be reviewed from both the perspective of consequences to the child and parental behavior. Focusing on neglect requires this dual perspective, since developmental outcomes for the child may not be observable for years.

Child Physical Neglect

Child physical neglect is seen as an act of omission by a caregiver responsible for the child, whether intentional or not, that results in physical, emotional, social, or cognitive harm, either presently or in the future. Many variations in the definition of neglect exist in the literature and subtypes can be found, but no definite consensus exists. Some researchers have divided neglect into subcategories of physical, emotional, or both (Gustavsson & Segal, 1994), while others have divided neglect into physical, emotional, medical, mental health, and educational subcategories (Erickson & Egeland, 2002).

Zuravin (1991) provides one of the most comprehensive sets of definitions for child neglect, including eight types of omissions in care by caregivers that may or do result in physical, emotional, social, and/or cognitive harm to the child or harm to others or property. The eight categories are:

1. *Physical health care.* Failure to obtain or a delay in obtaining medical attention for acute illnesses, injuries, physical disabilities, and chronic problems, or failure to comply with professional recommendations (medical, school, or social work regarding treatment).
2. *Mental health care.* Failure to obtain or delay in obtaining professional attention for *obvious* mental health problems and developmental

problems; or failure to comply with professional recommendations regarding treatment.

3. *Supervision*. Inadequate supervision of child activities both inside and outside of the home—parent is in the home with the child but is not monitoring the child's activities closely enough to keep the child from behaving in ways that could have negative consequences for the child, others, and/or property, or parent is not aware enough of the child's activities when he/she is out of the home to assure that the child is not at risk for negative personal consequences or engaging in behavior that could harm others or others' property; includes truancy, being consistently late for school, and failure to enroll in school.

4. *Substitute child care*. Abandons child; leaves child alone to fend for him/herself; leaves child in the care of an inappropriate caretaker; leaves child with any caretaker for more than 48 hours without either telling the caretaker in advance that the child will remain for 2 days or calling during the first 2 days.

5. *Housing hazards*. For example, leaking gas from stove or heating unit, hot water/steam leaks from radiators, dangerous substances (household cleaning agents, insect and rodent poisons, medications, anything that if swallowed could cause death or serious illness), and dangerous objects (guns and knives) stored in unlocked lower shelves or cabinets, under sink, or in the open, etc.)

6. *Household sanitation*. Garbage is not kept in a receptacle but instead is strewn around the house or kept in bags that are rarely taken away; perishable foods are not refrigerated and are frequently found spoiling; roaches, mice, and/or rats are frequently seen in the home; toilets are not functioning, with human excrement spilling on floor; animal excrement is visible around the house, etc.

7. *Personal hygiene*. Constant and consistent inattention to child's personal hygiene (e.g., child's hair is matted or tangled and dirty; child's skin is dirty; child's teeth are encrusted with green or brown matter; infant/toddler's soiled diapers are not changed for hours/days; child's clothes, which are soiled and stained beyond cleaning, are worn for days).

8. *Nutrition*. Failure to provide regular and ample meals that meet basic nutritional requirements (meals have not been provided at all for several days, children eat spoiled food or nonfood items like starch, dog food, or cat food, or are frequently seen begging for food) and failure to provide the necessary rehabilitative diet to a child with particular types of physical health problems (lead poisoning, severe diarrhea, etc.).

Emotional or Psychological Abuse

Emotional abuse of children occurs in all forms of maltreatment and an individual phenomenon, but it remains one of the most difficult forms of maltreatment to define and measure. The term *psychological abuse* is preferred because it encompasses cognitive and affective meanings of maltreatment, as well as acts of omission and commission by the perpetrator (Hart et al., 2002; O'Hagan, 1993). In CAPTA, 1974, psychological maltreatment was captured under the term *mental injury*. Since that time there has been a great effort to better characterize psychological abuse (APSAC, 1995; Garbarino, Guttman, & Seeley, 1986).

A broad definition of psychological maltreatment presented by the American Professional Society on the Abuse of Children (APSAC) (1995, p. 2) is as follows: "Psychological maltreatment means a repeated pattern of caregiver behavior or extreme incident(s) that convey to children that they are worthless, flawed, unloved, unwanted, endangered, or only of value in meeting another's needs."

The International Conference on Psychological Abuse of Children and Youth (1983) developed this definition:

> Psychological maltreatment of children and youth consists of acts of omission and commission, which are judged on the basis of a combination of community standards and professional expertise to be psychologically damaging. Individuals commit such acts, singly or collectively; who by their characteristics (e.g., age, status, knowledge, and organizational form) are in a position of differential power that renders a child vulnerable. Such acts damage immediately or ultimately the behavioral, cognitive, affective, or physical functioning of the child. (as cited in Hart et al., 2002)

One of the most widely used categorizations of the activities subsumed in psychological maltreatment was developed by Garbarino, Guttman, and Seeley (1986). Behaviors included are:

Rejecting. The adult refuses to acknowledge the child's worth and legitimacy of the child's needs.

Isolating. The adult cuts the child off from normal social experiences, prevents the child from forming friendships, and makes the child believe that he or she is alone in the world.

Terrorizing. The adult verbally assaults the child, creates a climate of fear, bullies and frightens the child, and makes the child believe that the world is capricious and hostile.

Ignoring. The adult deprives the child of essential stimulation and responsiveness, stifling emotional growth and intellectual development.

Corrupting. The adult "mis-socializes" the child, stimulates the child to engage in destructive antisocial behavior, reinforces the deviance, and makes the child unfit for normal social experience.

Other forms of psychological abuse that have been identified include destroying personal possessions and torturing or destroying a pet (Wiehe, 1990) and degrading and denying emotional responsiveness (Hart et al., 2002).

SCOPE OF CHILD MALTREATMENT TODAY

Child abuse and neglect is a persistent national problem. Data provided from two national studies underscore its pervasiveness. The Child Maltreatment 2002 Report (CM-2002) presents national data about child abuse and neglect that was known to CPS agencies in 2002. The Third National Incidence Study of Child Abuse and Neglect (NIS-3) presents data from a nationally representative sample collected in 1993 and 1994 from various community agencies and professionals. This report includes data from CPS agencies, as well as data on children seen by community professionals who were not reported to CPS or who were screened out by CPS.

In order to make sense of the data, it is important to properly define the standards used in these studies. The CM-2002 study considered children as victims of child maltreatment if they were found to have experienced or to have been at risk of experiencing abuse or neglect after having been subjects of an investigation or assessment. The NIS-3 report, on the other hand, does not focus on whether children's cases were investigated. It used two different standards to decide whether to include a case of maltreatment. The first, more rigid standard is the *harm standard*. Under this standard children are considered maltreated only if they had already experienced harm from the abuse or neglect. The second standard is the *endangerment standard*, which considered children maltreated if they experienced abuse or neglect that put them at risk of harm.

Reports of Maltreatment

The CM-2002 notes that in 2002, two-thirds (an estimated 1,726,000) of referrals were screened in as needing an investigation or assessment by CPS agencies. Of these screened-in referrals, 56.1% came from "professionals" such as educators, legal and law enforcement, social services, and medical personnel. The most common sources of reports were from education personnel (16.1%). The other 43.9 % of referrals came from parents, relatives, friends, and neighbors.

The NIS-3 points to similar report sources. Overall, school staff was the predominant source of recognition of maltreated children under both the harm standard (59% of recognized children) and the endangerment standard (54%). The NIS-3 also notes that other important sources of maltreatment recognition were hospitals, police departments, social service agencies, and the general public.

Types of Maltreatment

According to the CM-2002, almost three million children were the subjects of a CPS investigation or assessment in 2002. Approximately 30 percent of these were found "to have experienced or to have been at risk of experiencing abuse or neglect" (p. 23). This 30 percent of children are considered victims of child maltreatment. The estimate for the total number of victims in 2002 is 879,000.

Table 1.1 shows the number of children found by CPS to have been *victims* of child maltreatment. The numbers for neglect in the tables include both the general neglect and the medical neglect categories. The table totals reflect the reported numbers based on 49 reporting states and not the CM-2002 general estimate (879,000), which includes all 50 states.

Overall, using the harm standard, the NIS-3 reports that 743,200 children were abused and 879,000 children were neglected during 1993 and 1994. The NIS-3

Table 1.1 CPS Victims of Child Maltreatment

Type of Maltreatment	CPS Victims 2000		CPS Victims 1996–2000	
	Number of Victims	Percentage of Victims	Number of Victims	Percentage of Victims
Physical Abuse	166,232	19.3	949,789	22.7
Neglect	541,242	62.8	2,453,653	58.8
Sexual Abuse	87,480	10.1	490,013	11.7
Emotional Maltreatment	66,293	7.7	281,634	6.7
Total Victims	861,247		4,175,089	

reports include slightly different categories. Neglect is broken down into physical and emotional neglect. Table 1.2 presents figures using both the harm standard and the endangerment standard. Of note is the fact that the endangerment standard broadens the scope of the report. Consequently, numbers presented under this standard include those presented under the harm standard.

When comparing the reports, it is evident that neglect is the most common type of maltreatment, followed by physical abuse. The reports had mixed results in terms of the degree of emotional and sexual abuse. This is probably due to differences in the definition of emotional abuse under both reports.

Response by Agency

As noted above, the CM-2002 reports that CPS agencies screened in 61.7% (estimated 1,726,000) referrals in 2002. This means that 38.3% (estimated 1,070,000) of referrals were screened out and not investigated by CPS. According to the NIS-3, CPS investigated only 28% of recognized children in their data who met the harm standard. Overall, CPS investigated only 33% of children whose maltreatment met the endangerment standard based on NIS-3 data. It is, of course, important to note that there is a seven-year difference between reports. Nonetheless, it is

Table 1.2 NIS-3 Reports of Child Maltreatment

Type of Maltreatment	Using Harm Standard		Using Endangerment Standard	
	Number of Children	Percentage	Number of Children	Percentage
Physical Abuse	381,700	33.2	614,100	18.2
Physical Neglect	338,900	29.4	1,335,100	39.7
Emotional Neglect	212,800	18.5	585,100	17.4
Sexual Abuse	217,700	18.9	300,200	8.9
Emotional Abuse	Not Available		532,200	15.8
Total	1,151,100		3,366,700	

noteworthy that the figures represent a substantial difference in the percent of children being investigated.

Additionally, NIS-3 reported drops in the number of investigations from their prior reports. Specifically, the percent of children receiving investigation using the harm standard dropped from 44% in NIS-2 (1986) to 28% in NIS-3, and from 51% in NIS-2 using the endangerment standard to 33% in NIS-3. The NIS-3 report does note that the numbers of countable children investigated by CPS remained stable. The NIS-3 includes other significant figures. For example, schools recognized the largest number of children maltreated under the harm standard, but only 16% of these children were investigated by CPS. Furthermore, CPS investigated only 26% of children found to be seriously injured and 26% of those found to be moderately injured by their reporting source. The percent of those who received CPS investigations represented less than one-half of the maltreated children in all categories of maltreatment except fatalities.

In terms of actual response based on investigation, the CM-2002 reports that 1,863,556 children and 643,093 families received CPS preventive services in 2002. The CM-2002 report also includes data on receipt of postinvestigative services. Victims of multiple maltreatments were more than twice as likely to receive services as victims of physical abuse only. Furthermore, victims of sexual abuse were less likely than victims of any other type of maltreatment to receive services.

Recidivism

The NIS-3 does not provide information on recidivism; however, the CM-2002 does. According to the CM-2002, recurrence is defined as having a second incident within a 6-month period. Overall, 8.6% of abuse or neglect victims had a recurrence within 6 months. Furthermore, neglected children were 27% more likely to experience recurrence than those who experienced physical abuse. Also, sexual abuse was less likely to recur than physical abuse and neglect.

Child Fatality

Child fatality is not discussed extensively in the NIS-3. However, the report does note that the incidence of fatally injured girls had declined slightly since its prior NIS-2 (1986) study, while incidence of fatally injured boys rose. The CM-2002 report, on the other hand, has data on child fatalities. The rate estimate for the year 2002 is 1,400 child deaths from abuse and neglect. Based on a sample of N = 708 for the year 2002, Table 1.3 shows a breakdown of fatalities based on type of abuse.

CONCLUSION

This chapter has given a historical and current overview of the issues surrounding child maltreatment. Definitions of the types of maltreatment were presented and will be referred to throughout the book. Evidence was provided to support

Table 1.3 Child Fatalities by Type of Abuse

Type of Maltreatment	Number of Fatalities	Percentage
Neglect Only Fatalities	247	34.9
Physical Abuse Only	197	27.8
Physical Abuse and Neglect	157	22.2
Neglect and Any Maltreatment	32	4.5
Physical Abuse and Any Maltreatment	28	4.0
Any Type Except Physical and Neglect	12	1.7
Unknown Type of Maltreatment	35	4.9
Total	708	

the recognition that physical and sexual abuse and neglect, in all their forms, are prevalent in our world. We need strategies to identify, combat, and treat families and children who are experiencing child maltreatment.

In this context, the book will focus on the developmental consequences of child maltreatment and present an ecological and developmental assessment framework that views child maltreatment in a complex web of transacting systems. Intervention strategies are offered that focus on the developmental stage the child/ren are experiencing and based on the nature of the maltreatment.

Chapter 2 will present the overall theoretical and philosophical framework for the book.

2

THEORETICAL OVERVIEW
OF UNDERSTANDING CHILD MALTREATMENT

Since the growing awareness of child maltreatment in the 1960s, the professional literature has amassed and attempted to give us a clearer understanding of the etiology of child physical abuse, sexual abuse, and neglect. Child maltreatment encompasses many variations in its causes, outcomes, and treatment. Families and children that experience the different forms of maltreatment are not similar and need to be assessed and treated in a manner that will maximize their strengths and at the same time assure the safety and well-being of the child. In order to recognize child maltreatment as a multifaceted problem, a comprehensive theoretical approach is required, one that takes into account ecological risk factors, at varying systemic levels, and the transactions within each developmental stage of the child. The two major theoretical frameworks that are the foundation for understanding and treating child maltreatment are the ecological and the developmental perspectives. An ecological perspective allows for an interactional and conceptual understanding of human behavior and social functioning. A developmental perspective provides a framework for understanding growth and functioning of children in the context of the family. It views adaptive and maladaptive behaviors through developmental processes and how they relate to child maltreatment. In this chapter we will present an overview of these perspectives; we incorporate both frameworks in subsequent chapters.

Effective assessment and treatment of child maltreatment, by its nature, must take place within the context of the family. The family-centered focus has been emphasized as the most appropriate when working in the field of child maltreatment (DePanfilis, 1999; Gaudin, 1993; Pecora et al., 2000). As indicated in chapter 1, it is the center of all current child welfare policy. To respect the uniqueness of all families, three guiding principles underlie assessment and intervention with families who have maltreated their children: a family-centered principle; a strengths-based principle; and a cultural responsiveness principle. These principles must be integrated within the ecological and developmental framework. In this chapter key components of each principle will be highlighted. They should be used as a lens when considering all discussions of assessment and intervention throughout the book.

ECOLOGICAL AND DEVELOPMENTAL PERSPECTIVE

An ecological and developmental understanding of child maltreatment requires insight into the theoretical models that have been used to explain this complex phenomenon. The ecological model places an individual in an interdependent relationship with the culture and situation, where one influences the other. Developmental theories outline physical, social, emotional, and psychological development during critical periods throughout one's life. Therefore, development is affected by one's ecology and life experience, which makes an exploration of theoretical models of child maltreatment and development necessary. Additionally, any insight into child maltreatment requires an understanding of attachment theory, which helps explain the generational aspect of maltreatment. This chapter will first discuss historical and current theories of child maltreatment from psychological theories to more comprehensive theories. The second part of this chapter presents the ecological and developmental perspective on which this book is based.

THEORIES OF CHILD MALTREATMENT

All social scientists use conceptual frameworks, whether formal or informal, to guide their work (Tzeng & Jackson, 1990). Tzeng, Jackson, and Karlson (1991), in an analysis of 46 child abuse and neglect theories, found that the historical evolution of maltreatment theory falls into four progressive stages. The first is the "speculation" period of the 1960s when the phenomenon of child abuse and neglect first came into public awareness. The second is the "introspection" period of the 1970s when unidimensionality theories were prevalent; third is the "diversity" period that explored more ecologically based theoretical explanations. The 1990s was classified as "multidisciplinary integration" with the embrace of the ecological/transactional theory that guides much of maltreatment practice and research today. As the body of knowledge of child maltreatment matures, the methods and strategies to assess, treat, and research child abuse and neglect have also evolved.

Child maltreatment has largely been linked as one concept even though there are marked differences in the definitions of the types of maltreatment. Little attention has been devoted to the differences between different types of abuse and neglect in theoretical literature and empirical studies, and theoretical models have focused on the concept of child maltreatment as a whole. Despite the fact that different factors contribute to the absence of a behavior (e.g., neglect), compared to the act of a behavior (e.g., physical abuse), the theoretical and empirical research largely link child abuse and neglect together as a single phenomenon (Wolock & Horowitz, 1984). Thus, the theoretical discussion presented in this chapter focuses on child maltreatment as a single concept.

Since Kempe and his colleagues (1962) coined the term *battered child syndrome*, many theories have been used to explain child maltreatment. Prior to the 1970s, most of the theoretical models focused on one-dimensional and linear constructs, beginning with psychopathology and then broadening to other social factors (Garbarino, 1977; Garbarino & Gilliam, 1980). Since the 1980s, the theoretical viewpoint of maltreatment has focused primarily on two etiological theories: the ecological model (Belsky, 1980) and the transactional model (Cicchetti & Rizley, 1981).

What separates the ecological and transactional models from other theoretical models is their deviation from single-focused processes to holistic and multilevel explanations. The major problem with single-focused theories is that they fail to explain the exceptions. That is, they fail to explain the socially disadvantaged families that do not maltreat their children (Buchanan, 1996). The ecological/transactional model, however, places an individual in an interdependent relationship with the culture and situation. In order to understand child maltreatment, an exploration of all the levels is necessary. This chapter presents the major theoretical models that have been used in determining the etiology of child maltreatment, with special focus on the ecological/transactional model.

HISTORICAL MODELS OF CHILD MALTREATMENT

Kempe and his colleagues' landmark paper on child abuse brought child maltreatment to the attention of the public and research community as a major social issue. Since that time, the professions of medicine, psychology, sociology, and social work have been trying to identify the etiology of child maltreatment. The major theories that have been offered to identify the causes of maltreatment fall into four broad categories: (1) psychological, (2) sociological, (3) social learning, and (4) ecological. Each category contributes to a better understanding of maltreatment, and the ecological model incorporates to some degree components of each (Pecora et al., 2000). While no one theory has been identified as a conclusive unifying framework—largely due to the inability to empirically test them—the ecological/transactional model is widely embraced due in part to its integration of many theoretical perspectives (Cicchetti & Rizley, 1981; Carolson et al., 1989; Cicchetti & Lynch, 1993; Pecora et al., 2000).

Psychological Models

During the 1960s parental psychopathology was identified as the leading cause of child maltreatment (Ammerman, 1990). The parental psychopathology view suggests that parents who maltreat have a clinically diagnosable mental condition, such as a personality disorder or psychosis. This idea grew primarily out of the connotation associated with the term *battered child syndrome*, indicating a narrow connection of parent-as-perpetrator with an "illness" (Spinetta & Rigler, 1972). This linear view fit well with the contemporary philosophy that personality traits determine human behavior (Buchanan, 1996), but it was eventually refuted due to a lack of supporting research. Research that compared abusive and nonabusive parents showed no abusive personality type (Ammerman, 1990), and only a small percentage of those who maltreated experienced any psychopathologic disorder (Kempe & Kempe, 1978). More importantly, when this theory has been applied in researching child maltreatment, methodological problems prevail, such as inadequate control groups and weak dependent measures (Nash et al., 1993). Beyond psychiatric illness, however, parents may find it difficult to parent when they do not have their own needs met. Even without a mental illness, a parent who cannot sufficiently meet her/his own needs or is excessively needy may be unable to meet the needs of her/his own child. Lacking supporting research to fully explain psychological influences on maltreatment, a theoretical exploration of child maltreatment continued.

Sociological Models

Sociological models of child maltreatment emphasize social factors such as poverty, socioeconomic status, social status, isolation, and the acceptance of violence in society as causes of child abuse and neglect. Resource theory, for example, focuses on power differentials in relationships where inequity lies in the economic disparity of the partners. The basic premise is that males have historically been the primary wage earners and therefore hold decision-making power, which is predictive of intimate partner violence (IPV). As a result, IPV is associated, either directly or indirectly, with increased abuse of children (Buchanan, 1996). Strain theory maintains that maltreatment occurs because of society's emphasis on economic success combined with a failure to provide equal opportunity for achieving that success. For example, maltreatment rates are higher in areas plagued with lower incomes and unemployment. Social support is also a component of sociological models of maltreatment. Many families who experience maltreatment have fewer organizational networks to provide support; and they have fewer connections to organizational or social support, which exacerbates stress within the home and creates an environment for abuse or neglect (Giovannoni, 1970).

Much research exploring sociological variables has only been able to show indirect and often weak support for explanations of abuse (Sweet & Resick, 1979). For instance, while economic disadvantage does place children at greater risk of maltreatment, it does not show a causal link between poverty and maltreatment since most families living in poverty neither abuse nor neglect their children. The relationship between sociological variables and maltreatment lacks linear prediction.

Social Learning Theory

Social learning theory (Bandura, 1977) includes many of the aspects of behavioral theory and cognitive theory. Social learning theory provides insight into the generational transmission of maltreatment and acceptance of interpersonal violence through vicarious reinforcement. To clarify, children who are exposed to violence, either directly or indirectly, learn that violent behavior causes a desired response. Additionally, exposure to violence can reinforce children to accept violence as a "normal" and appropriate way to handle situations, express emotions, and resolve conflict. Further, watching violent behavior can lead to repeating that behavior at a later time, referred to as modeling. Daro (1998) adds that children model the behavior around them especially if they identify with the perpetrator. This can carry through to adulthood, as well as into one's own parenting practices. In light of this, however, social learning theory lacks explanatory power since it is easily refuted with the awareness that many individuals who witness or experience violence fail to become perpetrators of violence.

While psychological, sociological, and social learning theories provide insight into child maltreatment, they fail to singularly render the multidimensional and complex explanation of maltreatment that is necessary to understand the phenomenon. They fail to explain the exception, and therefore any single microtheory is inadequate. Failing to integrate the multiple determinants of maltreatment, researchers began viewing maltreatment from an ecological perspective that integrated individuals, social and cultural factors, and their ecological connections.

Ecological Models

Bronfenbrenner (1979) proposed an ecological perspective on human development, and Belsky (1980) applied the model to child maltreatment. What separates the ecological model from other theoretical models is its deviation from single-focused processes to a transactional and multilevel explanation. Integrative and ecological models of maltreatment have been noted as the best theoretical models for explaining child maltreatment (Garbarino, 1977). Despite limitations in its capacity due to its descriptive nature and its difficulty to test empirically, the ecological model is accepted in the field as the most explanatory model of maltreatment to date. Even with the difficulty in empirical validation, this perspective guides maltreatment research and practice.

Belsky's primary contribution to the ecological framework is the addition of the ontogenic level. The underlying foundation of the ontogenic level was borrowed from the 1951 work of Tinbergen and modified to provide an additional context for maltreatment. Belsky coupled the theoretical models of Bronfenbrenner and Tinbergen to develop the ecological model. It is explained in four levels: (1) ontogenic, (2) microsystem, (3) exosystem, and (4) macrosystem. Each level is ecologically nested within the next, and maltreatment is determined by the interaction of, and between, levels. Therefore, an understanding of maltreatment is only possible by examining all levels and their interaction; any one level provides an insufficient etiology for maltreatment. Each level is additionally influenced by the culture in which the family lives. Parental and child behavior must be understood within the cultural context in which behavior is learned and displayed (Peterson, 2000). Culture exerts an influence on the attachment relationship, the expectations of children and parents, the family's immediate social environment, the larger social connectedness of the family within their smaller communities, and the larger social fabric of the environment in which they live.

Ontogenic Development

Ontogenic development explores the childhood histories of abusive parents (Belsky, 1980). The purpose of this exploration is to assess how a particular parent grows to behave in an abusive manner. The occurrence of abuse or neglect in childhood alone is insufficient to explain the phenomenon of child maltreatment, because the majority of those who were maltreated fail to maltreat their own children. Yet the developmental history of the parents may predispose them to respond to certain situations in the microsystem or exosystem.

One well-known issue in the ontogenic development is attachment (Cicchetti & Barnett, 1991). Research shows that maltreated children are more likely to have insecure attachments, and many have disorganized-disoriented (Type D) attachment patterns (Crittenden, 1988; Carlson et al., 1989; Egeland & Sroufe, 1981; Main & Solomon, 1986). Bowlby (1982) explained that children form mental representations of their relationship to others based on their attachment to their primary caregiver, which includes affect, cognition, and expectations about future interactions. This primary relationship provides an internal working model (IWM), which serves as a template for other interpersonal relationships. One's expectations and views of relationships are impacted by the IWMs that began during childhood. This places parents who were maltreated with a possible predisposition to maltreat, depending upon circumstances in the other levels of the ecological model. Attachment theory is discussed in detail later in this chapter.

Microsystem

Many of the additional factors that interact with the parents' developmental history occur within the family itself. The microsystem is the immediate context in which child maltreatment takes place and includes the family system, the maltreatment itself, and both parent and child characteristics.

> *Parents.* Characteristics of the parent can impact the likelihood of maltreatment. Parents who maltreat are more likely than nonmaltreating parents to have a history of abuse or neglect themselves (Kaufman & Zigler, 1989). Trickett, Aber, Carslon, and Cicchetti (1991) found that parents who maltreated were less satisfied with their children and perceived parenting as less enjoyable and more difficult. In addition, social isolation is more characteristic of neglecting parents, while social conflict is indicative of abusive parents (Crittenden, 1985). The marital relationship can also influence the occurrence of child maltreatment. Domestic violence and spousal abuse have been shown to be related to child maltreatment (Rumm et al., 2000; Widom, 1989).
>
> *Child.* Certain characteristics can serve as contributors to a child's own maltreatment. Children can be at greater risk of maltreatment if they are born prematurely (Klein & Stern, 1971; Fontana, 1971); have a less attractive appearance to the parent (Frodi & Lamb, 1980); or have physical and mental disabilities (Gil, 1970; Ousted et al., 1974). Child interaction styles also affect the parenting relationship. Burgess and Conger (1978) found that maltreated children exhibit more negative behavior than matched controls of nonmaltreated children, which may predispose them to engage

parents differently. Therefore, characteristics of the child can make parenting difficult and unrewarding (Green, 1968).

Family system. Within a family, both the child and parent influence one another's behavior and responses. It is important to note that within the microsystem, child maltreatment must be considered an interactive process (Belsky, 1980). While children may play a role in their own maltreatment, they cannot cause it themselves. As evidenced within the microsystem, child characteristics can influence parental behavior, but the context of maltreatment must be viewed within the larger social milieu. For example, a colicky child may elicit an episode of maltreatment if the parent is predisposed to respond in an abusive manner within a stressful environment.

Exosystem

The exosystem encompasses the individual and family within larger social structures, including both formal and informal structures. Belsky (1980) primarily focuses on the influences that two primary structures exert on the family: work and neighborhood. However, other social structures include school, formal and informal support networks, socioeconomic status, and social services. This level also includes Bronfenbrenner's (1977) mesosystem, which comprises the interaction and interconnections between exosystem structures.

Several aspects of the exosystem have been correlated with child maltreatment. Poverty and socioeconomic status are risk factors for child maltreatment (Gelles & Strauss, 1988; Wolfner & Gelles, 1993). Unemployment has been shown to be associated with child maltreatment (Gil, 1970; Light, 1973; Wolfner & Gelles, 1993). Steinberg, Catalano, and Dooley (1981) found that increases in child abuse were preceded by periods of high job loss, and resulted from family stress (Cicchetti & Lynch, 1993) that unemployment brings.

Also a component of the exosystem, the neighborhood in which the family lives, can contribute to likelihood of the occurrence of child maltreatment. Based on socioeconomic conditions alone, Garbarino and Sherman (1980) found that some neighborhoods have higher maltreatment rates than expected, and others have lower rates than expected. In neighborhoods with equal socioeconomic disadvantage, neighborhoods with more social resources, whether formal or informal, experienced less child maltreatment than neighborhoods with fewer social resources. In addition, families that lack a connection to their community have fewer opportunities for exposure to child-rearing practices that could improve their own parenting skills (Trickett & Sussman, 1988). Without this social filter and opportunities for parental learning, parents lack a connection to emotional and material support during stressful times. Garbarino and Sherman (1980) also found that in neighborhoods where abuse and neglect were lower than expected, the families perceived their neighborhood with greater satisfaction and as a place for child and family development.

In addition, social isolation from other social networks and extended family is associated with maltreatment (Corse et al., 1990). Mothers who commit physical abuse are shown to have fewer peer relationships, more difficulties with extended family and less social contact within their community than nonabusing mothers (Corse et al., 1990). Less social contact results in less conformity to social and community parenting standards (Belsky, 1978; Garbarino, 1977).

Evaluating the influence of the exosystem on the microsystem requires that the actual influence be explored. Much of the influence that the exosystem has on the microsystem, as well as their ecological embeddedness, is the stress and pressure that structures in the exosystem exert on the family system, including family dysfunction (Cicchetti & Lynch, 1993). To the extent that family stress is already high, parental developmental history can predispose negative parenting, especially when those factors are coupled with exosystem influences that increase the probability of child maltreatment (Cicchetti and Lynch, 1993).

Macrosystem

The macrosystem examines the embeddedness of the individual, community, and family within the larger cultural fabric. The United States, compared to other countries, tolerates violence to a certain degree (Christoffel, 1990), and the line between violence and punishment is ambiguous. Physical punishment is widely practiced and condoned, and the fact that the culture is willing to accept violence creates an environment ripe for maltreatment in the microsystem and exosystem (Cicchetti & Lynch, 1993). For example, countries with the lowest rates of death from maltreatment also have low rates of adult homicide; similarly, countries with high levels of child death have high adult homicide rates, reflecting a larger social fabric of violence (UNICEF, 2003). In addition, a ban of corporal punishment in schools has been adopted by many industrialized nations with the exception of Australia, Canada, Mexico, and the United States, which continue to be experience high rates of child maltreatment and maltreatment-related death (ibid., 2003).

Similarly, cultural differences exist with regard to the value placed on physical punishment for child discipline. For example, Park (2001) found Korean parents to report negative attitudes toward physical abuse but positive attitudes about the use of physical punishment as a discipline. In general, Korean parents tend to feel that physical punishment is necessary for punishing children (Chun, 1989). Other differences may arise in regard to socioeconomic disparity. For example, research has shown that working-class parents are less likely to promote curiosity and to use reasoning in discipline, while middle-class parents encourage child inquisition and provide greater detail in their explanations to their children (Wolkind & Rutter, 1985).

Racism is an integral component of the macrosystem. Racism places undue stress on families, as well as limiting the educational and economic opportunities and the distribution of resources. When institutional discrimination of the larger culture blocks minority access to educational and employment opportunities, stress and frustration arise. Stress, coupled with factors within other levels of the ecological model presented, can create a maltreatment-prone situation. The child welfare system also experiences a reporting bias with minority clients. Minorities are overrepresented, which lends credence to the institutional racism that is still a part of American society.

The ecological model of child maltreatment lends itself to a multidisciplinary approach to the phenomenon by drawing from the fields of psychology, medicine, sociology, and child development (Ammerman, 1990). The ecological perspective has much strength for both practice and research. Contrary to psychological and other unidimensionality theories, the ecological model avoids deterministic cause-effect explanations of behavior and allows for many different ways to view patterns of relationships and the context of maltreatment (Payne, 1997). The ecological model also allows for interactive thinking, which concentrates on the ecological place of each individual rather than focusing on the internal thoughts and feelings of a single perpetrator or victim.

The appropriate application of the ecological model emphasizes the role of culture in examining each of the levels. Parent, child, and family expectations may differ depending upon the family's culture. Family conflicts may be explained by culture-prescribed role expectations and issues surrounding acculturation. The macrosystem must be explored within the context of the family's values regarding parenting and discipline, but it must also include issues of racism and discrimination. The ecological model, however, does not explain why things happen. It fails to explain why the system levels are ecologically nested and how each affects one another, ultimately limiting the opportunity for empirical validation (ibid.). Yet the ecological model is still a good perspective for research and practice because of its multilevel structure.

Ecological/Transactional Model

Cicchetti and Lynch (1993) drew upon Belsky's (1980) ecological model and Cicchetti and Rizley's (1981) transactional framework to develop the ecological/ transactional model of child maltreatment. The ecological/transactional model presents a broad and integrative framework for explaining the processes associated with child maltreatment, in addition to the consequences on child development (see Figure 2.1). While the ecological model focuses on the etiology of child maltreatment, the transactional model focuses more closely on the outcomes of child maltreatment, with special attention to developmental outcomes for children (Cicchetti & Lynch, 1993).

The underlying assumption of the framework is that children's multiple ecologies influence one another, affecting children's development (ibid.). Thus, the combined influence of the individual, community, family, and larger culture affect the developmental outcomes for children; parent, child, and environmental characteristics combine to shape the probabilistic course of the development of maltreated children. Cicchetti and Lynch integrate community factors that influence all levels of the ecological model. Violence in the community influences violence in the family, which in turn directly influences the likelihood of child maltreatment. The outcome of community and family violence manifests in developmental problems for children. However, the way in which children respond to violence is apparent in their own ontogenic development and internal working model, which ultimately affects their adaptation to the situation.

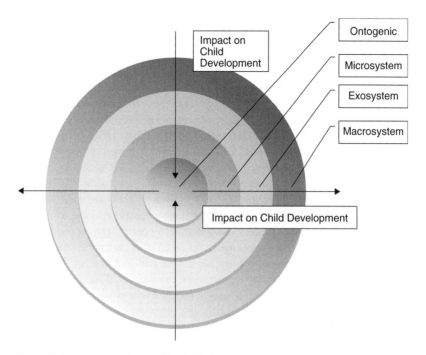

Figure 2.1. Ecological/Transactional Model

The transactional/ecological model takes Belsky's (1980) ecological model a step further by focusing not only on the etiology of maltreatment, but also on the developmental consequences to the child. The model offers both risk and compensatory factors at each of the four levels of the ecological model, as well as prescriptions for the sequelae of maltreatment and community violence. It is important to understand that the presence of violence at one level does not sentence children to poor developmental outcomes. The existence of community violence at the exosystem can be overcome by compensatory factors in the microsystem, which can protect the child against any adverse developmental outcome.

Both Belsky's ecological model and Cicchetti and Lynch's transactional/ecological model provide a comprehensive method for examining the etiology of child maltreatment by focusing on the interaction between the ecological systems. Cicchetti and Lynch expand the ecological perspective by focusing on the developmental outcomes to the child and the protective factors that can compensate for other risk factors that may be present at each ecological level. Different risk and protective factors are prominent at different developmental stages; therefore risk and protective factors will be presented at each stage of development and built upon in each age group. Additionally, a broad range of parent, child, family, and social factors have been identified as risk factors. Protective factors have also been identified that moderate the effects of risk factors, therefore reducing the likelihood of child maltreatment. Each chapter will state risk and protective factors across the ecological domains.

In conclusion, four broad historical theories of child maltreatment have been presented: psychological, sociological, social learning, and ecological. As evidenced in this review, the ecological/transactional model serves as a comprehensive theoretical model for explaining the etiology and sequelae of child abuse and neglect. It requires integration and an appreciation for the ecological embeddedness of each of the four levels within one another. It requires that a comprehensive view of the maltreatment situation, individuals, culture, and larger social environments be explored. Single and one-dimensional explanations prevalent during the 1960s and 1970 have proved insufficient. Psychological theories focused primarily on the psychopathology of the parent, but they were disputed with advances in research, which indicated that few parents who maltreat have psychiatric conditions. Sociological theories gained support initially but ultimately failed to provide causal connections, especially with the difficulty in measurement and the indirect relationships on which the conclusions were based. The social learning model focused on parental learning of violence but again failed to provide an explanation of the environmental context that is necessary for maltreatment to occur. Most importantly, no one-dimensional theory explains the exceptions of its premise, and the unidimensionality of single-focused theories mandates a multidimensional etiological model of child maltreatment. Currently, the most comprehensive and rigorous explanatory model is the ecological/transactional model. While this framework has limited ability to be used as a testable theoretical model, it provides a descriptive approach and theoretical guide for both assessment and intervention.

DEVELOPMENTAL PERSPECTIVE OF CHILD MALTREATMENT

Understanding healthy child development within an ecological framework has implications for both assessment and intervention. Developmental stages of human growth change throughout the life cycle. This book presents developmental periods than encompass infancy to adolescence and the tasks associated with each. Insight into how development changes with time by focusing on biology, psychology, and social and cultural contexts has tremendous implications for the child who experiences child maltreatment. The framework of this book, therefore, focuses on the developmental consequences of child maltreatment within an ecological context.

Child development is affected by not only genetics, but also by environmental influences, including parenting, stress, neighborhood, culture, and social policy. The major developmental theories presented in this book afford the reader an understanding of healthy child development so that deviations from healthy development can be understood in relation to child maltreatment. Developmental theory is complex and not linear. The key theories presented in this book include Freud's stages of psychosexual development, Erickson's theory of psychosocial development, John Bowlby's theory of attachment, and Piaget's theory of cognitive development. Other developmental concepts are equally as important to assessment and intervention, including play, peer relationships, academic achievement, and school. Therefore, the developmental component of the ecological framework used throughout this book examines three domains: (1) physical, (2) cognitive-behavioral, and (3) socioemotional. It is difficult to separate development into three distinct categories because, for example, what affects cognitive development also affects social development. However, our attempt is to delineate development as clearly as possible, although some overlap between domains will undoubtedly occur.

Physical development includes the growth and change that occurs to a child's physical body. It includes gross and fine motor skills, movement, and genetics. Cognitive behavioral development includes the mental processes that underlie thinking, learning, and information processing. The cognitive-behavioral domain includes the work of Jean Piaget, who sought to uncover how an individual's thinking affected their behaviors, attitudes, and beliefs. Finally, social development includes emotions, relationships, personality characteristics, and attachment. Social tasks change depending on developmental level and chronological age. For example, friendships change throughout one's development and by adolescence can have a major impact on an individual's behavior. An integral component of the socioemotional domain is attachment theory. The importance of attachment (see Table 2.1), especially to child maltreatment, is a theme throughout this book and has serious implications for child development.

ATTACHMENT THEORY

Attachment theory has informed child maltreatment practice and research for the past two decades (Aber & Allen, 1987; Bolen, 1999; Brazelton, 1988; Carlson et al., 1989; Cicchetti & Lynch, 1993; Egeland & Sroufe, 1981; Perry, 1994; 1999). It is well established in the empirical literature that the quality of early caregiver-child interaction has important implications for child development (Beckwith, 1990; Belsky, Rovine, & Taylor, 1984; Brazelton, 1988; Carlson, 1998; Coates & Lewis, 1984; Erickson, Sroufe, & Egeland, 1985; Wachs & Green, 1982).

Attachment begins at birth and occurs during the first three years of life. The infant relies totally on the primary caregiver, and in the context of this primary dependence, the caregiver's response to the dependence is how the attachment relationship is established (Perry, 2000). In order to form and maintain quality attachment relationships, primary caregivers need to provide continuous, sensitive, and responsive care to the infant. In doing so, the primary caregiver establishes a quality bond with the infant. In the field of infant development, the attachment bond has several key elements: "an attachment bond is an enduring emotional relationship with a specific person; the relationship brings safety, comfort, soothing, and pleasure; and loss or threat of loss of the person evokes distress" (Perry, 2000).

The attachment relationship is hypothesized to be dyadic and reciprocal. The sensitive parent reacts to an infant's crying and learns to differentiate among the infant's various cries; for example, different rhythmical cries indicate hunger, anger, and pain. The infant, in turn, experiences the pleasant sensations of having its basic needs met and responds with smiles. This, in turn, is gratifying to the

Table 2.1 Primary Developmental Tasks: Infancy to Adolescence

Period	Age	Task
Infancy and Toddlerhood	0–36 Months	Dramatic changes in all areas of development. The most important task of the infant is with the parent and the development of attachment. Infants and toddlers need not only food and good nutrition, but also environmental stimulation in order for healthy cognitive, physical, and socioemotional development.
Early Childhood	3–6 Years	With increases in cognitive, motor, and social skills, the primary objective of children is to play and practice their new skills and abilities. Language development expands, and children begin to establish peer relationships.
Middle Childhood	6–11 Years	The basic orientation of middle childhood is the onset of attending school. Gross motor skills become better, and reaction time decreases. Athletic abilities increase, and peer relationships begin to become more important. Cognition increases with reading, writing, and literacy.
Adolescence	12–18 Years	Puberty leads to sexual development, and peer groups and friendships become even more important. Adolescents spend increasingly more time with peers than parents. Adolescents focus on establishing a sense of self, self-identity, and establishing a place in the world. Adolescents are capable of hypothetical and logical reasoning, which can contribute to the increase in parent-child arguments.

parent, increasing his/her attachment and increasing sensitivity to the child's needs, and so it goes (Bowlby, 1982).

Cultural variations are especially important to examine with regard to attachment theory. Children who are raised in multiple mothering environments may not respond to their mothers as children raised in more nuclear-family environments. To illustrate, African American children are often raised in a multiple-caregiver community consisting of both blood and nonblood relatives (Jackson, 1993). While a strength of the African American community, this pattern of attachment may lead to erroneous attachment conclusions if the social worker fails to pay attention to the role of culture in a child's development. A child may not react to her/his mother in the expected European American manner and instead responds to several caregivers (Woody, 2003).

On the other hand, children who are raised solely by a primary caregiver and have little contact with substitute caregivers or strangers may be extremely anxious at their mother's departure. This child may respond with great anxiety, but the context of the child's rearing must be understood within the culture the child has been raised. Extreme anxiety would be appropriate if the child has little contact with anyone but her/his primary caregiver. This would not necessarily indicate an insecure attachment but perhaps a lack of experience and exposure to strangers.

The reciprocal nature of attachment is important to understand. Many factors may interfere with the attachment experience, and problem areas to explore may be related to the infant, the primary caregiver, the environment, or the fit between the infant and caregiver.

Infant Characteristics

Infant characteristics, including infant temperament and the goodness of fit with the parent, can affect the attachment relationship. The fussy, nonaffectionate child or the passive child who does not react does not reinforce the parent's responsiveness and may contribute to attachment problems with the parent. The temperament of the child may be antithetical to the parents. The child may be active and the caregiver passive. The infant may remind the primary caregiver of the father who is no longer in the home and thus bring negative feelings to the caregiver. The same may be true for mentally or physically handicapped infants who do not respond in ways that are gratifying to the parent.

Nonetheless, it is important to mention that the role of temperament and the attachment relationship has been a source of debate. Some purport that the temperament of the infant does not influence the attachment relationship *directly* since infants with difficult temperaments who receive consistent and sensitive care can have secure attachments; and infants with "easy" temperaments may develop insecure attachment relationships when provided insensitive care (Sroufe, 1985). The counterargument suggests that the temperament of the infant directly affects the attachment relationships, where more temperamentally difficult infants are more likely to be classified as insecure because of the impact distress exerts on mother-infant interaction (Chess & Thomas, 1982).

Primary Caregiver Characteristics

Characteristics of the primary caregiver can impact attachment. The sensitivity of care the primary caregiver, often the mother, provides to the child is critically important to the development of secure attachments (Ainsworth, 1973). Infants must receive sensitive and responsive care from a primary caregiver in order to develop a sense of trust that they can rely on the care and compassion of others. Without this sense of security, children develop an insecure attachment, discussed in detail later in this chapter. The caregiver may be insensitive and unresponsive to the child because of substance abuse, depression, maltreatment history of the parent, or overwhelming problems that interfere with the ability to be nurturing to the child.

Environment

The environment of the family, such as overcrowding and violence in neighborhoods, may lead to distress and the inability to engage in a supportive relationship.

Exposure to domestic violence may arouse fear in both the child and her/his caregiver, thus affecting the quality of the parent-child relationship. These circumstances should be explored in assessing the ontogenic level and attachment relationship between parent and child because they could lead to problems in attachment (Scannapieco & Connell-Carrick, 2002).

The Fit Between the Infant and Caregiver

Another area that can affect the attachment relationship is the goodness-of-fit of personality, temperament, and behavior between parent and child. The temperament of the child may be antithetical to the parents. The child may be active and the caregiver passive. The infant may represent the loss of a loved one or a painful relationship and thus produce negative feelings in the caregiver, which can lead to problems in attachment (Scannapieco & Connell-Carrick, 2002).

Categories of Attachment

Attachment can classify into two major categories: secure and insecure, which has three classifiable subtypes. Attachment has historically been studied using the "strange situation" (Ainsworth et al., 1978), which involves a laboratory setting and a series of separations and reunions between child and primary caregiver (attachment figure). The strange situation is generally thought to be a good measure of the quality of caregiving that infants received during the first year of their life (ibid.). However, newer techniques are currently being used and tested, including the Waters and Deane Q-Sort (Waters & Deane, 1985), separation anxiety tests, and doll-play stories (Bretherton, Ridgeway, & Cassidy, 1990). During infancy, patterns of attachment include the following:

Secure. The securely attached child uses the caregiver as a secure base. The child explores freely in the caregivers presence but "checks" on the caregiver periodically either through eye or physical contact. When the caregiver leaves, the child's reaction to the separation ranges from little to extreme distress. However, upon reunion, the child actively positively greets the caregiver, seeks physical contact, and then continues playing.

Insecure – Avoidant. The insecurely avoidant child "avoids" the caregiver in her/his presence. The child appears not interested in the caregiver and explores his/her environment without interest in the caregiver's presence. When the caregiver leaves, the child is minimally distressed. Upon reunion, the child again continues to ignore the caregiver.

Insecure – Resistant/Ambivalent. The insecure resistant/ambivalent child is preoccupied with the caregiver when the caregiver is in the room; the child has great difficulty separating from the caregiver. These children have great difficulty leaving the caregiver to play or explore. Upon separation, ambivalently attached children tend to be extremely distressed. At reunion, they again become preoccupied with the caregiver and seek physical contact.

Insecure – Disorganized/Disoriented. Initially, only two categories of attachment patterns were developed, but several cases remained unclassified. Main and Solomon (1986; 1990) reviewed those cases and found another pattern: disorganized/disoriented. Children with insecure–disorganized/ disoriented attachment patterns utilize a disorganized coping strategy for dealing with separation from their primary caregiver. Children with disorganized/disoriented attachments also have difficulty managing arousal patterns, and either fail to or seem confused about approaching the caregiver when distressed. Characteristics of this type of attachment pattern include odd behaviors in which the child appears confused or scared of the caregiver and her/his presence. These children are the most distressed upon separation from the caregiver.

Finally, some children do not fall into any of the aforementioned categories and are therefore placed in an "other" category, but this is rare (Goldberg, 1995). Similarly, researchers have also expanded the primary attachment categories according to developmental periods, such as school age, adolescence, and adulthood (Crittenden, 1992; Main & Cassidy, 1988; Main, Kaplan, & Cassidy, 1985).

One of the most compelling aspects of attachment theory is the mental representation of the primary attachment relationship, which manifests in an internal working model for future relationships. Bowlby (1982) purports that children form mental representations of their relationship to others based on their attachment to their primary caregiver, which includes affect, cognition, and expectations about future interactions. This primary relationship provides an internal working model (IWM), which serves as a template for other interpersonal relationships throughout one's life (Bowlby, 1982). One's expectations and view of relationships is impacted by the IWM that began during childhood. To illustrate, an infant even by 3 months of age may fail to cry because she/he has already learned that crying elicits no response from the caregiver. The child may be developing an insecure attachment relationship, which would likely be the case with a nonresponsive and insensitive caregiver. Therefore, the child's internal working model allows the child to feel that she/he cannot rely on the compassion and care of others. The child learns not to expect others to meet her/his needs. The child's IWM, then, does not demand respect and compassion of others, but rather expects little from those in her/his life. Similarly, a parent who was maltreated as a child may have a predisposition to maltreat, depending upon circumstances in the other levels of the ecological model.

Relationship of Attachment and Child Maltreatment

Child maltreatment affects all areas of a child's development, not only at the time of the incident, but also across the lifespan. Research shows that approximately two-thirds of maltreated children have insecure attachments, and most have disorganized-disoriented (Type D) attachment patterns (Crittenden, 1988; Carlson et al., 1989; Egeland & Sroufe, 1981; Main & Solomon, 1986). Interestingly, maltreated children have a more stable attachment pattern than children with secure attachments (Schneider-Rosen et al., 1985). On the other hand, about two-thirds of nonmaltreated infants have secure attachments, which are more stable than insecure attachments in this population (Lamb et al., 1985). As always, it is important to focus on the culture of the family and the child in order to assess the attachment relationship so that mislabeling of healthy, secure attachment is avoided.

Additionally, it is important to recall that a representational model develops from this primary attachment relationship, which serves a template for future relationships. While the internal working model can be altered throughout the course of one's life, early competence and successful adjustment facilitates future adaptation, just as early incompetence allows for challenges to healthy adaptation through the lifespan (Cicchetti & Toth, 1995). The individual's sense of self and worthiness is altered due to this primary relationship. Therefore, examining the attachment pattern of the parent gives insight into a current maltreatment situation of the family, as well as insight into the attachment between parent and child.

While it is important to assess the attachment relationship of all victims of maltreatment, it is essential to assess neglect. Neglect is often difficult to identify because it requires a measure of an omission of behavior. Neglect is characterized by a lack of care regardless of income. As a result, separating neglect from poverty requires an examination of the relationship between parent and child. Although several different subtypes and definitions of neglect exist, neglect is primarily the result of an impoverished relationship between parent and child. The parent fails to meet the needs of an infant through a lack of care, which then manifests in developmental consequences for the child (Scannapieco & Connell-Carrick, 2002) and even death (USHDDS, 2002). The child who experiences neglect in the first three years of her/his life will experience problems with attachment that have developmental consequences spanning the range of physical, behavioral, cognitive, and social functioning throughout the lifespan. Parental behavior affects attachment, which then affects child behavior. When parents fail to nurture and bond with their child, it alters the child's behavior. This cycle is signified by poor attachment, ultimately increasing the possibility of neglect and children at risk of harm.

Assessing Attachment

Assessing the attachment between a caregiver and child without a laboratory setting can be a daunting but not impossible task. In natural settings it takes a very observant professional who has expertise in child development and attachment theory. Attachment can be approximated in natural settings, such as home or office, by carefully examining the interaction of parent and child. It is also necessary to determine some characteristics of the child before assessment, including asking about the child's temperament. If a child is naturally energetic, she/he will display that in interaction with a caregiver, and a similarly self-descriptive reaction can be expected from a passive child. It is also important to focus on cultural issues that pertain to the family. As previously mentioned, the traditional use of multiple caregivers in African American families may lead a child to appear less excited about her/his mother. This behavior may not be an indication of indifference toward her; rather the child understands of her/his multiple caregiver arrangement. Similarly, anxiety may appear in children who have very little contact with anyone other than their primary caregiver. Recognizing this family dynamic would avoid mislabeling the attachment.

Assessing attachment in infancy requires tremendous skill since the child lacks the ability to crawl until about the 6th month of age. However, observing the parent-child interaction will provide a tremendous amount of information regarding the type of relationship. By 3 months, attachment to the primary caregiver is visibly evident. The securely attached child will be more excited to interact with his/her primary caregiver, either by waving his/her arms or kicking her/his legs, than to strangers or less familiar people.

Between 6 and 12 months, the child is becoming increasingly mobile by crawling and eventually walking. Children will return to their caregiver in times of distress, seeking physical contact and ensuring that the caregiver is present through eye contact and physical means. Stranger anxiety and separation anxiety may appear where infants are wary of strangers and distressed at separation from their parents. Separation and stranger anxiety occur and increase in frequency between 12 and 16 months of age and then decline as the child's cognitive maturity increases. It is important to keep in mind that the extent to which stranger and separation anxieties occur is multiply determined by the child's temperament, the situation in which the child meets the stranger(s), and past experience with strangers. It is equally important to remember that stranger and separation anxieties, and the associated fear seen in children, are self-preservation mechanisms. They serve to keep the child in close proximity to those whom she/he trusts. Cultural variations also exist with respect to stranger anxiety and separation anxiety. Some cultures and families expect their children to demonstrate greater independence and to control their emotions better than others. For example, Harwood (1992) compared Puerto Rican and Anglo mothers and found that Anglo mothers expected their children to manage their anxieties with strangers while separated from them, while Puerto Rican mothers expected their children to cling to them for support.

Another method for assessing attachment is social referencing, where the child uses the facial expressions of others as a guide for his/her own emotions. Using these concepts, assessing attachment becomes easier. For example, if the child falls while at your office or while you are in their home, whom does the child look to in order to determine how to react (social referencing)? As always, in assessing children and families, a cultural understanding of the family is paramount to any good assessment. If the family is part of a culture in which the use of multiple caregivers is valued, you may find the child looking toward a grandmother or aunt, rather than always to her/his mother, for information in uncertain situations. This should not lead the caseworker to conclude that the child is unattached or poorly attached to the mother, but rather to recognize that the child is attached to a number of caregivers. The child may be cared for by several different caregivers, all of whom love and protect the child. In such a circumstance, you would find a child looking for one of her/his attachment figures.

As the child increases in mobility from walking to running, attachment becomes obvious by examining who the child uses as a secure base. According to attachment theory, children use their attachment figure(s) as a secure base—an individual that the child demonstrates proximity behaviors toward. A securely attached child on the playground will explore freely but will seek proximity to the caregiver frequently for a few moments (this is called anchoring) and then return to play. A child will also seek the physical contact of their attachment figure as a secure base during times of distress. Securely attached children are more easily soothed by their attachment figures during distress, and they calm down faster with this individual than any other. Assessing attachment by focusing on whom the child seeks in times of distress is a good approximate of the attachment relationship, even in early and middle childhood, as well as during adolescence.

Historically, the most widely used setting to assess attachment in a laboratory setting is the strange situation (Ainsworth et al., 1978). The strange situation involves a standard laboratory setting in which the child experiences two separations from her/his primary caregiver and is accepted as a good indication of the type of care the child received during the first year of life. While a laboratory setting is most appropriate for research purposes, supervised visits between parent and child are a good approximate of this type of setting. When children are removed from their homes due to abuse and neglect, parents are often given supervised visits with their children in a child protection or psychotherapeutic setting. During the visit, the caseworker can watch the reunion between parent and child. It is important to focus on both parent and child behavior during the interaction, as well as on how each reacts at separation. It is important to explore the following questions:

- Who does the child go to in terms of distress?
- Does the child or parent seek physical contact at reunion?
- Is the child preoccupied with the parent (ambivalent attachment)?
- Does the child actively ignore the parent (avoidant attachment)?
- What happens at separation and the subsequent reunion?
- What cultural factors may influence the separation and reunion of a parent and child?

Assessing attachment in a natural setting requires knowledge of many factors, including the child's temperament, family cultural norms, and history with strangers, to name a few. It is paramount, however, to working effectively with families who have experienced maltreatment. With a strong foundation of attachment theory and child development, child welfare professionals can approximate the type of attachment relationship in order to develop a treatment plan for the family that focuses on ameliorating the effects of an impaired attachment.

Consequences of an Impaired Attachment

The consequences of an impaired attachment relationship in early childhood have both immediate and long-term effects. The cost to the individual ranges from the most severe loss of the capacity to form any meaningful relationships, to mild interpersonal, social, or emotional problems. The *Diagnostic and Statistical Manual of Mental Disorders (DSM-IV)* indicates that lack of adequate care can lead to Reactive Attachment Disorder (RAD) of Infancy or Early Childhood. It is important to note the diagnosis of RAD is controversial. Primary reasons for the controversy lie in the fact that the diagnosis pathologizes children and that the diagnosis of and treatment for RAD lack empirical support (Werner-Wilson & Davenport, 2003). However, at this time RAD is still a diagnosable condition in the DSM-IV. At any rate, the provision of basic nourishment alone to an infant without tactile and cognitive stimulation will impede healthy child development, which is why focusing on the relationship between child and parent is vital.

An impaired attachment relationship in infancy can have long-lasting consequences, primarily because of the relationship's influence on the child's internal working model. Children with secure attachments feel confident that the world will meet their needs; they trust that the world is a place for them to explore through physical and emotional means. Children with insecure attachment do not have that same understanding of the world. Thus, a child with an insecure-avoidant attachment might interpret "neutral or even friendly behavior as hostile and show inappropriate aggressive behavior" (Widom, 2000, p. 351). Research has shown that the experience of physical abuse in childhood may lead to aggressive behavior because the individual's internal working model includes a tendency to process information through deficient and hostile-influenced mechanisms (Dodge, Bates, & Pettit, 1990).

Similarly, children with insecure attachments cope with their environments less well than children with secure attachments. They often behave more impulsively and lack problem-solving skills. Sometimes substance abuse becomes a major form of coping in order to escape from a current abusive environment (Harrison, Hoffmann, & Edwall, 1989; Kazdin et al., 1985), to deal with depression (Harrison, Hoffmann, & Edwall, 1989; Kazdin et al., 1985; Yamaguchi & Kandel, 1984), and to medicate oneself (Cavaiola & Schiff, 1988; Harrison, Hoffmann, & Edwall, 1989). Other maladaptive means of coping include running away, especially for abused and neglected adolescents. However, it is difficult to ascertain the actual causes of maladaptive coping and behavioral patterns since an impaired attachment affects all aspects of development. Treatment issues and intervention strategies concerning attachment will be discussed in each developmental stage. Next we will discuss the guiding principles that underlie assessment and intervention.

THREE GUIDING PRINCIPLES FOR ASSESSMENT AND INTERVENTION

Family-Centered Principle

Assessment and intervention must focus on the family as key to understanding the dynamics of child maltreatment and provision of services to ameliorate the conditions that lead to the problem. The family-centered principle is critical to working with children and families in the child welfare system (Pecora et al., 2000). Family is defined broadly as "two or more people who are joined together by bonds of sharing and intimacy (Meyer, 1990, p. 16, as cited in Hepworth, Rooney, & Larsen, 2002). Using this definition, family encompasses a wide array of formations, which may include kinship families, stepfamilies, same gender couple families, and single parent families.

Individuals can best be understood within the context of the family. Assessment must examine every person in the family and the reciprocal relationships with each of the other members of the family. It is also important to directly assess the subsystems within the family, such as the partner relationship, parent-child, and sibling. Effective intervention to resolve the issues surrounding child maltreatment is based on a comprehensive assessment of the family and its ecology.

All families, as well as the type and extent of child maltreatment, are different. Therefore, no one type of intervention will be effective in all situations. In respect for family differences, family definitions of self, and cultural differences, treatment must be customized to the specific needs of individual families.

Strength-Based Principle

The strength-based principle highlights practice strategies that promote effective functioning of children, parents, and families. From the strength principle, parents who maltreat their children should be viewed as persons with the ability and motivation to grow and achieve competence (Pecora et al., 2000). It recognizes that families have a number of competencies and builds on developing the abilities and resources of the family (Saleebey, 1992). Existing competencies and resources are built upon to promote healthy family functioning. This perspective contrasts with the more traditional pathology or deficit model. It emphasizes family capability and partnership with the family.

In agreement with prior literature (Fraser, 1997), strengths are conceptually and operationally defined as *protective factors*. Protective factors are those at each level of the family ecology that help the family and child resist or ameliorate risk. Assessment, from the strength principle, focuses on the multifaceted relationship of both risk and protective factors related to all levels of the ecological model. Through the assessment, conditions contributing to child maltreatment will be understood and intervention strategies directed to strengths and deficits within and outside of the family. Treatment is not directed at pathology, but support is directed at assisting the family in maximizing their potential for gaining skills and developing a sense of mastery and control.

Cultural Responsiveness Principle

The principle of cultural responsiveness describes a set of knowledge and skills that a practitioner must develop in order to be effective with multicultural families and children (Lum, 1999). Underlying the principle is the understanding that societal attitudes and biases affect individuals and families. Therefore our assessment and intervention decisions cannot ignore cultural difference or the impact societal attitudes have on people of different cultures. Assessment must gather sufficient information so we may understand the experience of the individual or family and how living in their culture affects them today. Cultural differences cannot be ignored; it is important to understand them and integrate them into the overall approach to assessment and intervention.

Practitioners working in the child maltreatment field need to be culturally competent for three reasons, outlined by DePanfilis (p. 218, 1999). First, the United States is experiencing increased cultural diversity and minorities have been shown to be overrepresented in the child welfare system. Second, there is under-representation of professionals reflective of the families treated in our helping institutions. Finally, there is inadequate delivery of services to maltreated child and families of color.

Cultural responsiveness is addressed, but it is beyond the scope of this book to adequately infuse all of the information needed to address cultural responsive-ness across developmental levels and maltreatment type. In the appendix, we pro-vide a cultural responsiveness guide to refer to in order to gain further information.

CONCLUSION

Children neither develop nor are maltreated in a vacuum. The ecological per-spective provides a manner in which to assess and intervene with children who have been maltreated by focusing not only on the child, but also the parent-child relationship, social environment, culture, and macro influences. In order to ade-quately assess child maltreatment, an exploration of all ecological levels is neces-sary. Furthermore, child maltreatment has developmental consequences that can be both subtle and overwhelming. Ecological and developmental perspectives on child maltreatment, integrated with the three principles above, provide a broad framework for examining predictors, consequences, and risk and protective fac-tors that influence and result from child maltreatment.

3

INFANCY AND TODDLERHOOD
Child Development and Maltreatment

Infancy and toddlerhood is a period of great cognitive, physical, social, and behavioral growth. At birth children enter the world with basic reflexive capabilities, and by 3 years of age they are able to jump, run, and talk. They learn the foundations of how relationships work from their primary relationship with their caregiver(s); they learn to regulate their own emotions and how to manage their own bodies through toilet training. This developmental period is tremendous and magnificent. Never again during the course of human development is the brain developing so rapidly, and never again do so many important developmental tasks occur. Many believe that the first three years are the most important in one's life. The foundation for personality and future behavior is laid, and child maltreatment can seriously disrupt the course of healthy development (Scannapieco & Connell-Carrick, 2002).

EXPECTED DEVELOPMENT ACROSS DEVELOPMENTAL DOMAINS

In order to understand the developmental consequences of child maltreatment, an understanding of healthy child development is necessary. This chapter will present the major developmental theories, including Freud's theory of psychosexual development, Erickson's stages of psychosocial development, social developmental theories, attachment theory, Piaget's theory of cognitive development, and physical and motor development (see Table 3.1). The developmental milestones of children in infancy and toddlerhood will be discussed in relation to socioemotional, cognitive, and physical developmental domains. Since Freud and Erickson are psychodynamic theorists, they will be presented first, but their contribution covers all areas of the child's development, with special attention to socioemotional and cognitive domains. After healthy child development is presented for children ages 0 to 3, the developmental manifestations of physical abuse, sexual abuse, and neglect will be presented. Keep in mind that child development and the manifestations of child maltreatment must be understood within a cultural context.

44

Table 3.1 Infant and Toddler Development

	Psychodynamic		Social	Cognitive	Language	Physical
	Freud	Erickson		Piaget		
0–6 Months			• eye contact • preference for the human face over other objects • turns head to sound • differential response to caregiver than less-known persons • all basic emotions present at birth • reflexive emotions; social smiling; anger, surprise and sadness; laughing; increasingly leads to organized emotional expressiveness	*Primary circular reaction:* Coordination of senses and schemes; voluntary behavior	• startle response to sharp noises • interest in sounds and voices • responds to sound • vocalizes two vowel sounds	• head erect; elevate self by arms; grabs, rolls over • should double birthweight by 4 months; increasingly develops more adult sleeping patterns • sits with support

(continued)

45

Table 3.1 continued

	Psychodynamic		Social	Cognitive	Language	Physical
	Freud	Erickson		Piaget		
6–12 Months	*Oral stage:* Primary pleasurable and stimulating activity is sucking. If oral needs are unmet, it may manifest in nailbiting, thumb sucking, chewing behaviors.	*Trust vs. mistrust:* Warm and responsive care fosters trust and confidence. Child learns to be able to rely on the care and compassion of others when trust develops. When mistrust develops, child learns that her/his needs may not be met by others.	• cooperates in games • looks at self in mirror and smiles • emotional expressions are related to social events • anger and fear due to stranger and separation anxiety • social referencing • attachment to caregiver is evident	*Secondary circular reactions:* Object oriented; imitation of behaviors; coordinate schemes; intentionality; outward direction of actions; physical causality	• babbling, cooing, with the purpose of attracting attention of caregiver • vocalizes different vowel sounds • imitates sounds • makes vocal expressions that mimic conversation	• sits alone, crawls, pulls oneself to stand; attempts to walk alone • should triple birth-weight and increase length by 50% • perception of facial expressions • sits alone momentarily to sitting alone • transfers objects from hand to hand • looks at pictures in a book
12–18 Months			• uses caregiver as a secure base • laughing • engages in games and may initiate game	*Tertiary circular reactions:* Increased curiosity and exploration; trial-and-error learning;	• first words; holophrases • vocalizes both vowel and consonant sounds • relies on gestures for communication	• builds blocks, scribbles • walks • turns pages of a book • uses gestures to make wants known (pointing)

Age	Psychosexual (Freud)	Psychosocial (Erikson)	Social-emotional	Cognitive (Piaget)	Language	Physical/Motor
18–24 Months	*Anal stage:* Focus on holding and releasing; anus is the focus of pleasurable activity; toilet training is the most important activity. If parents demand too much from their children, they may appear extremely orderly or extremely messy, which arises over conflicts over control.	*Autonomy vs. shame and doubt:* Children increasingly want to do things for themselves, such as getting dressed, eating, and other self-care skills. Children who are not allowed to become independent feel shameful and do not feel competent in their abilities.	• self-conscious emotions appear—shame, embarrassment, pride • emotional regulation appears • beginning of empathy may appear	*Internalization of schemes:* Internalization of sensory images or words that represent events; ability to think about concrete events; object permanency; deliberate approach to world	• two-word phrases; begins to learn the role of language • relies on combination of words and gestures for communication	• jumps in place; walks on tiptoes • feelings of contempt and guilt • uses words to make wants known • combines words and gestures • walks up stairs with help • throws ball • sleeps 12–13 hours • decline in appetite and change in eating habits • smoother and rhythmic movements
24–36 Months			• emotional regulation improves • self-conscious emotions become more common • interactive play • instrumental aggression common • beginning of self-esteem and self-concept	*Preoperations stage:* Physical control and intentionality; mental representations of reality; symbolic play with imitation	• uses two-word phrases • two-word sentences • increasingly uses words to make wants known • able to understand distinctions between words • invents words for objects • meaningful phrases	• jumping; feeding; dressing; open doors • identification • jumps • runs with coordination • kicks ball • fine motor development is much better—putting on clothing, zipping, using eating utensils

Psychodynamic Theories

Freud's Psychosexual Stages of Development

Freud's psychosexual theory of development proposes two stages from 0 to 3 years of age. The first stage occurs from 0 to 1 and is called the oral stage. The primary source of pleasure during the oral stage is the mouth, and the primary activity is sucking. Infants receive instant gratification from sucking a breast and bottle or substitute (i.e., pacifier). When sucking needs are either unmet or overmet, Freud proposed that the individual becomes orally fixated, which may manifest in nail biting or thumb sucking. The second stage of psychosexual development occurs from ages 1 to 3 and is called the anal stage. The primary source of pleasure is the anus, and the primary activity is the holding and releasing of urine and feces. As the child gains greater physical and cognitive skills, she/he becomes more actively involved in her/his environment. Toilet training becomes a major developmental task. When toilet training becomes either too strict or results in a power struggle between parent and child, long-term negative consequences may develop. For example, a child or adult may become excessively orderly or messy; she/he may seek control of self or others and desire extreme regularity, commonly referred to as an "anal personality."

Freud also proposed that the mind and personality are structured by three parts: the id, ego, and superego. The id is present at birth and is the largest part of the mind. It is the source of basic biological drives and needs; it is driven by what Freud called the pleasure principle. The ego develops in early infancy and is the rational, conscious component of the mind, driven largely by the reality principle. The id is primarily sexual and is biologically driven, while the ego is more rational. The ego is guided by the reality principle because it seeks rational decisions that take into consideration the outside world and drives; it has the ability to delay pleasure. On the other hand, the id is impulsive and is considered primarily with the self. The ego helps to redirect the child's id from its impulses onto appropriate objects. The final component of the mind, the superego, develops in the next developmental period and will be discussed further in chapter 5. While Freud's theory is not employed in modern society as much as it once was, it is important to understand because of its influence on the origins and foundations of all child development theory.

Erickson's Psychosocial Stages of Development

Similar to the stages in Freud's theory of psychosexual development, Erickson proposed that children must resolve two psychosocial crises from 0 to 3: (1) trust vs. mistrust, and (2) autonomy vs. shame and doubt. The crisis of trust vs. mistrust occurs from birth to age 1. During this stage, the infant learns whether she can trust her environment; whether her needs will be met by those around her. If the infant learns that she can trust her environment and the people in it, she understands that the world is a safe place in which she can rely on the care and compassion of others. She begins to understand that her basic needs will be met and develops a sense of security. On the other hand, when a child is intermittently attended to or has to wait a long time to be fed, the child cannot be certain that his needs will be met. This child learns that he cannot rely on predictability in his environment and develops a sense of mistrust in his surroundings. With the positive resolution of Erickson's first psychosocial crisis, the child feels confident exploring her world, which becomes even more important in the next psychosocial crisis.

The second psychosocial crisis is autonomy vs. shame and doubt and occurs from 1 to 3 years of age. Toddlers want to govern their own bodies and actions; they want to get dressed themselves, decide what to wear, and eat by themselves. Toilet training is also a part of this stage, where children learn to control their bodily functions and how to manage them. Children in toddlerhood have new gross motor capabilities that allow them to walk, and they should feel that their world is safe for their exploration, within limits. The negative resolution of this crisis is the emergence of shame and doubt. If the child's environment is too restrictive, the child may fail to develop a sense of autonomy; the child may feel shamed or doubtful of her/his actions and abilities. Erickson, however, eventually proposed the resolution of his crises as less dichotomous and more of a middle ground between each extreme.

Development must be understood within a cultural context, and some argue that Erickson's theory focuses too much on individualization. An underlying component of the theory is that the child develops a separate identity from the family, which may be antithetical to collectivistic societies (Woody, 2003). Children in societies and cultures that emphasize collectivity may not demonstrate the individuation evident in Erickson's theory.

Social Development

While Erickson's theory grew out of psychodynamic theory, it certainly contributes to our understanding of the social development of the child, which is tremendous from 0 to 3 years of age. Many of the social developmental tasks in infancy and toddlerhood coincide with both physical and cognitive development. All of the basic emotions are present at birth: happiness, sadness, and fear—those emotions that you can behaviorally see. For example, children express distress by crying, which alerts the caregiver to hunger or pain. Smiling is reflexive in the first few months of life, but by 6 to 10 weeks the infant has a social smile. Social smiling occurs when the infant smiles in response to a pleasing stimulus, and laughing occurs by 4 months. Smiling is a social construction; though it is initially reflexive, it eventually becomes elicited by a social circumstance.

Furthermore, while all the basic emotions are present at birth, more sophisticated and self-conscious emotions emerge between 18 and 24 months. Toddlers begin to express shame, guilt, embarrassment, and pride behaviorally. To illustrate, a toddler might cover his face with his hands or a blanket if he is embarrassed. An ashamed girl might hang her head or lower her eyes. The importance of such emotions is culturally driven. When being proud of an accomplishment is valued, children learn to celebrate their actions; when celebrating behavior is seen as boastful, such behavior is seen as shameful.

As children mature, self-regulation becomes more important to toddlers' long-term development and their acquisition of social norms. At approximately 24 months, children become better at managing their emotional experiences. Emotional regulation becomes a way for toddlers to learn socially responsible ways of expressing their feelings. Temper tantrums can be important learning tools for infants, because they provide the opportunity for caregivers to demonstrate socially acceptable ways of expressing emotions. As children mature and enter school, those who lack the ability to emotionally regulate themselves have difficulty in the classroom. They often have behavioral problems as they enter structured situations, such as school, and demonstrate more frustrations with peers. Cultural differences also exist with regard to children's emotional regulation. Different cultures have different expectations for child emotional regulation. Harwood (1992), for instance, found that Anglo mothers expected their children to manage their own emotions, while Puerto Rican mothers expected them to cling to them for emotional support.

Self-awareness

Children in the first three years of their lives become increasingly self-aware. Children develop self-conscious emotions and come to understand themselves as reflective observers. While infants see themselves as subjects separate from other people, they eventually see themselves as reflective observers and as objects of evaluation. With time, this understanding of oneself as an object of evaluation extends to others. Toddlers and children begin to appreciate and understand others' perspectives, which is the foundation of empathy. They understand their feelings, and they begin to extend those feelings to others. It is remarkable that the foundation of empathy begins so early in life.

Stranger and Separation Anxieties

It is generally rare for children to show physical affection for unfamiliar adults in infancy (Ablus & Dozier, 1999). As infants age, however, they may come into more contact with unfamiliar persons. Infants between 9 and 15 months become wary of strangers. Stranger anxiety begins to emerge around 6 months and peaks between 10 and 14 months. However, the extent to which stranger wariness is observed depends on a number of factors, including culture, the infant's past experience with strangers, the circumstance in which the infant meets the stranger, and the parent's reaction to the stranger. For example, the child who has been largely with her/his parent and has met few strangers will likely be more scared than a child who has met many strangers and has an active social life.

Separation anxiety occurs when the infant is fearful and experiences anxiety at being separated from the primary caregiver, usually the mother. Separation anxiety usually begins at 8–9 months and peaks at 14 months. Again, a child's response to separation from a caregiver depends on a number of factors, including the infant's past experiences and the way in which the caregiver departs. The extent to which separation and stranger anxiety is seen is also affected by culture. Children who grow up in a home with multiple caregivers may be less wary of strangers and separating from any one caregiver. On the other hand, intense fear of strangers and separation may exist among children who are cared for solely by one person with little contact with anyone else. Both behaviors would be appropriate given the culture in which the child has been raised.

Attachment

The most important emotional relationship between 0 and 3 is the infant's relationship with her/his primary caregiver. No discussion of infancy and toddlerhood is adequate without a discussion of attachment. Since chapter 2 is largely devoted to attachment theory, a brief overview will be presented here. Attachment begins at birth and occurs during the first three years of life. The infant relies totally on the primary caregiver for all forms of care. Some cultures, however, utilize multiple caregiving arrangements so that the idea of a primary caregiver is shared among several persons. The attachment relationship is reciprocal, but the responsibility is on the parent initially to develop, maintain, and nurture the relationship. The sensitive parent reacts to an infant's crying; the infant, in turn, experiences the pleasant sensations of having its basic needs met and responds with smiles or cooing. This, in turn, is gratifying to the parent, increasing his/her attachment and sensitivity to the child's needs, and so it goes (Bowlby, 1983). Many factors may interfere with the attachment experience, and problem areas to explore may be related to the infant, the primary caregiver, the environment, or the fit between the infant and caregiver, as discussed in chapter 2.

The development of attachment is essential to the development of trust, as proposed by Erickson's psychosocial theory of development. As the infant matures, autonomy and exploration become more important as social developmental tasks. When children feel confident and secure in their environments, they willfully and energetically explore their surroundings, learning how they act upon this world and how it reacts to their influences.

Furthermore, as children become more mobile, visibly seeing the attachment relationship becomes easier. Even by 3 months of age a child will respond differently to her/his attachment figure(s) than to anyone else. For example, a 3-month-old infant may kick her/his arms and legs vigorously when seeing or interacting with a caregiver; when interacting with a stranger or other person, the infant may respond but not show excitement. As the child ages, the visible reaction of the child is easier to observe. Once children begin to crawl or walk, they will return to their caregivers in times of distress, using caregivers as a safe base. Similarly, the securely attached child will "anchor" away from her/his attachment figure when playing on a playground, but will return back occasionally to make sure her/his attachment figure is there and to seek physical contact before resuming play. This pattern of returning to a caregiver in times of distress and for emotional and physical comfort is relatively stable. Even adults often return emotionally or physically to their attachment figures in stressful times for comfort and security.

Social Referencing

Infants learn early on the connection between emotional expressions and the tone of the caregiver. By the time the child reaches 7 to 10 months, the infant understands facial expressions as organized patterns. As a result, infants and toddlers begin to look toward trusted persons in their environment to direct them how to respond emotionally in uncertain situations, and this is a powerful tool for learning. For example, when an 11-month-old falls down when trying to move from the sofa to the table, she may look to a trusted person to direct her how to react—the trusted person shows her the appropriate emotional expression by her own reaction. If the trusted person covers her mouth as if the child got hurt, the child may start crying. On the other hand, if the trusted person acts as if nothing happened, the child will likely get up and keep playing. In such circumstances, the infant is engaging in social referencing—looking toward one's environment in order to demonstrate the appropriate emotional response to an uncertain situation. One other aspect of social referencing is that it provides a learning opportunity for toddlers; it allows them to compare their assessments of novel events to the responses of others.

Cognitive Development

Over the first three years of life, an infant grows from a primary reflexive being to a walking and talking toddler. Children develop language, memory, increased capacity for thought, and a change from physical to cognitive problem solving. Piaget's theory of cognitive development begins with the sensorimotor stage, from birth to two years, which includes six substages of increasing complex behaviors and different understandings of the world (see Table 3.2). The primary means of

Table 3.2 Sensorimotor Stage of Development: Substages 1–6, Birth to 2 years

Name	Age	Characteristics
Substage 1: Reflect Activity	Birth–1 month	Infant responds through reflexes (i.e., sucking)
Substage 2: Primary Circular Reactions	1–4 months	Infant repeats responses that bring pleasure
Substage 3: Secondary Circular Reactions	4–8 months	Infant reacts to and interacts with environment more than before
Substage 4: Coordination of Secondary Circular Reactions	8–12 months	Infant has object permanence and goal-directed behavior, anticipates events
Substage 5: Tertiary Circular Reactions	12–18 months	Toddler solves problems through physical means and trial-and-error learning
Substage 6: Mental Representation	18–24 months	Toddler solves problems through mental representation and thinking skills

solving problems in the sensorimotor stage is through physical means. In substage 1, which occurs from birth to 1 month of age, the infant primarily responds through reflexes. Infants may suck or grasp over and over, and through this they learn about the world. During substage 2, which occurs from 1 to 4 months, infants learn to extend what they learned in stage 1 to other activities, primarily through accommodation and assimilation. For example, infants learn to suck differently on a pacifier, which does not provide them nourishment, than from a bottle or breast. Similarly, an infant that is primarily breast-fed can learn to suck from a bottle—extending his/her knowledge of sucking to another object.

The next two stages within the sensorimotor stage are called secondary circular reactions and last from 4 to 8 months with two substages. Substage 3 occurs from 4 to 8 months. Infants react to their environment more than they did before; they babble and react more energetically when others respond to them. In substage 4, which extends from 9 to 12 months, two important cognitive gains take place: goal-directed behavior and object permanence. Prior to this, infants only have accidental behavior, but substage 4 is marked by goal-directed behaviors. Babies can intentionally solve problems with sensorimotor means, such as by sucking their thumbs to self-soothe. Similarly, children learn that objects exist even if they cannot see them; this is called object permanence. A distinguishing quality of object permanence is that a child will look only in one place to find a hidden object, rather than looking in multiple places. If you hide a beloved teddy bear behind your back, the child will look for it behind your back. However, if you move it from behind your back to under the sofa, the child will not continue searching for it. Infants also become better at anticipating events, and as a result they might try to change those events. To illustrate, if an infant sees her mother getting her coat, the infant knows that getting a coat means that her mother is leaving. She may protest or cry to try to maintain her mother's proximity.

Substages 5 and 6 are called tertiary circular reactions and extend from 12 to 24 months. In substage 5 (12 to 18 months), a toddler's actions become more creative, although he/she continues to solve problems through physical means. This stage is marked by trial-and-error learning; children approach the world in a deliberate manner, trying to solve problems and play in combination with their new physical gains. Children will try to perform activities to provoke new effects. For example, a toddler may push a car into the sofa over and over before it eventually turns to go in the direction she/he wants. The child may throw a ball downstairs, roll it down the stairs, and bounce it off the wall in an attempt to learn how the ball rolls in different ways. In addition, object permanence extends, and the toddler will look in more than one place for a hidden object. The final substage extends from 18 to 24 months, during which the child gains greater mental representation. Instead of using trial-and-error learning, toddlers in substage 6 use mental combinations rather than physical means to solve problems. Instead of pushing the car against the sofa, the toddler has now learned that if she/he stops and moves the car, then the car will go in the direction she/he wants. She/he will briefly stop and think about what she/he has learned and move the car. Another cognitive gain in substage 6 is deferred imitation. Mental representation allows children to remember and copy a behavior they have seen. For example, if a child sees a peer throw a temper tantrum today, she/he may act out that same temper tantrum the following day; or the child may watch a parent sweep the driveway today and imitate that same act in a few days. Finally, make-believe play emerges, in which the child acts out familiar activities, such as pretending to be asleep or pretending to eat.

The second stage of Piaget's theory of cognitive development is called the preoperational stage and occurs from ages 2 to 7 (this is presented in more detail in chapter 5). This stage is characterized by the greater mental representation seen in toddlers' play, language, and behaviors. Make-believe play becomes more of a sociodrama. Make-believe play initially begins through pretending to do ordinary and familiar activities (i.e., pretending to sleep). Even by 2½ years of age, a child may assume roles and act out familiar scripts. For example, a child may pretend to be a doctor and act out a complex plot. Objects that a child plays with also change and extend beyond their function. A coat rack may be a control tower for a child pretending to be an astronaut and then become a goal post for an imaginary soccer game.

In addition to the acquisition of new cognitive abilities, children become skilled at applying their abilities in various ways. A child between 24 and 36 months of age begins to understand that the causes and consequences of behaviors better. A child may know that she/he must look both ways before venturing into the street but may fail to remember until she/he is already in the middle of the street.

Language Development

Language development and language understanding begin at birth. Infants initially have the ability to reflexively communicate through crying, and soon after with coos, differential crying, and fussing. Newborns prefer high-pitched "baby talk" over normal speech; and babies communicate with coos and cries before they babble. At 6 months of age, all infants begin babbling, including deaf babies. Babies understand language long before they can speak it. Between 10 and 12 months, children begin to use gestures to make their wants known; for example, they will point at the refrigerator if they want water or milk. First words are spoken around the age of 12 months, and between 13 and 18 months language acquisition develops slowly. Children this age learn about 1 to 3 words a month. Initially, language development builds on sensorimotor activities. To illustrate, a child will put her/his hands in the air and say "up" or wave good-bye while saying "bye bye."

Between 18 and 24 months, language acquisition explodes and toddlers learn 10 to 20 words a week and 3 or more words a day. By the end of this period, children know about 200 words and begin to use their words to make their wants known. Initially children begin using holophrases, or one-word phrases; two-word phrases begin at approximately 21 months. During this time, children leave out all of the unimportant words and include only the most important words to convey a meaning, such as "more cookie," referred to as telegraphic speech. Two grammatical errors generally occur as children acquire language. One error is underextension, where children use a word only to refer to a certain thing even though the word actually represents more than one object. For example, a child might call her/his favorite stuffed animal a "doll" but fail to call any other stuffed animal a doll; those objects would be called something else by the child. A second, more common grammatical error is overextension. Overextension occurs when a word is overextended and applied to more objects than is actually intended. For example, a child might call any object with wheels or that transports people a "car," which would include bikes, cars, airplanes, buses, and trains.

Physical Development

The most obvious signs of growth and development in children ages 0 to 3 occur in physical growth. Babies become rounder and plumper for the last few weeks of gestational life to their 9th month. During the first few days of life, infants generally lose weight, but they quickly regain it as they begin eating regularly and become adjusted to life outside the womb. By the 4th month of life, infants generally double their birth weight. It is normal for the child's head to be bigger in proportion to the rest of the body until approximately age 2, when a child's body mimics an adult body. Infants should get taller and stronger; they should gain weight and height. Physical growth decreases in the second year and even more so in the third year, when appetite and sleep decline.

Motor Skills

Infants progress from simple reflexive beings to mobile and industrious toddlers. Gross motor skills involve large muscle groups. At birth, newborns are not strong enough to hold their heads up, but they quickly gain the strength to do so by approximately 6 weeks. At 1 month, an infant should be able to thrust her/his arms in play, and at 2 months infants will make crawling movements when placed on their stomachs. Infants attempt to bring their hands to their mouth at 3 months and can sit with support at 4 months. Five-month-old infants push their weight to their arms when on their stomach. Infants can usually sit alone by 6 months; they begin attempts at crawling, which most achieve on all fours by 8 months. Once children learn to crawl, they begin to pull themselves up on furniture and learn to climb. They start making attempts at walking, first with help from parents and then on their own. Most children are able to walk alone between 12 and 13 months. Oftentimes, walking children will resort to crawling when they desire speed until they become more adept at walking. Toddlers increasingly become better and more coordinated walkers. As they master this task, they become good at running, skipping, walking on tiptoes, and gross motor movements, such as kicking a ball and throwing.

During their first year of life, children gain almost an inch in height every month; and the average North American infant weighs 22 pounds and is 30 inches long by 12 months of age (Behrman, 1992). Most children are able to walk by 13 months and eventually run. Toddlers can walk up stairs with help at 16 months, as well as throw a ball while standing. By 23 months, toddlers should be able to jump in place.

Between 24 and 36 months, children generally become slimmer and some body fat diminishes. They add 2 to 3 inches and about 5 pounds during the year. A child will likely experience a decrease in appetite due to the slowdown in growth, as well as a decrease in sleep.

The gross motor skills of toddlers ages 26 to 36 months continue to develop. They keep practicing the skills they have already acquired—running and jumping—but there are changes. Toddlers begin to walk better and more rhythmically; their feet are not as widely spaced, and they will swing their opposite arm. Hurried walk changes to a true run, and they might jump down from step to step. They'll begin to ride push toys with their feet and with steering.

Gross motor skills develop before fine motor skills, because fine motor skills require small and sophisticated movements. Fine motor skills are more difficult than gross motor skills for infants and toddlers. While grabbing is initially reflexive, infants increasingly gain more control over their grasping behaviors. At 4 months, infants begin to inspect their own hands, and grabbing and reaching improves by 6 months. Infants with even a mild amount of visual stimulation reach for objects earlier than infants who lack visual stimulation. By 6 months, the child should be able to hold an object in her/his hand and bang on something. The child should be able to hold a rattle and even transfer an object from one hand to another. At 6 months, children will reach and grab for anything—eyeglasses, earrings, hair. Fine motor skills allow children to explore their environment and see how things in the world work. Babies develop a pincer grasp, a grasp with their thumb and forefinger that allows them to pick up even the smallest objects. The development of fine motor skills can be a dangerous time for parents as children become increasingly mobile and then have the ability to pick up small objects.

Fine motor skills continue to develop from 12 to 24 months. Toddlers are able to hold a pencil or crayon, use building blocks, and scribble. They should have a well-coordinated pincer grasp that allows them to pick up fine objects, such as pieces of grass, as well as the ability to open and close boxes and turn knobs. Fine motor development is also reflected in their play, such as putting small objects into boxes.

At 24 to 36 months, toddlers' fine motor skills become increasingly refined and are easily seen in an increase in self-help skills. Toddlers should be able to use a fork and spoon and get dressed/undressed with simple items of clothing. They are often very excited about their ability to manage their own skills and bodies. They should become better at scribbling and drawing. Toddlers should also be able to build towers of blocks, and their play changes with their new physical and cognitive skills.

Culture and ethnicity do influence motor development in young children, and understanding culture's role in human development is essential to an adequate developmental assessment. Within certain cultural groups, parents expect greater physical independence at an earlier age from their children (e.g., Bartz & Levine, 1978). When this expectation exists, children tend to walk and perform self-care skills earlier.

Brain Development

The brain in an infant and toddler is closer to its adult size than any other structure. A newborn's skull is larger than the rest of its body because it has to hold the brain, which is already 25% of its adult weight (Berger, 2001) and takes up 25% of the infant's total body length (Berk, 2001). By age 2, the brain is approximately 75% of its adult weight and occupies 20% of the total body length. The brain grows faster than the rest of the body because it makes the development of other areas possible.

More important than the brain's weight is the brain's communication system. At birth, the brain is composed of hundreds of billions of neurons that transmit and store information, and the production of neurons is nearly complete by the end of the second trimester of pregnancy. A small gap between neurons, called synapses, assists neurons in sending information to one another. During a child's first two years, the growth of neurons and the synaptic connections increase at a remarkable rate (Moore & Persuad, 1998), and this phenomenon is referred to as transient exuberance (Nowakowski, 1987). It is called transient because the rate of neural growth and synaptic connections decreases with age, and exuberant because of the enormity of the growth of the neural connections. An important aspect of this brain growth is stimulation. Neural pathways that are stimulated by the environment and exercised become stronger and larger; the neural pathways develop more connections (Berger, 2001), and they form elaborate communication systems that allow the child complex abilities. On the other hand, neural pathways that are not stimulated or exercised atrophy and die. Therefore, experience and a stimulating environment are necessary for the development of neural pathways, which allow for the acquisition of skill and complex abilities. Deprivation of early stimulation can have lifelong implications for the developing person.

Brain development also corresponds with the physical, social, and emotional development of a child. The first part of the brain that develops is the brainstem, which controls body temperature, heart rate, and blood pressure. The last part of the brain to fully develop is the cortex, which controls abstract and concrete thought. Obviously, the brain grows in an important sequence, with the lower brain controlling functions necessary for life (i.e., heart rate) and higher parts controlling more sophisticated tasks (i.e., abstract thought). In addition, the parts of the cortex that control auditory and visual functioning have a synaptic growth spurt from age 3–4 months until the end of the 1st year, when tremendous visual and hearing gains occur (Berk, 2001). Other areas, such as the frontal lobe, develop later to assist with self-control and regulation. Infants have less mature frontal lobes and are unable to control their sleeping patterns during the first few months of life. Later, as the child nears age 1, the frontal lobe is better developed and can assist in the regulation of sleeping and eating patterns. Eventually, the frontal lobe helps the child with emotional regulation, which is an important component of social development in toddlers (Berger, 2001).

The brain is also referred to as "plastic" because the environment plays a role in its development. Many neural pathways are prewired at birth. For example, our brains prepare us for responding to speech (NCCAN, 2001). Neural pathways that are used and stimulated are strengthened and increase, while those that are not used become weak and are eventually discarded. If the neural pathways are discarded completely, then the expected functions may not ever occur. Therefore, a stimulating environment in the early years of life is paramount to lifelong healthy development, including brain development. Birth to 3 years of age presents sensitive periods for tremendous brain growth and development, and such opportunities begin to decrease after the age of 3 (Shore, 1997). Thus, the first three years of a child's life lays a foundation for future functioning.

DEVELOPMENTAL CONSEQUENCES OF CHILD MALTREATMENT FOR CHILDREN 0 TO 3 YEARS OF AGE

Infants and toddlers make tremendous developmental gains from 0 to 3 years of age. They evolve from primarily reflexive beings to walking and talking toddlers. Child maltreatment affects all areas of a child's development. Child victims suffer devastating consequences at such a crucial developmental time. More children die from maltreatment between the ages of 0 and 3 than during any other time (USDHHS, 2002). Besides death, children may suffer developmental delays, social, emotional, and physical problems. Infants and toddlers who enter the state's custody due to child maltreatment have been shown to be at risk on developmental screenings (Dale, Kendall, & Humber, 1996) and significantly below average on Bayley Scales of Infant Development (Urquiza et al., 1994).

The consequences of maltreatment can affect a child's development, which may not be recoverable with age. While all three forms (physical abuse, neglect, and sexual abuse) of maltreatment overlap to a certain extent, especially when discussing such young victims, each type results in developmental consequences to its victims. This section presents the consequences of physical abuse, sexual abuse, and neglect. Neglect occupies the greatest attention since it is the most likely to be confirmed and has the most devastating consequences for the youngest of victims.

Physical Abuse

One of the most obvious signs of development is the child's physical development, and child physical abuse can result in devastating consequences to a child who should grow from an infant into a mobile and energetic toddler. Children evolve from babies into active, playful toddlers whose approach to the world is exploratory. Child physical abuse is often the result of harsh discipline and corporal punishment in order to control the playful toddlers' behavior, but it extends beyond the point of discipline to physical injury or the risk of physical injury. Families from all socioeconomic, racial, and educational backgrounds commit physical abuse, but it is most often confirmed for single parent and poor households (Belsky & Vondra, 1989; Whipple & Webster-Stratton, 1991).

Cognitive-Behavioral

Even in the first few years of life, infants and toddlers who have been physically abused and maltreated in general may exhibit signs of post-traumatic stress disorder (PTSD). The result of physical trauma may manifest in both cognitive and behavioral changes. For example, a child who has been severely sexually abused may appear "catatonic" when placed in foster care and demonstrate extreme re-sistance to physical contact, which is certainly contrary to the expectation when children are developing attachments with others in their environment. Physical contact is more important during infancy and toddlerhood than in other devel-opmental periods. Infants, even as early as 3 months of age, can learn to expect regularity in their environment, but they can also learn that their environment is irregular and unpredictable. When a physically abused infant is placed in a safer environment, she/he may maintain the detachment that was necessary to cope with her/his chaotic and abusive environment. Coping with chaos is apparent in the child's behavior (i.e., detachment), especially with preverbal children and children with limited language development.

As children develop representational memory in their 2nd year, they may show their trauma through play or drawings (Gaensbauer & Siegel, 1995). Physically abused children may act out or draw a circumstance that depicts trauma and their abuse in play. As children become more verbal, they may provide verbal inter-pretation of a traumatic event shown in their play or behavior (ibid.), although physically abused children have been shown to have delayed language develop-ment (Oates, Peacock, & Forrest, 1984).

Socioemotional

The importance of attachment and its consequences have been explored in chap-ter 2. Children who have been physically abused have been shown to be at risk of establishing an insecure-avoidant attachment pattern with caregivers (Ainsworth et al., 1978). In relationships with peers, physically abused children are more likely to use avoidant behaviors with caregivers and other children, as well as increased aggression with peers (George & Main, 1979). With age, such children are also likely to show resistant behaviors. Compared to neglected children, physically abused children show more aggression toward others (Egeland, Sroufe, & Erickson, 1983), and physically abused toddlers respond less positively toward friendly gestures (George & Main, 1979). Similarly, internal working models, which are developed from one's primary attachment relationship in infancy, can be negatively affected by the impairment physical abuse may bring to the attachment relationship. Chil-dren who have been physically abused may have problems with achieving autonomy, Erickson's 2nd psychosocial task (see Table 3.1), because of their insecure attach-ment and failure to develop trust in their environment (Houck & King, 1989). Autonomy allows the child to explore her/his environment and feel competent in her/his social abilities—a cornerstone of healthy development in infancy and toddlerhood.

The extension of emotions to others and the development of empathy begin to develop in the 2nd year of life. A child who has been physically abused may act aggressively toward other children in peer relationships. A physically abused child, when presented with an opportunity to exhibit empathic behaviors, may demon-strate a lack of emotional understanding and empathic responding (Straker & Jacobson, 1981). When given the opportunity for prosocial behavior, the physi-cally abused child may react with resistance rather than assistance or concern

(Howes & Eldredge, 1985). For example, a physically abused toddler might kick sand on a child crying on the playground.

Similarly, play is an important part of toddlerhood, which changes from solitary play to make believe and dramatic play. Maltreated children tend to have similar frequencies of dramatic play as nonmaltreated children, but their themes are different. Maltreated children demonstrate concrete and parental role themes, rather than fantasy themes that are seen among nonmaltreated children (Alessandri, 1992). Abused toddlers may act out an abusive situation or take on the role of an abusive parent toward their dolls. Thematic details tend to be less fantasy and make-believe oriented, and more concrete and realistic.

Physical

Death is one consequence of child physical abuse in infancy and toddlerhood. Almost 28% of all child deaths were the result of physical abuse in 2002, and 44% of all fatalities were for children under the age of 1 (USDHHS, 2002). Infants and toddlers who have been physically abused may have burns, bite marks, bruises, fractures, and injuries, often in uncommon sites (i.e., burn marks on genital areas; a burn mark on inner part of arm where area was immobilized; bruises on buttocks). In many circumstances the parental explanation is inconsistent with the injury. Therefore, the parental explanation is of the utmost importance in assessing physical abuse in infants and toddlers due to the victims' limited vocabulary and language capability.

Physically abused children may have a host of medical problems, including failure to thrive (Famularo et al., 1992), brain injury (Bruce, 1992), and abdominal injuries (Ricci, 2000). In addition to experiencing immediate symptoms, which may include lethargy, vomiting, and irritability (Perry et al., 2002), physically abused infants and toddlers may also experience long-term effects. Severe infant physical abuse can manifest in developmental delays, retardation, and paralysis (Perry et al., 2002). Similarly, children may exhibit a high pain tolerance. When a child falls on the playground and hurts himself/herself, a child who has been chronically physically abused may fail to cry or show appropriate emotional reaction to the apparent injury.

In addition to medical problems, physically abused children may also have delayed physical development. A physically abused child may lag behind other infants and toddlers in both gross and fine motor skills. An infant who has experienced physical abuse may be delayed in or fail to hold her/his head up, crawl, and walk. Physically abused infants may have either new or untreated fractures that make gross motor movement painful. Old fractures that have not healed properly may make movement painful and sometimes awkward-looking. Fine motor skills may also be affected by physical abuse, such as holding a book with both hands, using eating utensils, or dressing oneself. However, Reams (1999) found that children entering the state's custody due to maltreatment showed deficits in motor skills least often compared to other developmental areas for 0- to 3-year-olds.

The brain is also affected by physical abuse in infancy and toddlerhood. The brain allows the infant or toddler to organize and adapt to the trauma she/he has experienced (Perry, 1997). The brain will develop in accordance with the environment in which the child victim lives. Children whose cries are met with abuse learn different lessons from children whose cries are met with comfort (NCCAN, 2001). Unpredictable and prolonged stress has a negative impact on the developing child's brain, which may result in overdevelopment of areas of the brain involved in anxiety and fear responses (ibid.). Consequently, neural pathways in other areas of the brain may then be underdeveloped. Children who are chronically physically abused may grow up in a constant state of fear (Perry, 1997).

As child victims of chronic physical abuse grow, they often exhibit behaviors indicative of fight or flight responses or dissociation. Infants, however, are not capable of fight or flight responses (Perry & Pollard, 1998). Instead, an infant will use crying, facial expressions, or body movements to indicate discomfort. The infant requires the assistance of a caregiver to manage and overcome the perceived threat. Yet such behaviors in maltreated infants may not elicit a comforting response from their environments; they may actually receive a threatening response with physical violence or no response at all, as with neglect. As a result, a child will learn, even by 3 months, that crying elicits no response or a negative response and will fail to cry. Infants, in particular, with limited fight or flight response options, may use dissociation as a means to manage unpredictable stress (ibid.). Children who have been physically abused may appear to use survival tactics to navigate everyday life, especially when the threats perceived at home are unpredictable and chaotic. In toddlerhood, they may become aggressive in an attempt to control the predictability of physical abuse, rather than wait for it to happen (Perry, 1997). Physical abuse influences the brain to focus its resources on the child's survival and in response to environmental threats (NCCAN, 2001).

After prolonged, unpredictable physical abuse, a child's brain will adapt and be ready for danger (NCCAN, 2001). When the neural pathways involved in fear are constantly activated in a child, the child may cognitively perceive the world as a threatening place and will act accordingly for survival. Even in circumstances where a threat is minimal, the child's brain is organized to perceive the world as hostile with the child in need of protection. The brain becomes hyperaroused to danger, which is especially common later in life among males and older children (Perry, 1996). One way that physically abused children adapt to such a world is by provoking aggression in an attempt to manage the predictability of it (Perry, 1997); children learn that it is better to control when the abuse happens because they "know" that it is going to happen. As a result, they may provoke aggression to elicit the predictable response.

One specific type of child physical abuse, commonly referred to as shaken baby syndrome, results from vigorously shaking a baby usually between 0 and 1 year old. Such infants present to the hospital with seizures, vomiting, lethargy, drowsiness, and death, to name a few symptoms. Shaken babies often show retinal damage and brain injury. The physical consequence of shaken baby syndrome is usually brain injury, but it can also result in spinal cord injury and subsequent paralysis. Either consequence, however, affects all areas of one's development.

Neglect

In 2000 in the United States, 62% of all confirmed victims of maltreatment were victims of neglect (USDHHS, 2002). Neglected children are more likely to be younger, and the highest rate of victimization is between the 0 and 3 age group (USDHHS, 2002). The most devastating consequence of neglect is death, and in 2000 the majority of deaths due to maltreatment were due to neglect. Overall, child fatality due to neglect ranges from 32% (Delambre & Wood, 1997) to 48% (Wang & Daro, 1998) of all reported child death cases. One aspect of neglect that separates it from physical abuse or sexual abuse is that it tends to be chronic rather than episodic. Neglect tends to be a lifestyle rather than an event. An impoverished parent-child relationship is at the core of the definition of neglect. Children ages 0 to 3 need a consistent and responsive caregiver to meet her/his physical, cognitive, and emotional needs. An infant has few other outlets to receive nurturance and care. As a result, the consequences of neglect in young children span all areas of a child's development (Scannapieco & Connell-Carrick, 2002).

Cognitive-Behavioral

A child who has been neglected may be delayed in her/his cognitive development (Scannapieco & Connell-Carrick, 2002). One specific type of neglect, failure to thrive, has specific manifestations on an infant's cognitive development, and will be expanded upon in chapter 4. However, children who have been hospitalized for failure to thrive with low weight have been shown to have poorer cognitive functioning than normal weight children (Singer, 1986). The cognitive deficits of nonorganic failure-to-thrive infants who have been given psychosocial intervention still persist at 3 years of age (Singer, 1986). Similarly, infants and toddlers who experience both neglect and failure to thrive show more severe cognitive deficits than infants who experience only one type of maltreatment or none at all (Mackner, Starr, & Black, 1997).

Infants suffer cognitive deficits as a result of neglect, and research shows that children who are placed in environmentally enriching and stimulating homes can make up for the developmental and cognitive delays of impoverishment. One study of Romanian orphans who were reared in an emotionally and physically deprived environment found significant developmental differences at the age of placement into adoption (Rutter et al., 1999). All infants placed in adoption were doing poorly at initial placement, but those who were placed prior to 6 months had greater developmental improvements than those adopted between 6 and 24 months. Thus, if identified early enough, the developmental delays of neglected children may be recoverable.

The cognitive deficits of neglected children seem to cumulate with time (Gowen, 1993). Infants and toddlers are generally interested in their surroundings and enjoy looking at human faces and hearing noises. A neglected child may appear apathetic and disinterested in her/his environment. Children have beginning forms of mental representation even by 6 months of age, and this may be lacking in a neglected child who has failed to receive environmental stimulation. For example, if you make an "O" with your mouth to a 5-month-old child, you should see them looking intently at your face and trying to imitate your facial expression. While they may not actually make the "O," they should begin moving their mouth in an attempt to make your expression. Experiencing new things is how the infant learns; an infant must have a stimulating environment in addition to good nutrition and an available caregiver.

Children at 3 months of age begin to anticipate events. If a child wakes from a nap at 3 months of age, she/he may begin to cry. When her/his mother (caregiver) comes into his room, she/he will stop crying because she/he knows that she/he is going to be picked up. However, neglected children may either fail to cry or cry indiscriminately. The child may not cry because he/she has learned that crying elicits no response. Or the child may cry without trying to convey a message to a caregiver. A child who has experienced neglect, even at 3 months, has already learned that she/he cannot rely on others to meet her/his needs.

Between 6 and 12 months, infants begin to have goal-directed behaviors, and they can coordinate specific activities that are deliberate (such as thumb sucking). As children mature, they become increasingly interested in their environment, and this may not be apparent in neglected children (Scannapieco & Connell-Carrick, 2002). They may not have self-soothing intentional behaviors but may appear indifferent to their surroundings.

Children at 6 months also should be babbling, and there should be a progression from first words to phrases during the first three years. Severe neglect has been shown to be related to a number of language delays (Culp et al., 1991). Neglected children show declines in both expressive and receptive language skills (Gowen, 1993). Maltreated toddlers develop and use language differently than nonmaltreated toddlers. They use language less frequently for social or affective exchanges than nonmaltreated toddlers (Cicchetti & Lynch, 1993). Neglected children will likely babble, but their language development afterward may fail to develop as expected. They may fail to use gestures to convey wants from 6 to 12 months, and they may not understand simple dialogue (e.g., "Where is your nose?"). One way that the caregiver facilitates language development in a child is to attach a word to the gesture; neglected children may not have a caregiver who is responsive to their needs in this way, and language development may be delayed. From 12 to 24 months, and especially around 18 to 24 months, language development should be markedly apparent and increasingly rapid; and this often does not occur for neglected children.

By the time children who are developing normally reach 24 months, they should have a vocabulary of approximately 200 words, but neglected children may already be behind in their language acquisition (Scannapieco & Connell-Carrick, 2002). You should expect to be able to talk to the child about something by 2 years of age, but keep in mind that children adopt the speech to which they are exposed. At 24 months, neglected children may not use two-word sentences, and their conversational skills may be poor.

Other expected developmental indicators include changes in play. Recall that toddlers from 12 to 18 months repeat actions with variation, provoking new effects; their approach to the world is exploratory. Children between 12 and 18 months who have been neglected may not exhibit an exploratory approach to the world with trial-and-error learning. They may appear indifferent and lethargic in a room full of toys. With the greater mental representation that is expected in children between 18 and 24 months, children are able to recall people, places, and events better, and neglected children may not be able to do this. For example, a child who is 30 months should be able to recall where you keep candy in your office after a few visits if you allow her/him to have candy every time she/he visits you; a neglected child may not do this. The neglected child, if accustomed to one-command statements, may have great difficulty understanding more complex sentences.

Socioemotional

In general, maltreated children are more likely to have attachment problems than other children, and those can range from mild interpersonal difficulties to the loss of capacity to form any meaningful relationship. While infants and toddlers who have been physically abused tend to develop insecure-avoidant attachment relationships, infants who have been neglected tend to develop insecure-resistant (Ainsworth et al., 1978) and anxious attachment patterns (Erickson & Egeland, 2002). Erickson and Egeland (2002) also found that by the age of 2, children who had experienced neglect displayed avoidant or unaffectionate behaviors toward their mothers. With age, both physically abused and neglected children are eventually likely to be classified as disorganized-disoriented because both groups have been found to display resistant and avoidant behaviors in the presence of their caregiver. Attachment should also be viewed in its cultural context since attachment behavior may vary depending upon the type of caregiving arrangement the family uses or the child's frequency of contact with strangers or separation from the caregiver.

Attachment should be assessed by inspecting both the parent and child. One indication of a poor attachment is when a child fails to use crying as a means of communication; they either fail to cry or cry indiscriminately. As the child matures, she/he may fail to return to their caregiver/attachment figure in times of distress, and fail to use her/his caregiver as a secure base. The child may either ignore their caregiver or be preoccupied with her/him, both of which are indicators of avoidant or ambivalent attachments. The child may similarly act confused or dazed in the presence of a caregiver, an indication of a disorganized attachment pattern. One of the primary social tasks of the first year of life is the development of trust, and neglected babies may appear distrustful and hopeless in their surroundings.

While smiling is reflexive during the first few weeks of life, it eventually becomes socially constructed. By the 6th to 10th week, smiling is elicited by a human face, someone smiling at the infant, or the visual recognition of a caregiver. Neglected children are often not offered the stimulation to evoke a social smile, and the neglected child may fail to smile. Neglected infants may not laugh, which also requires active stimulation.

Virtually all infants experience stranger and separation anxiety, but many neglected infants fail to do so, especially around 7 to 10 months. If the neglected toddler does not have a real understanding of who is supposed to take care of her/him, she/he will respond indiscriminately to any stranger or being left with any person. The neglected child will not expect someone to meet her/his needs. The degree to which stranger and separation anxiety is seen is multiply determined, however, by culture, the child's temperament, past experiences with strangers, and the situation in which the infant meets the stranger. Neglected children are often not cared for consistently by a caregiver, and therefore they do not experience anxiety when separating from their caregiver. Stranger and separation anxiety serves a self-preservation function for infants because they induce fear. Fear keeps children close to those who are supposed to protect them. Children should become more skilled at social referencing and looking to a known person for information on how to respond in an uncertain situation. Neglected children may not have a specific person to look toward to give them such information, and they may not social reference at all.

It is important, however, to assess attachment and separation and stranger anxieties within a cultural context. The manner in which the infant is raised may affect the child's reaction to separation from a caregiver and interaction with strangers. For example, children who are taken to child care while their parent works may not demonstrate the same level of anxiety at their caregiver's departure and return. They may have become accustomed to the separation and reunion with their caregiver and seem to be unaffected by it. Similarly, children raised in a multiple caregiving format run the risk of being mislabeled with regard to attachment. Traditional in the African American community (Jackson, 1993), children become accustomed to having multiple caregivers—usually blood and nonblood relatives. Therefore, the responses seen from such children at separation and reunion do not typically conform to Eurocentric and single/dual caregiver patterns of behavior.

Children who have been neglected may also show developmental delays between 24 and 36 months. Such children may lack the vocabulary to talk about emotions and lack the ability to regulate their emotions in general. The behavioral expression of emotions also may not be evident in neglected children. They will not hang their heads when ashamed or hide their faces when embarrassed, or even have an understanding of such emotions.

Neglected children may have problems interacting and playing with others. They may fail to extend their knowledge of emotions to others, as is expected of children ages 24 to 36 months. Instead, they may act angry (Erickson & Egeland, 2002) and aggressively, such as behaving forcefully towards a hurt and crying child on the playground, indicating a lack of empathic behavior. They may also have general problems in relating and playing with peers and fail to demonstrate make-believe play. Neglected toddlers also tend to be easily frustrated, impulsive and show little enthusiasm towards play (Erickson & Egeland, 2002).

Emotional abuse is often linked with neglect since neglect cannot occur in infancy and toddlerhood without some emotional consequence to the child, although the link between emotional abuse and maltreatment is equally relevant to any discussion of physical abuse and sexual abuse. Equally noteworthy is an infant or toddler who witnesses the abuse of a parent, such as in cases of domestic violence. Children understand language far earlier than they can speak it, and witnessing fights, whether physical or verbal, between one's caregiver and another can be traumatic. Children respond with more post-traumatic stress symptomatology when a caregiver is threatened, including fears, aggression symptoms, and hyperarousal (Scheeringa & Zeanah, 1995). While a caregiver may feel like she/he is protecting an infant during a domestic disturbance, often the child will fear harm to her/his caregiver and exhibit PTSD symptomology.

Physical

The most obvious signs of development in infancy and toddlerhood occur with physical maturity, but neglected children are often smaller and weigh less than other children. Neglected children experience inadequate physical care (Gowen, 1993). Failure to thrive is one of the most devastating physical manifestations of neglect in infancy and toddlerhood. Nonorganic failure-to-thrive infants (NOFTT) are generally below the 5th percentile of relative growth for infants at a given age, and the diagnosis places children at significant risk of poor developmental outcomes (Casey, Bradley, & Wortham, 1984). While one would expect a child to increase in both height and weight, neglected children and NOFTT infants may decrease and fall down the growth curve. Neglected children often fail to get round and plump, as is normal for children until the age of 9 months. Failure-to-thrive infants often fail to gain weight at all and will continue to be smaller and weigh less even as they mature (Kristiansson & Fallstrom, 1987). The skin of children who have been neglected may also appear dull and their hair thin.

Children who have been neglected may fail to develop their gross motor skills as well as other children do (Scannapieco & Connell-Carrick, 2002). The neglected infant may not be able to keep her/his head erect, as expected at 6 weeks. Neglected infants may not elevate themselves by their arms, sit with support, roll over, or crawl, as expected. Some neglected infants are placed for long periods in one position, and their body develops differently or abnormally. For example, a child who virtually lives in a car seat will have an extremely flat head; and a child who is placed in a bouncing swing will only develop leg muscles but will be unable to sit because of a failure to develop back muscles. The neglected infant may not walk on time, and the child may be behind in gross motor development with no medical explanation. The toddler who has chronically experienced neglect may not run or jump, as is expected when there is a progression from walking to more sophisticated gross motor behaviors.

Children who have been neglected may fail to develop fine motor skills, such as grabbing, reaching, and picking up objects, at the rate of nonmaltreated children. They may be unable to hold an object, such as their bottle or rattle at 6 months, or something larger, like a book at 12 months (Scannapieco & Connell-Carrick, 2002). Children between 12 and 23 months may be unable to hold a crayon, throw a ball, or pick up small objects. The child who is neglected may not be able to use a fork or dress oneself in his/her 2nd year of life, as is expected and developmentally appropriate for a toddler.

Effects on the Brain

Chronic neglect in infancy and toddlerhood has a devastating effect on the developing child and the child's brain. As discussed previously, during the first three years of life the brain is rapidly developing, with the tremendous growth of neural pathways. Babies' brains grow and develop as they interact with their environments and learn how to function within them (NCCAN, 2001). For appropriate neural pathways to develop, a child must have a stimulating environment. Pathways that are not stimulated decrease, whereas pathways that are stimulated flourish. The later functioning of the child may depend upon the development of critical pathways during infancy and toddlerhood. The brain of a child in an environment in which a child is ignored without proper stimulation for growth may develop to focus only on day-to-day survival and fail to develop other important areas, such as cognitive and social growth. When neural pathways die, the child may not be able to achieve the expected developmental milestones, which is often seen among chronically neglected children (NCCAN, 2001).

Children must be provided the opportunity to develop their neural connections during infancy and toddlerhood. Babies who are not spoken to may not develop language at the same rate as other children. When a child's cries are not responded to or are met with hostility, the child learns early that crying does not elicit a desired response and may fail to cry. Consequently, when a child is not offered attention or positive interaction, she/he may not then know how to deliver comfort and kindness to others. Such capacities often fail to develop because the child lacked the environmental, and thereby neural, stimulation necessary for such pathways to develop (NCCAN, 2001). In extreme cases of neglect where the child experiences overall sensory deprivation, the brain may be smaller, fewer neural pathways may exist, and the child may be permanently damaged intellectually (Greenough, Black, & Wallace, 1987; Perry & Pollard, 1998).

One of the most important tasks of infancy is the development of attachment. The ability to form an attachment relationship may also be a function of early brain development. The lack of appropriate affective experiences in early life results in the misorganization of attachment capabilities (Perry, 1997). Early neglect may result in the lack of empathy because the part of one's brain that understands connectedness to others fails to develop. Lack of empathy or the lack of connectedness one feels to others may have tremendous consequences to the child as well as society. Perry maintains that the ability to feel empathy, remorse, and sympathy are experience-dependent capabilities. A child who experiences a lack of comfort and care may fail to develop such emotions. Children may then grow to behavior in ways consistent with their upbringing (i.e., without remorse or concern for others).

In addition to affective difficulties seen in many neglected children, neglect has a profound influence on a child's cognitive capability. Cognitive stimulation allows the brain to develop critical neural pathways. Conversely, a lack of stimulation may result in brain size and capability differences. The cortex regulates the functioning of lower parts of the central nervous system. Its growth and ability to make synaptic connections is dependent upon the type, quality, and quantity of sensory experience (Chisholm et al., 1995). When a child lacks sensory stimulation and cognitive experience, as is often the case with neglect, the cortex may be smaller in size and have fewer neural pathways, resulting in long-term negative consequences for the developing child (Perry, 1997).

This discussion of the consequences of neglect may seem somewhat extreme given that the scope of neglectful behaviors is broad. Not all neglect is characterized by extreme deprivation; some neglect *may* be more benign, such as the case with incidents of neglectful supervision or merely a dirty house. For example, the majority of children who live in dirty homes are well cared for. Some caregivers may be excellent caregivers but forgetful or preoccupied at times. A well-cared-for child living in a dirty home would not show many or any of the aforementioned developmental manifestations. This discussion of neglect, however, focuses on the consequence to the child when lack of care of the infant or toddler is central to the maltreatment. This discussion centers on the impoverishment of care inherent in serious child neglect, which is a devastating event in a young child's life. As discussed further in chapter 4, protective factors may mediate the negative consequences seen even in the worst of neglect cases. Emotional deprivation to an infant or toddler, however, is cause for great concern and results in negative child developmental outcomes.

Sexual Abuse

Sexual abuse of infants and toddlers can include fondling, digital penetration, object insertion, oral sex, and intercourse. Physical contact and touch is more important from 0 to 3 years of age than it is in other developmental periods. Infants need more physical contact and tactile stimulation for optimal development than children in other developmental periods. While physical contact is necessary for healthy growth, perpetrators of sexual abuse cause harm to the developing child. Some argue that since the infant's memory is developing, the child will not remember what has happened. However, infancy and toddlerhood is a time of great learning about the world, its safety, and its predictability. The relationships formed with one's caregiver(s) lay a foundation for future relationships. Children learn even in the first months of life how their world works, and who is safe and who is not. Their bodies respond physiologically to changes and distress, and they understand the world before they can talk about it. The difference between adults and infants is that an infant's brain is just organizing itself, while adult trauma changes how one's brain organizes events (Perry, 1994). Thus, children understand and organize victimization even though they may not be able to verbalize it, which has long-lasting consequences for development.

It is important to mention that no specific disorder characterizes the child who has been sexually abused. Some children show no symptoms, while others show a variety of symptoms that make the identification of a sexual abuse syndrome impossible (Kendall, Williams & Finkelhor, 1993).

Cognitive-Behavioral

It seems reasonable that infants and toddlers who have been sexually abused before the age of 3 may experience no effects or even remember the incident(s) of abuse. However, infants are able to "recall" prior traumatic events even if they have no concrete awareness of them; they have no tangible "memory" of the event, but their bodies respond physically to danger and fear that manifests from sexual touching (Perry, 2003). Perry argues that infants have physiological memories rather than the ability to recall an event.

Behavioral responses to traumatic events often manifest in patterns of activity that begin in birth, even though the infant or toddler may be preverbal and seemingly unaware of events. Infants and toddlers who have experienced sexual abuse may associate genital touch with fear if they have been sexually abused (Perry, 2003). This association, although the child may not have specific awareness of it, may impact future sexual development. An adult who was sexually abused as a child may also fail to truly understand her/his sexual problems because she/he does not recall a sexually abusive incident, but rather has unconsciously associated genital touching with fear that began in infancy. Similarly, when the abuser is an attachment figure or caregiver who is supposed to create an environment of safety and security, the child's understanding of relationships becomes one of exploitation and abuse. Changes in development occur when the primary attachment relationship is disrupted (Perry, 2003). This may impact all future relationships according to the internal working model proposed by Bowlby and discussed in chapter 2.

Sexually abused children also have delayed language development (Oates, Peacock, & Forrest, 1984). When faced with trauma, children are forced to respond often with a consequence to their development. Their brain resources are hyperaroused to deal with the trauma and may be less available for developmental achievements.

Children begin to adapt to their environment from the moment of birth, and those who experience trauma may use dissociation as a primary coping mechanism when faced with enduring and repeated stressful situations, such as with sexual abuse. Again, children during infancy and toddlerhood are beginning to organize their responses to their environment (Perry & Pollard, 1998). Such patterns of adaptation continue throughout one's life in order to cope with emotional experiences too traumatic or painful to confront.

Socioemotional

According to Erickson's theory of psychosocial development, primary social tasks during infancy are the development of trust and attachment. When a caregiver sexually abuses an infant or toddler, the child lives at a heightened sense of awareness and in an environment that is often unpredictable and unsafe. The sexually abused infant or toddler, therefore, cannot develop trust in his/her caregiver or the safety and predictability of his/her environment. Similarly, Erickson's 2nd psychosocial task maintains that the development of autonomy is important in toddlerhood. Toddlers who have been sexually abused may not have developed a secure attachment with their caregivers, which affects their ability to fully embrace the task of autonomy. A toddler's primary job is play, and toddlers with insecure attachment may appear avoidant of or preoccupied with their caregiver, both of which impede the development of autonomy. Toddlerhood should be a time of great exploration and the development of trust in one's competencies and abilities. When children are preoccupied or resist their caregiver(s), they are not able to discover their abilities on their own and develop a sense of competence.

Physical

Sexually abused infants and toddlers have physical manifestations in addition to cognitive-behavioral and socioemotional consequences. Many of the physical manifestations are similar to that of preschool-age children, including injury to their genitalia; difficulty sleeping; difficulty eating; problems walking and sitting; bleeding genitals; itching genitals; genital odor; pain in the genital area; anal trauma; and difficulty with bowel movements. Because of the overlap with preschool consequences, the physical manifestation of sexual abuse will be expanded upon in chapter 5.

Brain development is also affected by sexual abuse. Because the brain is developing and organizing during a child's first three years, the brain is influenced by early sexual experiences. The brain creates memories of a traumatic event, and these memories are reactivated when a reminder of the traumatic event (e.g., specific perpetrator) is presented (Perry & Pollard, 1998). These memories may alter the child's perception of the world in which she/he lives. For the child, this perception seems like reality and may be very difficult to change even when the environment improves (NCCAN, 2001). Therefore, the child may physically respond to a perceived threat and may maintain a status of hyperarousal similar to what is seen among physically abused children. The stress of sexual abuse may cause a child to focus his/her brain resources on survival and perceived environmental threats, which may make it less likely for her/him to focus energies on more adaptive and sophisticated learning (ibid.). Sexually abused children may be hypervigilant and ready for danger; their primary way to navigate their environments may be with survival in mind.

CONCLUSION

Infants and toddlers who experience child abuse and neglect suffer devastating consequences to their development. Children from 0 to 3 make tremendous developmental gains, with the primary tasks including attachment, motor development, and intellectual development. One of the most devastating, but rare, consequences to infants and toddlers is death, which occurs more often to this age group than any other. Besides death, however, the consequences of maltreatment include disability and pervasive academic and social problems. Similarly, the attachment relationship has tremendous impact on the developing infant immediately and in the future. Therefore, from age 0 to 3 children need not only an available caregiver, but also a stimulating environment that nurtures their optimal development. Child abuse and neglect, and general child trauma including witnessing violence, alter normal child development and can have lifelong consequences without intervention.

4

INFANCY AND TODDLERHOOD

Ecological and Developmental Assessment of Maltreatment and Intervention

High prevalence of maltreatment for infants and toddlers denotes a significant number of children who will experience negative developmental outcomes, possibly throughout their lifespans. In the first three years of life a child experiences enormous growth in all the developmental domains. As discussed in chapter 3, the consequences of maltreatment during this developmental phase are devastating and long lasting. Assessment of children who may be experiencing child maltreatment during this age period is the most challenging yet the most critical in preventing physical, emotional, and cognitive damage.

This chapter will first present the risk and protective factors, within the ecological framework, that are most applicable to this developmental stage. As discussed, all assessment must be culturally responsive. If the social worker is not familiar with the child's culture, a cultural guide should be used to help in the assessment.

Recall that many risk and protective factors cut across all developmental stages; the ones that most apply to infancy and toddlerhood will be presented here. Child maltreatment is usually persistent and is rooted not only in individual behavior but in familial, societal, and cultural circumstances; therefore the need to examine factors from an ecological perspective is key. Much of the research on child maltreatment has focused on factors from each of the ecological levels and how they interact to increase the likelihood of maltreatment. Social-cognitive and affective processes of the caregiver have also been assessed to be related to the risk of maltreatment. (See Tables 4.1 and 4.2.) These processes will be presented when applicable.

Assessment and intervention strategies for families with children ages 0 to 3 who have experienced maltreatment are presented.

RISK AND PROTECTIVE FACTORS

Ontogenic Level

Factors at the ontogenic level are related to the childhood histories of the parent or caregiver. Developmental history has a significant influence on parenting. Since the

Table 4.1 Risk Factors

	Infant and Toddler
Ontogenic Microsystem	• Parent experienced child maltreatment as a child
Child	• Age itself
	• Born prematurely
	• Physical or mental disability
	• Infant tests positive for AOD
	• Race
Parent	• Not satisfied with the child
	• Biological or genetic factors
	• Does not enjoy parenting
	• Young parent
	• Not understanding role as caregiver
	• Lack of knowledge of child development
	• Substance abuse
Family	• Poverty
	• Stress in family environment
	• Interpersonal conflict between partners
	• Single parent
Exosystem	• Lack of social support
Macrosystem	• Cultural values that support violence
	• Attitudes toward how mothers should behave as a parent

parent-child relationship is so critical at this stage of development, the factors related to risk must be identified and addressed. Infants require nurturing and protective adults in order to survive. The infant and toddler are unable to feed, clothe, or take care of themselves and must rely on the caregiver for the most basic needs. What the parent brings from their own childhoods often influences their ability to parent.

A paramount risk factor is that the parent experienced maltreatment as a child. Caregivers who were physically abused, sexually abused, or neglected by their caregivers have been identified as more likely to maltreat their own children (Boyer & Fine, 1992; Cantrell et al., 1990; Haynes et al., 1984; Herrenkohl, Herrenkohl,

Table 4.2 Protective Factors

	Infant and Toddler
Ontogenic Microsystem	• Parent experienced secure attachment
Child	• Temperament
	• Goodness of fit with the parent
Parent	• Secure attachment as a child
Family	• Supportive significant other in the home
Exosystem	• Social support
Macrosystem	• Cultural value of protecting children

& Toedter, 1983; Straus, 1983). This factor needs to be viewed in context of the dynamics of the abuse experienced. In the assessment section of this chapter, we explore the type of questions asked to best understand the impact of this risk factor on infants and toddlers. A protective factor would be that the parents did not experience abuse or neglect as children and that they experienced secure attachment to their parents or caregivers; or if caregivers have resolved their issues surrounding their own maltreatment as a child.

Microsystem Level

Many of the additional factors that interact with the parents' developmental history occur within the family itself. The microsystem is the immediate context in which child maltreatment takes place and includes the family system, parenting styles, the maltreatment itself, and both the parent and child characteristics. The factors that most influence an infant or toddler's risk of abuse or factors that protect against the effects of maltreatment are presented in three areas: parent, child, and family system characteristics. The focus on protective factors is to emphasize family strengths in the context of the assessment.

Parental (Caregiver) Characteristics

Some characteristics and attitudes of the parent have been found to distinguish nonmaltreating parents from maltreating parents. The following are most relevant to infants and toddlers.

RISK FACTORS   Parents who maltreat are more likely than nonmaltreating parents to have a history of abuse or neglect themselves (Conger, Burgess, & Barrett, 1979; Kaufman & Zigler, 1989; Straus, 1983; 1994). This is not to say that all parents who have experienced maltreatment as a child will abuse their children. Most abused children do not become abusive parents (Kaufman & Zigler, 1989; Widom, 1989). Mothers who have genetic or biological factors that result in physical problems during pregnancy or delivery have been linked to an increased risk of physical abuse or neglect (Barth, 1991; Finkelhor, 1986). Like all risk factors discussed in the book, the influence this factor has on the occurrence of maltreatment has to be evaluated within the context of ecology of the family, including broader environmental risk factors.

Social-cognitive and affective processes of the parents that are related to the parent-child relationship have distinguished parents who maltreat and those who do not (Erickson & Egeland, 2002). The less satisfied the caregiver is with their children and the more he/she perceives parenting as less enjoyable and more difficult, the greater the risk of maltreating their infant or toddler (Trickett et al., 1991). Exacerbating these and other parental characteristics is the age of the parent. The younger the parents, the more likely they are to maltreat (Cadzow, Armstrong, & Fraser, 1999; Straus, 1983). Lack of experience and knowledge at younger ages may result in the omission of adequate care or heighten frustration leading to physical abuse.

During this developmental stage of the child, another parental social-cognitive and affective process that places the child at risk for maltreatment is the parents' lack of understanding about their role as caregiver and their feelings about caring for the needs of an infant (Pianta, Egeland, & Erickson, 1989; Scannapieco & Connell-Carrick, in press). Parents often misunderstand and misinterpret the behavior of the child because of their lack of knowledge of the child's developmental level. Also, as stated earlier, the developmental history of the parent may contribute negatively to the parent-child relationship. If the parent has not resolved earlier dependence and trust issues, they may seek to meet their own emotional needs through the child. When these are not met, the parent may exhibit aggression toward the infant or toddler.

Parental substance abuse is a risk factor for maltreatment during infancy and toddlerhood in a number of ways. Most alarming is the connection between substance abuse and child fatalities. It has been shown that as many as two-thirds of all child fatalities involve a substance-abusing caregiver (Chance & Scannapieco, 2002; Reid, 1999; Scannapieco & Connell-Carrick, in press).

Infants who experience prenatal exposure to alcohol and other drugs may experience negative developmental outcomes, the worst of which is death (New York City Child Fatality Review Panel, 1995, as cited in Kelley, 2002). The research is not conclusive on the impact of drugs on long-term negative developmental effects (Frank et al., 2001). Not all infants who experience prenatal drug exposure go through drug withdrawal. Opiate-exposed infants, especially those exposed to heroin and methadone, have been documented to experience neonatal withdrawal, but cocaine-exposed infants have not (Kelley, 2002). Given how critical attachment is to the parent-infant relationship, an infant experiencing neonatal withdrawal may contribute to difficulty in the bonding process.

Infants exposed prenatally to alcohol seem to have the most serious effects. Of all the substances, alcohol has been proven to have negative developmental effects that include mental retardation and neurological deficits (Kelley, 2002).

PROTECTIVE FACTORS   Parents whose pasts are free from violence are less likely to contribute to maltreatment of their infant or toddler. Parents who have not experienced child maltreatment are more likely to have experienced a secure attachment with their own caregiver. Caregivers that come to this relationship experiencing secure attachment are more likely to have a healthy parent-child relationship.

Child Characteristics

What the child brings to the parent-child relationship is now widely recognized as a determinate of the nature of that relationship (Belsky & Vondra, 1989). Certain characteristics can serve as contributors to a child's own maltreatment by influencing caregiver behavior, such as colic or physical disabilities.

RISK FACTORS   Infancy and toddlerhood as a developmental stage in and of itself is a risk factor because young children are so dependent on the parent. Infants are reported to child protective services more than any other group (Berrick et al., 1998; Scannapieco & Connell-Carrick, under review). Children ages 0 to 3 are at high risk because they rely solely on the care of an adult to survive. Severity of children's injuries is associated with being an infant or toddler. As one example, most child deaths, as a result of child maltreatment, occur to children under the age of 3 (Chance & Scannapieco, 2002; Delambre & Wood, 1997; McClain et al., 1993). Other risk factors during infancy and toddlerhood related to maltreatment include premature birth (Belsky, 1980; Klein & Stern, 1971; Fontana, 1971; NCCAN, 1994) and physical or mental disabilities (Gil, 1970; Ounsted, Oppenheimer, & Lindsay, 1974; Sullivan & Knutson, 1998). Infants who test positive for drugs at birth are also at increased risk, especially if they exhibit withdrawal symptoms (including vomiting, poor feeding, marked tremors, a high-pitched cry, and seizures) (NCCAN, 1994).

Race is also a risk factor for infants and toddlers. African American infants are more likely to be reported as maltreated than any other ethnic group (Berrick et al., 1998; Scannapieco & Connell-Carrick, in press). In the maltreatment literature, there is concern that this may be a product of reporting bias, not only of ethnicity but also of economic status. It has been found that families from lower socioeconomic backgrounds are more likely to be reported than those from higher socioeconomic backgrounds (Goerge & Lee, 1999; Hampton & Newberger, 1985; Lindsey, 2004), mainly because they are more visible in the system. It is difficult to distinguish the impact of poverty from ethnicity. African American families are disproportionately poor (U.S. Census, 2000) and are disproportionately reported for maltreatment (NIS-3, Scannapieco & Connell-Carrick, 2003).

PROTECTIVE FACTORS   The temperament of the infant or toddler may buffer them from harm. Temperament is a major factor in escalating the chances that a child will experience problems or, alternatively, be protected from stressful home environments (Seifer et al., 1996; Thomas & Chess, 1977). Three general temperamental styles have been identified: the easy child, the difficult child, and the slow-to-warm-up child (Thomas & Chess, 1977). Of these three the easy child temperament will be most protected. This infant quickly establishes regular routines, is generally cheerful, and adapts easily to new experiences.

Infant and toddler risk and protective characteristics must be kept in the context of the overall child maltreatment assessment. Caregivers who have a "goodness of fit" with their child will experience better outcomes than those who do not. Many child attributes can lead to healthy parent-child relationships as long as the caregiver sensitively adjusts her/his behavior to fit the baby's needs (Belsky, Lerner, & Spanier, 1984; Seifer & Schiller, 1995; Sroufe, 1985). If, on the other hand, the parent does not have this capacity because of her/his own personality or substance abuse, the children will be at greater risk of maltreatment.

Family Characteristics

Poverty is in the family characteristic section since all members are affected and since all are calculated into most measures of family income. Since neglect is prevalent in maltreatment cases of infants and toddlers we will discuss this risk factor here. In addition, it is important in the microsystem level to explore the relationship among the individuals in the immediate family. The relationship between the parent and her/his partner or her/his partner relationship with the children is significant. Risk and protective factors can be identified within this context.

RISK FACTORS   Poverty and low income have been found to be highly associated with child maltreatment (Brown et al., 1998; Chaffin, Kelleher, & Hollenberg, 1996; Coulton et al., 1995; Drake & Pandey, 1996; Gelles, 1992; Jones & McCurdy, 1992; Lee & Goerge, 1999; Sedlak & Broadhurst, 1996; Scannapieco & Connell-Carrick, in press; Sedlak, 1997). The increased risk for child maltreatment attributed to poverty among the studies ranged from 20 to 162 times in families with less than $15,000 in income (Sedlak, 1997); 40 to 48 times when measured by the harm standard or endangerment standard, respectively, in families with incomes less than $15,000 (Sedlak & Broadhurst, 1996); and 6 times in substantiation (Lee & Goerge, 1999). Other studies added that the combination of income of less than $15,000 and single parenthood contributed to child maltreatment (Jones & McCurdy, 1992). Coohey (1998) found that mothers who do not provide adequate supervision to their children were significantly more likely to have been homeless within the last year and were also more likely to currently have inadequate housing than comparison mothers.

The combination of high poverty and young maternal age was also found as a risk factor (Lee & Goerge, 1999). Children born to mothers 17 years of age or younger who lived in high poverty areas were 17 times more likely to have a substantiated case of child maltreatment than children born to mothers who were 22 years of age or more in low poverty. In addition, the higher the poverty, the higher the incidence of child maltreatment substantiations, compared to low poverty areas (Drake & Pandley, 1996).

Although there is a significant correlation between poverty and maltreatment, most families living in poverty do not abuse or neglect their children (Pelton, 1989). Although there has been speculation that reporting bias occurs against poor families, this has been shown not to be the case in several studies (Ards & Harrell, 1993; Osborne et al., 1988; Zellman, 1992).

Stress in the family environment may serve as a catalyst for escalating a challenging situation into an abusive one (Cadzow, Armstrong, & Fraser, 1999). Many theories that explain child abuse include stress (Wolfe, 1999) as a factor contributing to child maltreatment. Most parents do not resort to violent behavior in most situations. It is not the type of stress that seems to aggravate the level of conflict between family members but the presence of a stress-filled family environment (ibid.).

Interpersonal conflict between the parents (parent and partner) may act as a barrier to effective parenting (Emery & Forehand, 1994). Marital discord is more likely to be found in families who maltreat their children (Scannapieco & Connell-Carrick, in press; Strauss, Gelles, & Steinmetz, 1980). This conflict often takes on the form of domestic violence that can escalate the stress-filled environment where the infant resides and increase maltreatment of the infant or toddler (Appel

& Holden, 1998; Dubowitz, 1999). This coupled with other risk factors in the microsystem places the infant or toddler at additional risk.

Many infants and toddlers who experience maltreatment are from homes of a single parent, usually the mother (Scannapieco & Connell-Carrick, in press). The lack of support and diminished economic level within the microsystem adds to the stressful life events of being single and caring for an infant.

PROTECTIVE FACTORS   Families that experience financial and marital stability during the early formation of the parent-child relationship are associated with non-maltreating families (Wolfe, 1999).

Significant others in the microsystem, such as father, partner, or sibling, can mediate the negative effects of a debilitated primary caregiver, primarily the mother. These individuals do not remove the consequences of parental risk factors altogether but help mediate the effects on the child by increasing her/his ability to cope and develop competency (Farber & Egeland, 1987). The protective factor, a supportive partner at the time the mother becomes a parent, distinguishes between mothers who maltreat and those who do not (Egeland & Erickson, 1990). Having one supportive adult in an otherwise hostile early environment has been identified consistently in the literature as a buffering factor in later developmental outcomes (Dutton, 1998).

Exosystem Characteristics: Risk and Protective Factors

The exosystem encompasses the individual and family within larger social structures, including both formal and informal structures. Belsky (1980) primarily focuses on the influences that two primary structures exert on the family: work and neighborhood. However, other social structures include school, formal and informal support networks, socioeconomic status, and social services. This level also includes Bronfenbrenner (1979) Mesosystem, which comprises the interaction and interconnections between exosystem structures. Recall that much of the influence that the exosystem factors have on the family (microsystem) is the stress and pressure that structures in the exosystem exert on the family system, including family dysfunction (Cicchetti & Lynch, 1993). During infancy and toddlerhood, the usual dominant exosystem structure is the support systems, both formal and informal, the family has in place. The support that families receive outside their home and their connections to society can be as important as the support received from within. In future chapters other elements of the exosystem, such as school, church, and employment, will be discussed.

Social support is at once a risk factor and a protective factor. The lack of social support, which is also an indication that the family is isolated, has been found to be a strong predictor of emotional stress and depression and to characterize families in all maltreatment categories (Colletta & Gregg, 1981; Erickson & Egeland, 2002; Scannapieco & Connell-Carrick, in press). Mothers receiving high levels of social support, both emotional and concrete, report the lowest levels of emotional stress and depression (Colletta, 1983). Mothers who neglected their children had fewer parental resources and individuals within their social networks

(Coohey, 1996; Gaudin et al., 1993; Scannapieco & Connell-Carrick, in press), and received less social and emotional support from their social networks (Brayden et al., 1992; Coohey 1996; Gaudin et al., 1993).

Macrosystem Level

The macrosystem examines the embeddedness of the individual, family, and community within the larger cultural fabric. There is little empirical evidence suggesting that specific cultural values are associated with child maltreatment. Physical punishment is widely practiced and condoned, and the fact that the culture is willing to accept violence creates an environment that condones maltreatment in the family microsystem. Attitudes about mothers and how they should react and behave with a newborn are also a contributing factor.

MALTREATMENT ASSESSMENT OF FAMILIES WITH INFANTS AND TODDLERS

Following the ecological and developmental model presented in chapter 2, child maltreatment is viewed as an outcome of the transactions between child, parent, and environmental risk and protective factors. It is the awareness that factors within one ecosystem (e.g., parent developmental history) may affect behavior across ecosystems (e.g., family) that enables an adequate assessment of the family. Factored into the assessment model is the acknowledgment that the natural settings where the family resides are best for observing behaviors, such as the home or day care.

In each assessment chapter we will pay special attention to the child and her/his developmental stage and the behavioral effect on development that maltreatment might have. This is referred to as "soft signs of abuse" in medical or forensic environments (Ferrara, 2002) and often needs to be corroborated by hard evidence such as medical documentation or eyewitness for prosecution. In the context of the ecological model and based on the developmental theories presented, appraisal suggestions will be given for the child domains of cognitive-behavioral, socioemotional, and physical. The behavioral indicators may be an outcome of neglect, physical abuse, or sexual abuse. It is important that the practitioner also explore behavioral change that may indicate a disturbance in development. Often it is only through behavior that assessment can be made when placed in the context of the overall ecological assessment model. Physical indicators, or hard evidence, of child maltreatment will also be discussed in the microsystem level.

Indicators from the ontogenic, the microsystem, and the exosystem level will be presented in each chapter, in the context of the developmental phase under discussion. Although many of these indicators are relevant at various developmental stages, the ones presented are more directly related to the particular age of the child. The macrosystem level will not be discussed in the assessment section of the chapter, but rather in the risk and protective section since the book is not addressing macrolevel interventions. Inferences about the macrolevel of assessment can be easily made from that discussion.

Ontogenic Level

The key assessment question at this level is whether the caregiver was maltreated as a child. It is important to ascertain not only if the parent was maltreated as a child but the extent, duration, and type of maltreatment. Risk of maltreatment to the infant or toddler is increased the longer and more serious the parent's maltreatment. Other areas of assessment to explore are the caregivers' experience with early development. Questions related to this area of assessment are the following:

- What was the nature of her/his parenting?
- Did her/his parent use physical discipline?
- What was her/his parent's philosophy of child rearing?
- Has the parent made any resolution around his/her own maltreatment?

Microsystem Level

Parent

In assessing the microsystem, caregiver characteristics and reactions to the inquiry of child maltreatment must be viewed in combination with what the child is presenting. We have discussed risk factors that have been found to distinguish maltreating from nonmaltreating parents and that were most relevant at this developmental stage. These factors should lead the assessment of the parent and should be referred to in decision-making and case disposition. Some of the questions that would need to be answered are:

- What is the age of the parent?
- Does the caregiver enjoy being a parent and is she/he satisfied with her/his child?
- Does the caregiver understand her/his role as a parent?
- How does the parent feel about caring for her/his infant?
- Does the parent have a good understanding of what is developmentally appropriate for the infant or toddler?
- Does the parent have unresolved dependence or trust issues that he/she is trying to get met through the child?

Child

As discussed in chapter 3, knowledge of normal and appropriate child development is essential to understanding any abnormal delay in child development. If child maltreatment is present in a child's home, then awareness of normal child behavior provides the practitioner a heightened understanding of the child's developmental level, whether normal or abnormal. It is also necessary to break down the age of the child into six-month increments for the first two years. Children learn much during the first two years of their lives. During the child's third year, development begins to slow and observable changes are less drastic, and thus the 24th to 36th months are not divided into six-month increments.

Behavioral Indicators of Child Maltreatment

Neglect, the most predominant form of child maltreatment, is difficult to assess because it is indicated by the absence of behavior and it is a challenge to measure what is absent. Table 4.3 provides an assessment tool to evaluate child maltreatment through behavioral indicators based upon the theories of child development presented in chapter 3. These indicators, in the overall context of the assessment, may provide support that the child is being neglected or physically or sexually abused. The assessment areas are divided into three categories: cognitive-behavioral, socioemotional, and physical.

Cognitive-behavioral assessment is combined since cognitive development manifests in observable behaviors, such as attention span and goal-directed behaviors, in young children lacking extensive verbal ability. Socioemotional development includes an assessment of the attachment relationship at various stages, as well as the child's ability to interact with others in her/his environment. Of paramount importance in any assessment of infants and toddlers is an assessment of normal physical development, which is one of the least subjective and more observable indicators of maltreatment. Using the behavioral indicators provided in Table 4.3, children ages 0 to 3 can be assessed even without the verbal and communicative abilities of older children by using appropriate child development as a guide.

Physical Indicators of Child Maltreatment

Other assessment areas that need to be understood are the nonbehavioral areas. Injuries to the infant or toddler that are nonaccidental need to be recognized by the practitioner. Given the inability of an infant to move about on its own, any traumatic injury or any poisoning should be considered suspicious. Again, based on the development of the child there are certain injuries that are not possible for an infant or toddler to sustain accidentally. For example, it is next to impossible for an infant to fracture a femur (upper thigh) (Besharov, 1990).

A suspicious injury is at the core of child battered syndrome (Kempe et al., 1962). As discussed in chapter 1, Kempe and associates first identified the phenomenon, which is now an accepted medical diagnosis in cases that meet certain criteria. An infant or toddler who exhibits evidence of fracture of any bone, subdural hematomas, failure to thrive, soft tissue swelling or skin bruising; in any child who dies suddenly; or where the degree and type of injury is at variance with the history given regarding the occurrence of the trauma would be diagnosed as a battered child (ibid.). Many of these injuries, such as head, abdominal, or skeletal injuries, will need to be confirmed by a medical practitioner, but it is important for the practitioner to understand that they deviate from normal expected injuries.

Certainly less serious injuries to the child should also be suspect, particularly those that would not ordinarily be sustained without an act or omission of the parent, such as slap mark on the face. Recall the definition of physical abuse in chapter 1. For an injury to be considered physical abuse a child younger than 18 years of age must have experienced an injury (harm standard) or risk of an injury

Table 4.3 Assessing Children Ages 0-3

	Cognitive-Behavioral	Socioemotional	Physical
0–6 months	• Does the child imitate adults' facial expressions? • Does the child repeat chance behaviors that produce pleasure for the child? • Can the child recognize people and places? • Does attention become more flexible with age? • Does the child babble by the end of this period?	• Does the child show a range of emotions, including happiness, sadness, and fear? • Does social smiling and laughing emerge? • Can the child imitate adult emotional expression during interactions? • Does the infant begin to distinguish self from others (the emergence of an "I")?	• Does the child have rapid height and weight gain? • Can the child hold her/his head up, roll over, and reach for objects? • Can the child hear sounds, with increasing sensitivity to sounds of own speech with age? • Does the child begin to habituate toward fixed stimuli? • Is the child sensitive toward motion?
6–12 months	• Does the child have goal-directed and intentional behavior? • Can the child find hidden objects? • Can the child imitate adults' actions? • Can the child combine sensory and motor activities? • Does the child babble, including sounds in the child's spoken language? • Does the child show preverbal gestures, such as pointing?	• Does the child show stranger and separation anxiety? • Does the child use the caregiver as a secure base? • Can the child engage in social referencing? • Does the child show definite attachment to caregivers?	• Can the child sit alone, crawl, and walk? • Can the child organize stimuli into meaningful patterns?
12–18 months	• Does the child sort objects into categories? • Can the child find hidden objects by looking in more than one place? • Does the child show trial and error learning in play? • Does the child have an improved attention span? • Can the child talk, at least saying first words? • Does the child use overextension and underextension of the words she/he knows?	• Does the child recognize an image of himself/herself? • Does the child play with siblings and familiar adults? • Does the child show signs of empathy? • Does the child engage in turn-taking behaviors when playing? • Does the child understand simple directives?	• Does the child continue to grow, but less rapidly than during the first year? • Can the child walk better with more coordination? • Can the child stand alone in one place? • Can the child manipulate and play with small objects, improving coordination? • Can the child use a spoon or cup?

18–24 months

- Can the child take turns when playing interactive games (peek-a-boo)?
- Does the child experiment with different behaviors to see the result and find new ways to solve problems?
- Can the child find objects that are out of sight?
- Does the child try to fully imitate adults' actions?
- Does the child engage in make-believe play?
- Does the child move objects into categories during play?
- Does the child recall people, places, or objects better than before?
- Does the child use two-word phrases?
- Can the child scribble with crayons or pencils?

- Does the child express self-conscious emotions, such as shame and embarrassment?
- Does the child have a vocabulary that includes emotional terms?
- Does the child use vocabulary in order to emotionally regulate himself/herself?
- Can the child increasingly tolerate the absence of a caregiver?
- Does the child use own name as labeled image of oneself?

- Can the child jump, run, and climb?
- Can the child manipulate small objects with good coordination?
- Is the child walking alone?
- Is the child able to push or pull something while walking?
- Can the child feed herself/himself?
- Can the child partly undress herself/himself?

24–36 months

- Can the child point to and name body parts?
- Is make-believe play less self-centered and more complex?
- Does the child have a well-developed memory recognition?
- Does the child have a more developed vocabulary?
- Can the child use sentences with increased usage of grammar?
- Does the child display conversational skills?
- Is the child able to follow simple directions?
- Can the child tell simple stories?
- Is the child able to answer questions?

- Can the child distinguish one's intention and unintentional actions?
- Can the child understand causes and consequences of behaviors?
- Does the child exhibit cooperative or aggressive behaviors?
- Is the child beginning to engage in parallel play?

- Can the child get dressed or undressed partly by oneself?
- Can the child use a spoon or fork?
- Can the child run, jump, hop, and throw objects?
- Can the child pedal a tricycle/big wheel?
- Does the child gain weight and height but less so than during the first 2 years?

(endangerment standard) as a result of having been hit with a hand or other object or having been kicked, shaken, thrown, burned, stabbed, or choked by a parent or parent-surrogate (as cited in Kolko, 2002).

The following are examples of injuries that an infant or toddler may present that a caregiver may inflict. This is not meant to be an exhaustive list, but simply illustrative.

- Pressure bruises on the neck that resemble fingertips, whole fingers, and entire hands. This may occur from the parent grabbing the child and shaking her/him in an attempt to stop her/him from crying.
- Extensive pinch marks. Some children have difficulty feeding. Pinching the child's face may be an attempt to get them to feed.
- Multiple inflicted injuries in different stages of healing. Indication that the parent has, over time, repeatedly beat the child.
- Distinctively shaped dry or contact burns. If a caregiver were to force the child against a radiator to stop them from crying, the shape of the heater would be apparent on the infant or toddler.
- Small circular lesions suggesting that the child was burned with a cigarette, cigar, or match tip.
- Injuries involving the mouth that may be a result of forced feeding or an attempt to make the infant or toddler stop crying.

  Torn or lacerated frenulum (the membrane connecting the gum and lips and the tongue with the floor of the mouth). Neither structure is likely to be injured accidentally in a child who is not yet walking (Giardino & Giardino, 2002).
  Swollen lips.
  Marks, bruises, or lacerations at the corners of the mouth suggesting that the child was gagged.

- Retinal hemorrhages and detachments, when accompanied by other evidence of severe shaking, such as subdural hematomas. Parent will shake the baby to stop them from crying and often does not realize how rigorously he/she is shaking.
- Any bone fracture

A special syndrome that would come under nonaccidental physical injury to an infant or toddler is shaken baby syndrome (SBS). Shaken baby syndrome is a form of abusive head trauma that is a result of severe shaking or slamming of the infant that often results in permanent, irreparable brain damage or death. Babies are susceptible to whiplash shaking injuries for several reasons. When infants are shaken, weak neck muscles cause their relatively large heads to "whip" back and forth. The brain moves in the opposite direction, causing the brain tissue to shear and blood vessels to rupture (Brooks & Weather, 2001). Head injuries are the most common cause of traumatic death in infants under 1 year of age (American Academy of Pediatrics, 1993). Child abuse that results in central nervous system injuries is the leading cause of morbidity and mortality (Caniano, Beaver, & Boles, 1986). The most common trigger for the shaken incident is the baby's crying.

Assessing SBS can be difficult at first because there are often no external signs of abuse. Symptoms are frequently nonspecific and can range from irritability, lethargy, and vomiting to more severe cases of seizures and unconsciousness. SBS must be diagnosed medically, using a computed tomography (CT) scan or MRI. The diagnosis includes determining if the child has sustained retinal hemorrhage, subdural or subarachnoid hemorrhage, and associated fractures (Brooks & Weathers, 2001; Loiselle, 2002).

Infants and toddlers presenting with nonspecific symptoms coupled with histories that seem to be at odds with the physical findings should be placed under suspicion until thorough assessment can be made. Along with the medical evaluation, a history surrounding the circumstances of the incident should be taken from all individuals connected to the infant. Antecedent activities such as crying, feeding problems, or toileting issues should be noted since these are often the triggers to abuse. Consistency among caregivers is also important. If the history of the event does not seem plausible, continued assessment and monitoring should take place. In light of the need to be continually culturally responsive, this issue must be viewed in the context of the family's culture.

Neglect

Insufficient physical growth, or failure to thrive, of infants and toddlers is one of the most common presentations of neglect (Joffe, 2002), but it is not always a result of omission of care. There are many organic reasons leading to insufficient growth not related to neglect, such as problems with intake and retention of adequate nourishment. Recently the medical profession is moving away from the terms "organic" or "nonorganic failure to thrive" to a more interactional model (Joffe, 2002). In recognition that the condition needs to be assessed within the ecological context, the medical profession is aligning with the theoretical perspective of child maltreatment presented in chapter 2.

Although organic and nonorganic causes of failure to thrive may coexist in infants and toddlers, neglect assessment areas concerning the care of the child are similar. Most of the current assessment literature still dichotomizes severe insufficient physical growth into organic or nonorganic failure to thrive. We will focus on the assessment of nonorganic failure to thrive; for cases presenting with organic reasons for insufficient growth in families who are unable to meet the child's needs, the assessment discussion is relevant.

Nonorganic failure to thrive is associated with deprivation of necessities, often from parent-child relationship problems that disturb feeding and eating. Failure to thrive occurs most frequently but not exclusively in children ages 0 to 3. Assessment criteria that designate nonorganic failure to thrive are the following:

- Weight below the 3rd percentile with subsequent weight gain during presence of nurturing and a subsequent fall in percentile
- Height below the 3rd percentile
- Developmental delays with subsequent acceleration of development following appropriate stimulation

- No evidence of disease or abnormality to account for the initial growth failure
- Clinical signs of deprivation improve with nurturing
- Significant environmental psychosocial disruption

Other physical and behavioral indicators that a practitioner might observe in the assessment of nonorganic failure to thrive are:

- Failure to grow, gain weight, or to develop physically
- Vomiting or diarrhea
- Anemia
- Rashes
- Fever
- Weakness, tiredness
- Little affect. The infant is unresponsive and withdrawn, and may fail to smile at a human face or respond to a coo
- Lack of crying or aggressive behaviors
- Infant is too easily subdued in the presence of sustained attention
- Infant is submissive but not cooperative

The caregiver-child interaction is primary to assessing whether failure to thrive is a result of neglect. Some indicators are:

- Caregiver does not spend enough time with the baby
- Caregiver is frequently depressed/preoccupied with other problems
- Caregiver will often prop the child's bottle
- Caregiver may reveal that other children were also "small"
- Baby is kept with the rest of the family and is not isolated
- Often child is part of a sibling group; other children will be relatively healthy if they are old enough to get their own food
- Caregiver often forgets to feed the infant due to her preoccupation

Based on the discussion above, questions that should be asked during an assessment are:

- Who feeds the child?
- What does the child eat? (Get specific information about type of food and amount given to the child.)
- When does the child eat?
- Have there been similar problems with low weight gain in other children in the family?
- When did the caregiver first notice that the child was losing weight or failing to gain?
- What did the caregiver do about the child's weight loss or failure to gain?
- Was the child showing any signs of illness?
- Was the child taken to a doctor for medical attention?
- What have other family members said about the child's weight?

- How is the formula mixed? (If parent is of limited capacity, get them to demonstrate.)
- Is there food for the child in the home?

Sexual Abuse

As difficult as it is to believe, infant and toddlers are also victims of sexual abuse. Although the rate of sexual abuse is very low for 0 to 2-year-olds, it is relatively constant for children ages 3 and older (USHHS, 1996). The great majority of sexual abuse cases of infant and toddlers do not involve violent or forced physical assaults. The behavioral indicators discussed earlier may be one sign of this victimization, but without physical evidence it is next to impossible to assess that sexual abuse has occurred. Without a witness to the assault or a confession by the perpetrator, physical indicators need to be present. The following are some physical manifestations that should be considered suspicious for sexual abuse:

- Genital area is infected, irritated, or ruptured and is not attributed to diaper rash
- Genitals are excessively reddened
- Genitals are unrealistically blistered
- Genitals exhibit tears or bruises on the surface
- Anal areas that are swollen, torn, lacerated, or infected
- Bite marks on or around the genitals
- Sexually transmitted disease (STDs can be transmitted at child birth, such as genital warts and chlamydia)

Family

Family characteristics along with the relationships among the family members in the microsystem need to be explored to determine if maltreatment has occurred and the current level of safety for the child and later risk. Some of the questions that guide family assessment are:

- Is the family living in poverty?
- Is it a single-parent household?
- What is the level of housing?
- What is the history of housing?
- Has the family experienced a number of stressful situations?
- Is there interpersonal conflict between the caregiver and her/his partner?
- Is there domestic violence in the family?

Exosystem Level

The social structure in which the infant or toddler and her/his family are embedded is an important area of assessment, particularly in determining safety. The key areas of evaluation are the formal and informal social supports the family has in place and what type of influence they exert of the family. As discussed earlier, social supports are critical in reducing the risk of child maltreatment. Some of the main questions that would need to be explored are:

- Does the caregiver have extended family in the area?
- How often does the caregiver have contact with her/his extended family?
- What is the nature of this contact?
- Does the parent find her/his extended family supportive?
- Does the extended family provide any resources (emotional and concrete)?
- Does the extended family assist in caregiving of the infant or toddler?
- Does the parent have any close friends that he/she can rely on?
- Is the caregiver receiving any parenting services?
- Is the parent or partner working?
- Does the caregiver engage in any social or religious activities?
- Are they affiliated with a place of worship?
- Do they access any community services or resources in the context of her/his culture?

Summary

Assessment is a process in which information is gathered and analyzed in order to determine the origin and extent of critical risk-related problems, the strengths that will enhance the potential for change, and the barriers that will hinder this potential. The ecological-transactional model of assessment divides individual risk factors into the different system levels. The intent is that this conceptual framework will help practitioners to think about the overall family functioning and the information they need to gather, as well as guide their assessments.

The physical indicators are variables that are easier to act upon and are indicative of increased risk. These are the cases in which we most often do a good job in protecting children. The behavioral and relational variables are harder to act upon but are as indicative of increased risk. These characteristics are most likely to be overlooked or to be considered insufficient for protective action. They are harder to act upon because they are often related to the parent or child characteristics that are more difficult to recognize.

It is important to consider the combinations of soft and hard indicators of child maltreatment. These combinations characterize conditions in which strong safety plans for children should be developed because they are in danger of increased risk.

INTERVENTION

In each chapter, a sampling of intervention strategies will focus on the developmental stage of the child in the context of the ecology of her/his family. It is beyond the scope of this book to present a comprehensive overview of intervention strategies; rather, we give guidance to areas for further learning.

Child welfare is usually the first professional field involved in reports of child maltreatment. Once the determination is made that the child has been maltreated and the family is in need of services, a service plan is developed to ensure the safety and well-being of the child. Since safety is the number one priority of child welfare services, sometimes the child is removed from the home to prevent recurrence of abuse. The intention of this book is to provide intervention strategies for practitioners who are working with families and children whether the child is in the biological home or in an out-of-home placement.

The conventional child welfare intervention continuum will be briefly discussed in this chapter. In subsequent chapters more specific treatment issues related to the developmental stage of the child will be presented.

CONTINUUM OF CHILD WELFARE INTERVENTION

Children who experience maltreatment by a parent or caregiver are provided services primarily by and through the public child welfare system. Many states, counties, and regions have adopted a differential response system that may direct some cases to private child welfare agencies. This may occur through the provision of services or assessment by a private child welfare agency funded through the public system. Whether the provision of services is provided by the public or private child welfare agency, the continuum of child welfare interventions is applicable.

Since CAPTA was enacted in 1974, mandating the identification and reporting of child maltreatment to designated social service agencies, states have formed public social service systems that are responsible for the investigation, assessment, and provision of services for families and children that experience child maltreatment. Public child welfare agencies collaborate with various multidisciplinary fields in all stages of intervention, from law enforcement to the medical profession, to the school system, and several others. But the primary responsibility for the safety and well-being of the child is held by the public or private child welfare agency.

After there has been a case disposition that indicates some form of child maltreatment has occurred in the family, child protective services follows a decision-making process based on risk and safety. The primary mission of public child protection services is to ensure the child's safety, permanency, and well-being. Within this context, services are provided to children and families that promote the healthy development of the child through her/his lifespan. Services that advance the child's development are the focus of the intervention chapters in this book.

Underlying the continuum of child welfare services is the principle of permanence. When the state intervenes in a child maltreatment case it is not only responsible for the safety and well-being of the child and family, but also must make sure that the child is raised in a stable, continuous, and secure family. The Adoption Assistance and Child Welfare Act of 1980 (PL 96-272) and the Adoption and Safe Families Act of 1997 (PL 105-89) sets out permanency planning guidelines for child welfare practice and the service continuum. The following guidelines assist the decision-making process related to the selection of services for children who have been maltreated:

- If the decision is to remove the child from her/his home for risk and safety reasons, placement options begin with exploring relative placements and move through a continuum starting with the least restrictive.
- Brothers and sisters, whenever possible, should be placed together.
- Children have the right to be safe in a permanent living situation within 12 months.
- The original reason a child came into substitute care needs to be continuously reexamined to determine the earliest time that safety and/or risk has been sufficiently controlled to allow a safe return.
- Determine if identified safety and/or risk factors can be managed with the child in the home.
- Determine family and community resources that would help the parent control risk factors and carry out a safety plan.
- Determine if older children in substitute care may have developed social or protective skills that would allow a safe return to their family.
- Concurrent planning is essential. Public child welfare agencies must be working on more than one permanency goal for children who are placed outside their home.
- If parents do not demonstrate the changes needed to reduce risk in 6 to 12 months, another permanency goal must be determined.

Once it has been determined that there is significant risk to a child's well-being and when the family resources indicate a need for services, a determination of what the family requires must be made. The assessment that was conducted, often in collaboration with other professionals, is the guide in determining what services will be provided. In current child welfare practice the child safety and well-being is paramount and the family is always the focus of intervention, which means that along the continuum of services the family is always engaged until such time that it is determined that parental rights should be terminated. From the least intrusive to the most, the family is seen as an integral component in the intervention. The following is the permanency continuum of options that guide child welfare intervention:

- Family preservation services (referred to in various ways in different states). These are family-centered services that are delivered in the home with the primary focus being the prevention of removal of the child and recurrence of maltreatment. The family system must be amenable to services and working in collaboration with the child welfare practitioner to resolve the issues that placed the child's well-being at risk. Some key child welfare practice principles are as follows:

  View the problem from the family's perspective.
  Empower the family to build on their strengths.
  Services are accessible and are provided in the home.
  Family may have 24-hour access to the worker.
  Concrete, emotional, and advocacy support is provided.
  Services are time-limited.
  Services are culturally appropriate.

- Family foster care. Child welfare professionals acknowledge that the best environment to maximize a child's development is in a family setting, whether their own or another. The decision to remove a child should occur only when there is no reasonable way to protect the child from abuse or neglect in the immediate or short-term future without removal. The intent of foster care is to provide temporary care for the child. Once the decision has been made to remove the child from her/his family, the following are the placement options based on best permanency planning principles:

  Kinship foster home. This may be a relative or a close family friend that to the child is considered family. Depending on the state, these homes may be licensed or unlicensed, but they all go through some assessment to determine their appropriateness as a placement for the child. Relatives or family friends are usually in a better position to meet the child's needs for nurturing, stability, and continuity of care.

  Family foster home. A private home of a family that has been trained and licensed as a foster home. Their level of specialty often divides family foster homes. Some homes are considered therapeutic and provide more intensive services or more sophisticated medical services.

- Residential care. A residential setting is usually the last alternative for children and the most restrictive. Children placed in these settings have usually demonstrated an inability to reside in a foster home or have behaviors that would be difficult to handle in a family setting. Residential services vary and may be placed on a continuum of institutionalized services. The main types of residential treatment facilities are as follows:

  Diagnostic center. Children may be placed in a diagnostic center if it is unclear what type of treatment will be most helpful to the child. Assessment is the center's key function and the child is usually there for a short period of time.

  Group home. Children who may not respond to being in a family setting because of the trauma they experienced may need intensive therapeutic treatment before they can be placed with another family. Group homes are residential care facilities that provide foster care for a limited number of children, usually between the ages of 7 and 12.

  Residential treatment centers. Children are placed in residential treatment centers for similar reasons as group homes but are assessed as needing more services. Residential treatment centers offer a therapeutic milieu that provides an integrated approach to residential, educational, and psychological services.

- Family reunification services. The desired outcome, when possible, of all out-of-home placements is the child's reunification with the family. When the child welfare practitioner has assessed the risk and safety to be such that the child's well-being is no longer in danger, services are provided to begin the transition of the child back into her/his home. As proposed by Maluccio, Warsh, and Pine (1993) family reunification does not have to be viewed as an all-or-nothing proposition but rather as a "reconnect-ing" of children with their family system. It is not always the goal that the child resides with her/his family, and this is one reason concurrent planning is important.

- Adoption. If the decision is to terminate parental rights, the child wel-fare worker will move to relinquishment and toward the identification of an adoptive home. Adoption is a means of providing a child both legal and emotional security. It is a socially and legally sanctioned method of providing a child a permanent home when the biological parent has been unable or unwilling to assume her/his role effectively.

Within the continuum of services are a number of services that may be con-tracted from private child welfare agencies, mental health agencies, the commu-nity, and others. Some of these are individual or group counseling, martial or family counseling, day care, homemaker services, parenting education programs, and domestic violence and substance abuse programs. The next section focuses on the specific interventions that infants, toddlers, and their families may benefit from based on the predominant forms of child maltreatment for this age group.

INTERVENTION FOR INFANTS AND TODDLERS WHO HAVE BEEN MALTREATED

As stated earlier, the assessment guides the specific therapeutic services provided to the infant or toddler and her/his family. Foremost in any assessment is the safety and well-being of the child. Whether the child remains in her/his own home, or is placed with kin or in foster care, the therapeutic strategies discussed in this chapter can be applied in all settings. Once safety and well-being are established, other interventions may be offered.

Not all child maltreatment affects all infants and toddlers in the same way. Key determining factors in decision making are how the child was functioning before, her/his temperament, support systems, and the reaction of the nonoffending caregiver. Other factors are the type of maltreatment, the severity of maltreat-ment, the duration of the maltreatment, and the prior relationship between the child and the perpetrator.

Child maltreatment has adverse effects on attachment with implications for development across the child's life span. Since the quality of the parent-child relationship is so critical during the earliest years, the focus of this section will be therapeutic strategies to improve the attachment relationship. Attachment will be addressed in future chapters as well.

Although there is a large empirical knowledge base demonstrating the adverse effects of maltreatment on development, intervention strategies based on attach-ment theory are rare (Cicchetti & Toth, 1995). Intervention discussion will be based on various strategies that apply attachment theory. Within this area, treatment goals focus on knowledge of child care and child development and stimulation of the infant or toddler through interaction with the caregiver. The setting of the intervention is based on the needs of the family. Often these services are home-based.

ATTACHMENT

When treating infants or toddlers that have been traumatized, attention must focus on the parent, family, and larger system because the developmental capacities of children this young is dependent on adults. Parents, in their own childhood, often have experienced child maltreatment and issues with quality attachment. There is disconnecting between their own experiences as children and their current emotional and behavioral response as parents. Intervention around attachment as a result may be twofold, focusing on attachment issues of the parent and her/his attachment experience with the infant or toddler. The work with the parent should focus on changing her/his representational model of relationships or restructuring this model (Azar, Breton, & Miller, 1998; Egeland & Erickson, 1990; Fraiberg, Adelson, & Shapiro, 1979). Psychotherapy with the parent should focus on the role that early parental history has on the current quality of caregiving (Lieberman & Pawl, 1988). The focus here is not with solely the parent but with attachment-guided strategies with the parent and child.

The abuse or neglect the infant or toddler has experienced is a form of disruption to attachment and without intervention may have long-term developmental consequences. The empirically based developmental antecedents of attachment were discussed in chapter 2. We pointed out that the issue of sensitive care for children by their caregiver is the strongest predictor of the quality of the child's attachment. Thus it is logical that promoting caregiver sensitivity is the first goal of intervention efforts.

Erickson and Kurz-Riemer (1999) have operationally defined sensitivity based on the developmental research as follows:

- Recognizing the infant's ability to signal needs
- Accurately reading and interpreting cues
- Responding contingently
- Responding consistently and predictably.

Much of the work with parents in this area focuses on educating them on normal expectations of the infant and on understanding what the infant is trying to say through her/his behavior.

Parents may not recognize the ability of infants to signal their needs. The practitioner must help the parent recognize the way in which the infant is communicating her/his needs. It is helpful to direct the parent's attention to the facial expressions, gestures, postures, and cries of the infant and what they may be communicating. Erickson and Kurz-Riemer discuss parenting education programs that may be resources for parents who want to enhance their sensitivity to their infant or toddler. Steps Toward Effective, Enjoyable Parenting (STEEP) begins the work prior to the birth of the child, teaching parents to pay attention to how their activity affects the baby's activity in utero, thus building a foundation for the understanding of the reciprocal nature of the parent-child relationship. Another key strategy of STEEP involves videotaping the parent-child interaction as a learning tool for the parent. Other early intervention programs have successfully adopted this strategy across many settings (Erickson & Kurz-Riemer, 1999).

By teaching parents how to respond sensitively to their infant, the infant will experience responsive care and will begin to develop confidence that others will react appropriately to his/her needs. This is also the foundation of the reciprocal nature of the parent-child relationship.

Sumner and Spietz (1994, as cited in Erickson & Kurz-Riemer 1999) developed a table of common signals that babies give to indicate how and if they want to engage in activity with the caregiver. A sampling of these cues follows:

ENGAGEMENT CUES
Head rising. Elevation of head with eyes directed upward toward caregiver.
Alerting. Increased muscle tone of face, possibly with flushing to cheeks; eyes
    usually sparkle.
Face gaze. Looking at the parent's face.

DISENGAGEMENT CUES
Facial grimace. Combination of frown, eye tightening, and upper lip rising.
Eyes clinched. Eyes tightly shut.
Head lowering. Chin brought in toward chest, eyes usually lowered.
Pulling away. Moving torso and/or head away from caregiver or object; that
    is, withdrawing and increasing distance from caregiver or object.
Crying (three types)

- Hunger or ordinary cry. Somewhat low in volume, of short duration (1–2 seconds); rhythmical, with vocalization and 1–2-second pause, vocalization and 1–2-second pause, and so forth.
- Angry cry. A more forceful version of the hunger or ordinary cry; remains rhythmical.
- Pain cry. A vocalization of sudden onset, of long duration (approximately 7 seconds); loud, followed by audible expelling or air, gulping in air, repetition of above.

Recall that the infant or toddler crying often precipitates shaken baby syndrome. Parents often feel inadequate when their child cries and believe that they should be able to do something to stop the crying. Crying is consistent across cultures, and by 2 months the baby averages about 3 hours of crying a day. Crying is a baby's work and the only way they have to communicate with the caregiver. Infant and toddlers cry to relieve stress or to communicate something to the caregiver. Educating the caregiver on the different types of crying will help their frustration. It is important to emphasize that if the caregiver is becoming frustrated or angry, they should put the child down in a safe place. The parent should know to give him or herself permission to take a break and to regain control. If they are angry with an infant who is continuing to cry, caregivers should not touch the child. It is important to focus intervention on teaching the parent how to cope with crying, not on the cessation of crying.

Parents who learn that their infant cues and who therefore can provide consistent, predictable care will develop secure attachment. This relationship teaches the child that she/he has influence with others to effectively get her/his needs met.

As the caregiver and infant tailor their behavior to each other, they form a mutual attachment that affects the child's development throughout his/her early years (Bowlby, 1969).

Parents who maltreat their infant or toddler are often unable to understand the child's behavior. Neither all children nor caregivers will be responsive to cues and subsequent behavior. Infants who respond unpredictably to daily routines will elicit frustration and feelings of inadequacy in the parent. Caregivers who have poor attitudes or misconceptions of parenthood may provide inferior quality of care to their child. Strategies that alter the parent's tolerance and expectations while increasing the child's social responsiveness through stimulation and reinforcement can improve the attachment relationship (Swetnam, Peterson, & Clark, 1983).

As discussed in chapter 3, toddlers respond to social situations with an ever-expanding array of vocalizations and behaviors. They express anger, delight, affection, and disgust with facial expressions and body postures; they initiate interaction by touching, smiling, and vocalization. Toddlers who have been maltreated often express ambivalence toward social interaction. The impaired relationship between the parent and toddler contributes to the child's fear of new situations. As the parent learns how to provide the toddler with a safe, sensitive environment, the child will experience more successful developmental outcomes. Some strategies to teach the caregiver are:

- Providing clear communication of requests and appropriate positive attention.
- Allowing safe exploration of her/his environment
- Giving positive attention to the toddler when he/she shows objects to the parent.
- When toddler indicates wants by pointing and vocalization, the parent responds appropriately.
- Sharing objects with the toddler.
- Use of songs and stories.
- Game playing.

Though not always easy or straightforward, teaching parents appropriate expectations based on the child's developmental stage and within their cultural behavior patterns and how to be responsive, sensitive care providers will improve the quality of the parent-child relationship, which will facilitate cognitive, emotional, and physical development.

CONCLUSION

In this chapter we began to introduce the numerous ecological risk and protective factors that contribute to child maltreatment. When the risk factors outweigh the protective factors, abuse is likely to occur, as is the risk of future maltreatment. In later chapters, we expand on the impact of ecological correlates and their transactions within and between systems.

Early childhood is a critical developmental stage for intervening with families. Children ages 0 to 3 are at the highest risk of experiencing devastating consequences of physical abuse and neglect. Assessment is focused on the interaction between the infant or toddler and the caregiver. During this stage of development, the practitioner must rely heavily upon observations of the child's behavior and the interaction between the child and the caregiver. Special attention was given to shaken baby syndrome and failure to thrive.

The development of secure attachment between the parent and infant or toddler is key to continued healthy development. Intervention strategies were discussed to encourage and teach parents how to make consistent, stable, and nurturing connections with their child. Strategies focusing on understanding age-appropriate expectations for the child were presented, as well as behavioral cues the infant gives to the parent.

Chapter 5 will focus on the normal developmental expectations of the preschool child, age 3 to 6. Consequences of child maltreatment will be presented in the three developmental domains: social, cognitive-behavioral, and physical.

CASE: CINDY SMITH

Principal Information

Cindy Smith (6 months old), female alleged victim

Melissa Smith (18 months old), female alleged victim

Jamie Smith (30 months old), male alleged victim

Randy Brown (22 years old), male parent partner, alleged perpetrator

Erika Smith (21 years old), female parent, alleged perpetrator

Allegation

Physical neglect of all three children by mother

Case Summary

The household consists of the three victims: 6-month-old female, 18-month-old female, and 30-month-old male. Mr. Brown is not the father of any of the children. He and Ms. Smith have known each other for approximately one month and have been living together for most of that time.

Home Environment

Ms. Smith, Mr. Brown, and the three children live in a house with two bedrooms, a living room, and a kitchen. The house has one bed. Sometimes all five persons sleep in one bed, but many times Jamie and Melissa sleep on the floor. Cindy also sleeps in her crib sometimes, but Ms. Smith prefers her to sleep in the bed so she doesn't have to get up at night. The house has a television set and radio. The house has some toys. The house appears dirty; there are piles of clothes and rags in one corner. Another corner in the living room has a pile of dirty disposable diapers. The house has roaches, and Ms. Smith said that she has talked to her landlord about that. She says that the roaches don't bother the children. The kitchen counters had food sitting out including lunchmeat, moldy bread, mayonnaise, and packages of cookies and crackers. There is no formula in the house, and Ms. Smith denies breast-feeding Cindy. She said that she just has to run and get some, but that Cindy doesn't eat as much as other infants. Even her doctor told her so, she says. Ms. Smith also reports she is in a TANF ready-to-work program, which also subsidized her day care.

During the caseworker's visit to the home, Cindy did not fuss and was quiet. Ms. Smith did not interact with her unless being prompted by the caseworker. Ms. Smith boasted that she got lucky because Cindy is such a "good and quiet child . . . she never cries or fusses." Cindy smells because her diapers need to be changed. There is a pile of dirty disposable diapers in the bathroom. Neither Ms. Smith nor Mr. Brown ever seemed upset with the children during the visit; they did not seem to pay much attention to them.

Ms. Smith reports that her father physically abused her when she was a child, and she was placed in foster care for three years. Her mother abandoned them when she was 6 months old, and she hasn't seen her since. After foster care, she went to live with an aunt and uncle whom she barely knew, and then she moved out on her own at 15. She reports that she liked foster care a little but that she did not like living with her aunt and uncle and all their "rules."

Victim

Cindy, 6 months, has a very bad diaper rash and is dirty. The day care reports that she attends day care with a diaper from the previous day several times a week. They have sent notes to Ms. Smith, who tells them that she does change Cindy's diaper. Cindy's weight seems appropriate, but she is small for her age. She is able to hold a rattle but had difficulty holding her bottle. She is very "easy-going" and does not cry very much. When Ms. Smith comes to pick Cindy up, she always seems in a hurry. She picks up the child and rushes out the door. She does not inquire about the Cindy's day or interact with the child much.

Case Exercise

1. What are the normal developmental expectations are for the child?
2. Consider each child's developmental level. What developmental manifestations can you identify that may be an indication of child maltreatment in the following domains?

   - Physical development
   - Cognitive-behavioral
   - Socioemotional

3. What role does culture play in the child's development?
4. Expand your assessment of each child's developmental level to the over-all ecological model. Assess the family's risk and protective factors in the context of the ecological model.

   - Ontogenic level
   - Microsystem
   - Exosystem
   - Macrosystem

5. What intervention strategies might you employ to facilitate develop-ment of the child?
6. What intervention strategies might you employ with the caregiver?
7. What cultural aspects of the family are important to consider for both assessment and intervention?
8. Since you cannot rely on interviewing Cindy to obtain information about her neglect, what will you do?
9. How will you obtain information from the parent?
10. Think of Cindy and her developmental level. What developmental manifestations can you identify that may be an indication of neglect in the following domains?

    - Physical development
    - Cognitive-behavioral
    - Socioemotional

11. Expand your assessment of Cindy's developmental level to the overall ecological model. Assess the family in the context of the ecological model.

    - Microsystem
    - Exosystem
    - Macrosystem
    - Ontogenic level

12. What intervention strategies might you employ to facilitate develop-ment of the children?

5

EARLY CHILDHOOD
Child Development and Maltreatment

Early childhood is often called the "play years" and includes children from 3 to 6 years of age. Children in early childhood have expanded thought and language capabilities, as well as more coordinated gross motor and fine motor skills. Equally important, they begin to develop peer relationships and friendships. The ability to engage and play with peers is extremely important as the child's social development matures. This chapter will present healthy child development according to the major developmental theories. Second, it will present the developmental manifestations and consequences of child maltreatment specific to physical abuse, sexual abuse, and neglect.

EXPECTED DEVELOPMENT ACROSS DEVELOPMENTAL DOMAINS

Understanding healthy child development is essential to understanding the developmental consequences of child maltreatment. Consistent with other chapters in this book, major developmental theories presented include Freud's psychosexual theory of development, Erickson's psychosocial theory of development, social developmental theories, attachment theory, Piaget's theory of cognitive development, and physical and motor development. The developmental milestones of early childhood will be discussed in relation to children's socioemotional, cognitive, and physical development (see Table 5.1). Psychodynamic theories will be presented first since their contribution covers all areas of the child's development, with special attention on socioemotional and cognitive domains.

Psychodynamic Theories

Freud's Psychosexual Stages of Development

Freud's psychosexual theory of development from approximately ages 3 to 6 is called the phallic stage. The erogenous zones for children include the penis for

Table 5.1 Early Child Development

	Psychodynamic		Social	Cognitive	Physical
	Freud	Erickson		Piaget	
3–4 Years			• Emotional self-regulation improves • Self-conscious emotions (pride, guilt, embarrassment) emerge • Play with others increases	*Preoperational stage:* Development of language and make-believe play emerges • Children use	• Walks up stairs with alternate feet • Jumps and hops • Pedals and steers tricycle • Fastens and unfastens buttons • Uses scissors • Draw first pictures of person
4–5 Years	*Phallic Stage:* Most important body part is the genitals • Children find pleasure in their genitals	*Initiative vs. guilt:* • Children want to perform more adultlike activities • A child's self-esteem is defined by their skills and competencies that show their independence • If children overstep parental limits or a parent does not set reasonable limits, they will develop a sense of guilt in their own abilities and competency	• Advances in peer sociability and first friendships emerge • Instrumental aggression appears and continues from 2 to 6 years	symbolic thinking and language to understand the world • Thinking is still egocentric, but becomes less so as the child ages and develops	• Walks downstairs • Skips with one foot • Throws ball and catches with body rotation and transfer of weight on feet • Uses fork effectively • Cut with scissors following a line
5–6 Years	• Toilet training becomes a major developmental task • The Oedipus complex and Elektra complex explain identification with same-sex parent • The id, ego, and superego are established; basic personality is developed		• Relies on language to express emotions, including empathy • Acquisition of morality, including rules and behaviors • Ability to influence others' emotional reactions improves	• Imagination develops more fully and becomes a means of self-expression • Characteristics of preoperational thought include centration, egocentrism, inability to conserve	• Increased running speed • Engages in true skipping • Rides bicycle with training wheels • Ties shoes • Copies some numbers and words • Draws person with six parts

boys and vulva for girls. While different for boys and girls, each begin to identify—to ally oneself—with one parent or the other. Freud postulated that children identify with the same-sex parent as a result of their physical attraction to the opposite-sex parent, as explained by the Oedipus and Elektra complexes. The Oedipus complex is characterized by boys' attachment toward their fathers that manifests in response to the jealousy boys have for their father's sexual relationship with their mother. Boys become aware that they have a penis and that girls do not and, therefore, boys fear castration. As a result of their fear of castration and their jealousy of their father, they identify with their father. Boys realize they cannot replace their fathers, so they strive to be like them.

Similar to the Oedipus complex for boys, Freud theorized that girls experience the Elektra complex. Girls also realize they are different from boys; they realize they do not have a penis and become jealous of boys. Furthermore, girls realize that their mother also does not have a penis, and they become angry with her for this apparent "inadequacy." Freud argued that girls have sexual feelings for their fathers, because they have penises. The result of this conflict is that girls identify with their mothers because they realize that their mother is the object of their father's affection and sexual attraction. Since the girl cannot replace her mother, she tries to be like her.

Freud's Oedipus and Elektra complexes may be seen in more applicable examples, such as when children play together. Children may play "dress up" during this time and choose clothes that represent their same-sex parent. Children may display stereotypical gender-specific behaviors more than before; they may play stereotypical gender-specific games, depending upon the gender-stereotypes they see in their same-sex parents.

During the phallic stage, the child's superego develops. Freud postulated that one's personality is comprised of three components. The id is present at birth and is comprised of basic instincts and drives. Sexual desire is one example of an id drive present at birth. The id is primarily satisfied when it seeks irrational, impulse-driven pleasure, which is called the pleasure principle. The id seeks libidinal pleasure regardless of the external world. The second part of the personality to develop is the ego, which develops out of the id and is the rationalizing component of the personality. It attempts to distinguish self from other. The ego is driven by the reality principle because it seeks rational decisions that take into consideration the outside world and drives. It also has the ability to delay pleasure. The final component of the personality to develop is the superego, which develops during the phallic stage. The superego is the moralizing component of the personality. It develops out of the ego and guides the child to make moral decisions out of their internalization of parental values. Children are not born "moral," but they become moral through the influence their superego exerts on their personality. The ego mediates the id, the irrational, impulsive part of one's personality, and the superego, the moral component of one's personality. During the phallic stage when the child identifies with a parent, they internalize their values and morals. The internalization of parental and societal values helps develop the superego, which exerts an influence on both the ego and id. While Freud's theory is not used in modern society as much as it once was, it has contributed to our understanding of internal psychological processes, intrapsychic conflicts, and the origins and foundation of child development theory.

Erickson's Psychosocial Stages of Development

During the previous 36 months, children who are developing adequately have positively resolved Erickson's first two stages of psychosocial development: (1) trust vs. mistrust, and (2) autonomy vs. shame and doubt. If a child has positively resolved each of the previous conflicts (trust and autonomy), he/she is ready to face the current crisis: initiative vs. guilt. With increased motor ability and language skills, the child has a wider range of opportunities for exploration. A child's primary job during this stage is to explore and discover a sense of purpose and confidence in her/his abilities. A child who takes the initiative to seize opportunities and successfully masters new skills develops a sense of competence. This child gains a sense of confidence in his/her abilities, which prepares the child for pursuing goals and feeling good about her/his ability to achieve them.

The negative resolution of this stage is guilt. If a parent disallows their child to explore or to try new things, the child develops a sense of guilt in her/his abilities and competence. Similarly, if a parent demands too much self-control or perfection, the child may feel less competent in her/his abilities and possibly cease exploration. A child who resolves this psychosocial conflict with guilt will be hesitant in her/his abilities and less likely to explore freely and confidently. The importance of positive resolution is best seen by the child's confidence, where the child continues to pursue goals until she/he achieves them.

Social Development

Other social developments occur in children in their early years. When children obtain greater physical motor skills and cognitive skills, parenting can become more difficult. Children are able to move all over the house but often do not consistently process safety or danger, nor know their limitations. As a child's cognitive and social development matures, parents are able to discuss a wider range of topics with them. Preschoolers begin to feel stronger and more skilled, and as a result they begin to develop a better self-concept. Children ages 3 to 6 have generally optimistic opinions of themselves, frequently overestimating their abilities. They often believe that they can "win" regardless of the task or race, and they await grand adulation for the smallest achievements. However, as children reach the end of this stage, they begin to incorporate the evaluations of others into their self-concept and approach slightly more realistic self-evaluations.

Another important developmental indicator that emerges in early childhood is the ability of the child to regulate his/her emotions. Emotional regulation involves the ability to modify one's feelings in order to achieve one's goals. As a society, we expect children to regulate their emotions and frustrations to a certain extent during the preschool years, and children become quite good at this. They begin to delay aggression; to decrease the intensity or occurrence of temper tantrums; and to accept the negotiations of parents to delay gratification. Children begin to think before acting and to display appropriate emotions. The ability to regulate one's emotions is also taught, and the best teacher is the parent who leads by example. If a child throws a temper tantrum, the parent can teach the child appropriate behavior or a better way to manage the situation by her/his own behavior. If the parent responds to her/his 5-year-old child's temper tantrum with an adult version of a temper tantrum (angry outbursts, overreaction, throwing objects, etc.), the child sees the adult tantrum as an appropriate way to behave. On the other hand, if the parent responds calmly and uses words to settle the child, the child will see that behavior as a model of appropriate behavior and emotional management.

Attachment can also affect a child's ability to regulate her/his emotions (see chapter 2 for a detailed discussion of attachment). Children with insecure attachments have more difficulty regulating their emotions than children with secure attachments. Children with insecure attachments respond abnormally in distress (Sroufe, 1996). Insecurely attached children may respond aggressively to a sick or hurt child, by calling the child names or punching her/him in the stomach. During friendly (or unfriendly) encounters, the insecurely attached child might respond abnormally with excessive friendliness, such as seeking physical contact (sitting on lap or holding hands) with strangers. Neglected children, in particular, might seek physical touch from a child protection worker—excessively touching the worker, holding hands, wanting to sit on the worker's lap, wanting to go home with the worker. This is especially disturbing given that the child protection worker is a stranger coming into the family's home without invitation and often unexpectedly. The lack of fear of strangers and excessive friendliness can put a child at greater risk of other forms of maltreatment, especially among sexual predators.

The play years are also characterized by an increase in prosocial behaviors. Children begin to engage in more behaviors that have no direct benefit to them, such as sharing more with friends. As children become more self-aware and as they understand the expressions and emotions of others, they become capable of empathy. When a child is hurt on a playground, children in early childhood are capable of identifying that the child is hurt and may respond by patting the child on the back or by giving the injured child a hug. This demonstration of prosocial empathic behavior is tremendous, especially given that the origins of empathy begin so early in life. However, not all children exhibit prosocial behavior; some exhibit antisocial behavior, which is often correlated with a lack of emotional regulation (Eisenberg et al., 1997).

One form of antisocial behavior is aggression. As children develop increased self-awareness, they often use some form of aggression to defend their interests and needs. One common form in the early years is instrumental aggression, which is aggression with the purpose of obtaining a desired item. Since this type of aggression has a purpose (obtaining something), it is of less concern than aggressive behavior that lacks emotional regulation. Unprovoked aggression is especially disturbing when a child attacks another for no other purpose than inflicting harm.

Cognitive Development

Marked differences exist between the cognitive ability of a child in the sensorimotor stage of Piaget's theory of cognitive development, which occurs from 0 to 2 years of age, and the preoperational stage, which occurs from 2 to 6 years. Children during the preoperational stage are able to use symbolic thought, which is the ability to use words, gestures, and actions to represent objects, ideas, or behaviors. To illustrate, a child will be able to point to a dog in a book and label it "dog," may crawl on the floor and bark, and can point to her/his own dog and label it "dog." Children are still, however, restricted by their perception of things. Children are prelogical; that is, they are not ignorant but are not yet capable of true logical thought.

Several principles guide the preoperational stage. One principle is centration, in which children focus on only one way of perceiving rather than exploring alternatives. They may perceive their brother only as a brother and struggle with the concept that their brother is also a son, cousin, and grandson. Children continue to be egocentric because they perceive the world only from their own perspective. Again, a child will see her/his brother in his role as a brother and not in any other role. Children also display animistic thinking where they attribute human qualities to inanimate objects. A child might ask, "Is the sun sad when it is raining?"

Another characteristic of preoperational thought is appearance-base, which is when the child's focus is centered on the appearance of an object to the exclusion of other objects. Appearance-base is best demonstrated through Piaget's conservation tasks. In such experiments, Piaget tried to determine if children understood that the amount of substance in a glass is unaffected by its changes in appearance. He would show children two equal glasses of liquid and then pour the contents of one of the glasses into a taller glass. He would then ask the child which glass had more liquid, and preoperational children would respond that the taller glass had more liquid. Therefore, preoperational children adhere that appearance affects substance. Preoperational thinking tends to focus only on one aspect of the object—which is taller or shorter—rather than on other principles.

A final characteristic of preoperational thought is irreversibility. Children are not able to mentally reverse actions. For example, if you give a child an ice cream cone with sprinkles on it, she might cry because she didn't want sprinkles on her ice cream. The child lacks reversibility and fails to realize that scraping the sprinkles off the ice cream cone will result in a sprinkle-free cone.

Another component of early childhood cognitive abilities is the concept of private speech. Private speech is internal dialogue or "talking to oneself." Children in early childhood use private speech to help them solve problems, think, and learn how to accomplish tasks without soliciting the assistance of others. Private speech initially occurs aloud, where the child is usually unaware of the speech, and later it becomes silent even in adults.

As children gain cognitive skills, their language ability also increases. By 2 years of age, children know about 200 words; by age 6 they know about 10,000 (Anglin, 1993). By age 5 children can learn almost any word and use the word regardless of whether they truly understand its meaning. Children also acquire an under-standing of grammar during early childhood. They form plurals, begin to use tenses correctly, and use possessive forms of pronouns. One common grammati-cal error is overregularization. Overregularization occurs when children apply grammatical rules incorrectly, even though they never hear the incorrect usages. For example, a child might say they "broked their airplane," when they have never heard the word "broked." They have taken grammatical rules and misapplied them in an effort to master their language.

Physical Development

Cognitive, socioemotional, and physical development are intimately tied to one another. As mentioned previously, playing and the emergence of friendships be-come important developmental tasks during early childhood. Children need the motor skills, both gross and fine, and social skills to play with others and engage in games.

Children from 3 to 6 years of age continue to mature in their motor develop-ment, refining both gross and fine motor skills (Table 5.1). Overall growth de-creases from the first 36 months and continues at a slower rate. Muscles undergo more rapid growth; children begin and continue to run, hop, and skip. By the end of this period, a child can perform even difficult gross motor tasks, such as walk-ing on a balance beam. Fine motor skills also advance, with children being better able to print, scribble, and draw pictures of a person. As the child nears the end of this developmental period, she/he should be able to print her/his name, tie their shoes, and ride a bicycle with training wheels. Some children are even able to ride a bicycle without training wheels quite well by the time they reach 6 years old. Children begin to be able to perform self-help skills more competently, such as feeding themselves with eating utensils and getting dressed.

Child maltreatment disrupts the healthy course of development. Children who have been maltreated during early childhood show maladaptive coping patterns that can impede many of the developmental milestones that indicate healthy development.

DEVELOPMENTAL CONSEQUENCES OF CHILD MALTREATMENT FOR CHILDREN AGES 3 TO 6

The consequences of child maltreatment during the early years span cognitive, socioemotional, and physical development. Physical abuse, sexual abuse, and neglect, which may coexist, have specific effects on the developing child. The child between 3 and 6 should have greater motor capacity and a better ability to regu-late emotions. He/she should be able to use words to communicate and have a greater understanding of grammatical and conversational rules. Overlap exists between the developmental manifestations and effects of physical abuse, sexual abuse, and neglect, but each type of abuse also has unique manifestations.

Physical Abuse

Children who have been physically abused between age 3 and 6 have problems in all areas of development. While major motor tasks, such as walking, were developed in the previous stage, children should continue to develop their gross and fine motor skills, becoming increasingly coordinated, speedy, and agile in their movements. Children should similarly display their social and cognitive gains in their play. Physical abuse of children, however, disrupts normal development.

Cognitive-Behavioral

Cognitive impairments are evident in children who have experienced physical abuse in early childhood. They show more impulsivity and aggressive behavior (Egeland, Sroufe, & Erickson, 1983; Kolko, Moser, & Weldy, 1990). They also exhibit attention problems (Wodarski et al., 1990) and lower intellectual functioning (Erickson, Egeland, & Pianta, 1989; Perez & Widom, 1994; Wodarski et al., 1990). Physically abused children have also been shown to lack initiative in completing tasks and decreased motivation, contrary to what is expected for healthy child development (Aber & Allen, 1987).

Children learn acceptable and unacceptable behaviors early in life. Culture, environment, and caregivers are important socialization tools for teaching appropriate behavior. Evidence suggests that children who have been exposed to physical abuse demonstrate a greater acceptance for the use of physical punishment (Carlson, 1991). One explanation for this is the child's own experience. The environment of children in physically abusive families conveys that aggression is an acceptable problem-solving tool (Dodge, Petit, & Bates, 1997). Culture also plays a role in children's behavioral and emotional development. Living in a neighborhood plagued with poverty and violence has an impact on the developing child, including difficulty coping with conflict and poor social skills (MacLennan, 1994). These children may hear gun shots, witness fighting, and experience the death of loved one, which impacts the social, cognitive, and perhaps even physical development of the child.

Physically abusive parents also tend to have high and unrealistic expectations of their children's behavior (Azar et al., 1984). As children mature, they increasingly want to try out their new cognitive, social, and physical skills, but their skills are still limited. It may take several attempts and much patience before a child masters riding a bike or even pouring milk into a cereal bowl. If parents have unrealistically high expectations, as shown among physically abusive parents, normal behavior from children can lead to harsh physical punishment and abuse. As a result, the child may respond by decreasing her/his activities and may appear unmotivated and lacking initiation.

Socioemotional

Physically abused children have poor peer and interpersonal relationships (Kolko, 1992), which may be related to their tendency to demonstrate higher levels of aggressive behavior than unabused children (Alessandri, 1991; Ammerman, 1989; Howes & Espinosa, 1985). Even compared to neglected children, physically abused children are shown to be more verbally and physically aggressive (Hoffman-Plotnik & Twentyman, 1984). Both abused and neglected children have been shown to exhibit higher levels of aggression than nonmaltreated children. Compared to neglected children, however, physically abused children show more aggression in fantasy and open play (Reidy, 1977). It is important to mention that instrumental aggression is natural from 2 to 6 years of age, but unprovoked aggression is concerning. Haskett and Kistner (1991) found that abused preschool children exhibited more negative behaviors and fewer positive interactions than nonabused children during play. Abused preschoolers also tend to cause more distress in their peers than nonabused children (Klimes-Dougan & Kistner, 1990).

Physically abused children also have been shown to have less social competence (George & Main, 1979) and lower self-esteem (Allen & Tarnowski, 1989). Child victims of physical abuse have been found to have negative affect (Schneider-Rosen & Cicchetti, 1984), and their poor range of affect has been shown to be related to cognitive skill deficiencies (Camara, Grow, & Ribordy, 1983). Interesting, however, is that parents who physically abuse have also been shown to have limited positive affect and low social behavior (Kavanagh et al., 1988; Salzinger et al., 1986).

As mentioned in chapter 2, children with insecure attachments (about two thirds of maltreated children have insecure attachments) tend to interpret even friendly behavior as hostile. A child may react aggressively at another's benign attempt at interaction. As a result, the child may become ostracized by peers who exhibit prosocial behaviors because of the abused child's tendency to appear angry and mean in play. Similarly, abused children tend to react to friendly behavior by peers with anger and hostility (Howes & Eldredge, 1985). Maltreated children in early childhood demonstrate less positive and friendly interaction when playing with peers (Kaufman & Cicchetti, 1989), more negative affect (Schneider-Rosen & Cicchetti, 1984), and poor anger management (Beeghly & Cicchetti, 1994). Alessandri (1991) found that preschool maltreated children engaged in less group play and performed more repetitive motor play than nonmaltreated preschoolers.

As children become more self-aware and as they understand the expressions and emotions of others, they become capable of empathy, but physically abused children are less able to exhibit empathic behaviors (Burgess & Youngblade, 1989). Abused preschool children have difficulty discriminating the emotional expressions of others (Frodi & Smetana, 1984), which should be established by this time. As presented in chapter 4, social referencing involves looking toward a trusted person in one's environment to provide emotional information, and this extension of emotional understanding should continue to mature and develop in the early years.

Another developmental indicator during early childhood is an increased likelihood of gender-stereotypical play and identification with the same-sex parent, based on psychodynamic theory. While this concept has been discussed in this chapter as well as the controversy about the applicability of psychodynamic theory in current practice, it is worth addressing again. Children who witness violence in their home may identify with either the perpetrator or victim, depending upon their gender. Some physically abused children externalize their trauma through increased aggressiveness, while others internalize it through depression and low self-esteem. If the physically abused boy sees his father as the perpetrator, he may become angry at his mother for failing to protect him, while acknowledging the power his father has over the family. During early childhood, a child's identity and interpretation of the event(s) are shaped by the child's experiences. Research has shown that internalizing symptoms are associated with self-blame, while externalizing symptoms are associated with external attributions of the physical abuse (Brown & Kolko, 1999). Thus, the way in which the child perceives the abuse affects his/her attributional style. Fantuzzo et al. (1998) found higher levels of internalizing among abused preschool children.

Physical

The most severe physical consequences of physical abuse in early childhood include traumatic brain injury and death (USDHHS, 2000). While death is more prevalent in those 0 to 3, children ages 3 to 6 are still at risk (ibid.). Studies have revealed that children who have traumatic brain injury before the age of 6 have worse long-term outcomes than children who experience the event later (Costeff, Grosswasser, & Goldstein, 1990; Kriel, Krach, & Panser, 1989). Physical abuse may render a child disabled or incapable of play because of pain or injury from abuse.

Children from 3 to 6 should be playing actively, running, jumping, and demonstrating an increase in agility and speed. Between 4 and 5, children should be able to play catch. They should also be practicing their fine motor skills, such as dressing, coloring, and drawing. Children who have been severely physically abused may be unable to perform such activities if they have untreated injuries or too much pain. Medical attention is often necessary if the child has not been treated for current and untreated injuries. The child may experience limited movement due to injury and be unable to participate in games and play.

Sexual Abuse

Sexual abuse is a distinct type of maltreatment, and it differs from both physical abuse and neglect in important ways. Children usually fail to disclose their abuse immediately (Finkel, 2000), and in many cases offenders try to induce fear and use threats to deter victims from disclosure (Elliott & Briere, 1994). Because children may not disclose promptly, physical evidence may be absent. In addition, some forms of sexual abuse, such as fondling and oral sex, may leave no physical indicators even if the abuse is disclosed. As a result, the ability to obtain diagnostic and forensic evidence is a challenge to child welfare professionals, who have to rely on the child's statement rather than physical evidence in certain circumstances. The developmental consequences of sexual abuse, therefore, differ from those for neglect and physical abuse.

It is important to mention that the degree to which sexual abuse affects a child is multiply determined. Some children experience immediate effects, and others experience little or no effect. Some children do not experience any immediate effect but have difficulties at the onset of puberty. Sexual abuse can also occur with no immediate observable effect to the child's mental or physical health. The degree to which sexual abuse affects a child depends on many factors. The following presents some of the variables that should be considered.

The duration of the abuse. The results are mixed on the extent that the duration of the sexual abuse affects outcomes. Generally, the longer sexual abuse occurs, the more negative the outcomes for the child. One exception is when a single incident involves sadism and violence (Beitchman et al., 1992).

The type and extent of sexual activity. Children who experience more severe forms of sexual abuse, including penetration, tend to have worse outcomes than children who experience less severe forms of abuse, although this is not always the case (Ruggerio, McLeer, & Dixon, 2000).

The age the sexual abuse began. While Berliner (1991) concluded that the age of onset has not consistently been associated with severity of outcome, Beitchman et al. (1992) maintain that the consequences vary depending upon the developmental stage of the victim. How the child perceives the event may be related to their developmental level. Older children who have greater cognitive functioning tend to experience greater distress (Shapiro et al., 1992).

The relationship of child and perpetrator. The more intense the relationships between the child and perpetrator, the more negative the outcome for the child. Intense emotional relationships generally include family members, fathers, father figures, or a trusted member of one's family. Maternal support can also affect outcomes to the child. Maternal support is most often compromised when the offender is a live-in boyfriend or stepfather (Elliott & Briere, 1994).

The existence of multiple forms of maltreatment. Children who experience other forms of child maltreatment in addition to sexual abuse generally manifest more negative effects.

Attributional style of child. Children do less well when they have a negative general attribution style (Kress & Vandenberg, 1998; Mannarino & Cohen, 1996). Negative attributions often involve internalized distress and self-blame, resulting in more psychological distress over time (Mannarino & Cohen, 1996).

The above list is not exhaustive, and many other variables can affect a child's response to sexual abuse, including the disclosure experience, temperament, and personality, to name a few. It is also important to keep in mind that children experience sexual abuse differently than they do other forms of maltreatment. They often feel "involved" in the act since this form of maltreatment sometimes feels good to the child. Victims sometimes feel like a co-conspirator with the perpetrator or feel "special" with the attention or gifts they receive from the perpetrator. It is important to reiterate that even with the absence of diagnostic or forensic evidence and the absence of immediate observable effects to the child, child sexual abuse can still occur and validation should be attempted.

Cognitive-Behavioral

Children in early childhood have greater mental capacity, and play becomes an important part of cognitive development. Sexually abused preschoolers exhibit sexual play more than other children. Their make-believe play and play with dolls may surround sexual situations and behaviors. During early childhood, sexually abused children may play with adults by grabbing their genitals or stroking them in a sexual manner. As make-believe play emerges and sociodramatic play increases, the scenes sexually abused children perform may reflect a sexual nature. The frequency of dramatic play does not differ among maltreated and nonmaltreated children, but the thematic events of the play differ (Alessandri, 1991). Sexually abused children's language may be wrought with sexual terms, and their talk may be characterized by compulsive sexual talk (Olafson & Boat, 2000).

Cognitive distortions can arise from child sexual abuse. The child is forced to make sense of her/his abuse and the perpetrator through an "abuse dichotomy" (Berlinger & Elliott, 1996). For example, the child is forced to decide whether the perpetrator is the bad person, or whether the child herself/himself is the bad person. Children are taught obedience of parents and caregivers, and the child may internalize the abuse and that she/he must be at fault (Briere, 1989). As a result of internalizing the sexual abuse, children may develop a sense of shame and badness. The research is mixed regarding the occurrence of self-blame among sexually abused children. Hunter, Goodwin, and Wilson (1992) found that most children do not blame themselves for their victimization, while Einbender and Friedrich (1989) found that self-blame was a manifestation of sexual abuse. When self-blame is present, however, more severe outcomes may result and may continue throughout development (Berlinger & Elliott, 2002). Moreover, since early relationship templates are formed in a child's early years, sexually abused children may perceive other adults and their environments as unsafe and dangerous (Cole & Putnam, 1992).

Socioemotional

Children in early childhood may feel "shamed" and as if they are damaged goods due to their sexual experiences, especially around the ages of 3 and 4 when more sophisticated emotions like shame and embarrassment emerge. Overall, the effects of stigmatization may manifest in sexually abused children: shame, distrust, and self-blame (Einbender & Friedrich, 1989). Sexually abused children may begin to view their body differently and have concerns about their body image (Byram, Wagner, & Waller, 1995). While these body image concerns become more pronounced later and manifest frequently in anorexia, obesity, and body distortions, they begin to emerge during early childhood as the child understands his/her separateness and the complexity of his/her emotions.

Some sex play is normal during this stage, but sexually abused children have play that reflects intimate knowledge of sexual behaviors. Young children will display a wide range of sexual behavior that reflects their keen sense of curiosity. However, their intent is not sexual gratification and is not motivated by sexual arousal, as among adults (Chaffin, Letourneau, & Silovsky, 2002). The sexual behavior seen among sexually abused children is a unique consequence of sexual abuse and is not seen as frequently among other types maltreatment (Friedrich, 1993; Mannarino & Cohen, 1996). The play of sexually abused children may be overtly sexual with both peers and adults; they may make sexual overtures toward playmates and show their genitalia in a sexually suggestive manner. Their play and fantasy may be of a sexual nature. While nonsexually abused children may fondle themselves during play, children in early childhood may excessively masturbate.

Sexually abused children may play with dolls in a sexual manner and reenact a sexual event through pictures or dolls. Children who have been sexually abused are also more likely to draw sexual pictures than nonvictims (Hibbard, Roghmann, & Hoekelman, 1987; Yates, Beutler, & Crago, 1985). Characteristics of the drawing may include the minimization or maximization of the genitals, or phallic imagery. Sexually abused children have been found to be 6.8 times more likely to draw genitals than comparison children (Hibbard, Roghmann & Hoekelman, 1987). Sexually abused children display more sexual behaviors than neglected, physically abused, and psychiatrically disturbed children (Gale et al., 1988; Friedrich, 1993; Kolko, Moser, & Weldy, 1988) and have more sexual content in their drawings than nonvictims (Hibbard, Roghmann & Hoekelman, 1987; Yates, Beutler & Crago, 1985).

Children age 3 to 6 or 7 commonly display exploratory sexual behaviors (Volbert & Van der Zanden, 1992). It is normal for preschool-aged children to be curious about body parts and genitalia, but they are generally not inquisitive about intercourse or sexual interactions for which they have no context. They are more often curious about the physical differences between males and females, where babies come from, and anatomy in general (Sandnabba et al., 2003). Unless they have been exposed to sexual activities, they will generally not ask about specific aspects of sex for which they have no frame of reference, such as intercourse or oral/anal sex. However, a sexually abused child may behaviorally demonstrate sexual intercourse or may mimic sexual acts such as inserting an object into a vagina or anus (Friedrich et al., 2001), or displaying sexual acts with anatomical dolls (Everson & Boat, 1990). It is important to mention, however, that Friedrich (1993) maintains that not all sexually abused children exhibit problems in their sexual behavior.

Emotionally, sexually abused children exhibit anxiety, depression (Kolko, Moser, & Weldy, 1988; McLeer et al., 1992; Mannarino & Cohen, 1996), and overall emotional disturbances (Basta & Peterson, 1990). Children may also have nightmares and difficulty sleeping. They may appear clingy and fearful. Sexually abused children may also experience interpersonal problems, such as being less socially competent (Mannarino & Cohen, 1996) and more withdrawn (Friedrich, Beilke, & Urquiza, 1987), and they may have difficulty trusting others (Mannarino, Cohen, & Berman, 1994).

According to Erickson's theory of psychosocial development, the development of initiative, and subsequently a child's competence in her/his abilities, are primary social tasks during early childhood. The development of initiative allows children to explore freely and confidently, understanding their own abilities and competence. The negative resolution of this conflict is guilt, in which one does not have a sense of competence. Sexually abused children are not offered appropriate sexual limits and boundaries; in fact, their boundaries are completely disregarded by the sexually abusive situation. They may be physically restricted or hypervigilant due to the sexual abuse. Sexually abused children may feel guilty and shameful themselves; they may feel embarrassed by their involvement in the abuse and the secrecy. However, it is important to remember that not all children self-blame for their abuse (Hunter, Goodwin, & Wilson, 1992). Nonetheless, when sexually abused girls do feel shamed, higher rates of depression and lower self-esteem emerge (Fiering, Taska, & Lewis, 1998).

Physical

Sexually abused children may have physical manifestations of the abuse in addition to cognitive-behavioral and socioemotional consequences. As previously mentioned, diagnostic and forensic evidence may be lacking in child sexual abuse cases. Children who have been sexually abused often do not disclose the abuse immediately or will delay disclosure until they feel safe, which may be years after the abuse has stopped. As a result, physical evidence may be lacking at the time the abuse is disclosed. Even without disclosure of the abuse, however, sexually abused children often complain of headaches and stomachaches, and have difficulty sleeping and eating. A child's physical abilities may be compromised by their sexual trauma through pain or problems with walking or sitting, which may impact their ability to play, as other children do. Children may also have problems walking and sitting due to sexual trauma. Their genitals may bleed and itch; they may have genital odor and report pain in their genital area. Sexually abused children may contract sexually transmitted diseases and urinary tract infections (Kunin, 1978) and have anal trauma and difficulty with bowel movements.

By early childhood, children should be toilet trained, but not all sexually abused children have complete control over urinary and bowel functions. Other indications of sexual abuse in early childhood are encopresis, which is important to explore in children who have experienced anal trauma (Finkel, 2000), and enuresis. Another physical consequence of sexual abuse is gastrointestinal disorders (Drossman et al., 1990; Walker et al., 1995; 1993), which may not be identified until the child is older.

Neglect

Similar to the unique circumstance surrounding sexual abuse, neglect is a distinct subtype of child maltreatment. What separates neglect from physical or sexual abuse is its omission of behavior. Neglect is marked by the absence of behavior rather than an act itself. As a result, neglect has developmental manifestations that differ from both physical abuse and sexual abuse. Neglect is more chronic rather than episodic, which further complicates the developmental consequences because they arise from a lifestyle rather than an incident. Recall from chapter 3 that children who are neglected in the first 36 months of life may fail to meet developmental milestones at the rate of other children. Since development is a progressive process, neglected children between 3 and 6 may already be behind in their development. Compared to abused children who were shown to have mild developmental delays, neglected children have significant developmental delays (Crittenden & Ainsworth, 1989).

Cognitive-Behavioral

Children who have experienced neglect may have delays in their cognitive development. By 3 years of age, children should be using language more and understanding better; however, neglected children demonstrate language delays (Katz, 1992). Many neglected children have not been offered the environmental stimulation in order to facilitate language development. Neglected children are often not spoken to or only given directives ("Put your bowl away"). As a result, they may not be able to understand more complex statements ("Please join the group. Bring your crayons and draw a picture of your family, please."). They will understand part of the complex statement but not all of it, so they appear confused and seem to not follow directions. Having been spoken to with only simple commands, their confusion stems from their inability to process so much information at once rather than over defiance or ignorance.

Children who have been neglected often appear inattentive and lack interest in learning (Erickson & Egeland, 1996; 2002). They tend to be impulsive in the classroom, noncompliant, and dependent upon teachers, and to have problems adjusting to a classroom setting (Erickson & Egeland, 2002). Neglected children also demonstrate less maturity and have difficulty developing trust (Herrenkohl et al., 1984). Furthermore, they have been shown to remain isolated in opportunities for play (Crittenden, 1992), when engaging in play with others is developmentally expected.

Socioemotional

Early childhood is primarily characterized by play and children's energetic exploration of their environments due to new cognitive, motor, and emotional skills. During the early years, neglected children have been shown to exhibit less eagerness in play with others and to avoid opportunities for early learning (i.e., early school learning) (Erickson & Egeland, 1996; 2002). Children who are neglected may not exhibit this eagerness for their environment; and they may not engage others as freely and frequently as other children. Overall, neglected children interact less with their peers than either abused or non-neglected children (Hoffman-Plotnik & Twentyman, 1984), and they exhibit more withdrawal and avoidance of peers (Dodge, Pettit, & Bates, 1994; Hoffman-Plotnik & Twentyman, 1984). They also lack creativity and appear more unhappy than their non-neglected playmates (Erickson & Egeland, 2002).

Neglected children are more likely to be insecurely attached (Erickson & Egeland, 1996). They are also often not well liked by peers (Erickson & Egeland, 1996; 2002). They may interpret others words and behaviors in a negative way, even when the intent of the other person was friendly and engaging. As a result, neglected children are generally less well liked by peers, thus reinforcing their internal working model that their environment is unfriendly and unreliable.

Neglected children show less positive affect than other children, including abused children (Erickson & Egeland, 1996).

One of the developmental milestones that continue from toddlerhood into early childhood is emotional regulation. Children who have been neglected at 4½ years of age have been shown to lack impulse control, an important component of emotional regulation (Erickson & Egeland, 1996). The ability to regulate one's emotions is important and sets the foundation for good school performance and school behavior, which becomes even more important in the next developmental period. Having begun in toddlerhood, emotional regulation should be much better in early childhood.

Physical

Neglected children may have a host of chronic medical-related problems, including developmental delay (Halfon, Mendoca, & Berkowitz, 1995; Hochstadt et al., 1987; Moffatt, Peddie, & Stulginskas, 1985), anemia, infectious diseases, and asthma (Flaherty & Weiss, 1990). Neglected children often fail to grow at the rate of other children due to their emotional and physical deprivation, and many are of short stature or fail to thrive (Halfon, Mendoca, & Berkowitz, 1995; Hochstadt et al., 1987; Moffatt, Peddie, & Stulginskas, 1985). Consistent with the lack of care neglected children receive, many neglected children have untreated dental, hearing (Dubowitz et al., 1992; Hochstadt et al., 1987), and vision problems (Hochstadt et al., 1987).

Children who have experienced chronic neglect may not meet their physical milestones as expected. Between the ages of 3 and 4, the child may neither be walking nor walking with better coordination; he/she may not jump or hop. Neglected children may exhibit little interest or ability to provide self-care, such as dressing oneself. They may have difficulty holding or using a pencil or crayon or drawing pictures. A 5-to 6-year-old child who has been neglected may fail to develop sophistication in gross motor skills, such as failing to run fast and/or skip. A neglected child may fail to use eating utensils or scissors, or to tie her/his shoes. Finally, the neglected child will not only be unable to perform such tasks, but may also lack the desire and enthusiasm to try.

CONCLUSION

Child abuse, sexual abuse, and neglect have devastating consequences to the children whom they affect. This chapter has focused on the developmental consequences of child maltreatment, but it is also important to explore all levels of the ecological model in determining the antecedents and sequelae of maltreatment. While it is imperative to focus on the consequence of maltreatment to the victims, parental behavior, environmental influences, and social support should also be explored. Ecological influences can mediate and moderate the effects of maltreatment as easily as they can exasperate them. However, a primary focus should be on the consequence to the child in order to ameliorate the effects of abuse and stop the cycle of maltreatment.

6

EARLY CHILDHOOD

Ecological and Developmental Assessment of Maltreatment and Intervention

Early childhood is the developmental stage of a child's life that should be filled with play and amusement with others. For many young children ages 3 to 6 this is not the case. Young children are more likely to be reported for child maltreatment than older children (Berrick et al., 1998), and physical abuse tends to peak in the 4- to 8-year range (Whitman, 2002). Consequently, these young children do not have the opportunity to experience a safe and secure environment that would allow them to maximize the development of core emotional, cognitive, and physical traits that lead to healthy functioning as an adult. Abuse and neglect experiences in early childhood rob the child of vital social learning opportunities, as well as an otherwise playful time of life.

In this chapter the focus on early childhood and maltreatment will be placed in the ecological context for both assessment and intervention. The discussion of risk and protective factors that began in chapter 4 will be expanded to include those factors that are most salient at this development stage (see Tables 6.1 and 6.2).

RISK AND PROTECTIVE FACTORS

Ontogenic Level

As discussed in chapter 5, young children's development is focused on learning social skills and self-initiative. The parent's own experience (her/his ontogenic development) as a child during this developmental stage affects how the parent will provide care for the child. If the parents did not achieve independence, they may seek to have their needs met through the child, interfering with the child's negotiation of the central issues of this developmental period. Since the caregiver is the primary agent in teaching and role modeling appropriate social skills, parents who had difficult childhoods and a history of maltreatment may not appropriately guide and support the young child through her/his developmental milestones.

Table 6.1 Risk Factors

	Infant and Toddler	Early Childhood
Parental Ontogenic	• Parent experienced child maltreatment as a child	• Parent experienced poor parenting during their early childhood • Attachment issues
Microsystem		
Child	• Age itself • Born prematurely • Physical or mental disability • Infant tests positive for AOD • Race	• Excessive health or medical problems • Developmental delays
Parent	• Not satisfied with the child • Does not enjoy parenting • Young parent • Not understanding role as caregiver • Lack of knowledge of child development • Substance abuse	• Perceptions of child • Inappropriate child expectations around development • Lower educational level • Authoritarian • Substance abuse • Depression • Aggressive behavior
Family	• Poverty • Stress in family environment • Interpersonal conflict between partners • Single parent	• Coercive child-rearing practices • Little positive interactions • Family lacks leadership, closeness, and negotiation skills
Exosystem	• Lack of social support	• Caring individual in the child life • Neighborhood lacks both informal and formal social supports • Living in a violent community • Lack connection with the community
Macrosystem	• Cultural values that support violence • Attitudes toward how mothers should behave as a parent	• Culturally promoted attitudes and behaviors about parental rights to physically punish

What the parent brings to the parent-child relationship throughout all stages is a critical influence on the child's achievement of competence and adaptation.

Continued risk concerning the attachment of the caregiver and the preschool child is applicable. Maltreated preschoolers are significantly more likely to have insecure attachments than nonmaltreated preschoolers (Cicchetti & Barnett, 1991), and parents who have attachment issues with their children are more likely to maltreat them (Scannapieco & Connell-Carrick, in press). Additionally, parents who witness or experience violence as a child may learn to use aggressive

Table 6.2 Protective Factors

	Infant and Toddler	Early Childhood
Parental Ontogenic	• Parent experienced secure attachment	• Parent experienced appropriate parenting during early childhood • Continued to be securely attached to caregiver
Microsystem Child	• Temperament • Goodness of fit with the parent	• Competent behavior • Positive temperament • Child is perceived as affectionate • Child is perceived to have high cognitive ability
Parent	• Secure attachment as a child	• Adequate knowledge of preschool child development • Adequate developmental expectation of the child • Quality child-rearing conditions
Family	• Supportive significant other in the home	• Mothers who are happy with their partner relationship • Structured, consistent daily routine • Presence of father or father figure
Exosystem	• Adequate formal and informal social support	• Adequate formal and informal social support • Living in a nonviolent community • Connections with the community
Macrosystem	• Cultural value of protecting children	• Culture that promotes non-physical forms of punishment

methods of disciplining their young child (Dolz, Cerezo, & Milner, 1997; Straus & Smith, 1990).

Microsystem Level

Parental (Caregiver) Characteristics

RISK FACTORS Young children, by nature, are still dependent upon their parent for all their physiological and psychological needs. At the same time, the preschool child is becoming increasingly independent of caregivers in observing, experiencing, and internalizing environmental stimuli (Ferrara, 2002). Parents must be willing on the one hand to allow the child a safe environment to play and explore but on the other hand to provide for the child's basic needs. The parental risk factors presented in chapter 4 continue to be of concern during this stage of child development (see Table 6.1) with the addition of the following parental risk factors, which may be most relevant at this stage.

Several risk factors that distinguish between maltreating and nonmaltreating parents are related to social-cognitive and affective processes that are tied to the parent's perceptions of her/his preschool child. Caregivers who incorrectly attribute causes to particular child behaviors are more likely to be abusive (Azar, 1997; Crittenden, 1993; Wolfe, 1985). When the child is protesting separation from the parent, for example, the parent may view this as spoiled behavior instead of understanding that the child has an attachment to the parent and a feeling of safety. Another example may be a child who constantly says "no." The parent may view this as defiant behavior instead of the child asserting her/his independence. Parents who lack parenting knowledge and skills, and who have inappropriate child expectations and the belief that the child is intentionally annoying the parent, are more likely to abuse their young child (Bauer & Twentyman, 1985; Larrance & Twentyman, 1983; Scannapieco & Connell-Carrick, in press). Related to these distortions in social-cognitive and affective processes may be the risk factor of education. Parents with a lower educational level distinguish those who may maltreat from those who may not (Cadzow, Armstrong, & Frazer, 1999).

A parent who relies heavily on authoritarian and other coercive discipline strategies is at higher risk of physically abusive behavior (Drach & Devoe, 2000). Abusive parents rely on power-assertive techniques (Oldershaw, Walters, & Hall, 1986) and view their authority and will as being of primary importance. Challenges to this authority by the preschool child attempting to assert her/his independence are duly suppressed, often through severe physical punishment.

As indicated earlier, the young child is still reliant on her/his caregiver to meet basic needs. If the parent is abusing alcohol or other drugs, this may undermine her/his ability to parent appropriately and increase the risk of child maltreatment. Substance abuse has been found to be related to or the cause of child maltreatment in up to 80% of all cases (Chance & Scannapieco, 2002; Dore, Doris, & Wright, 1995; NCCAN, 1993; Reid, Macchetto, & Foster, 1999; Scannapieco & Connell-Carrick, in press). The alcohol or drug may reduce the parent's inhibition of aggressive impulse, and the substance abuse may interfere with the parent's judgment, thus resulting in a neglectful or abusive situation (Ammerman et al., 1999).

Other parental risk factors contributing to child maltreatment during early childhood are parental affective disturbances, such as depression or hostile and aggressive behavior (Lahey et al., 1984; Simons, et al., 1991).

PROTECTIVE FACTORS   During the early childhood years, development proceeds, literally, by leaps and bounds. Parents who have adequate knowledge of preschool development and subsequent expectations are less likely to maltreat their children (Cicchetti & Lynch, 1995; Werner, 1993). As indicated in chapter 5, according to Freud, the phallic stage begins during the third year of life. During this developmental stage, parent-child conflict may develop over masturbation, which many caregivers treat with punishment and threats (Rathus, 2003). If a caregiver has adequate knowledge of children's normal sexual development and experimentation, he/she would be less likely to punish a child for masturbation.

As in infancy, preschool children need proper stimulation and attention from their parents. Quality child-rearing conditions promote self-efficacy and self-worth through the continued development of a secure parent-child attachment. A parent who is able to provide safe opportunities for her/his young child to play and grow is more likely to optimize healthy child development.

Child Characteristics

RISK FACTORS   Children who have a disability or excessive health or medical problems are at greater risk of maltreatment in all its forms: physical abuse, neglect, and sexual abuse (Belsky & Vondra, 1989; NCCAN, 1993; Sullivan & Knutson, 1998). During the preschool years, parents' patience is challenged even for children who do not have any disabilities or health issues. The excessive parenting responsibility that is imposed on parents of children with developmental delays may increase parents' stress level, resulting in neglect or an abusive incident.

Gender is a risk factor for physical abuse during early childhood. The highest physical abuse rate for boys occurs between the ages of 4 and 7 (USDHHS, 2000).

PROTECTIVE FACTORS   Young children who have competent behavior and a positive temperament and who do not act aggressively are at lower risk of maltreatment (Garbarino et al., 1992; Wolfe, 1994). A child who is perceived as affectionate and of higher cognitive ability is more likely to be safeguarded from maltreatment (Garbarino et al., 1992; Radke-Yarrow & Sherman, 1990). These characteristics are associated with increased resilience, enabling the preschool child to use her/his internal resources effectively.

Family Characteristics

RISK FACTORS   As stated earlier, family determinants of child maltreatment are an integral part of understanding how the child and parent characteristics interact to bring about an abusive incident. Abuse occurs in the home where the child plays and sleeps. The risk factors discussed in chapter 4—poverty, stress in the family environment, interpersonal conflict between partners, and being a single parent—are significant predictors of maltreatment during early childhood and infancy. Additional family risk factors applicable to the preschool years are related to parent-child interactions.

It has been found that abusive parents are more coercive in their child-rearing practices (Azar, Barnes, & Twentyman, 1988; Oldershaw, Walters, & Hall, 1986). In these families, few positive interactions are present and there is more reliance on oppressive behaviors and lack of or manipulative communication between the child and caregiver. It is important to remember that within the microsystem, child maltreatment must be considered an interactive process (Belsky, 1980). A relationship may evolve whereby the child becomes oppositional in order to gain attention from the parent, which may elicit abusive behavior by the parent. This is not to say that the child is to be blamed for the physical abuse; it may be the only way he/she has learned to get attention. While children may play a role in their own maltreatment, they cannot cause it themselves.

These types of dysfunctional interactions between the preschool child and the parent also have implications for the child's overall recovery from the abuse, especially when there is not a nonoffending "protective" caregiver present. When a parent has betrayed the child through physical abuse, neglect, or sexual abuse, the child's sense of trust is compromised and she/he may be more vulnerable to stress and anxiety.

The last risk factor, overall family skills, is most associated with early childhood and the likelihood of the family experiencing child maltreatment. Maltreating families demonstrate less family leadership, less closeness, fewer clear negotiation skills, and less willingness to assume responsibility for their feelings (Gaudin et al., 1996), which all impact how successful the family is at meeting the needs of preschool children.

PROTECTIVE FACTORS   Mothers who are happy with their partner relationship are more likely to provide responsive, stimulating care to their preschool child (Belsky & Vondra, 1989). Families that are able to provide a more structured, consistent daily routine for their children are less likely to maltreat them.

The presence of a father or father figure has been found to decrease the likelihood of neglect (Dubowitz et al., 2000). Father figure or father involvement resulted in less neglect when the duration of the relationship was longer, involvement in household tasks and childcare was less, and they had a greater sense of parental efficacy.

Exosystem Characteristic: Risk and Protective Factor

Just as substance abuse is a risk factor across all developmental stages, social support and its different functions serve as a risk or protective factor across the lifespan. The correlation between informal social support and child maltreatment was discussed in chapter 4 and will be addressed here as well. The presence of a caring, supportive adult in the child's exosystem has been consistently identified as a protective factor for children (Finkelhor & Berliner, 1995; Kirby & Fraser, 1997). The preschool child is least likely to have contact with an unrelated adult, such as a teacher or coach, who might serve as this support. Grandparents, aunts, uncles, or other kin, who provide caring, responsive nurturing in the context of the child maltreatment, will help the child recover from child maltreatment. Role modeling prosocial behavior and skills also may protect the child from adverse developmental outcomes and is a good influence on the young child (Maluccio, Abramczyk, & Thomlison, 1996; Masten, 1994; Wolfe, 1994).

Families who live in neighborhoods with strong informal social support networks are less likely to experience child maltreatment and more likely to have positive parenting practices (Pelton, 1994). Formal social supports, such as churches and hospitals, also play a protective role in child maltreatment. Inaccessible and unaffordable childcare and health services in a family's community have been positively correlated with incidents of child maltreatment (Garbarino & Kostelny, 1992). Families who lack both kin support and formal social support are at higher risk of experiencing child maltreatment.

Living in a violent community may further hamper the parent's ability to provide appropriate child-rearing practices and may interact with troubled family characteristics and contribute to child maltreatment. Parents who live in constant fear may deny their preschool child normal developmental transitions. During this stage of development, the young child is beginning to initiate independence. If the parent does not trust that the neighborhood or housing community is safe, the parent may not allow or encourage appropriate independence of the child (Osofsky, 1999). Living in violent communities and coming from unstable homes, children are far more likely to suffer adaptational failures, such as relating to peers and behavior problems in school (Richters & Martinez, 1993).

Families lacking a connection to their community have fewer opportunities for exposure to child-rearing practices that could improve their own parenting skills (Trickett & Sussman, 1989). Without this social filter and opportunities for parental learning, parents lack a connection to emotional and material support during stressful times. Garbarino and Sherman (1980) also found that in neighborhoods where abuse and neglect were lower than expected, the families perceived their neighborhood with greater satisfaction and as a positive place for child and family development.

Macrosystem Level

Culturally promoted attitudes and behaviors about the rights of parents to physically discipline their child may influence parents' willingness to use harsh punishment. The parent, family, and community are a reflection of the larger cultural structure. As long as our society condones harsh treatment of children, families will continue to be at risk of maltreating their children.

MALTREATMENT ASSESSMENT OF FAMILIES WITH CHILDREN IN THE EARLY CHILDHOOD YEARS

Child maltreatment assessment for young children, using the ecological framework, must be based on the developmental principles outlined in chapter 5. Preschool children make great gains in social, emotional, and cognitive domains but still lack some abilities. For example, the child is unable to perceive a person in more than her/his one role. Although children make great gains in language from when they were toddlers—200 words to 10,000—the young child remains egocentric and can only perceive the world from her/his own perspective. It is essential to ground the assessment, which includes interviewing the preschool child, in the context of her/his developmental stage.

The assessment can move away from relying solely on observation of the child's behavior and her/his interaction with the caregiver to interviewing the preschool child. Behavioral indicators still play a key role in assessment, but the child is also a dependable source of information given the developmental limitations previously discussed and the experience of the child welfare professional.

In this section we will build on the evaluation techniques and suggestions presented in chapter 4. Many of the assessment areas presented for infants and toddlers are applicable here as well. The risk and protective factors offered in this chapter are the ones most applicable to the young child and her/his ecosystem, though many of these indicators are relevant at various developmental stages.

Ontogenic Level

Broad questions concerning the parent's own child maltreatment and attachment patterns cut across all developmental periods. In addition, depending on the age of the child under investigation for possible child maltreatment, the parent's own parallel developmental stage should be explored. The caregiver's own childhood experiences are primary to determining how she/he might parent her/his own child. At the ontogenic level the question to ask is how well the parent negotiated the central issues of her/his own preschool developmental period. The manner in which the developmental issues were handled plays a critical role in determining subsequent adaptation (Cicchetti & Lynch, 1993). Areas to explore with the parents concerning their own experience with adequate caregiving include the following.

- Were they punished for masturbatory activities?
- How was sexuality discussed in their family?
- What do they remember about their toilet training experience?
- Did their parents set limits when they were young children?
- Do they remember "make-believe" play?
- Were they able to ride a tricycle or bike when they were 3 to 6 years of age?

The responses to these and other questions based on the discussion in chapter 5 provide a framework to understand the caregiver's own ability to parent adequately.

Microsystem Level

Parent

The parent is a key element of assessment in the microsystem. Building on the caregiver assessment areas in chapter 4 (see Table 4.3), we will discuss more process-oriented characteristics of the parent-child relationship as a means of assessment of child maltreatment. Keep the other parental factors presented in chapter 4 in mind when assessing maltreatment of young children.

The risk and protective factors presented earlier in this chapter differentiate maltreating and nonmaltreating caregivers and are generally most relevant to preschool children. In determining child maltreatment, these factors can reinforce your decision of the disposition of the case. Some of the key questions to be answered are:

- How does the parent perceive the child? Affectionately? Warily?
- Does the parent think the child has a positive temperament?
- Does the parent think the child is bright?
- What is the parent's understanding of age expectations for children 3 to 6 years of age?
- At what age does the parent think the child should be toilet trained?
- What type of parenting style does the parent have? Authoritarian?
- Is the parent abusing drugs or alcohol?
- Does the parent seem depressed, withdrawn?
- Is the parent aggressive toward your intervention? The child? His/her partner? In general?
- Does the parent actively exclude the child from family activities?
- Does the parent engage the child in day-to-day activities?
- Is there a lack of affect in the parental treatment of the child?
- Does the parent leave the child without emotionally engaged adult supervision for long periods of time?
- Does the parent engage in conversation with the child at mealtimes?
- Does the parent give inappropriate reinforcement for aggression and precocious sexuality?

Child

Most young children can be interviewed concerning the behavior of their caregiver and their experiences in the home. There are limitations to the child's ability to effectively communicate; therefore awareness of normal and appropriate child development is important to understanding any indicators suggesting the child may be maltreated. These indicators, in the context of the ecological framework, may provide support that the child is being maltreated and that there are developmental consequences. Questions in the developmental perspective are divided into three categories: cognitive-behavioral, socioemotional, and physical.

Neglect

Child neglect assessment is not as straightforward as assessing whether physical abuse has occurred, although that is not always as simple as one may think. In Table 6.3 we suggest questions to ask about development that may be indicative of whether a caregiver is maltreating her/his child. The consequences of neglect are often not realized until months if not years after the neglectful conditions and often manifest in cognitive, social, or behavioral domains. As discussed in chapter 2, neglect takes on several forms. In assessing the different types of neglect—neglectful supervision and medical, physical, or emotional neglect—the following are indicators suggestive of neglect. Indicators of neglectful supervision are:

- Parent knows child is at risk and continues to allow access (i.e., to perpetrator of sexual abuse or physical abuse). The parent's act of omission is considered neglectful.

Table 6.3 Assessing Children Ages 3–6

	Cognitive-behavioral	Socioemotional	Physical
3–4 Years	• Does the child use words to make her/his wants known? • In problem solving, does the child focus on the appearance of an object solely and exclude other criteria? • Does the child commit grammatical errors, such as over-regularization? • Does the child increasingly pay attention to grammar and tenses in language?	• Can the child regulate his/her emotions? • Does the child show self-conscious emotions? • Does the child have generally optimistic opinions of self? • Does the child's caregiver serve as a secure base?	• Can the child walk better, with more coordination? • Can the child jump, hop, walk up stairs? • Can the child use scissors? • Can the child use eating utensils with coordination? • Can the child draw pictures of a person? • Can the child get dressed and undressed alone?
4–5 Years	• Does the child's vocabulary continue to expand? • Does the child primarily use grammar better and primarily use words to communicate?	• Does the child have friends? • Is the child more sociable among peers? • Does the child exhibit aggression that is unprovoked or purposeful?	• Can the child walk downstairs? • Can the child throw and catch a ball? • Can the child skip?
5–6 Years	• Does the child have a vocabulary of approximately 1,000 words? • Does the child understand grammar better than before and commit fewer grammatical errors?	• Does the child rely on language to express emotions? • Does the child have an understanding of socially agreed upon rules and behaviors?	• Does the child run with increasing speed? • Does the child skip with more coordination? • Can the child tie her/his shoes? • Can the child draw a person with six body parts? • Can the child ride a bike with training wheels? • Can the child walk on a balance beam or on a line?

- Parent leaves her/his child with caregiver who is unknown or essentially a stranger to the parent.
- A child, age 6 years or younger, is left alone.
- A child, age 6 years or younger, is left with a caregiver with mental or physical disabilities who is unable to protect him/her.
- Parent/caretaker is using a substance that may result in an inability to provide supervision for a child age 6 or younger.

Medical neglect indicators are:

- Routines or medical advice for chronic illnesses are not followed or are followed sporadically.
- Failure to seek medical treatment that poses a substantial risk of harm, including illnesses or optical or dental needs. Cultural beliefs may inhibit the parent from seeking care for her/his child.

Physical neglect indicators are:

- Lack of adequate clothing and good hygiene.

  Children dressed inadequately for the weather or suffering from persistent illnesses like pneumonia, frostbite, or sunburn that are associated with excessive exposure.
  Children chronically dirty and not bathed.

- Lack of adequate nutrition.

  Failure to thrive was addressed in chapter 4 and is an area of assessment for children 3 to 6 years of age.
  Children lacking sufficient quantity or quality of food that appears to be leading to malnourishment. Children consistently complaining of hunger or rummaging for food.
  Child experiences significant weight loss indicating malnourishment that is unrelated to a medical condition.
  Children suffering severe developmental lags.

- Lack of adequate shelter.

  Structurally unsafe housing (broken glass, missing stair rails, worn, splintery floors, exposed wiring).
  Inadequate heating.
  Unsanitary housing conditions (insect or rodent infestation that impacts child, such as rat bites or roaches crawling out of ears, festering garbage, human or animal excrement on floors and furniture).
  No housing (homeless). This is not neglect itself but may result in safety concerns.

Physical Indicators of Child Maltreatment

In chapter 4 we outlined a number of physical indicators that may be suspect as nonaccidental injury to an infant or toddler. The play years bring with them many bumps and bruises as a result of normal exploration and exuberance. Children begin to jump and hop, ride bikes, run, play with scissors, and throw a ball. Many of these activities may result in accidental injury. It will be important to be able to distinguish the difference between accidental injury caused by play and non-accidental injury that is inflicted on the child by a caregiver.

One of the key milestones of early childhood is toilet training. The frustration parents experience during this process may lead to the parent physically and emotionally abusing her/his child. Expectations around the child's ability to control her/his bowels and bladder are often misunderstood and misguided.

The normal age for the child to have control over her/his bladder and bowels varies. The American Psychiatric Association (2000) places the cutoff age at 5 years. Most children in the United States are toilet trained between 3 and 4 years of age (Liebert & Fischel, 1990) but continue to have accidents, particularly at night, for up to a year. Toilet training is best delayed until the end of the second or the beginning of the third year. It is not until then that the preschool child can consistently identify the signals from a full bladder or rectum and wait until they can find a place to permit the muscles to open. Additionally, it is not until this age that the child can successfully pull her/his pants up. Starting any earlier will not produce a more reliably trained child; it will just take longer (Brazelton, 1997).

Toilet training is a peak period for abuse as the parent may become stressed over the child's inability to achieve competence due to normal development or possibly due to physical or emotional problems. As a consequence one type of maltreatment often observed is a burn to the child's genitals, buttock area, or hands or feet. A common example is a preschool child who repeatedly soils her or himself and is punished by being forced into hot bath water or held under boiling water. Burns resulting from this action result in particular patterns.

- The "glove" or "stocking" burns are circumferential burns of the hands or feet with a discrete area of demarcation marking the level of contact with the water.
- The "doughnut burn" is the result of the child being immersed into a bathtub of hot water. The doughnut shaped around the buttocks, perineum, or genitals suggest the child was held down in the hot water; the unharmed area is where the child came in contact with the bathtub.
- Burns on the back of the hand or on both hands and feet are indicative of abuse.

Preschool children are naturally inquisitive, which predisposes them to accidental burns. Scalding and contact with hot surfaces comprise the majority of these burns (Giardino & Giardino, 2002). Accidental burns may be differentiated from inflicted burns by the severity of the burn and the distinct boundary line between the burned and unburned areas, and the absence of splash marks suggesting the child was forced and held under the water. If a child accidentally burns her/himself, the child instinctively withdraws after touching or grasping the surface, so such burns are usually not severe.

As a guide, the American Academy of Pediatrics recommends that caregivers set the water temperature at a maximum of 120 degrees Fahrenheit. Children would have to be exposed to this temperature for 5 to 10 minutes before getting a second-degree burn. An immersion burn in tap water 140 degrees and above can produce a second-degree burn in 5 seconds or less.

Other burn features that may be indicative of abuse are:

- Burns in a geometrical shape, such as an iron or heating grate
- A flame burn, such as a lighter or candle held over fingers or toes
- Cigarette burns
- Scald burns on the back of the child
- Multiple burns at different stages of healing

Knowledge about the type and severity of the burn and the given explanation by the parent or child will be suggestive of whether abuse has occurred. A contact burn with a geometric pattern is not consistent with a reported story that the child had spilled a cup of hot chocolate on himself. Reports that a child stepped into a bath that was too hot and resulted in both feet having second-degree stocking burns with no signs of splash marks is not consistent with the physical evidence.

Several dermatological conditions may produce marks that resemble burns. Two of these conditions are impetigo and "scalded-skin" syndrome. Small, circular-looking marks, often thought to be cigarette burns, may be a case of impetigo. Lesions of various sizes that occur in groups; that have a pussy crust; and that increase in number while the child is under observation characterize impetigo. Another condition that may be mistaken as a hot water burn is scalded-skin syndrome or toxic epidermal necrosis, an infectious condition caused by the bacteria Staphylococcus aureus. It occurs predominantly in infants or preschool children (Giardino & Giardino, 2002) and is characterized by generalized red and tender skin and unexplained blebs at such scattered intervals that it would be impossible to have been inflicted with hot water. As with impetigo, they continue after observation. A medical practitioner as part of the overall assessment should verify both of these conditions.

Some cultural practices may also result in burns, such as placing hot coins on the body to rid it of infection. It is important to assess these practices in the cultural context of the family. In addition to burns, bruises on particular body locations of a young child are indicative of child maltreatment.

During the play years, children will sustain bruises as a normal course of life. The body locations most likely to be affected are the shins, knees, forehead, forearms, and elbows. Young children may also present with traumatic injuries that are not usually sustained unless inflicted as a result of punishment. An explanation inconsistent with the injury itself may be indicative of abuse. The following are examples of injuries suggestive of physical abuse:

- Distinctively shaped injuries such as a belt buckle or outline of an object like a paddle or belt.
- Switch marks produce red streaks that may resemble train tracks.
- Loop marks as a result of a cord that is folded over produce an elongated U shape.
- Human bite marks.

- Circumferential tie marks around the ankles, wrists, or waist, suggesting that the child was restrained.
- Mouth injuries that may indicate that the child was gagged, such as lacerations at the corner of the mouth, or force-fed.
- Puncture wounds that resemble the end of a fork, comb, or other distinctive object.
- Hair loss from parents pulling out clumps of a child's hair, resulting in bald patches on the scalp; often accompanied by surface bleeding.
- Spiral, transverse, or other injuries to arm and leg bones that suggest twisting, squeezing, or pulling. Specific categories of fractures are highly linked with abuse and can only be determined by an X-ray and diagnosis by a physician.

Preschool children are vulnerable to sexual abuse (Finkelhor, Williams, & Burns, 1988; USDHHS, 1996). Many children who experience sexual abuse will not disclose its occurrence, yet adults who are close to the child may suspect he/she is being sexually abused. Young children who do disclose may have no physical indication and developmentally may not be able to clearly communicate the abuse. Assessment of sexual abuse in young children must rely on age-appropriate interviewing techniques, as well as awareness of behavioral indicators of sexual abuse. A parent does not sexually abuse the majority of the time, but when sexual abuse is perpetrated by a birth parent, the child is most likely to suffer a serious injury or impairment (USDHHS, 1996). Given that there is often no physical evidence of sexual abuse (Adams, Harper, & Revilla, 1994; Reece, 2000), behavioral, emotional, and cognitive indicators may be evidence of an abusive situation.

By using certain behaviors as diagnostic tools, along with other evidence, the practitioner can strengthen her/his conclusion that abuse occurred. Behavior indicators alone are not sufficient evidence to determine if child maltreatment has occurred; there may be many alternative explanations to the behavior (i.e., divorce, open nudity in the family). Additionally, because the behavioral, emotional, and cognitive indicators are based on research done on symptoms experienced by the sexually abused child, research indicates that one-third of sexually abused children do not have symptoms or any one pattern of traumatizing effects (Kendall-Tackett, Williams, & Finkelhor, 1993). The degree of symptoms is also influenced by the relationship of the perpetrator to the child, the extensiveness of the abuse, the frequency and duration, and the response by the nonoffending parent and the other professionals involved.

One reaction young children witnessing or experiencing sexual abuse have is an increase in sexual behavior (Berliner & Elliott, 2002; Kendall-Tackett et al., 1993). Recall from chapter 5 that preschool children do engage in normal sexual exploration; it is the extent, type, and excessiveness of certain behaviors that is indicative of sexual abuse.

Young children will act out sexually inappropriate behaviors associated with genital sexual activity with their siblings or peers (Friedrich et al., 2001). These behaviors range from inserting objects in the vagina or anus to simulating intercourse. Preschool children will verbalize sexual behaviors that they would not have knowledge of, as well as act out behaviors suggestive of sexual acts that, unless experienced, they would not know. Behavior such as this should serve as a warning sign that a child may be experiencing sexual abuse. It should be noted that not all children who experience sexual abuse would act out sexually.

Other physical and behavioral indicators that a young child may be experiencing sexual abuse are:

- Undergarments that are blood-stained or show signs of semen
- Irritation, pain, or injury to the genital area
- Foreign objects in rectal or vaginal cavities
- Difficulty sitting or walking
- Difficulty with urination
- Venereal disease in a young child
- Repeated urinary tract infections
- Excessive fear of being approached or touched by persons of a certain sex
- One child being treated by a parent in a significantly different way from the other children in the family
- A return to bedwetting
- Repeatedly plays with or smears feces
- Purposely urinates on the furniture
- Regressive behavior such as acting infantile, crying excessively, sucking the thumb, and withdrawing into fantasy worlds
- Sexually oriented play activity, i.e., sex games with other children
- Sexually oriented artwork or drawing, i.e., genitals stand out as most prominent feature, drawings of sex act.

The young child's behavior, physical appearance, and emotional state must be assessed within the context of his/her family. The interchange between the child and her/his environment enables a satisfactory assessment of whether child maltreatment is occurring.

Family

Child maltreatment takes place in the context of the family. Interactions between and among family members may support or hamper the existence of child maltreatment. Factors that place a family at higher risk of maltreatment need to be examined during an assessment. In the preschool years, the child relies heavily on the family for physical, emotional, and cognitive support that will lead to normal or abnormal adaptation. The following factors may place the child at a higher risk of maltreatment than children whose families do not exhibit these characteristics.

- Does the family engage in coercive child-rearing practices?
- What type of interaction is there between family members?

  Do family members talk positively about one another?
  Do family members compliment each other?

Are there a lot of negative comments about each other?
Are family members supportive of each other?
Do they show kindness toward each other?

- Do adults in the home exhibit leadership?
- Do the family members appear close?
- Are they aware of one another's activities?
- Are family members able to negotiate?
- Does the mother express satisfaction with her partner or vice versa?
- Does the family have a structured, consistent daily routine?
- Is there a father or father figure in the home?

Exosystem Level

The social structure in which a family lives becomes even more important during the preschool years of a child's life. The child enters the world of school, neighborhood, church, and community. What the child and parent find in this world will be indicative of how well they function and adapt. As children grow, parents need information and resources directly related to the demands of the parent-child relationship. If the child is disabled, has attention-deficit hyperactivity disorder, and behavior problems; or if the parent is depressed, poor, and/or substance abusing, the nature of the social structure around them may be deterministic of child maltreatment. Information about child maltreatment is extremely complex, and gathering information from all systems in the ecological model will assist in determining the safety and well-being of the family.

The assessment of social support between the microsystem and the exosystem must take on two forms: the actual network (frequency of contact, accessibility, and closeness) and the perceived social support from friends and families (DePanfilis, 1996). Some questions to guide the gathering of this information are:

- Does the caregiver have a relative or friend in the area with whom they can constructively discuss child-rearing issues? Who can provide appraisal support (information relevant to the parent's self-evaluation)?
- Does the caregiver have a relative or friend who provides tangible support (e.g., assistance with food, money, and babysitting)? How often?
- Does the caregiver have appropriate relatives or friends with whom they engage in leisure and recreational activities? How often?
- Is there a relative or friend who serves the function of developmental remediation for the child (helps the child deal with the effects of child maltreatment)?
- What is the family's relationship with faith, school, community agencies, and employer?
- What is the family's relationship with neighbors?
- What is the family's relationship with cultural connections?
- Does the family live in a violent community? Is the neighborhood a high crime area?

- Does the community have adequate resources for the family, such as day care, medical facilities, grocery stores, schools, churches, community centers, parks, public transportation, and other such services?

Preschool children and their families who are reported for suspected child maltreatment need to be assessed thoroughly to ascertain the extent of abuse and to prevent future maltreatment. Children 3 to 6 years of age are often not exposed to many formal systems, such as school or recreational programs, that will monitor if the child is being well cared for by the parent. A report of child maltreatment is an opportunity for child welfare professionals to interact with the family and to assess the safety and well-being of the child. In this section, we have outlined the many ecological and developmental indicators that will assist in making an empirically grounded decision concerning whether child abuse or neglect has occurred.

When child maltreatment is not substantiated but the professional thinks there is continued risk, referrals to community programs can be made to alleviate the future threat of maltreatment. Families with young children need to be connected to resources since developmentally the child is still dependent on the caregiver and is not yet in school. The next section will present treatment issues and intervention strategies for the preschool child who has experienced maltreatment.

INTERVENTION FOR YOUNG CHILDREN WHO HAVE BEEN MALTREATED

Intervention strategies for young children who are maltreated by their caregivers will be most effective if directed at the multiple levels of the ecological system— the ontogenic, microsystem, and exosystem—and based on the needs of the family. This integrative approach to treatment is necessary because of the complexities of child maltreatment. As discussed in chapter 5 and earlier in this chapter, child maltreatment is rarely a single event resulting from individual behavior but usually includes longstanding patterns of familial and societal interactions and circumstances that foster the abuse. Through the ecological assessment of the family in respect to the risk and protective factors on each level; attention to the type, severity, and duration of the maltreatment; and the prior relationship between the child and the perpetrator, effective intervention can be established.

As discussed in the earlier framework for the book, all families are unique, with their own sets of strengths and challenges, as well as cultural differences. To effectively intervene with families, practitioners must have an understanding of the family system, their definitions of what kin means to them, and the meaning of the problem to the family. Families must be engaged in a way that empowers them to effectively manage the challenges in their ecosystem. In partnership with the practitioner, families can learn to identify their needs and the means to meet those needs.

Preschool children experience all types of maltreatment, but young children ages 3 to 6 are most often brought to the attention of child welfare professionals as a result of neglect (USDHHS, 1996). This type of maltreatment is often accompanied by many other factors, such as poverty, depression, isolation, lack of parent-child attachment, and substance abuse. Treatment outcomes for changing patterns of neglect in families have been modest (Berrick & Duerr, 1997; Daro, 1988; Gaudin et al., 1993), which is not surprising given our earlier discussion of the many ways that lead parents to maltreat their young children. No one intervention approach is empirically supported over another, but there are some strategies and principles that have been effective for practitioners. These strategies will be discussed in the context of the preschool developmental stage, with special attention to the issues of attachment, cognitive-behavioral methods of intervention (using toilet training as an example), and building social supports.

Attachment

Young children who have experienced maltreatment at the hands of a parent or significant caregiver may experience disruption in attachment. As stated previously, not all children are affected by maltreatment in a predictable or consistent fashion, but whether it is physical, neglect, sexual, or emotional abuse, attachment and its subsequent impact on development are often impaired. Unfortunately the majority of the work on attachment relationships of maltreated children has focused on the infant or toddler (Cicchetti & Toth, 2000). The studies of preschool children have found that young children who have been maltreated are more likely to be insecurely attached (Cicchetti & Barnett, 1991; Crittenden, 1988) and give us reason to focus on intervention strategies that may improve the parent-child relationship.

Similar to intervention strategies during infancy and toddlerhood, focus on the parent-child relationship remains important. Attachment-guided strategies with the parent and child must center on the developmental task of the child. The young child has enhanced cognitive, social, emotional, and physical capabilities that allow the relationship between the parent and child to become more interpersonal, while the increase in the child's independence reduces the need for constant care (Cicchetti & Barnett, 1991).

Play is a central theme during the preschool years. Parents should be encouraged to engage in play activities with their child as a way of enhancing the attachment relationship. Through teaching the parent activities to engage in with her/his child, the practitioner will also be teaching appropriate developmental expectations for the child, which is often related to the cause of maltreatment.

Practitioners cannot assume that the caregiver is equipped with the skills and knowledge to engage in appropriate play with her/his young child. The parent should be provided guidance around play that is culturally and developmentally appropriate. There are many resources available to practitioners and caregivers through parenting programs (cited in chapter 4), community libraries and schools, and the World Wide Web. Some examples of interactional play activities that may enhance attachment relationships between the parent and child are:

- Preschool-level books that ask questions to the child (i.e., what sounds do animals make?)

- Crafts that the caregiver and child can engage in together
- Introducing colors to the child
- Introducing letters and numbers to the child
- Reading to the child, books, nursery rhymes, jokes, tongue twisters, etc.
- Teaching a child to ride a bike
- Drawing or coloring with the child
- Playing ball, skipping, running with the child
- Guessing games (What is in the box? I spy? Categories)
- Listening to music or playing musical instruments
- Baking or cooking together

Beginning in the preschool years, individual child therapy is also seen as important in influencing the child's processing and integration of her/his relationship experience with her/his caregiver (Cicchetti & Toth, 2000) and helping her/him not to generalize this to all relationships. Young children who have experienced inconsistent and abusive care may believe that all adults are not trustworthy and will ultimately reject them. A child who establishes a relationship with a responsive practitioner or other adult figure may be able to recover some of her/his ability to accomplish developmental tasks.

Individual work with the parent is also critical during the preschool years. As stated in chapter 4, work with the parent should focus on changing her/his representational model of relationship or restructuring this relationship model. The role her/his early childhood experience exerts on her/his current quality of parenting is paramount. Often the model of relationship these parents have formed, as a result of their own deprivation as a child, is closed to new information, so tremendous effort must go into the formation of relationships with the parent (Cicchetti & Toth, 2000). This is an important aspect to consider when intervening with parents. We often expect parents to respond to the system of care in a positive manner when in reality these caregivers are unable to form and maintain interpersonal relationships. Great care and patience needs to be placed on the development of positive connections and trust with the parent.

Cognitive-Behavioral Methods and Toilet Training

Toilet training is a peak time for abuse, as the caregiver may become stressed over the child's inability to achieve competence due to normal development or possibly physical or emotional problems. Behavior is often a function of what parents know and believe about child development. Parents often overestimate the capabilities of preschool children and attribute their lack of control to intentional behavior or negative attributions, when in reality the child is not able to perform such tasks at this stage. Specific suggestions around toilet training will be addressed later. First a discussion of cognitive-behavioral principles and strategies will be presented as a means of intervention with parents who abuse and neglect their children.

As we have discussed, parents who maltreat their children manifest social-cognitive problems that are seen as the cause of countless skill deficits. Interventions for parents who maltreat have increasingly relied on cognitive-behavioral approaches that address child-management skills (Azar, 1997; Miller-Perrin & Perrin, 1999) and have been found to be empirically effective with some types of families (Azar & Siegel, 1990; Dawson et al., 1986; Lutzker et al., 1987; Wolfe & Wekerle, 1993). Parents who have long-standing psychiatric disorders may need more intensive long-term treatment.

Most parents do not see themselves as having a problem and are most likely coming to treatment as an involuntary client. As a result the practitioner often experiences the parent as resistant and unwilling to change. This issue needs to be addressed in order for treatment to move forward. Many strategies discussed in the chapter 1 address ways to socialize parents into a collaborative partnership, therefore reducing resistance to intervention. A cognitive-behavioral solution to this resistance would be to restructure the problem so it is more "acceptable" to the caregiver. This is often called "reframing" the problem or behavior.

Instead of stating the problem as child maltreatment, it may be reframed as difficulty dealing with stress, anger, or child management, lack of social supports, and lack of adequate resources. Another use of reframing to reduce potential resistance is to address thoughts the parents may have about themselves, e.g., you might be worrying you might be called a bad parent. The practitioner may want to state that there are no bad parents, just as there are no bad children; parents do the best they can. This also lays groundwork for later reframing their work with their children; she/he is doing the best they can (Azar, 1997).

Reframing is not meant to minimize the problem or to collude with the parent around denial of the problem, but to reduce the parents fear and anxiety around the intervention. Other cognitive-behavioral techniques that encourage participation and attendance, which have been found empirically effective are:

• Incentives, movie tickets, McDonald's coupons
• Provision of transportation and child care
• Behavioral contracts with clear objectives
• Court-ordered treatment attendance (Azar & Wolfe, 1998)

Once the parent and child have been engaged, the problem area targeted, and the setting for intervention established, a number of cognitive-behavioral interventions methods can be employed. These will be briefly presented.

Behavioral Rehearsal. Behavioral rehearsal involves the use of role playing or simulating social exchanges. In this method, specific verbal and nonverbal behaviors to be changed are identified. Behavioral rehearsal offers opportunities to practice skills or behaviors in a safe and structured environment. The practitioner explains certain skills and demonstrates their use. The client then practices and receives continuous feedback from the practitioner. The feedback is constructive and immediate, thereby giving the client an opportunity to learn from the role-play experience. Clients are allowed to practice and experiment with different approaches to any given situation. An important component of behavioral rehearsal is identifying specific skill levels and building on these. Behavioral rehearsal can help at-risk parents by improving parenting skills through practice and receipt of constructive feedback.

Cognitive Restructuring. Cognitive restructuring is a method in which dysfunctional thinking patterns are identified as being illogical and/or as producing undesirable consequences. Looking at the evidence, creating client awareness of the distortion, and exposing false value judgments that may exist challenge faulty cognitions. The client is trained to monitor faulty thinking and track the consequences of that thinking. Once distortions are identified, the client is guided to modify the faulty thinking and replace it with an alternative thought. This method is focused on increasing a client's ability to consider alternative explanations or meanings to replace the distorted or unproductive thoughts and beliefs. In work with at-risk parents, this method may involve modification of general thinking errors associated with parenting, as well as identifying specific distortions parents may have used to excuse, rationalize, and justify abusive behaviors.

Feedback. Feedback is a method that provides sensory or verbal information in response to certain behavioral processes. The practitioner gives verbal feedback to the client about a specific target behavior. Sensory feedback involves the identification of actual physiological responses in the client. This is generally referred to as biofeedback and involves the use of electronic equipment to provide information about physiological responses. The idea is that if a client can become aware of his/her physiological responses, he/she can more readily learn to gain control over responses that may have previously been seen as involuntary. Biofeedback is most frequently used to treat physical reactions to stressful situations. Many at-risk parents experience high levels of stress that may lead to child maltreatment. Biofeedback may be used to facilitate the development of healthy coping mechanisms.

Skill Training. Skill training is a model that focuses on the acquisition of a set of skills that can be used to address a wide range of problems across different settings. This training can be done in a group setting but may also involve some individualized training through specific feedback to clients about applying the skills to a particular problem. However, the main focus of this method is on mastery of skills rather than on solutions to a particular problem. In this model, actual mastery of skills through practice and feedback plays a more important role than mere provision of information. This model is typically used to provide parent training. Parents receive training in a standardized package that might include training on skills such as the use of appropriate consequences or time-out.

Treatment of Antecedent Conditions. Treatment of antecedent conditions involves changing or rearranging cues that feed an undesired response. This is done because addressing antecedents of behavior can be as important as addressing the consequences of behaviors. Cues for desired behaviors are strengthened while cues for undesired behaviors are removed or reduced. Changing certain aspects of the environment as well can alter antecedents of behavior by altering specific behaviors that are associated with the target behavior.

Toilet Training Strategies to Employ with Caregivers

Toilet training is a learning process, but unfortunately many parents see it as a power struggle with their child. The average age for children in the United States to achieve toilet training completion is 3 years, and this does not include night-time dryness. This means some children do not achieve complete toilet training until 4 or 5 years of age. Additionally, when working with families it is important to understand any cultural differences concerning the nature of toilet training.

The child first must understand the bodily sensations, getting to the bathroom, and getting her/his clothes off. The mastery of these skills comes with an adult patiently teaching a child what is expected of them. The practitioner working with a caregiver can help them identify when the right time for training might be. Some helpful tips to ask the parent are:

- Does your child know when she/he is about to go?
- Are her/his bowel movements predictable?
- Does the child understand when she/he has eliminated and the names of the bodily functions (e.g., pee, poop)?
- Does the child show a preference for dry diapers?
- Does she/he want to wear underwear?
- Can she/he pull her/his pants down and then back up?
- Does she/he say when she/he has to go potty?

A number of behavioral-intervention toilet-training programs have been found to be empirically effective (Baker et al., 1976; Hobbs & Peck, 1985; Richmond, 1983). Although these programs have been developed for children with mental retardation, the behavior principles are applicable to training any child.

The behavioral principles underlying these programs are:

- Taking the child into the bathroom with you to expose them to what toileting is (helpful to begin changing child in the bathroom at around age 2).
- Keeping a toileting chart (diagram when the child usually empties her/his bladder and bowel), so caregiver will be able to prompt the child at the correct time to use the toilet
- Toileting at scheduled times on a consistent basis (after knowing the child's schedule, placing the child on the toilet when the bladder or bowel is full)
- Providing reinforcement for successful eliminating and being dry (can use a star system on the chart, or immediate positive reinforcement, being the child's cheerleader)
- Teaching the natural sequence of toileting (e.g., pulling pants down, sitting on the toilet, voiding, wiping with toilet paper, pulling pants up, flushing). (Handen, 1998)

It is important for the practitioner to provide support for the parent during this period. It is a stressful time, and for families with limited resources, both physical and emotional, it becomes even more stressful. Children love to learn and become independent, but it must be done on their time schedule.

Social Support Development

Families who experience maltreatment are more likely to be isolated and in need of assistance in developing social support networks (DePanfilis, 1996; Gaudin et al., 1990). Social support, both from informal and formal sources, is particularly important for families with young children because they provide nurturance and strengthening in dealing with the everyday strains of raising a child. Children ages 3 to 6 years require a connection with their environment in order to fully achieve their developmental competencies. Additionally, the support parents receive is crucial in how parents apply the knowledge they receive, such as the discussion above on toilet training. It is not enough to teach parents what a child needs. The parent needs to learn how to overcome barriers, as well as be supported both in the home (by a partner) and outside the home (practitioner, day care, mother) in order to follow through on what is best for the child. Stress that is not balanced out with support may lead to a higher risk of maltreatment (Brayden et al., 1992; Coohey, 1996; 2000; Gaudin et al., 1993).

During the assessment phase, the practitioner has identified the current and needed resources with the family. DePanfilis (1996) and Dunst, Trivette, and Deal (1994) have categorized various functions of social support networks. They are:

- Material support (money, food, clothing)
- Physical and environmental (adequate housing, safe neighborhood)
- Medical and dental care
- Vocational (opportunities to work)
- Transportation and communication (getting where they need to go and ability to make contact)
- Knowledge information
- Appraisal support (information pertinent to self-evaluation)
- Education (adult and child)
- Child care
- Recreational, social, and cultural
- Emotional and companionship (sense of belonging to family or group)

Important to the success of working with a family to access the needed resources is a collaborative, trusting relationship with the parent. It is important for the practitioner to understand the cultural difference in families and the type of social supports that are needed. Some families may be more comfortable going to a faith-based group for needed support than to a more formal community agency.

Once the support needs have been assessed, interventions may range from personal social networks (family and friends) to neighborhood and community groups that connect parents together (paraprofessionals, church, self-help groups, parent groups), to professional programs (schools, medical facilities, day care, housing programs, libraries), and finally specialized professional services (early intervention, family preservation, substance abuse). The choice of group or individual support intervention must be based on the skills of the parent. Caregivers who lack good communication or social skills may not benefit from a group setting, while other parents may need the group setting to motivate them to make change. The goal is to connect families and help them overcome barriers to accessing and sustaining the connection long after your involvement with the young child and the family.

The first step in this process is to provide clear and realistic information to the parent about available resources and services in her/his community. Providing them with a community resource book or other types of language-appropriate materials is important so they can refer to the materials when needed. Caregivers who have abused their children or who are the nonoffending parent are under a great deal of stress, and information and referral alone will not be enough. The practitioner may need to role model and coach parents on how to go about applying for services and what the relevant questions to ask are. Reflecting back on our discussion of cognitive-behavioral strategies, parents may need cognitive restructuring around their ability to be successful. Often parents come to this process not having much success getting their needs met and will need some coaching to reinforce their abilities. To encourage their participation, the practitioner may need to provide concrete services such as transportation and childcare.

CONCLUSION

Families who maltreat their preschool children present many challenges to professionals. Through an assessment of protective and risk factors and the provision of services that address those factors, young children's safety in their own home will be heightened. More importantly, their development and mastery of developmental milestones will be enhanced and potential for functioning in the future improved.

CASE: JACKSON FAMILY

Identifying Information

Jamie Jackson (5 years old)

Lewis Jackson (3 years old)

Sondra Jackson (21 years old), mother

Tamika Jackson (45 years old), grandmother

History of Referrals

The agency has worked with Tamika Jackson on many occasions. Prior referrals usually involved physical neglect of Sondra Jackson and her five brothers by

Tamika Jackson. An ongoing case was open for about 18 months, with minimal improvement noted prior to case closure.

CPS became involved with Sondra and her children when the nearest neighbor responded to a call for help from Sondra one day. The stove caught fire and Sondra could not get it out. Tamika Jackson, the children's grandmother, was gone. Sondra ran down the road to get help, leaving the two children asleep in the bedroom. There was concern because of the children's appearance, rashes, and limited speech. The neighbor, who was the only collateral, did not know that Sondra had children because he had never seen them. Neither Sondra nor her mother was able to provide the worker with other collaterals.

Level of Functioning

Sondra does not work, does not drive, and is dependent on her mother for shelter and food. Sondra does receive TANF and food stamps, which she gives to her mother. Sondra does not like crowds and does not go shopping with her mother. She will keep TANF appointments when scheduled. She has one friend in high school but has not kept in touch with her. She likes to watch TV and play Nintendo. She cannot say what her life goals are. She has difficulty reading and writing, and may be mentally retarded. She complains of often being tired and has little energy. She takes vitamins and "sometimes takes some of [her] mother's little white pills." We do not know what the pills are. Tamika Jackson calls them "nerve pills."

Tamika Jackson reports that she has chronic health problems of an unknown nature. It is believed that she may be an alcoholic. She states that she has trouble helping Sondra supervise the children because of her poor health. Mrs. Jackson's husband abandoned the family when Sondra was 2 years of age. There are five older brothers, all of whom have left the home or are in jail. Mrs. Jackson says that her sons will help her "fix up the house."

Case Exercise

1. What are the normal developmental expectations for the children?
2. Consider each child's developmental level. What developmental manifestations can you identify that may be an indication of child maltreatment in the following domains?

   • Physical development
   • Cognitive-behavioral
   • Socioemotional

3. What role does culture play in each child's development?
4. Expand your assessment of each child's developmental level to the overall ecological model. Assess the family's risk and protective factors in the context of the ecological model.

   • Ontogenic level
   • Microsystem

- Exosystem
- Macrosystem

5. What intervention strategies might you employ to facilitate development of the children?
6. What intervention strategies might you employ with the caregiver?
7. What cultural aspects of the family are important to consider for both assessment and intervention?

7

MIDDLE CHILDHOOD

Child Development and Maltreatment

Middle childhood extends from 7 to 11 years of age. During this time, children enter formal school, and academics becomes increasingly important. Overall, primary developmental tasks of middle childhood focus on the acquisition of new skills—cognitive, social, and physical—and children have school as a new forum for exploration. Sometimes called the "school years," children not only learn the foundations of math, reading, writing, and science, but also develop more sophisticated physical and social skills.

EXPECTED DEVELOPMENT ACROSS DEVELOPMENTAL DOMAINS

A strong knowledge of child development is necessary to explore the impact of child maltreatment on the normal course of development. Human development follows a relatively consistent course. Children walk before they run and babble before they talk. By the time a child who has been maltreated enters middle childhood, she/he may already have significant developmental delays if intervention and strong protective factors are absent. Consistent with other chapters in this book, major developmental theories presented include Freud's psychosexual theory of development, Erickson's psychosocial theory of development, social developmental theories, attachment theory, Piaget's theory of cognitive development, and physical and motor development. The developmental milestones of children in middle childhood will be discussed in relation to their socioemotional, cognitive, and physical development (see Table 7.1). However, it is important to keep in mind that developmental delays may be more marked if maltreatment has been occurring for many years, and they may be more subtle if the maltreatment is just beginning.

Psychodynamic Theories

Freud's Psychosexual Stages of Development

Freud's 4th stage of psychosexual development is called the latency stage and occurs between 7 and 11 years of age. During the latency period, sexual instincts

Table 7.1 Middle Childhood Development

	Psychodynamic		Social	Piaget	Cognitive	Physical
Freud	**Erickson**					

Freud column:

Latency:
- Sexual instincts decrease
- The superego develops further with less influence from family and more from peer relationships
- Children put their energy into activities, such as school and sports, and their sexual needs become dormant

Erickson column:

Industry vs. inferiority:
- Children busily try to master the activities valued by their culture
- The positive resolution of this crisis is the development of industry where children feel competent and productive in their ability
- Children continue to master new skills and continue to develop social skills and friendships
- The negative resolution of inferiority manifests as children feel unable to do anything well

Social column:
- Organized games with rules
- Social cognition emerges—children begin to understand their social world
- Peer groups become increasingly important, which helps develop self-concept and self-competence
- Acceptance by peer groups is valued, but personal friendships are more important
- Perspective-taking increases
- More realistic level of self-competence and self-esteem
- Peer interaction becomes more prosocial

Piaget column:

Concrete Operational Stage:
- Reasoning and logical thought begin
- Children are able to conserve and organize objects into hierarchies
- Children have the ability to interpret experiences objectively rather than intuitively
- Children understand logical principles and apply them to concrete situation, not hypothetical situations
- They understand identity, reversibility, seriation, and spatial reasoning
- Children still fail to have abstract reasoning

Cognitive column:
- Improvement in memory including an ability to remember facts over a period of days
- Memory strategies improve—rehearsal, organization, elaboration
- Vocabulary at age 6 should be 10,000 words
- Selective attention develops, which becomes important for school and learning
- Metacognition develops, which is the ability to evaluate a cognitive task to determine whether it is difficult or not
- Code switching in language emerges: formal and informal codes in communicating with friends and adults

Physical column:
- Children grow more slowly
- Slimmer bodies with stronger muscles
- Gross motor skills of running, jumping, batting, kicking are performed more quickly and with better coordination
- Reaction time improves in relation to cognitive development
- Flexibility, hand-eye coordination, balance, force, agility, and judgment of movement improve
- Fine motor development improves: building models, weaving small looms
- Printing improves from large letters to smaller letters
- Drawing improves with two-dimensional shapes, depth, converging lines

subside and become dormant. Instead of putting their energy into psychosexual activities, children focus on tasks such as school and sports. In previous stages, children are influenced primarily by their parents, but during the latency stage children are influenced by peers, teachers, and leaders of their organized activities. As a result of these external influences, their superegos continue to develop.

Erickson's Psychosocial Stages of Development

The psychosocial conflict that Erickson proposed during middle childhood is that of industry versus inferiority. During middle childhood, children try to master new cognitive and physical activities. Children learn to cooperate, share, and problem solve with other children, and as a result a sense of industry arises. Children with a resolution of industry feel competent at accomplishing tasks alone and with others. However, when children do not acquire the ability to work with others or they have negative experiences in completing solitary activities, they develop a sense of inferiority. In some cases, children have not been prepared well for school or lack emotional maturity to succeed in school, or they have had negative experiences when attempting tasks. Children who resolve the psychosocial crisis with inferiority feel incompetent and incapable of doing things well.

Social Development

In addition to the influence Erickson's psychosocial crises have on a child's social development, many other developmental activities affect a child's social development in middle childhood. Children become more complicated social beings as they enter school when new social opportunities arise. Changes in self-esteem, self-concept, and peer relationships occur.

As children mature, they become more interested in peer relationships and more independent. Their relationship with their parents is still important, but school relationships and lifelong friendships emerge. "Playing together" as a means of friendship changes, and qualities of true friendships such as trust and loyalty begin to define relationships. After children are able to identify friends with more mature characteristics, they use these friendships to practice conflict resolution and joint problem solving. Consistent with the understanding of internal characteristics and corresponding to gains in cognitive development, children also make social comparisons; children begin to more realistically appraise their own behavior compared to their peer's behavior or skills. Children understand how "good" they are at something compared to another, which is influenced by their cognitive development and their expanding social worlds. Friendships during middle childhood tend to be gender-segregated and occur around shared activities.

With more realistic self-appraisals, children adjust their self-esteem to fit their perceptions and evaluations of self. As a result, self-esteem tends to drop during the first years of elementary school, but it increases again from 4th to 6th grade. By age 6, children have separated their self-esteem into three different domains: academic, social, and physical. They are able to appraise themselves on each of the three areas; for example, a child may have high academic self-esteem but lower social self-esteem.

As children begin to understand themselves better and in relation to their peers, their interactions with peers often change. Some amount of aggression continues to be common in middle childhood, but to a lesser degree than in the previous developmental period. By middle childhood, children have learned the cultural and social rules that govern acceptable behavior. As a society, we also expect children to be better able to control their anger by the time they reach middle childhood. Girls and boys tend to express their anger in different ways. Girls tend to use more relational aggression—nonphysical aggression aimed at damaging another's self-esteem or peer relationships. For example, a girl might try to ostracize another child or belittle her among friends. On the other hand, boys tend to use more physical force to express anger. However, in both sexes, retaliatory aggression aimed at acting against someone who has harmed you increases. Although peers accept retaliatory aggression, it is not accepted by parents, teachers, and coaches.

Peer groups also become an important component of middle childhood. While true friendships are valued, acceptance by peer groups is also sought. Peer groups tend to be informal and cohesive, with their own language, vocabulary, and special identity. The peer group has collective goals, leadership, and loyalty. Often, the peer group can take the form of organized activities—such as soccer and basketball teams. Children switch their language when speaking with adults and peers to reflect the formality of the situation. Additional examples of the influence of peer groups will be discussed in the section on cognitive development.

Cognitive Development

Children in middle childhood focus both on physical attributes and inner traits of a person, which is not seen before this developmental period. A child might describe a person physically (e.g., tall, short) but add that the person is "dull" or "kind," referring to inner traits. Children at this stage are capable of perspective taking—the ability and capacity to understand what others may be thinking or feeling. They take the perspective of another person in relation to their own thoughts and that of others, and this helps them to understand consequences, such as getting in trouble or offending a friend. They develop a more sophisticated form of empathizing. Acquiring a more mature level of perspective taking is important because it helps children to avoid offending peers and further isolating themselves from social relationships.

According to Piaget's theory of cognitive development, children enter the concrete operational stage between 7 and 11 years of age. This stage is marked by the child's ability to distinguish reality over perception. During this period, children are capable of more logical thought; they are able to process operations that require compliance with logical rules. For example, children can pass conservation tasks where they can focus on more than one aspect of a task in order to solve the problem appropriately. In the previous stage, if a child were asked to choose between two beakers with equal amounts of liquid but with different shapes, the child would choose the taller beaker. In this stage, the child would recognize that "taller" does not mean that the beaker had more liquid, but that the shape of the glass affects the appearance of the liquid. Also achieved in middle childhood is the ability to reverse both physical and mental actions. For example, a child who has tomato on his hamburger realizes that if he removes the tomato it makes the hamburger just like he wants it. Seriation is also possible: children can line objects in order of size or appearance, such as lining pencils from tallest to shortest. However, children are not yet capable of solving hypothetical and abstract problems at this time. To illustrate, they are unable to figure out word problems that ask whether hypothetical people are taller than one another (e.g., If Katie is taller than Ann, and Ann is taller than Jen, who is the tallest?).

Children between 7 and 11 years of age experience an improvement in memory. Children can retrieve stored information for lengths of days or longer. They also demonstrate selective attention, where they are able to screen out distractions and focus on the important information. For example, during class a 10-year-old should be able to pay attention to the teacher while ignoring and forgetting disruptions from nearby classmates. Thus, the child selectively attunes to the important information being presented by her teacher. Children also begin to use strategies to improve their memory, such as rehearsal, elaboration, and organization. Rehearsal involves repeating information over and over in an attempt to remember it, and this begins early in this period. Elaboration involves creating a shared meaning—elaborating—on the information to be remembered. For example, if a child wants to remember the words "snake" and "lollipop," the child might imagine a snake with a lollipop in its mouth. Elaboration does not appear until the end of this period because it is quite a sophisticated memory strategy. Finally, children use organization to improve memory, where they mentally organize related items together. If making a pie crust, they might organize the dry and wet ingredients together to recall the recipe or "remember" how you make a pie crust.

The influence of peer relationships is also seen in the child's language and dress. In middle childhood, children begin to switch dialect from one group to another depending upon the situation and the formality of the circumstance. Children will talk in "formal" code when speaking with teachers and parents and use proper vocabulary and appropriate sentence structure. While speaking with friends, children will switch to an informal code with informal language structure, fewer words, and gestures to communicate meaning and shared understanding. For example, a 10-year-old girl talking with friends might use words such as "like" and "you know," frequently indicating group membership and social acceptance. However, among teachers at school the girl would use a more formal pattern of speech. Peer groups often develop their own languages and dress, and acceptance into the "group" requires conformity to the group's social rules.

Physical Development

Children ages 7–11 grow more slowly than before; they average 2–3 inches in height and gain about 3–5 pounds per year. Girls experience their adolescent growth spurt before boys, which may result in girls gaining both height and weight quickly toward the end of this period. Children's bodies become slimmer, and the lower portions of their bodies grow the fastest. Children may grow out of their jeans faster than their jackets, as their legs increase in length. Common during middle childhood are "growing pains" where children complain of nighttime aches and pains as their muscles grow and adapt to their changing bodies. They should continue to receive regular medical and dental check-ups, as primary teeth are gradually replaced by permanent teeth.

During middle childhood, children continue to develop both their fine and gross motor skills. Gross motor development improves with children being able to successfully play organized activities and group sports with rules. Throwing, swimming, and climbing improve. These skills are demonstrated with better co-ordination and more quickly than ever before. Children also become better at activities that require good coordination, such as riding a bicycle, swimming, and ballet.

Children ages 7–11 have greater flexibility, balance, agility, and force. The combination of their gross motor changes and their cognitive changes allow some children to play sports well; they are able to make quick decisions with skilled and swift movements. For example, playing baseball affords school-age children several opportunities to demonstrate their physical, cognitive, and social skills. Swinging a baseball bat with a strong, quick, flexible swing allows school-aged children the oportunity to play an organized sport, demonstrate their ability to play with peers, and abide by the rules.

Fine motor development continues throughout middle childhood. Children should begin to write print letters and learn cursive handwriting. They should be able to print and write stories, and written words become clearer with age. Similarly, drawing improves, and by the end of this period children should be able to make second and third dimensional drawings with attention to detail, depth, and lines. Some sex differences do exist with respect to motor skills. Girls perform some fine motor skills better than boys, such as drawing and handwriting, as well as some gross motor skills that require balance (Berk, 1999). On the other hand, boys do better than girls on most gross motor skills such as throwing, kicking, dribbling, and catching (Cratty, 1986), which may be due to environmental influences and practice rather than genetics.

DEVELOPMENTAL CONSEQUENCES OF CHILD MALTREATMENT FOR CHILDREN AGES 7 TO 11

Many of the developmental effects of maltreatment during middle childhood concur with the effects of earlier periods. Children during the school years are increasingly involved with others outside the family–school, sports, and play. School-aged children are sometimes first identified and reported for child maltreatment because this may be the child's first opportunity for consistent contact outside the home. The effects of maltreatment are also observed in school with more academic and physical opportunities.

Physical Abuse

Many of the developmental effects of physical abuse during middle childhood continue from previous periods if physical abuse has been chronic. The observed effects of maltreatment, however, also correspond to new developmental gains. Children are increasingly outside the home among teachers at school who not only observe them on a daily basis, but also assess their academic and social skills. Developmental manifestations of physical abuse are observed within cognitive, socioemotional, and physical domains.

Cognitive-Behavioral

Cognitive impairments may develop in children who have experienced physical abuse in middle childhood. From 7 to 11 years of age, children have entered formal schooling and are challenged with academic performance and peer relationships. Children who have experienced physical abuse may have lower language and intellectual functioning (Alessandri, 1991; Tarter et al., 1984), which becomes an important problem for children in school, especially when undiagnosed. Child victims of physical abuse also have more difficulty than nonmaltreated child with problem-solving skills, perceptual motor skills, and communication abilities (Friedrich, Enbender, & Luecke, 1983), as well as less motivation (Azar & Wolfe, 1989). Research has also shown that abused children have lower verbal IQ scores than nonabused counterparts (Howe, Tepper, & Parke, 1998).

Child victims of physical abuse may also have difficulty with academic adjustment and achievement. These children have lower academic achievement than nonabused children (Salzinger et al., 1984), including working slower and at lower levels than nonabused students (Howing et al., 1993). They also have more difficulty identifying solutions to hypothetical social problems (Haskett, 1990). Similarly, physically abused children are more likely to repeat a grade (Eckenrode, Laird, & Doris, 1993; Howing et al., 1993), have learning disabilities, and receive special education (Eckenrode, Laird, & Doris, 1993).

Victims of physical abuse have also been reported to have more behavioral problems, trouble following school rules, and more frequent discipline by the school (e.g., paddled, suspended, or expelled) (Howing et al., 1993). School-aged children who have been physically abused have been shown to have more discipline referrals than either neglected or sexually abused children (Eckenrode, Laird, & Doris, 1993). They have also been shown to have six times more suspensions from school than nonmaltreated children (ibid.). The consequences of child physical abuse, therefore, can become lifelong for the child victim unless appropriate assessment and intervention occur. The child's academic endeavors are just beginning, yet she/he may already be suffering cognitive difficulties and decreased intellectual functioning.

Socioemotional

School-aged victims of physical abuse tend to have poor relationships with peers, teachers, and parents, as well as low self-esteem (Allen & Tarnowski, 1989). With the introduction of formal schooling, both peers and academics become primary developmental pathways for healthy growth. Physically abused children have difficulty adjusting to the entry and structure of school. Children who have been physically abused have been found to exhibit behaviors of aggression and noncompliance (Erickson, Egeland, & Pianta, 1989). Compared to nonmaltreated children, abused children have more difficulty with peer relationships (Rogosh, Cicchetti, & Aber, 1995), which is partially explained by the increased likelihood of insecure attachment. Children with insecure attachments tend to avoid or resist their parents; their parents do not serve as a safe base for them to express their problems or seek comfort.

The influence of attachment is evidenced by its effect on a child's perception of relationships, including friendships. Children who have insecure attachments may not trust other children. They may not know how to interact socially with them or may act too aggressively. These interactions force them into peer groups of other aggressive children or isolation. Neither antisocial peer groups nor isolation are good developmental signs for a child who lacks compensatory factors (see chapter 8). Abused school-aged children have difficulties making friends (Alessandri, 1991; Gelles & Straus, 1990), getting along with peers (Howing et al., 1993), and developing positive social interactions with peers (Fantuzzo, 1990), and they have low social competence (Rogosch et al., 1995). Although Howing et al. (1993) found that abused children had as many friends as nonmaltreated children, other research has found that they have greater peer isolation (Dean et al., 1986). They have also been shown to have lower social status and more peer rejection (Salzinger et al., 1993), which is especially concerning because peer rejection has been linked to dropping out of school. In addition to the child's perception of friendships, abused children have been rated by teachers as having less social competence and as demonstrating more negative and fewer positive behaviors (Howe, Tepper, & Parke, 1998). Similarly, abused children have difficulties in using appropriate emotional responses in interpersonal situations (Rogosch, Cicchetti, & Aber, 1995), which can affect their peer, family, and social relationships.

In addition to poor social interactions, abused children tend to have problems with emotional adjustment and self-esteem. When children enter school, they become better at making social comparisons. In early childhood, children consistently rate themselves as the best on most tasks, but when children enter middle childhood they become capable of making accurate social comparisons. They recognize they may not make the best grade in the class or be the best at swinging a baseball bat. As a result, self-esteem tends to decrease slightly when children enter school, but then increases again at around 4th grade. Howing et al. (1993) found that school-aged abused children scored low on measures of behavior, intellect, physical, anxiety, popularity, and happiness; and they scored the lowest on the behavior, happiness, and satisfaction scales.

Abused children perceive themselves as less competent (Vondra, Barnett, & Cicchetti, 1989), which may reflect a more accurate, although negative, self-perception. They also tend to be rated as less socially competent by parents and teachers (Levendosky, Okun, & Parker, 1995). Interesting, however, is that gender differences may exist between maltreated boys and girls. Maltreated girls tend to rate themselves more socially competent than nonmaltreated counterparts, although this perception is inconsistent with ratings of teachers and parents (Levenkosky, Okun, & Parker, 1995). One possible explanation for this difference is that girls may be more attuned to relationships than boys, which may lead them to inflate their self-esteem as a defense mechanism toward their actual low social competence (Levenkosky, Okun, & Parker, 1995). Abused children have also been shown to be less adept at understanding emotional expressions when measured both by a teacher rating and also the abused child's quality of response to emotional statements (Howe, Tepper, & Parke, 1998).

Abused children have been shown to have low self-esteem (Allen & Tarnowski, 1989; Kaufman & Cicchetti, 1989). Howing et al. (1993) found that abused children were more likely to have thoughts about suicide or attempted suicide than nonabused children. Another consequence of abuse is attention deficit hyperactivity disorder or oppositional defiance disorder (Famularo, Kinscherff, & Fenton, 1992), whose diagnoses among school-aged children has risen dramatically in the past decade. Certainly not all children diagnosed have a history of child physical abuse, but the connection is noteworthy.

It is well documented that children who have been victims of physical abuse show increased anger levels and aggression (Ammerman, 1989; Hoffman-Plotkin & Twentyman, 1984; Howing et al., 1993; Reid, Kavanagh, & Baldwin, 1987), even when compared to neglected children (Hoffman-Plotnik & Twentyman, 1984). While the ability to regulate one's emotions was a developmental task in early childhood, abused children continue to struggle with this ability. They do not have the necessary self-control and often resort to aggression to solve problems. Delinquent behavior seen in middle childhood can continue into adolescence and adulthood, which can evolve into a life of antisocial tendencies and crime.

Physical

School-aged victims of physical abuse may experience difficulty in all areas of physical development, as well as medical problems. Certain types of physical abuse can result in disfigurement, head injury, fractures, and death. Between ages 7–11, children's physical activity includes more sophisticated movements and better coordination of gross and fine motor skills. Children can climb trees, play sports, and perform gymnastics. Children who have been victims of physical abuse may have pain or discomfort when trying to play with friends; they may make excuses for gym class or fail to participate at recess to hide their injuries and pain. A history of physical abuse may manifest as old burns, skin markings, and scars.

The developmental effects of physical abuse are circular because all areas of a child's development can be affected. When a child lacks social competence, acts aggressively, and lacks self-esteem, it is difficult for that child to master the developmental tasks of middle childhood. When a child is isolated from peers, gets in trouble with school, performs poorly academically, and has physical injury or pain from abuse, the child is disadvantaged in multiple ways and a comprehensive intervention is warranted.

Sexual Abuse

Sexual abuse is a distinct type of maltreatment, and it differs from both physical abuse and neglect in important ways that have already been discussed in chapter 5. The developmental consequences of sexual abuse for school-aged children, therefore, differ from those for neglect and physical abuse.

The degree to which sexual abuse affects a child is multiply determined. Some children experience immediate effects and others experience little or no effect. It is important to keep in mind that children experience sexual abuse differently than they do other forms of maltreatment. Victims sometimes feel like coconspirators with the perpetrator or feel special because of the attention or gifts they receive from the perpetrator. In many cases, the victim is fearful because of threats of violence against them or loved ones if they disclose the abuse (Saunders et al., 1999). However, it is important to remember that victims may experience a range of sexually abusive behaviors both in context and severity, which affects the observed manifestations.

Cognitive-Behavioral

Children in middle childhood have greater mental capacity; they have logical thought and greater reasoning than ever before. Sexual abuse can cause children to have distorted ideas about sexuality. While Freud purports that school-aged children are in a sexually latent phase, sexually abused children may exhibit sexuality in various ways. Because of the child's cognitions about sex and sexual abuse, their behavior may be overtly sexual, including repetitive, excessive masturbation; sex talk with adults and other children; and sex play with children and adults. Children who have been sexually abused tend to have more sexualized behaviors (Gale et al., 1988), even when compared to other maltreated children and psychiatrically disturbed children (Friedrich et al., 1997). They may have heightened awareness of sexual acts, acting them out in drawings, play, or behavior with friends. They may act out sexual activities on dolls or pets, reenacting sexual events behaviorally; some act out sexually on other children.

Sexually abused children differ from nonabused children in their perceptions of many factors of sexual abuse, including definitions of sexual abuse, descriptions of violators, and perceptions of potential consequences of the victim (Miller-Perrin, Wurtele, & Kondrick, 1990). They may perceive their world differently, and this is often seen through their behavior. When asked to describe vignettes, sexually abused children were more likely to describe rape or abuse, and the abuser as an older male relative who used threats or coercion in the victimization, with each description paralleling their own victimization (ibid.). Consequently, on one hand their behavior may be seductive, while on the other they may appear immature and seem to regress to earlier stages of development.

An integral component of sexual abuse is the control that the perpetrator has over the victim. The perpetrator has psychological and emotional control, and often physical control, over the victim, which allows the perpetrator to gain the trust of the victim and use it to her/his advantage. This trust is then manipulated to prevent the victim from disclosing the abuse, as well as making the victim feel "involved" or a part of the abuse. When the perpetrator is a parent or parent figure, the attachment relationship between the parent and child is altered; this can also occur if the child feels unprotected by a caregiver. The child may have difficulty separating from the parent, even though the parent-offender abuses the power to gain sexual control over the victim. Understanding the ambivalence the child feels toward an attachment figure who also offends helps us understand why some children have such difficulty separating from their offender, even though the abuse is occurring. The child may exhibit conflicted feelings toward the offender. When separation and disclosure do occur, the child may have tremendous feelings of guilt over "ruining" her/his family. Because of the misuse of power by the offender, sexually abused children may have difficulty being touched (Roesler, 2000), and this may be noticeable during physical exams by a physician or with interactions with schoolmates or family members.

School-aged children who have been sexually abused may have a number of cognitive distortions. They may perceive themselves as "different" from other children, and they may have less trust in themselves and their environment (Mannarino, Cohen, & Berman, 1994). The attributions the child makes about the abuse is equally important in understanding long-term effects. Negative attributional styles have been associated with poorer outcomes for sexually abused children (Kress & Vandenberg, 1998). Fiering, Taska, and Lewis (1998) found that high feelings of shame were correlated with more depression, lower self-esteem, and PTSD symptoms. Feelings of shame and a lack of trust in oneself is especially troublesome as children enter puberty and are exposed to consensual-sex decision-making.

Sexually abused children may also be cognitively impaired (Einbender & Friedrich, 1989) and may have learning difficulties and lower academic achievement in school (Rust & Troupe, 1991). They may appear to lack attention and concentration in the classroom, and their grades may decline. Compared to girls with no history of abuse, sexually abused girls do less well academically and have decreased cognitive ability overall (Trickett, McBride-Chang, & Putnam, 1994). In addition to appearing distracted in the classroom, sexually abused children may appear hyperactive. School-aged children who have been sexually abused also appear unpopular, anxious and extremely dependent upon their teachers (Erickson et al., 1989). Children who have been both sexually abused and neglected are more likely to repeat a grade in school, but sexual abuse alone has not predicted grade repetition (Eckenrode, Laird, & Doris, 1993). Similarly, research shows that children who have been both sexually abused and neglected have more discipline referrals and more suspensions than nonmaltreated children (ibid.). However, compared to physically abused and neglected children alone, sexually abused children do better in terms of academic achievement and school conduct but less well in social and behavioral domains.

School-aged victims of sexual abuse may perceive themselves negatively. Delinquent behaviors such as lying and stealing may emerge. They may also have concerns about the damage that was done to their body during the sexual abuse. Generally, children have limited understanding of how their bodies work. Some sexually abused children may misperceive the damage that has been done to them, especially when objects have been inserted into them. They may have concerns over whether they are pregnant or whether they can get pregnant from oral sex. Such concerns lead to increased anxiety, which can manifest in physical problems. Furthermore, while the relationship between child sexual abuse and depression in adults has been well established (Briere, 1989; Finkelhor, 1990), children who have been sexually abused are also more likely to be diagnosed with depression (Lanktree, Briere, & Zaidi, 1991; Mannarino & Cohen, 1996; Koverola et al., 1993). The onset of depression may occur immediately and in the beginning stages of disclosure in some children, but the onset of child depression does not seem to be related to the severity of abuse (Koverola et al., 1993). However, sexually abused children with low IQ and a high number of stressful life events may be at particular risk of developing depression following abuse (Koverola et al., 1993). Recent research on treatment has determined, however, that sexual abuse symptoms do not decrease at the same rates. Anxiety and depression appear to improve more quickly than dissociation, post-traumatic stress, and sexual concerns (Lanktree & Briere, 1995).

The degree to which each of these cognitions and behaviors manifest in a school-age victim is multiply determined and complex. In addition to cognitive-behavioral manifestations, children who have been sexually abused also have difficulties in social and emotional development.

Socioemotional

One aspect of sexual abuse is the stigma many children feel as a result of their victimization. Sexually abused children may feel "different" from their peers and like "damaged goods." Sexually abused children exhibit anxiety, aggression, hostility, and depression. Children may also have nightmares and difficulty sleeping. They may appear fearful and demonstrate phobias or obsessions. Sexually abused children often exhibit behaviors consistent with PTSD, such as fear, anxiety, re-experiencing, and difficulty concentrating (McLeer et al., 1992). In fact, children with a history of sexual abuse exhibit more PTSD symptomatology and are more likely to be diagnosed with PTSD than either physically abused or nonabused children (Deblinger et al., 1989; Dubner & Motta, 1999). Many of those who fail to receive a PTSD diagnosis exhibit PTSD symptoms (McLeer et al., 1992).

Sexually abused children also have interpersonal problems, such as being less socially competent (Friedrich, Beilke, & Urquiza, 1987; Mannarino & Cohen, 1996) and having peer or family conflicts. Friendships are important to school-aged children, and sexually abused children may have poor peer relationships or difficulty making friends. Developmentally, this is an important task of middle childhood and is worthy of attention in treatment.

As mentioned earlier, a decrease in self-esteem is common for children as they enter school, but a positive yet realistic self-appraisal generally emerges by 4th grade. Sexually abused children, however, tend to have lower self-esteem (Cavaiola & Schiff, 1988; Hotte & Rafman, 1992). Suicidal behavior (Lanktree, Briere, & Zaidi, 1991), anxiety (Kolko, Moser, & Weldy, 1988), and depression (McLeer et al., 1992; Mannarino & Cohen, 1996) are also seen among sexually abused children. It is important to mention that self-blame does not appear to be as common among victims as once thought. Most victims do blame their offender, but when self-blame is evident more severe outcomes manifest (Berliner & Elliott, 2002). While the child may not be able to explicitly indicate each of these emotions, they may be seen through the child's behavior, school work, or play. Sexually abused children may appear socially withdrawn or hyperactive. They have been shown to have behavior problems (Wind & Silvern, 1992), which can make the formation of teacher and peer relationships difficult.

According to Erickson's theory of psychosocial development, the primary social task during middle childhood is the development of the child's competence in her/his abilities. The positive resolution, the development of industry, indicates that the child feels competent and productive. The child feels she/he can master new skills and is good at them. For example, bike riding is one common activity for school-aged children. Children must fall off a bike many times before they can ride with skill and ease, but they keep trying until the task is mastered. This sense of mastery is important for social development and is a foundation for challenges that lie ahead. Social development is compromised when children do not feel that they can do anything well. The child feels inferior to her/his peers and may not want to keep trying to ride a bike or skate with friends. Children who have low appraisals of themselves with low self-esteem and little confidence will alienate themselves from their nonabused peers who keep trying to accomplish challenging tasks. Furthermore, sexually abused children tend to be less trusting of their environment and themselves (Mannarino, Cohen, & Berman, 1994). Such characteristics can lead to the child's negative resolution of Erickson's psychosocial crisis and result in further social and developmental difficulties.

Physical

Sexually abused children have physical manifestations in addition to cognitive-behavioral and socioemotional, although forensic evidence may be lacking in some cases. Sexually abused children may have a sexually transmitted disease due to their victimization and should be screened by a physician. School-aged children may not fully understand the implications of a sexually transmitted disease, which may contribute to their feelings of being damaged. This is especially important to explore if treatment and repeated tests are necessary. Children should be informed of their condition and treatment to the extent that their understanding permits. The physician conducting the physical exam should be sensitive and attentive to the trauma already experienced by the child to reduce further trauma. As mentioned previously, some sexually abused children have a hard time being touched by others, and this will impact the trauma experienced by repeated physical exams. Asthma has also been associated with sexual abuse (Felitti, 1991).

Enuresis and encopresis are also common manifestations of sexual abuse in school-aged children. Encopresis is especially common if anal trauma has occurred (Finkel, 2000). Regressive behaviors may appear in sexually abused children, and enuresis and encopresis are both indicative of regression, but they may be caused

by physical rather than emotional reasons. Sexual abuse can manifest in excessive physical complaints from the child. Physical complaints of sexual abuse in school-aged children include persistent stomachaches and headaches; the child may make repeated visits to the school nurse. Children may have genital pain and genital   ·
odor. Depending upon the abuse, they may have genital and anal injury and pain.

School-aged children increasingly play with peers on the playground, after school, and during recess. Both gross and fine motor skills are better during middle childhood; the child's reaction time and flexibility improve, and children have more coordinated physical movements. Sexually abused children may have problems playing with children for physical reasons and pain, and they may not be able to practice their new physical movements. They may have problems sitting, walking, or running. What may appear as a lack of interest in play or a tendency toward social isolation may be the result of physical trauma related to the abuse, and should be explored by a trained professional.

Sexually abused children may also display heightened sexual behaviors (Mannarino & Cohen, 1996), even more so that other physically abused children. They may engage in sexual activity, genital exposure, or "pretend" intercourse (Friedrich et al., 2001). However, not all sexually abused children exhibit sexual symptoms behaviorally. In fact, Friedrich (1993) found that only 1/3 of victims exhibited sexual behavior problems.

Neglect

Similar to the unique circumstance surrounding sexual abuse, neglect is also a distinct subtype of child maltreatment. Since neglect is often "embedded in a larger pattern of dysfunction and, in many cases, environmental chaos" (Erickson & Egeland, 2002, p. 9), it is impossible to separate the impact of neglect and the environment on the developing child. Therefore, a child who has been neglected from birth to school age will have many developmental challenges and delays that are already present as she/he enters school. Children who have been neglected also tend to have developmental deficits in overlapping domains, so that cognitive, social, and physical delays may be observed.

Cognitive-Behavioral

Children in middle childhood are assessed by academic standards, standardized tests, and their overall school performance, and neglected children have the most severe academic deficits of all maltreated children (Eckenrode et al., 1993). Erickson et al. (1989) found that children who have experienced neglect not only have cognitive deficits, but also are inattentive and lack initiative in school. Neglected children have been found to perform below average on standardized tests (Howing et al., 1993; Hoffman-Plotnik & Twentyman, 1984) and have more learning problems than other children. When children should be demonstrating their mastery of language and learning grammar, sentence structure, and advanced writing, children who have been neglected show language delays (Katz, 1992), low academic performance (Erickson & Egeland, 1996, 2002; Reyome, 1993), and overall academic problems (Hufton & Oates, 1977; Moffatt et al., 1985). Neglected children have also been shown to avoid early school opportunities, which may be due in part to low cognitive functioning at the onset of school (see chapter 5).

Howing et al. (1993) found that academic failure was the most dramatic and constant consequence for school-aged neglected children, and neglected children performed worse academically than abused children. Neglect has the most immediate and long-term negative consequences on academic achievement than other forms of maltreatment (Eckenrode, Laird, & Doris, 1993). Much research has found deficits in neglected children on language, math (Eckenrode, Laird, & Doris, 1993; Wodarski et al., 1990), and reading skills (Eckenrode, Laird, & Doris, 1993; Howing et al., 1993; Hoffman-Plotnik & Twentyman, 1984). Wodarski et al. (1990) found that neglected children scored even lower than abused children on language and reading skills, when controlling for socioeconomic status. Children who have been neglected are also significantly more likely to repeat a grade, and children who have experienced both neglect and sexual abuse have more discipline referrals and suspensions than nonmaltreated children (Eckenrode, Laird, & Doris, 1993).

Socioemotional

Children who have been neglected tend to have severe social and emotional developmental deficiencies. In addition to performing at a lower academic levels than other children, including abused children, neglected children interact less with their peers than other children (Hoffman-Plotnik & Twentyman, 1984). Neglected children tend to show passivity (Crittenden & Ainsworth, 1989); social withdrawal (Crittenden & Ainsworth, 1989; Erickson & Egeland, 1996) and even aggressive behavior in the early school years (Erickson & Egeland, 2002). In a longitudinal study of maltreated children, Erickson and Egeland (2002) found that neglected children showed high internalizing and externalizing behaviors. Similarly, while self-esteem decreases to a certain extent during the early school years, neglected children tend to have low self-esteem and more delinquent behavior overall.

Children in the school years expand their social circles and develop more sophisticated friendships than in the preschool years. However, neglected children tend to be more unpopular and unaccepted by peers (Erickson & Egeland, 1996; 2002). One explanation for this can be the enduring effect of an insecure attachment with a child's parent. When a child has an insecure attachment, as most maltreated and neglected children do, she/he may interpret friendly behavior as hostile. Such interpretations of teacher or peer behaviors can lead to a child's further alienation and social isolation. When children do not have the necessary social and coping skills, they lack the ability to join play groups successfully and win acceptance by peers. As a result, they either make friends with other socially inept peers or become isolated, both of which are not excellent alternatives for a child already disadvantaged by neglect.

In general, neglected children have poorer emotional health than other children (Erickson & Egeland, 2002). When a child's appraisal of her/himself is negative (i.e., low self-esteem), and when they limit their opportunities for social interaction, they have less of an opportunity to nurture a sense of industry—a sense that one can accomplish and master new activities. School requires a child to master an array of academic subjects, in conjunction with the social interaction among peers. Children who limit their social contact and lack self-esteem will continue to fall behind in these areas without intervention.

One the tasks of school-age children is the maturity of their sense of industry. Children should increasingly be mastering activities, such as school and sports. However, neglected children may lack the initiative to engage fully in school and social tasks. Neglected children often lack initiative and have difficulty doing the basic tasks of school, such as following directions and completing a task from start to finish (Erickson & Egeland, 2002).

Physical

One of the most devastating consequences of neglect is death (Wang & Daro, 1989), but neglected children may also show severe developmental delays (Crittenden & Ainsworth, 1989; Hochstadt et al., 1987). Growth delay is one of the most obvious signs of neglect (Hochstadt et al., 1987). Remember that school-aged children are flexible, coordinated, and strong, and as they practice their motor development they become better and better at age-appropriate tasks and games—such as soccer, gymnastics, climbing on monkey bars, and basketball, to name a few. However, neglected children show many other physical problems that can affect their ability to develop their gross and fine motor skills.

Neglected children may have significant medical problems and illnesses, including malnutrition. They also have been shown to have anemia and asthma (Flaherty & Weiss, 1990). Research on children in foster care show that hearing, vision (Hochstadt et al., 1987), and dental (Dubowitz et al., 1992) problems are often unattended among neglected children.

CONCLUSION

Child abuse and neglect have devastating consequences to the children whom they affect. This chapter has focused on the developmental consequences of physical abuse, neglect, and sexual abuse in children ages 7 to 11. School-aged children experience academic and social challenges. They enter formal schooling and are seen on a daily basis by teachers and school administration. Perhaps for the first time, children leave their home environment for several hours a day; and during that time they are learning the foundation of their academic future. As this chapter has demonstrated, school-aged victims of maltreatment have academic problems, experiencing both cognitive and intellectual deficits. They also have difficulty interacting with peers and being accepted by them. Delinquent acts are often seen among physically abused victims, while neglect victims may appear passive and withdrawn. The tremendous effects of maltreatment on development are devastating to the school-aged child. The long-term consequences to development are apparent, and the abused/neglected child may fall even further behind academically, physically, and socially, which paves the way for trouble as she/he enters adolescence.

8

MIDDLE CHILDHOOD

Ecological and Developmental Assessment of Maltreatment and Intervention

Moving from early childhood to middle childhood, or the school years, children are at a period of expansive imagination and are at the peak of wanting to learn new skills and knowledge. Children ages 7 to 11 want to know and understand things; they want to take part in the learning and to master creating things. Caregivers continue to be important influences in their lives, but growth and development is also shaped by the myriad of friends and schoolmates crossing their path.

Middle childhood, as discussed in chapter 7, is a time for learning many new social, physical, and cognitive skills. Success in mastering these skills reflects children's increasing physical maturity, personality factors such as self-confidence and persistence, an encouraging microsystem, opportunities to learn, and other encouragement from the exosystem. Competence in mastery of skills enhances children's self-esteem and acceptance by their peers. Children who experience abuse or neglect prior to or during middle childhood often are not ready to tackle the many challenges that school presents (Veltman & Browne, 2001). These children come to the school years unready to learn, fearful or angry, and behaving in such a manner that alienates peers. The joy of curiosity and imagination often escapes school-age children who have experienced child maltreatment.

In this chapter we will explore what places school-age children are at risk and what indicators assist us in determining whether child maltreatment is occurring. Often maltreatment has gone undetected prior to the school years because children are less observable to professionals. It is often not until the child enters the school system that child maltreatment is discovered. This may be one reason children in the middle years of childhood are at high risk of maltreatment (USDHHS, 1996). If maltreatment is prevented and intervention is provided, children will have a better chance of achieving the critical task of knowing how to learn.

RISK AND PROTECTIVE FACTORS

As discussed, Cicchetti and Rizley's (1981) transactional approach to conceptualizing the developmental process takes into account environmental forces, caregiver and child characteristics, and the influence they have on each other for developmental outcomes. This model focuses on the transactions among risk and protective factors for the occurrence of child maltreatment. We have discussed many of these thus far. Please refer to Tables 8.1 and 8.2 to refresh your understanding of the risk and protective factors already discussed. The ones presented in this chapter seem most appropriate for children 7 to 11 years of age, in families that are being assessed for child maltreatment. All the risk and protective factors are applicable across the lifespan and should be considered.

Ontogenic Level

The focus in this book is on the parent's ontogenic development and how this influences parenting ability. Along with what we have discussed in other chapters, the caregivers' own developmental adaptation and the influence of her/his environment on adaptation need to be assessed. Parents' adaptation to school is a critical task of their ontogenic development (Cicchetti & Lynch, 1993). Unsuccessful integration into her/his peer group and poor academic achievement are indicators that the parent may have experienced maltreatment as a child (Howing et al., 1993; Veltman & Browne, 2001) and did not resolve issues of middle childhood development. This may place the caregivers at risk of maltreating their child. Additionally, the parent may not provide the child with the needed support and motivation to be successful in school, therefore neglecting the child.

Parents who experienced successful adaptation to school, exhibited independence, and achieved positive relations with peers and teachers are more likely to provide the school-aged child with the appropriate support and encouragement to succeed.

The type of attachment the parent experienced during her/his middle childhood with her/his caregiver is indicative of the occurrence of maltreatment. As we have discussed in detail, an insecure pattern of attachment behavior influences the caregiver's current parenting. It has been found that as many as 30% of maltreated school-aged children reported having confused patterns of attachment with their mothers (Lynch & Cicchetti, 1991). Caregivers may persist in distorting their representational model of the parent-child relationship, placing the child at risk of maltreatment. Distorted perceptions of the parent's own history of care are associated with child maltreatment (Crittenden, 1988). Exploration into the patterns of attachment is one of the factors in the overall assessment in determining the level of maltreatment risk in the family.

Microsystem Level

Physical abuse and neglect are still a serious concern during middle-childhood. As indicated, children during this stage are at maximum risk of maltreatment (USDHHS, 1996). Since the median age for victims of sexual abuse fall within the middle childhood developmental phase, special attention will be given to sexual abuse.

Table 8.1 Risk Factors

	Infant and Toddler	Early Childhood	Middle Childhood
Parental Ontogenic	• Parent experienced child maltreatment as a child	• Parent experienced poor parenting during their early childhood • Attachment issues	• Poor adaptation to school • Lack of integration into peer group • Sexually abused as a child • Confused patterns of attachment with mother
Microsystem Child	• Age itself • Born prematurely • Physical or mental disability • Infant tests positive for AOD • Race	• Excessive health or medical problems • Developmental delays	• Age • Oppositional or problem behaviors • Inappropriate sexually behaviors • Gender • Low self-esteem • Depression • External locus of control • Introverted
Parent	• Not satisfied with the child • Does not enjoy parenting • Young parent • Not understanding their role as caregiver • Lack of knowledge of child development • Substance abuse	• Perceptions of child • Inappropriate child expectations around development • Lower educational level • Authoritarian • Substance abuse • Depression • Aggressive behavior	• Depression • Withdrawal • Anger • Aggression • Antisocial personality • Obsessive-compulsive disorder • Serious mental illness • Paternal psychopathology • Low self-esteem • Poor self-concept • Negative perception of own identity • Loneliness

(continued)

Table 8.1 continued

	Infant and Toddler	Early Childhood	Middle Childhood
Family	• Poverty • Stress in family environment • Interpersonal conflict between partners • Single parent	• Coercive child rearing practices • Little positive interactions • Family lacks leadership, closeness, and negotiation skills	• Lack of impulse control • Cognitive deficits and distortions • Unemployed • Substance abuser • Poor communication • Lack of emotional closeness • Social isolation • Disorganized • Less cohesive • Stepfather in the home • Victim not close to mother • No physical affection from father • Low income • Family isolation • Patriarchal family • Unemployment • Hostility between partners • Father-only homes
Exosystem	• Lack of social support	• Caring individual in the child's life • Neighborhood lacks both informal and formal social supports • Living in a violent community • Lack connection with the community	• Social supports • Neighborhood that lack resources • Fathers who do not access family social supports
Macrosystem	• Cultural values that support violence • Attitudes toward how mothers should behave as a parent	• Culturally promoted attitudes and behaviors about parental rights to physically punish	• Stereotype of male dominance in sexual relationships • Social tolerance for sexual interest in children • Barriers to women's equality • Denial by society that sexual abuse exists

Table 8.2 Protective Factors

	Infant and Toddler	Early Childhood	Middle Childhood
Parental Ontogenic	• Parent experienced secure attachment	• Parent experienced appropriate parenting during early childhood • Continued to be securely attached to caregiver	• Successful in school • Developed peer group • Secure attachment
Microsystem Child	• Temperament • Goodness of fit with the parent	• Competent behavior • Positive temperament • Child is perceived as affectionate • Child is perceived to have high cognitive ability	• Competent behavior • Competent social and cognitive abilities • Positive self-esteem • Easy temperament • Adequate knowledge of middle childhood development
Parent	• Secure attachment as a child	• Adequate knowledge of preschool child development • Adequate developmental expectation of the child	• Adequate knowledge around home management
Family	• Supportive significant other in the home	• Quality child-rearing conditions • Mothers who are happy with their partner relationship • Structured, consistent daily routine • Presence of father or father figure	• Brothers and sisters • Caregivers are emotionally supportive
Exosystem	• Adequate formal and informal social support	• Adequate formal and informal social support • Living in a nonviolent community • Connections with the community	• Strong social networks • Family social supports • Well-resourced neighborhoods • Family's perception of neighborhood is positive
Macrosystem	• Cultural value of protecting children	• Culture that promotes nonphysical forms of punishment	• Society that acknowledges the magnitude of sexual abuse • Value equality of the sexes • No tolerance for the exploitation of children

Parental (Caregiver) Characteristics

RISK FACTORS   Children in the middle-childhood years of development are becoming more independent and do not have to rely on caregivers to provide for all
their needs. School-age children can feed themselves, dress, bathe, use the toilet,
be left alone for short periods of time, and articulate their needs and wants. As
long as basic resources such as food are available, children can do much more for
themselves. Parent characteristics that place the child at most risk are not related
to biological needs but to cognitive-emotional and protective needs. The risk factors discussed in chapters 4 and 6 are still applicable but for different reasons.

The risk of a child being sexually abused is significantly elevated by parental
psychological distress (Berliner & Elliott, 2002). Psychological difficulty experienced by the caregiver is the single most influential risk factor associated with
child maltreatment (Thomlison, 1997). The risk factors subsumed under this
factor are parental affective disturbance, such as depression, withdrawal, anger,
and aggression; antisocial personality disorder or characteristics (Christensen
et al., 1994); obsessive-compulsive disorder (Chaffin, Kelleher, & Hollenberg,
1996); serious mental illness and paternal psychopathology (Brown et al., 1998);
and maternal and paternal sociopathic behavior (Brown et al., 1998; Ferrara, 2002).

Nonpsychiatric mental health correlates of child maltreatment include low self-
esteem and poor self-concept (Faust, Runyon, & Kenny, 1995; Christensen et al.,
1994); lack of self-confidence (Gaudin et al., 1993); negative perceptions of one's
own identity (Christensen et al., 1994); loneliness (Garbarino et al., 1992; Gaudin
et al., 1993); lack of impulse control under stress (Coohey, 1996; Gaudin et al.,
1993; Wolfe, 1985); and difficulty expressing feelings (Gaudin et al., 1993).

Parental cognitive deficits and distortions are associated with child maltreatment (Azar, 1997; Milner, 1993). Cognitive deficits can be defined as an absence
of thinking where it would be beneficial. Cognitive distortions are attributed not
to a lack of ability but to thinking involving bias and dysfunction (Wolfe, 1999).
An example of a cognitive deficit regarding middle childhood development is the
following: During the school-age years, parents may have unrealistic expectations
of the child's behavior that may lead to increased aggression. A parent may believe that a 7-year-old child should get her/himself up in the morning for school,
dress and feed her/himself, and get to the bus stop on time. Unsuccessful completion of these tasks may lead to severe punishment.

Another example of a cognitive distortion is a parent who misperceives a child's
behavior. Parents who maltreat are more likely to perceive child behavior as a
problem and attribute negative intent to the child (Milner, 1993), which leads to
justification for disciplining the child in a cruel manner.

The employment status of the caregiver is related to child maltreatment. Unemployment and underemployment were both correlated with child maltreatment. Compared to mothers who commit other forms of maltreatment, mothers
who neglected had the smallest percentage of full-time employment (Jones &
McCurdy, 1992; Raiha and Soma, 1997).

Substance abuse continues to be an issue during the middle-childhood years.
Given that over 80% of all cases substantiated by child protective services involve

substance abuse of a parent (Scannapieco & Connell-Carrick, 2004; Dore, Doris, & Wright, 1995), this risk factor cuts across all developmental stages of the child. Parenting may be compromised by substance abuse and lead to a higher risk of child maltreatment in middle childhood when alcohol or other drugs cause disinhibition of aggressive impulses or break down the internal inhibitors, leading a caregiver to sexually abuse the child (Ammerman et al., 1999; Finkelhor, 1984). Alcoholism is the most often reported precipitating factor among pedophiles (Greenfield, 1996).

PROTECTIVE FACTORS   Parents who have adequate skills coping with stress related to caring for a school-aged child and who have adequate knowledge of child development and how to stimulate her/his child are more likely to be healthy nonabusing caregivers (Wolfe, 1999). Another characteristic of appropriate parenting that may reduce the possibility of child maltreatment is a caregiver who has adequate knowledge and skills around home management (Wolfe, 1999). Parents who have an ability to do meal planning, budgeting, and provision of basic needs (e.g., shelter, clothing, etc.) may have reduced stress that lends itself to a protective force against child maltreatment.

Child Characteristics

RISK FACTORS   Age, similar to the infant and toddler stage, again is a risk factor for children 7 to 11 years of age. There is a disproportionate increase of maltreatment during the middle-childhood years (USDHHS, 1996). The median age for victims of sexual abuse falls within the middle-childhood years. Female victims' median age is 11 years while male victims' median is are 8 years of age (USDHHS, 2000). There is an increased risk of sexual abuse if children have lived without one of their birth parents for a period of time or if their mother is unavailable (Finkelhor & Baron, 1986; Finkelhor et al., 1990). The first year of school may offer the first opportunity for a professional to observe the child and become concerned about her/his condition.

School-aged children who exhibit oppositional or problem behaviors are more at risk of being physically maltreated (Eckenrode, Laird, & Doris, 1993; Ford et al., 1999; Howing et al., 1993). Boys with behavioral problems are more likely than girls to be physically abused (Rutter, 1987). Children misbehaving may impose extreme parenting pressure that may increase the potential for harsh discipline.

Child interaction styles also affect the parenting relationship. Burgess and Conger (1978) found that maltreated children exhibit more negative behavior than matched controls of nonmaltreated children, which may predispose them to engage parents differently. Therefore, characteristics of the child can make parenting difficult and unrewarding.

Inappropriate sexual behavior is also an indicator of sexual abuse (Friedrich et al., 2001) and may be considered a risk factor. If a child is demonstrating age-inappropriate sexual knowledge, such as inserting objects in her vagina, simulating sex acts with peers, siblings, or dolls, or genital exposure, she might be experiencing sexual abuse. These sexualized behaviors also place children at increased risk of having multiple episodes of victimization.

Gender related to risk of sexual abuse is a risk factor. Victimization rates for boys and girls are similar for physical abuse and neglect but not sexual abuse. Girls are at greater risk of sexual abuse than boys (USDHHS, 1996; 2000). Beginning at age three, children are consistently vulnerable to sexual abuse, with the median age for girls being 11 years (USHHS, 1996), and disclosure is more likely to occur once the child has entered school.

Other child risk factors associated with sexual abuse are low-self esteem, depression, external locus of control, socially isolation, and introversion (Faust, Runyon, & Kenny, 1995; Finkelhor & Baron, 1986).

PROTECTIVE FACTORS   In the middle-childhood years the factors associated with protection from child maltreatment are related to social and cognitive abilities. Children who demonstrate competent behavior and competent social and cognitive functioning promote more protective processes (Kinard, 1995). Positive self-esteem and easy temperament are also defined as protective factors (Kinard, 1995; Rutter, 1987; Wolfe, 1999).

Family Characteristics

School-age children require a supportive family, contact with classmates, and ample opportunities to learn and master their environment (Cicchetti & Lynch, 1995). Families need to move from control of the child to allowing the child more independence as her/his developmental progress dictates. It is difficult for healthy families to move smoothly through this process, and even more for families experiencing child maltreatment.

RISK FACTORS   Children who have experienced sexual abuse come from similar types of families (Berliner & Elliott, 2002). Some of the key family characteristics are poor communication, lack of emotional closeness, social isolation, disorganization, and lack of cohesion (Berliner & Elliott, 2002). Other major family risk factors associated with child sexual abuse are stepfather in the home, victim not close to mother, victim receive no physical affection from her/his father, low income, family isolation, and patriarchal family or father seen as domineering (Finkelhor, 1984; Pecora et al., 2000).

Unemployment has been shown to be associated with child maltreatment (Gil, 1970; Gelles, 1975; Light, 1973; Wolfner & Gelles, 1993). Steinberg, Catalano, and Dooley (1981) found that increases in child abuse were preceded by periods of high job loss and resulted from family stress (Cicchetti & Lynch, 1993) that unemployment brings. From both an individual risk factor as well as from a family perspective, unemployment in the home is a reason for concern.

Partners in the home who have high levels of hostility toward one another have been found to be linked to frequent use of punishment during the school-age years (Belsky & Vondra, 1989). It may be that the child is placed in the middle of these situations. Partners who rely on hostility and anger as a means of communication and problem solving are more likely to use similar techniques with their children.

The structure of the family also may contribute to child maltreatment. As discussed in chapter 4, single-parent status is a risk factor for abuse and neglect often because of additional stress and reduced resources. An additional factor related to single-parent status is for children who live in father-only homes; they are twice as likely to be physically abused as those living with the mother only (Sedlak & Broadhurst, 1996).

PROTECTIVE FACTORS   Families whose caregivers are emotionally supportive and are available to provide comfort and reassurance to their children provide a buffer from child maltreatment (Finkelhor & Berliner, 1995; Kinard, 1995). The presence of a sibling may protect school-aged children from stress and offer help in adjustment (Anthony & Cohler, 1987; Hegar, 1988) by providing a buffer to the abusive situation.

Exosystem Characteristic: Risk and Protective Factor

One factor found to safeguard against the effects of unemployment on the family system is strong relationships with family social supports (Garbarino, 1982). Strong social networks serve to support families in an emotional and tangible manner, providing nurturance and provision of material aid. The presence of family social supports functions to reduce stress resulting from unemployment and will thus reduce the risk of child maltreatment. Families who are socially isolated and lack social support, in both rural and urban settings, may be at higher risk of neglecting their children (DePanfilis, 1996).

Studies have found differences in how fathers and mothers access social support (Coohey, 2000; Kinard, 1996) and how it impacts the occurrence of child maltreatment. Abusive fathers were found to have less connection to their family social network (Coohey, 2000), but there was no difference found for abusive mothers (Kinard, 1996). Mothers who abused their children were no more connected to their families than mothers who did not abuse their children.

The middle-childhood years require the child to enter the formal exosystem for the first time. School-aged children no longer have to rely solely on informal social support. Children begin school and become involved in neighborhood and community activities, sports teams, cultural events, religious associations, and connection with other formal support systems. The more connected the child and family are to these social networks, the more they are buffered from the risk of child maltreatment.

The neighborhood in which the family lives can contribute to the likelihood of child maltreatment. Based on socioeconomic conditions alone, Garbarino and Sherman (1980) found that some neighborhoods have higher maltreatment rates than expected and others have lower rates than expected. In neighborhoods with equal socioeconomic disadvantages, neighborhoods with social resources, whether formal or informal, experienced less child maltreatment than neighborhoods with fewer social resources. In addition, families lacking a connection to their community have fewer opportunities for exposure to child-rearing practices that could improve their parenting skills (Trickett & Susman, 1989). Without this social filter and opportunities for parental learning, parents lack a connection to emotional and material support during stressful times. Garbarino and Sherman (1980) also found that in neighborhoods where abuse and neglect were lower than expected, the families perceived their neighborhood with greater satisfaction and as a place for child and family development.

Macrosystem Level

Several cultural attitudes in the United States help promote the sexual abuse of children. Some of these include the stereotype of male dominance in sexual relationships, social tolerance for sexual interest in children, and barriers to women's equality (Hay & Jones, 1994). One need only look at some of the advertisements in fashion and other magazines, where boys and girls are presented in sexual manners that support the idea that sex with children is acceptable.

Another disturbing and critical area is the denial of society that sexual abuse exists. Society has chosen to reject knowledge of sexual victimization of children rather than make the needed institutional changes (Bolen, 2001; Olafson, Corwin, & Summit, 1996). Prevalence studies have demonstrated that 30% of all females and 13% of all males in the United States have been sexually abused (Bolen & Scannapieco, 1999). When society accepts this knowledge and acts accordingly, children will be protected from the occurrence of sexual abuse and other forms of maltreatment (Nelson, 2000).

MALTREATMENT ASSESSMENT OF FAMILIES WITH CHILDREN IN THE MIDDLE-CHILDHOOD YEARS

An ecological and development assessment of suspected maltreatment for children in the middle-childhood years presents different challenges than with younger children and infants. The assessment discussions in earlier chapter are important and relevant to the overall assessment of child maltreatment. This chapter will focus more specifically on children in middle childhood.

Children ages 7 to 11 gain cognitive skills that may make interviewing more straightforward. Unlike younger children, they have the ability to distinguish reality from perception, are capable of logical thinking, and make improvement in memory.

With cognitive gains, the social domain becomes more complex. Children are still influenced by parents, but peers become more influential. Peer and teacher relationships need to be examined, social networks explored, and the child's perception of self and child transactions with caregivers, siblings, and others need to be assessed.

The middle-childhood phase is often the first opportunity for professionals to observe and interact with children. Many children entering the school system have experienced prior child maltreatment, but it has gone undetected. Professionals have the opportunity and the obligation to deter further maltreatment. It is important to be aware of the risk factors of the child, her/his microsystem, and exosystem that may inform you that they are experiencing physical abuse, neglect, or sexual abuse. In this section we will cover key assessment areas for children ages 7 to 11.

Ontogenic Level

Exploring both the mother and father's developmental history is important in determining if it presents risk to the child. What the offending and nonoffending parent bring to the situation is significant. As we have discussed many times, the parent's own experience with attachment, the style of child-rearing practices they were exposed to, and the conception they have of their childhood is directly related to how they parent and the beliefs they have about child rearing. The relationship the parent had with her/his caregivers is associated with her/his own developmental outcomes and potential for psychopathology (Garmezy, 1983).

An assessment of suspected maltreatment during the school-age years in reference to the ontogenic level should focus on the following questions:

- Did the parent experience physical abuse, neglect, or sexual abuse at any time during her/his childhood?
- What style of parenting were they exposed to?

  Authoritative. Parents who are both demanding and child-centered in their responsiveness (caregivers who are sensitive to their child's abilities and needs).

  Authoritarian. Parents who are demanding and parent-centered in their responsiveness (demanding and controlling but at the same time insensitive to their child's abilities and needs).

  Indulgent. Parents who are undemanding and child-centered.

  Neglecting. Parents who are undemanding and parent-centered (Maccoby & Martin, 1983).

- How do they describe their childhood?
- How do they describe their transition into school?
- How do they describe the school experience? Academics? Athletics? Social?
- Did they have many friends when they were 7 to 11 years old?
- Were their parents' alcohol or drug abusers?
- Were their parents hostile toward one another?
- Was there domestic violence in the home?

Microsystem Level

Parent

The early discussion of the parents' ontogenic development is crucial in a thorough assessment. Caregiver characteristics and behaviors and the parent's transactions with the child are essential assessment areas when determining if child maltreatment is occurring in the family. This chapter builds on earlier discussions about the risk and protective factors distinguishing between maltreating and nonmaltreating caregivers. During the school-aged years parents take on different and sometimes more complex child-rearing responsibilities. Practitioners who are evaluating whether parents maltreat their children in the middle childhood years should consider the following questions:

- Is the caregiver experiencing psychological difficulty?

  Is the caregiver depressed, withdrawn?
  Does the parent exhibit angry or aggressive behaviors?
  Does the parent have obsessive-compulsive disorder or another serious mental health disorder?

- Does the parent have low self-esteem?
- What is the parent's self-concept?
- Does the parent demonstrate self-confidence?
- Is the parent lonely?
- Is the parent able to appropriately express her/his feelings?
- Explore any cognitive deficits or distortions the parent may have. Does the parent have unrealistic expectations of the child? Do they attribute negative connotations to the child's behaviors?
- Is the parent employed? Underemployed?

Substance abuse cuts across all developmental stages and is present the majority of the time in families that maltreat. The following questions may be helpful in gathering information from the caregiver to determine if they are involved with alcohol or other drugs:

- Do you believe you have a problem with alcohol or drug use?
- Have you ever had a problem with alcohol or drug use?
- Has anyone in your family ever thought you had a problem with drug or alcohol use?
- At what age did you start drinking or using drugs?
- When was your last drink? When did you last get high?
- When do you usually use alcohol or drugs?
- Have you ever blacked out?
- Have you ever had the D.T.'s (delirium tremens)?
- What do you drink? What drugs do you take?
- How much do you drink?
- How frequently do you drink or take drugs?
- Have you had significant periods of sobriety?
- Where do you usually drink or take drugs?
- What happens when you stop drinking or taking drugs?
- What drugs have you taken this week? Today? What have you had to drink this week? Today?
- Have you ever received mental health services? When? For how long? Why did you stop?

- Have you ever been arrested while intoxicated? Any D.W.I.? (i.e., driving while under the influence of alcohol or other drugs)
- Has drinking/drug use ever caused problems with your job/family?
- Does anyone in your family use (or have they used) drugs or alcohol?
- What is your diet like?
- Have you or other members of your family been treated or hospitalized for alcoholism or drug dependency?

Child

School-aged children are firmly embedded in their ecological system for the first time. They are entering the world of school, community, and family independently and have continued to master many skills in the cognitive-behavioral, socioemotional, and physical domains. Behavioral and emotional indicators cut across all forms of child maltreatment, neglect, sexual abuse, and physical abuse. Although some behaviors are more indicative of sexual abuse (i.e., sexualized behaviors), others, such as oppositional behaviors, may be a consequence of any form of child maltreatment. Since the occurrence of child sexual abuse is paramount during the school-age years and in adolescents, we will spend substantial time in this chapter and in chapter 10 on the assessment of sexual abuse.

In chapter 7 normal middle-childhood developments are discussed, as well as developmental consequences of child maltreatment for children ages 7 to 11. In understanding what children should normally be going through, we may be able to detect signs of child maltreatment. Developmental and ecological assessment requires that these indicators be understood in relation to an assessment of all other systems within the ecological framework. For a list of questions along the three developmental domains that should be asked see Table 8.3.

The level of attachment the child has with the parent and other significant adults continues to be an important assessment matter and one that, in relation to all other areas, can provide insight into the occurrence of maltreatment. During evaluation of attachment, it becomes necessary to move beyond observing parent-child interaction. Indicators of attachment disorder occur along a continuum from mild to severe and can change in frequency and duration over the course of development. These symptoms are influenced by the following factors (Levy & Orlans, 1998, p. 105):

- Developmental stage at the time of disruption
- Length of disruption
- Nature and quality of attachment prior to disruption
- Nature and quality of attachment experiences following disruption
- Constitutional factors, including genetic background and temperament
- Protective factors, including support from extended family and positive out-of-home placement

Behavioral indicators of problems with attachment range from mild, such as clingy behavior, to more aggressive acting out, to the most severe, including self-destructive behaviors (self-mutilation), fire setting, and cruelty to animals (Levy &

Table 8.3 Assessing Children Ages 7–11

Cognitive-Behavioral	Socioemotional	Physical
7–11 Years		
• In describing another person, does the child include both physical and inner traits? • Does the child show perspective taking? • Is the child better able to distinguish perception over reality, such as focusing on more than one task in order to solve a problem? • Can the child reverse both physical and mental actions? • Does the child show an improvement in memory from previous developmental stages, including using memory strategies to remember information? • Does the child demonstrate selective attention? • Do children use an "informal" code when talking with friends and switch to a formal dialect when speaking to adults?	• Does the child make social comparisons between self and others? • Does the child have a peer group? • Does the peer group have similar language and a shared identity? • Does peer interaction become more prosocial? • Does the child exhibit a more realistic appraisal of self-competence? • Is the child able to play games with organized rules (i.e., soccer)?	• Does the child have quicker and more coordinated gross motor skills (running, jumping, kicking)? • Has the child's reaction time improved from the previous developmental period? • Does the child have better judgment of movement? • Does the child show increasing flexibility? • Can the child build models? • Child prints well with smaller letters? • Can the child write cursive letters well? • Can the child draw two-dimensional shapes with attention to depth?

Orlans, 1998). Moving beyond behavioral assessment, it is important to utilize assessments of the internalized representation of the parent-child relationship. Measurement of attachment focuses on the mental model of the attachment relationship (Cicchetti & Toth, 2000). A number of established measures have been developed with the school-aged child in mind to assess the quality of attachment. They are:

- Relatedness scale (Wellborn & Connell, 1987). This scale has been used in studies with children in the school years and range of risk levels (Lynch & Cicchetti, 1992; 1997; Toth & Cicchetti, 1996). The 17-item child-report scale assesses two dimensions of children's relationship experience: emotional quality and psychological proximity seeking. Emotional quality refers to the range of emotions a child experiences with the parent in an attempt to capture the overall emotional tone of the relationship from the child perspective. Specific emotions assessed include relaxed, ignored, happy, bored, mad, important, unimportant, scared, safe, and sad. Psychological proximity-seeking is the degree to which children desire to be psychologically closer to their caregiver. Items such as "I wish my mom paid more attention to me" and "I wish my dad knew me better" are included.
- Projective storytelling task (McCrone et al., 1994). This fairly open measure is qualitative in nature. The social worker begins by asking the child to tell a story: "Once upon a time . . . can you finish the story?" Themes of attachment are interpreted from the story told by the child.

Neglect

Chapter 6 discusses indicators of neglect. These indicators are applicable across all developmental stages but were presented in the preschool years because children are most vulnerable to negative consequences prior to the school-age years. Middle childhood brings a mastery of skills that enable the child to survive (i.e., ability to obtain food and water). Although at times extremely challenging and unfair, school-aged children do not need the level of supervision that younger children require. In addition to the relevant indicators discussed in chapter 6, neglect should be considered in the following circumstances:

NEGLECTFUL SUPERVISION
- A child aged 9 or younger left to babysit children ages 5 or younger
- A school-aged child left alone for long periods of time
- A child, aged 11 or younger, drinking or using drugs with parental approval or encouragement (this is based on the extent of parental involvement and risk of significant bodily harm from the use of the substance)
- Parent/caretaker leaving a child 15 years or younger to live without any adult supervision

MEDICAL NEGLECT
- Lack of medical attention for serious illness
- Routines for chronic illnesses are not followed or are followed only sporadically

- Any identified medical need, (i.e., glasses, dental care), not followed up on by the caregiver
- Required immunization shots have not been obtained for the child
- Lack of medical/psychological services that poses a substantial risk of harm, including not getting necessary pharmacological or psychological treatment

EMOTIONAL NEGLECT OR ABUSE

- The caregiver consistently communicates negative definitions of the self to the child (i.e., you are stupid, ugly, worthless)
- Purposefully and continually embarrassing the child
- Confusing the child's sexual identity (i.e., making little boys wear dresses).
- Not protecting children from assault by schoolmates, siblings, or other adults that is not normal developmental sibling rivalry or school fights.
- Showing no interest in the child's school performance (as an indicator of neglect along with others)
- Isolating the child from peers, not allowing the child to participate in school activities, normal family routine
- Locking child in her/his room or other area
- Excessive threats and psychological punishment
- Ostracizing child for not achieving far above normal abilities
- Involving the child sexually with other children or adults, exposing her/him to pornography

PHYSICAL NEGLECT

- Children who steal lunches at school, eat off other children's discarded trays of food
- Children who come to school infected by parasites or fungus, such as head lice or ringworm, and are not being treated
- Lack of personal cleanliness; child is chronically dirty and obviously does not take baths
- Inappropriate clothing, dirty, torn, or unseasonal (wearing shorts in cold weather)

In the cultural context of the family, other important questions and behavioral indicators when assessing child maltreatment in the school-age years are:

- Does the child exhibit oppositional or problem behaviors?
- Does the child present depressed?
- What is the child's view of self? High/low self-esteem?
- Is the child socially isolated or introverted?
- Is the child unduly hostile to school authority?
- Is the child violent toward classmates?
- Is the child disdainfully refusing to do or complete homework?
- Does the child come to school tired and unable to stay awake during class?
- Is the child chronically staying home from school to take care of a parent or other family member?

Physical Indicators of Child Maltreatment

The above behavioral and emotional indicators are not always sufficient reason in and of themselves to determine if child maltreatment has occurred and may be present in nonmaltreating families. Physical indicators along with the above will strengthen the final assessment determination. Many of the physical indicators of physical abuse have already been presented in chapter 4 and 6, along with some physical indicators of sexual abuse. In this chapter we will focus mainly on the physical, behavioral, and emotional child assessment of sexual abuse. First we will complete the discussion on physical abuse assessment of the child.

Physical Abuse

The most common places on a child's body for accidental injuries are areas of bony prominence. The following are highly susceptible to impact injuries: knees, shins, elbows, forehead, hands, chin, and nose. Bruises or other injuries to the body parts that would not be hurt in a fall, such as the upper arm, the genital or rectal area, back of the leg or torso, and the buttock, should be suspect. Additional physical indicators of physical abuse that should be suspected as nonaccidental injury to the child are:

- Pressure bruises on the neck that resemble fingers or whole hands, suggesting the child was strangled or choked.
- Slap marks that frequently leave linear, parallel bruises similar to the outline of fingers; these can cause loose teeth, abrasions to the inside of the mouth, ruptured eardrums, and eye injuries
- A narrow loop pattern with converging lines away from the loop, caused by a folded belt or extension cord
- Thick and thin marks in a looping fashion because of centrifugal force from a belt
- Areas of mass bruising that occur when both flexible and fixed objects are used; caused when several blows land in the same approximate area
- Two black eyes without accompanying injury to the nose
- Rib fractures, especially if accompanied by pressure bruises on the ribcage that resemble fingers or hands

Sexual Abuse

Recall that there is a distinction between incest and sexual molestation. Incest is generally defined as sexual abuse that occurs between family members (parents, grandparents, siblings, aunts, or uncles) or surrogate parent figures (foster parents or paramours). Intrafamilial sexual abuse, another term for incest, is characterized by the psychosocial dynamic of the familial relationship, which should be extended to the kinship role, regardless of blood ties. A nonrelated stranger or nonfamily member commits sexual molestation, or extrafamilial sexual abuse. Neighbors, family friends, priest, older children, and other individuals commit sexual molestation.

The majority of children are sexually abused by a family member, relative, or some other person they know (Elliott & Briere, 1994; Finkelhor, 1994; Russell & Bolen, 2000; Saunders et al., 1999). When sexual abuse occurs within the family, the repercussions to development and subsequent maladjustment in adult life are more severe (Russell, 1986). Children in middle childhood have been found to have the most severe short-term effects of sexual abuse (Tufts, 1984 as cited in Finkelhor, 1986).

As discussed in chapter 1, sexual abuse is very complex and has various patterns of occurrence. It encompasses a range of sexual behaviors, causes, types, and relationships. The after effects of sexual abuse are multiply determined. Some children experience immediate effects and others experience little or no effect. As discussed in chapters 5 and 7, it is important to remember that the effects of sexual abuse vary among victims, its context, and its severity, which inturn affect the manifestation of sexual abuse.

School-aged children who experience sexual abuse may not disclose it. Disclosure often happens as an accidental event, through a physical exam or based on the behavior of the child (i.e., sexually acting out). There are relatively few physical findings diagnostic of sexual abuse without a corresponding disclosure (Adams, 2001). This said, the assessment is multifaceted and requires knowledge of the dynamics of sexual abuse, as well as an understanding of the family context. In this chapter we will discuss a model developed by Finkelhor (1984) that groups risk factors into four preconditions that are required in order for sexual abuse to occur. This model is widely accepted in the literature and has been used for the past two decades. In chapter 10 we will focus on another model developed by Finkelhor and Browne (1986) that discusses four clinical dynamics (traumatic sexualization, stigmatization, betrayal, and powerlessness) that are unique to victims of sexual abuse.

The four preconditions provide us with a guide for assessing whether a child is being sexually abused. The preconditions and appropriate related questions will be presented.

Precondition 1. An adult or older adolescent with the motivation to sexually abuse a child. Assessment questions have to do with the perpetrator. Questions you would want to ask concerning the person suspected of molesting the school-aged child are:

- Is the person developmentally immature?
- Does the person have a need to control and dominate?
- Was the suspected perpetrator sexually abused as a child?
- Did the person have an early sexual experience that was traumatizing?
- Does the person possess child pornography or advertising that portrays children erotically?
- Does the person indicate heightened arousal to children?

Precondition 2. The absence of internal inhibitors. This condition also has to do with the suspected perpetrator. Questions to ask are:

- Is there evidence that the person was socialized with cultural values that do not inhibit sexual interest in children?

- Is the person using alcohol or other drugs? Did the child report that the person was using?
- Does the person have an impulse disorder?
- Was there a recent stressful event, such as unemployment?
- Is there frustration in the partner or other sexual relationship?

Precondition 3. Overcoming external inhibitors—the biggest one being an aware and protective parent.

- Is the nonoffending parent absent, sick, powerless?
- Is the nonoffending parent distant or not protective of the child?
- Is the nonoffending parent dominated or abused by the suspected perpetrator?
- Is the family isolated?
- Are there opportunities for the suspected perpetrator to be alone with the child?
- Is the nonoffending parent not supervising the child?
- Are the housing conditions crowded or set up to have easy access to the child?

Precondition 4. A breakdown of the child's resistance. Violence, threats, or bribes may be used more often than once thought. Violence to animals is sometimes used to scare the child.

- Is the child emotionally deprived?
- Is the child socially isolated?
- Does the child have knowledge of sexual abuse?
- Does the child talk about keeping secrets, secret games, and themes of secrecy?
- Does the child indicate that the suspected perpetrator threatened him/her with violence toward himself, nonoffending parent, sibling, or family pet?
- Does the child indicate that coercion was used? Were special gifts or activities provided by the perpetrator?
- Has the child been exposed to child or adult pornography (a means of desensitizing the child to sexual activity)?
- Does the child have a special fondness for the suspected perpetrator?

Children 7 to 11 years of age may also exhibit behavioral or physical signs symptomatic for sexual abuse. As previously discussed, these indicators must be placed in the context of the overall developmental and ecological assessment. In chapter 6, a number of indicators were discussed that are applicable to middle-childhood. Additional factors that should be considered in your assessment are as follows:

PHYSICAL SIGNS
- Vaginal or penile discharge
- Sexually transmitted disease
- Nightmares, sleep disorders

- Tearing around genital area, including rectum
- Visible lesions around mouth or genitals
- The presence of semen in oral, anal, or vaginal areas
- Bite marks on or around genitals
- Repeated cystitis (inflammation of the bladder), especially in middle-childhood girls

BEHAVIORAL SIGNS
- One child being treated by a parent in a significantly different way from the other children in the family
- Arriving at school early or leaving late
- Dramatic change in behavior or school performance
- Unusual accumulations of money, videogames, toys, etc.
- A return to bedwetting
- Sexual self-consciousness, provocativeness, or vulnerability to sexual approaches
- Regressive behavior, such as acting childishly, crying excessively, sucking the thumb, and withdrawing into a fantasy world
- Sexually oriented play activity
- Sexually oriented drawings (genitals stand out as most prominent feature, drawings of intercourse)
- Sexual behaviors with animals
- Repeatedly plays with or smears feces
- Talks about sex and repeatedly asks questions about sex
- Inability to make friends
- Sexualized behavior; has precocious knowledge of explicit sexual behavior and engages self or others in overt, repetitive sexual behavior
- Pseudomature; seems mature beyond chronological age
- Compulsive masturbation
- Enuresis or encopresis

It is important to understand that children ages 7 to 11 engage in healthy, natural sexual behaviors. As discussed in chapter 7, children in middle childhood will ask about genitals, breasts, intercourse, and babies. It is normal for children to play doctor and explore each others 'bodies, show others their genitals, touch their own genitals when they are going to sleep or are excited or anxious, and play games with same-age children related to sex and sexuality. When this behavior takes on extremes and involves coercion, it becomes a concern and a possible indication that the child is experiencing incest or sexual molestation.

In the discussion of the parent, family, and exosystem, evaluation of sexual abuse and indicators specific to those assessment areas will be discussed. Further discussion of sexual abuse assessment and treatment will also take place in chapter 10.

Family

There are family profiles shown to distinguish families that experience maltreatment from those that do not. During the middle-childhood years, some family assessment areas are more relevant than at other developmental stages. The preceding family assessment discussions are essential to any assessment. The current material builds on earlier chapters.

The following questions may assist you in determining the existence of child maltreatment in the family system. Again, it is important to the ongoing emphasis on cultural responsiveness that these questions are placed in the cultural context of the family.

- What is the family's communication style? Do they communicate well?
- Does the family demonstrate emotional closeness?
- Is the family socially isolated?
- Is the family organized?
- Is the family cohesive? Are family members helpful and supportive of one another?
- Is there a stepfather in the home?
- Are the child/children close to the mother?
- Does the child receive physical affection from the father?
- Is the family patriarchal?
- Is the family low-income?
- Is anyone unemployed in the family?
- Do the partners have hostility toward one another?
- Is it a father-only home?
- Are there siblings in the home?

Exosystem Level

The family's competencies and resources are important in determining the level of risk and safety to the child. Focus of assessment also has to take into account the family's interactions with the broader community and environment. We need to understand the contributing factors of the exosystem that may be associated with child maltreatment. Some of the questions that may assist in information gathering are:

- Does the family have strong relationships with extended family social support?
- Is the family socially isolated from formal and informal social supports?
- How often does each partner access social supports?
- What type of contact does the caregiver have with the school?
- Does the parent visit the school, go to teacher-parent meetings, and engage in school activities or outings?
- Is the family involved with their neighborhood?
- Is the family involved in any religious organization?
- Is the family involved in any sports or community activities?
- Does the community where the family lives have adequate resources for the family with a middle-childhood son or daughter?
- What are the community's beliefs about the care of children?

Summary

During the middle-childhood years, professionals often have the first opportunity to intervene in families who are experiencing child maltreatment. Children come to school, participate in sports and community activities, go to church, and are seen by multiple medical professionals. It is important for practitioners not to miss an opportunity to detect a child who is suffering from physical, sexual, or emotional abuse. In this section, we have outlined the many ecological and developmental indicators clueing professionals into the fact that a child is being maltreated. To reduce further developmental consequences, a thorough assessment that leads to effective treatment is fundamental. In the next section we will focus on treatment issues and intervention strategies for the school-aged child who experiences child maltreatment.

INTERVENTION FOR MIDDLE-CHILDHOOD CHILDREN WHO HAVE BEEN MALTREATED

In each chapter we focus on treatment issues and strategies that are most relevant for a particular developmental stage. Recall that different forms of maltreatment rarely occur in isolation of each other. Treatment strategies focus on the effects of maltreatment on children and families. Since it is difficult to distinguish effects of different types of maltreatment and the possible interaction effects among forms of maltreatment (Margolin & Gordis, 2000), many of the interventions presented are beneficial across all types of maltreatment.

Prior intervention strategies, such as the cognitive-behavioral techniques (CBT) discussed in Chapter 6, are applicable across the lifespan and can be applied to many different conditions and intervention methods. There is substantial empirical literature supporting the effectiveness of CBT for reducing many of the symptoms related to child sexual abuse (Cohen, Berliner, & Mannarino, 2000; Cohen, Berliner, & March, 2000; Deblinger & Heflin, 1996; Finkelhor & Berliner, 1995), and it seems to be a somewhat favored approach by African Americans, American Indians, Hispanics, and Asians (Paniagua, 1994, as cited in Olafson & Boat, 2000). A number of authors have provided specific CBT for child victims of sexual abuse and the nonoffending parent. See Cohen & Mannarino (1993), Deblinger & Heflin (1996), and Lipovsky (1992). In this chapter we will refer to the aforementioned references and expand our discussion to include treatment issues and strategies related to sexual abuse, children in the school system, and treatment for caregivers who physically abuse their children. In chapter 10 we focus our discussion on treatment related to sexual abuse and the adolescent child, and life-skills training for the child reaching independence.

Sexual Abuse

Sexual abuse is not a disorder or a syndrome (Finkelhor & Berliner, 1995). Children who are sexually abused may exhibit abuse specific effects, but there is no predictive group of symptoms to differentiate sexually abused children from children who have not been sexually abused (Kendall-Tackett, Williams, & Finkelhor, 1993). Children who have been sexually abused may experience a number of effects as a result of their victimization, but some children will exhibit no symptoms (ibid.). Although all children who have been sexually abused are victimized, not all children experience traumatization.

Children experience incest and molestation in diverse ways, and effective treatment needs to be based on an individual assessment of the significant impact issues for the child. Consequences of child sexual abuse manifest in both short- and long-term problems for the child (see chapters 3, 5, 7, and 9), so intervention may be warranted at different developmental stages to overcome the effects. Sexually abused children may show a reduction in symptoms of abuse during the course of treatment, but many will continue to experience significant symptoms at various times throughout their development (Oates et al., 1994). Some children have been found to experience more symptoms over time when at the initial assessment they had none (Kendall-Tackett et al., 1993). Treatment modalities also should be based on the developmental stage of the child.

The effects of child sexual abuse can be understood from a developmental perspective, with a focus on both attachment and the interpersonal consequences. Two main themes direct the development of symptoms: affective responses to the trauma and behavior patterns that are a result of social learning processes. Addressing these two areas is critical to treatment outcomes for the school-aged child (Cohen & Mannarino, 2000). In previous chapters we indicated that effects of maltreatment are based on several factors influencing healing and need for service. Those related to maltreatment are the type, severity, and duration of maltreatment, and the prior relationship between the child and the perpetrator.

There is a body of empirical literature describing the effects of sexual abuse on children. Porter, Blick, and Sgroi (1982) have outlined ten impact and treatment issues that should be considered when working with children who have been sexually abused. Although it has been 20 years since they outlined these issues they hold up today and continue to gain empirical support (see Berliner & Elliott, 2002). The first five are likely to affect most children who have been sexually abused, regardless of the relationship of the perpetrator to the child. The last five treatment issues are more likely to affect child incest victims (intrafamilial). Intervention strategies are suggested for each impact issue (Urquiza & Winn, 1993).

1. *"Damaged Goods" Syndrome.* The sense of being "damaged goods" may have to do with the possibility of real injury or fear of physical damage and retaliation. Community response such as pity, curiosity, or disgust may also reinforce this self-concept. Issues of body integrity, sexual or physical adequacy, injury, and changes in the body that might result from sexual abuse are important to identify and explore during treatment. To intervene with these concerns the practitioner can:

- Have the child undergo a thorough medical exam
- Discuss with the child what it feels like to be vulnerable or powerless
- Clarify anatomy, purpose, and function of the genitalia and sex organs

- Explain theories of sexuality and sexual orientation to the child and her/his caregiver
- Clarify age-appropriate interactions and intervene if the child is being exploited or abused
- Provide information on safe sex, sexual health care, and birth control
- Emphasize the positive aspects of the child's abilities and behavior

2. *Guilt*. After disclosure, guilt typically intensifies. The amount of guilt experienced is determined by the child's age and developmental level, as well as the response of significant others. The child usually experiences guilt on five levels:

- Feels responsible for the sexual behavior and her/his participation, particularly after he/she has experienced the societal response
- May feel guilty if she/he experienced any physical pleasure from the abuse
- May have experienced some covert power and feel guilty about using the secret to manipulate the perpetrator or other family member
- Feels responsible for the disclosure
- Feels responsible for the disruption in the family

The practitioner can help the child work through the guilt and feeling of responsibility by:

- Discussing with the child that the adult/older adolescent is the only person responsible for the behavior
- Increasing the child's understanding of why this kind of behavior is cruel to children
- Educating the child about the concept of consent
- Exploring with the child why he/she kept the secret and the circumstances of disclosure
- Educating the child in an age-appropriate manner about the physical nature of sexual response to explain the presence of physical pleasure
- Affirming the child's sense of power rather than focusing on victim status

3. *Fear*. Fears vary from child to child. Children experience fear of separation and abandonment, subsequent episodes of sexual abuse, and reprisals from the perpetrator. Sleep disturbances and nightmares may emerge as a result of such fears. Other regressive behaviors seen in young children are thumb sucking, bedwetting, and eating problems.

- The practitioner can reassure the child, to the best of her/his ability, that the child will be protected
- Routinely explore safety issues with the child
- Emphasize that the child deserves to be safe and protected
- If the child cannot be assured of safety in the home, she/he must be placed in out-of-home care
- Any current safety or protection issue alarming the child should merit immediate assessment

4. *Depression*. Most child victims will exhibit some symptoms of depression. Signs will vary from externalized, such as appearing sad, subdued, or withdrawn, to internalized, such as masked in the form of physical illnesses, tiredness, irritability, and fatigue. Some children will act out their hopelessness with self-mutilation and other suicidal gestures.

- The practitioner should address any repressed or unexpressed feelings
- Identify the child's capacity and willingness to experience and express her/his feelings
- Facilitate awareness and identification of feelings by providing a vocabulary and a sense of safety for the child
- Educate the child about feelings and the four groups of feelings: mad, sad, scared, and happy
- Encourage the expression of feelings

5. *Low Self-Esteem and Poor Social Skills*. Younger children especially may feel unworthy and undeserving. They have a limited understanding of their value as human beings and often feel inadequate. This, coupled with the feeling of damaged goods and society's response, will weaken the child's self-confidence. Due to the isolation typically associated with sexually abusive families, these children have had limited opportunity to learn more appropriate social skills. Children will often act out sexually as a result of lacking a repertoire of social skills. The practitioner can:

- Help the child acknowledge and accept her/his limitations by offering information about developmentally appropriate behavior
- Assist the child in identifying how she/he attempted to take care of her/himself and manage her/his feelings during the abuse
- Support the child's abilities to accomplish developmentally appropriate tasks
- Give the child permission to acknowledge her/his difficulties without losing esteem
- Use intervention strategies helping the child learn and master new skills
- Use intervention strategies allowing the child to practice decision making and experience a sense of control
- Use intervention strategies educating the child about social skills and educational tasks

The next five impact issues may affect children who have experienced sexual abuse within their family more than those experiencing it outside the family. If the extrafamilial abuse experience is with a perpetrator whom the child knows and trusts, it may generate the same treatment issues.

6. *Repressed Anger and Hostility*. Although the child may not appear outwardly angry, most children experience intense feelings of anger. The child is angry at the perpetrator and also with the caregiver who failed to protect them. Often the most difficult anger to express is the anger with the nonoffending parent. The practitioner can:

- Help the child express the anger and rage associated with victimization
- Help the child associate words with how they are feeling and to express her/his anger through vocabulary
- Help the child identify the thoughts and feelings that preceded her/his behavior
- Address the issues of loss and powerlessness that underlie the anger
- Model methods of managing difficult experiences

7. *Inability to Trust.* Once a loved and trusted caregiver has betrayed the child, her/his ability to trust again will be impaired. The degree of difficulty they have in developing a trust relationship will depend on a number of variables: the length of time and frequency molested, the identity of the offender, the type of relationship with the offender, the degree of pain/discomfort associated with the incident(s), the type of relationship with the nonoffending parent, the amount of disruption following the disclosure, and responses of others to the disclosure. The practitioner can help the child redevelop trust and intimacy by:

- Helping the child develop age-appropriate activities and relationships
- Helping the child increase her/his ease with interactions such as talking, listening, and sharing
- Modeling a close, reciprocal, trusting relationship and identifying qualities in the therapeutic relationship that can be transferred to other relationships
- Identifying behaviors supporting or interfering with developing meaningful relationships
- Helping the child recognize hurtful or abusive situations

8. *Blurred Role Boundaries and Role Confusion.* Inevitably children experiences confusion of roles when a family member has sexually abused them. Adults having sexual relations with children imply a deep disrespect for the usual societal role boundaries. Obscuring of roles occurs between mother and child, and father and child; often one finds mother-and-child role reversal. The practitioner can:

- Clarify appropriate parent-child responsibilities and roles
- Help the caregiver address issues of role reversal, boundaries, and setting limits
- Connect the child with appropriate adult role models in her/his ecosystem

9. *Pseudomaturity and Failure to Complete Developmental Tasks.* The sexual stimulation and preoccupation with sexual relationships disrupts the accomplishment of age-appropriate tasks, resulting in sexual abuse victims acting much older (i.e., dress, makeup, talk). Role confusion adds to this issue if the child prematurely takes on adultlike responsibilities as a result of the sexual abuse. Practitioners, through nurturing and teaching, can:

- Help the child behave in an age-and developmentally appropriate manner
- Practice problem-solving skills and help the child determine her/his needs and wants

- Reinforce the development of interest and curiosity in school and peer activities and support systems

10. *Self-Mastery and Control.* Sexual abuse involves a violation of the child's body, privacy, and rights of self-mastery and control. A sexually abused child believes she/he has no control over anything, especially her/his body (Porter et al., 1982). Refer to strategies under item 5, self-esteem.

Treatment Methods for the Child

Safety of the child is paramount in all treatment strategies addressing child maltreatment. As discussed in chapter 1, out-of-home care may be required to assure the safety of the child. Most child welfare professionals would argue that the sexually abusive offender should be the person to leave the home. But when the non-offending parent does not believe the child or does not seem willing to protect the child from the offender, foster care may be required. Treatment cannot be effective if the child is continuing to be molested or they do not feel safe. Whether the child is in her/his own home or in a foster home, treatment to reduce the symptoms of sexual abuse must be initiated.

As previously discussed, treatment choices need to be embedded in issues of race, ethnicity, and culture to be successful. Boys and girls respond to sexual victimization differently and therefore need to be engaged in different therapeutic strategies (Chandy, Blum, & Resnick, 1996; Friedrich, 1995). Many children who have experienced sexual abuse suffer from comorbid disorders, including depression, anxiety disorders, attention deficit hyperactivity disorder (ADHD), and disruptive behavior problems (Berliner & Elliott, 2002). As a separate entity of treatment, the comorbid disorders should be addressed with the most empirically effective modalities known in those areas. Other considerations in planning treatment strategy are how the family is reacting and how siblings are impacted.

Children often benefit from individual, family, and group therapy. In receiving different modalities, it is hoped that the victimized child will be able to integrate the abuse experience into her/his current life and effectively move forward developmentally (Gil, 1993, 1996; Mayer, 1991). The timing of group therapy should be assessed based on the child's ability to trust and her/his feelings of safety. A child needs to experience a trusting, one-on-one therapeutic relationship before they feel safe enough to disclose information in a group setting (Lanktree, 1994; Sgroi, 1988; 1989). Individual therapy provides children a safe time and place to begin to address the impact issues.

Sexual abuse treatment is based on the individual therapists theoretical orientation (cognitive-behavioral, psychoanalytic, feminist, etc). Guided by their theoretical orientation and practice perspective, especially effective techniques in individual therapy are play therapy, art therapy, guided imagery, poetry, and storytelling (Kelly, 1984; Mayer, 1991; Pecora et al., 2000; Porter et al., 1982). Play and art therapy may be ideal for school-aged children who have yet to develop the cognitive skills that would allow them to resolve their problems verbally.

Children may require a transition period before participating in both individual therapy and group or family therapy (Porter et al., 1982). For some children who have been extremely traumatized, group therapy may never be an option. They may never feel safe enough to disclose intimate details in a peer setting. Group therapy will be discussed in more detail in the adolescent chapter, since it is a particularly appropriate for adolescents.

School-Related Interventions

Middle-childhood affords a unique opportunity for professionals who work in the school system to intervene with children who have experienced child maltreatment. Prior to entering school, children may have experienced child maltreatment for years. Parents may not have had assistance with learning new and effective ways of child rearing or support in overcoming the many challenges of raising children with limited resources. The school can begin to provide the needed positive and secure relationships with peers and adults, as well as social support and connection to other forms of social support for the family. Teachers can provide opportunities for personal development, fostering accomplishment and boosting the child's self-esteem and mastery. They can help maltreated children to build self-confidence and to navigate the process of developing peer relationships.

Schools provide universal programs for all students that may offer protection from maltreatment today and prevention of maltreatment tomorrow (Veltman & Browne, 2001). Programs that focus on the identification of child maltreatment will help the child acknowledge the occurrence in her/his home and hopefully prevent future maltreatment. Other school programs, such as building self-esteem, sex education, and teaching parenting, will prevent maltreatment for future generations.

Cicchetti, Toth, and Hennessy (1993) have made the following recommendations concerning interventions with maltreated children in the school setting:

- Obtain an individual, comprehensive assessment of the maltreated child
- Begin intervention efforts with the children as soon as possible after the maltreatment has been confirmed.
- Recommend the most appropriate educational setting possible for the children
- Involve the nonoffending caregiver in the intervention and treatment process
- Encourage teachers to focus on the whole child, not merely on academic growth
- Help teachers understand how children are affected by maltreatment
- Help teachers learn how best to relate to maltreated children
- Work toward coordinating the services of the child welfare, special education, legal, and child mental health systems to help maltreated children
- Encourage researchers to conduct studies on how maltreated children function in schools
- Encourage schools to develop programs that can identify maltreated children

Often other support programs are associated with or provided by the school system with which a family interacts in their ecosystem. These programs can support and assist school-aged children and their families in coping with the impact of child maltreatment and relieve some of the stress families experience. Several selected programs are:

- After school programs focusing on social, recreational, educational, or therapeutic issues
- Problem-solving, assertiveness-training, or conflict-resolution programs
- Mentoring programs using adults for educational and social development
- Services for special needs children that focus on developmental and educational screening and advocacy for services such as transportation
- Counseling, either individual or group
- Parenting groups focusing on life skill development

Group Treatment for Parents Who Physically Abuse Their Children

Physical abuse of children must be viewed in the context of the family's ecology. Violence often occurs within the family, including partner abuse, child abuse, and within the community, which may tolerate abuse toward the child. Ecologically, other issues related to physical abuse must be considered, including unemployment, parent's childhood history of maltreatment, number of children, physical or developmental disabilities that are difficult to manage, and other caregiving responsibilities. Treatment of physical abuse is most effective when violence is addressed on all levels, especially in the family. Physical abuse of children is a family system issue, and all parts of that system must be treated to establish a healthy balance. It is also important to note that, as discussed earlier, many parents abuse alcohol or other substances. Substance abuse treatment must be initiated along with therapy that addresses the issues of physical abuse. Psychiatric disorders may also demand additional specialized treatment for the parent.

Two main areas for parent treatment are self-management, including anger management and self-control skills, and child behavior management, including parent education of developmentally appropriate expectations and alternative solutions to using physical discipline. The strength-based approach would dictate that the practitioner build on the assets the parent brings to treatment, with the parent involved in goal setting to reduce resistance. Whether the parent engages in individual or group treatment, the goals are the same. Crosson-Tower (2002) and Daro (1988) outline the following as goals for all parents who physically abuse their children:

- Cease battering behavior and learn alternative nonviolent methods of child behavior management
- Recognize the feelings or events that led to the initial abuse
- Recognize the warning signals that immediately precede the abusive behavior
- Learn alternative coping skills to handle anger and frustration
- Gain pride in themselves as parents

- Increase knowledge of child development and developmentally appropriate expectations for children
- Enhance parent-child bonding, emotional ties, and communication
- Improve communication within the family and with extended family
- Increase knowledge of home and child management
- Minimize or reduce environmental stressors
- Recognize and reduce their isolation
- Increase access to social and health services for all family members

Group work as a treatment modality may be an effective strategy for parents. Although there is not much empirical support for the use of group treatment and individual or family therapy may continue to be required to monitor child risk and safety, group treatment has been advocated for several reasons. Groups are thought to be useful in improving the parent's interpersonal skills, diminishing the stigma of being labeled inadequate, reducing social isolation, teaching parents to change their own behavior in order to foster prosocial skills in children, helping them develop positive interaction styles, and helping them replace antisocial behaviors such as aggression and noncompliance with prosocial behaviors that include self-control (Swetnam, Peterson, & Clark, 1983; Azar, Breton, & Miller, 1998).

Cognitive behavioral group treatment that is embedded into the ecological and developmental perspectives (see Azar et al., 1998) fits well into the theoretical framework of this book. Although the interventional strategies are directed at the caregiver's skill deficits, the interactions between these deficits and the family ecology are considered. Azar et al. (1998) discuss strategies used in their CBT group treatment model that all address the treatment goals stated earlier in this chapter. The CBT strategies are:

- Role playing
- Developmental education and training to increase developmental stimulation and play behavior
- Cognitive restructuring and problem-solving training
- Child management training
- Cognitive anger control
- Stress management
- Social skills training

Treatment for caregivers who physically abuse their children should also focus on meeting the needs of the child and reducing environmental stress. Parents who have the additional challenge of providing basic needs for their families may be more prone to lose their temper and strike out at their child. Attention to concrete services, such as financial benefits, housing, education, employment, health care, and social supports, is critical to reducing the risk of recurrence of child physical abuse. Addressing the physical and emotional needs of the child, individually and within the family, is important to improving the child's ability to correct developmental deficits and improve adaptation in the future.

CONCLUSION

In this chapter the school-age child and the family and environment have been explored as they relate to child maltreatment assessment and intervention. Focus was placed on the experience of sexual abuse and the subsequent sequelae and intervention needs. All forms of abuse have been linked to later depression, suicidal behavior, lowered self-esteem, eating disorders, and substance abuse (Bagley, Wood, & Young, 1994; Finkelhor & Browne, 1986; Gutierres & Todd, 1997; Mullen et al., 1993). Because there is a great deal of overlap in outcomes associated with various forms of abuse, intervention strategies are applicable to children who have experienced physical abuse, emotional abuse, neglect, or sexual abuse.

Chapter 9 focuses on adolescent development and the consequences of child maltreatment. In chapter 10 we continue to focus assessment and intervention on sexual abuse. In adolescence, sexuality becomes paramount; youth go through puberty, which leads them to developing full-grown bodies and sexual maturity. During this period youth are confronted with developing more mature peer relationships of both genders and developing a construct of self. If a child has been or is being sexually abused, these developmental challenges often bring it to the forefront.

CASE: GARCIA FAMILY

A referral was received on the Garcia family on September 27 involving sexual abuse of Maria, age 9, by her father, Michael Garcia. Maria made an outcry to her school counselor, who had observed a drop in Maria's grades within the past few weeks. She noticed that Maria was withdrawn and did not interact with other children. Maria has been observed behaving seductively around older boys and male teachers.

Maria was interviewed on September 27 by a Child Protection Services worker and disclosed being sexually abused by her father for the past year. She described incidents of fondling by her father of her breast and vaginal area on top of and underneath her clothes. Maria further described an incident that occurred approximately one month ago, when her father attempted to perform oral sex on her and her mother walked into the room. According to Maria, Mrs. Garcia instructed her husband to leave the room and was very angry with both her husband and her daughter about what she witnessed.

Mr. Garcia continued to remain in the home. Upon interview by the CPS worker, Mrs. Garcia stated that she did not recall seeing her husband attempting to perform oral sex on their daughter. She was quite angry with the CPS worker for indicating that she had prior knowledge of the abuse. Mrs. Garcia stated that she is a schoolteacher and is fully aware of the indicators of sexual abuse, and does not believe it is happening in her home.

Mr. Garcia was very difficult to engage during the interview process. He acknowledged that he and his daughter spend a lot of time together. Mr. Garcia only admitted to possibly touching his daughter's breast accidentally in showing affection or wrestling with her. Mr. Garcia drinks a six-pack of beer daily on average. He stated that his father physically abused him as a child.

In planning for the safety of Maria, Mrs. Garcia was adamant that their relatives not be involved at all in this case and refused to facilitate a placement with them. Mr. Garcia agreed to remain out of the home for four days and stay in a hotel. He is currently unemployed due to a layoff. There are no siblings in the home. Mrs. Garcia and Maria have a superficial relationship, possibly because Mrs. Garcia suffered from postpartum depression after giving birth to Maria. An uncle sexually abused Mrs. Garcia when she was 8 years of age, but she never told anyone about the abuse.

Giving birth to Maria triggered thoughts of the abuse for Mrs. Garcia. During the period of postpartum depression, she did not bond with Maria and refused to even hold her for several months after her birth. Mr. Garcia was basically the primary caretaker of Maria during this period. Mrs. Garcia did seek therapy for her depression and received medication. She stabilized when Maria was 2½ years of age. Mrs. Garcia has had no further occurrences of depression.

Both Mr. and Mrs. Garcia related that they have friends that they mainly socialize with at the Catholic church they attend. They visit with their extended family members, but they don't like them interfering in their lives.

Case Exercise

1. What are the normal developmental expectations for the child?
2. Consider the child's developmental level. What developmental manifestations can you identify that may be an indication of child maltreatment in the following domains?

   - Physical development
   - Cognitive-behavioral
   - Socioemotional

3. What role does culture play in the child's development?
4. Expand your assessment of the child's developmental level to the overall ecological model. Assess the family's risk and protective factors in the context of the ecological model.

   - Ontogenic Level
   - Microsystem
   - Exosystem
   - Macrosystem

5. What intervention strategies might you employ to facilitate development of the child?
6. What intervention strategies might you employ with the caregiver?
7. What cultural aspects of the family are important to consider for both assessment and intervention?

9

ADOLESCENCE

Child Development and Maltreatment

Adolescence is the bridge between childhood and adulthood. It begins at age 12 and ends around age 20, and is marked by changes that occur within and outside the individual. This chapter will focus on adolescents from ages 12 to 18, to include the changes of early adolescence to the time when a teen becomes a legal adult and is no longer involved with the child welfare system as a victim. The most obvious changes in adolescence are those that are physical, but the transition to adulthood also requires cognitive and social transformation. Adolescents begin to explore their own identities, trying to find out who they are and what they really believe. They are spending even larger amounts of time away from home with friends, who become even more influential and more important than ever before.

EXPECTED DEVELOPMENT ACROSS DEVELOPMENTAL DOMAINS

Human development follows a generally consistent course. By the time a child enters adolescence, she/he may have experienced years of maltreatment. For other adolescents, their maltreatment is just beginning. Adolescence is a period of tremendous transition and transformation as adolescents experience physical, emotional, cognitive, and social changes. In modern society, teens emerge from this period as adults who are capable of serving in the military, voting for public officials, and raising children. Consistent with previous chapters, the developmental milestones of adolescence will be discussed in relation to their socioemotional, cognitive, and physical development (see Table 9.1). It is important to keep in mind that developmental delays may be more marked if maltreatment has been occurring for many years, and they may be more subtle if the maltreatment is just beginning. Many people have explained the transition that occurs between childhood and adulthood. The most notable theories are Freud's psychosexual theory of development, Erickson's psychosocial theory of development, and Piaget's cognitive theory of development. Each will be discussed below, in addition to theories of social development and overall growth and maturation.

Table 9.1 Adolescent Development

Psychodynamic		Social	Cognitive		Physical
Freud	Erickson		Piaget		
Genital: • With puberty, sexual impulses to reemerge • The genitals are the focus of pleasure and the young person seeks sexual stimulation and satisfaction	*Identity vs. role confusion:* • Adolescents try to discover a self-identity through political, social, sexual, and career identities • The primary job of adolescents is to establish intimate ties with others • Adolescents who have had previous negative resolutions have difficulty establishing ties to others and are confused about their identity and roles	• Parent-adolescent conflict and moodiness increases, but varies depending upon age, gender, and culture • Friendships become even more important and influential • Peer groups are important and based on similar interests and values • Loyalty and intimacy are crucial to friendships • Peer pressure with both constructive and destructive abilities • Sexual and romantic relationships begin	*Formal operations stage:* • Adolescents have the ability for abstract thought and scientific reasoning • Hypothetical reasoning is possible, and problems are approached with logic and reasoning • Adolescents can think about ideas rather than only concrete events • As a result, ethics, social, and moral issues become more interesting	• Better ability to argue with increases in hypothetical and abstract thought • Metacognition and emotional regulation improves • With age, becomes better at decision making and planning • Adolescent egocentrism emerges where the adolescent focuses on self believing her/his thoughts, beliefs, and feelings are unique experiences • Invincibility fable—a way of thinking which adolescents feel immune to the dangers of behaviors	• Puberty begins • For girls, puberty sparks onset of breast growth, initial pubic hair, peak growth spurt, widening of hips, and first menstrual period • For boys, puberty sparks onset of pubic hair, growth of testes, growth of penis, first ejaculation, growth spurt, voice deepening, beard development • Average age of menarche is 12.5 years • For girls, motor performance peaks and then levels off • Average age of spermarche is 13 • Adolescent may have sexual intercourse

190

Psychodynamic Theories

Freud's Psychosexual Stages of Development

Freud's 6th stage of psychosexual development is the genital stage. Coinciding with the onset of puberty, an adolescent's primary focus is on sexual pleasure and stimulation. The major developmental task during this period is to achieve mature sexual intimacy. Since much of Freud's genital stage is focused on sexuality, it will be further expanded upon in the section on physical development.

Erickson's Psychosocial Stages of Development

Erickson proposed that the major psychosocial crisis of adolescence is identity versus role confusion. An important developmental task is the development one's identity—to determine a self-identity while still maintaining some form of group ideals. Teens who achieve this crisis positively enter adulthood with a set of self-chosen values, goals, morals, and political ideology. They are not confused about what role to play in various aspects of their life; they may have explored other identities during adolescence, but by the end of this period, they have usually settled on a self-chosen one. Individuals who negatively resolve this crisis appear directionless, confused, and shallow. As a result, they are often unprepared for the daunting task of adulthood. It is important to mention that previous developmental thought was that the search for an identity resulted in an identity "crisis," but current thought is that this is not a crisis at all (Grotevant, 1996). It may be difficult for loved ones to adapt to an adolescent's new behaviors, ideas, and thoughts. Teens are not in crisis, but are rather actively searching for an identity.

In general, adolescents do not initially arrive at a decision quickly, but they often search for an identity throughout this period. Four identity patterns emerge during adolescence, and teens tend to move in and out of various identities before deciding on one (Marcia, 1966):

> *Identity achievement.* Adolescents who have reached identity achievement have positively resolved the psychosocial crisis of deciding upon an identity. This adolescent has explored alternatives and has a set of self-chosen values, goals, and morals. These teens have critically looked at their belief system and accepted some parts of it while rejecting others. They have decided on a set on self-chosen ideals. A sense of psychological peace settles with this individual.
>
> *Identity moratorium.* Identity moratorium is characterized by a delay in identity achievement. This individual does not make firm commitments to an identity, but rather explores various thoughts and activities. Attending college is often thought as a socially constructed moratorium where students can try on different identities and behaviors until deciding on what is appropriate for them.
>
> *Identity foreclosure.* Identity foreclosure occurs when adolescents prematurely accept a set of values and goals that others have chosen for them. They fail to question traditional values and do not take the time to explore

various alternatives. An example of this is a teen who becomes a preacher because her/his father and grandfather were both preachers, and this decision is expected of her/him.

Identity diffusion. Identity diffusion occurs when adolescents are directionless. They are not in search of their own goals or values and have not committed to any. Many teens find the task of exploring their identity daunting and overwhelming and therefore fail to do so. They appear apathetic and may even have difficulty doing tasks that require thinking about the future. They may fail to commit even in friendships or romantic relationships.

Adolescence is marked by decisions concerning what an individual should do with her/his life—college, vocational school, work, personal values, goals, and aspirations. Teens who are able to fully explore interpersonal qualities and societal opportunities are prepared for the challenges of adulthood. It is also important to understand that identity discovery is culture-based. In cultures where there is virtually universal cohesion to social norms and roles, the transition of adolescence into adulthood is relatively short and easy. When few options exist, deciding on an identity is short and quick. Adolescence is a time of great self-exploration for many teens.

Social Development

In addition to Erickson's psychosocial crises, many other developmental activities affect a child's social development in adolescence. Even though the adolescent years can be trying for parents who are struggling to understand the changes in their child, children with strong attachments to their parents are able to weather the tasks of adolescence better than teens with poor attachments. In spite of the influence of peers, attachment to caregiver(s) remains strong during adolescence, and teens continue to share core values and beliefs with their parents (Kandel & Lesser, 1972). A strong attachment to parents is predictive of high academic achievement and good peer relationships (Black & McCartney, 1998). Similarly, who that have good relationships with their parents are less likely to use drugs both in adolescence and adulthood (Brook et al., 2000). However, teens and parents tend to bicker and argue more at home during adolescence. They fight about petty things, such as hair, clothing, and cleaning. Teens often try to obtain adult privileges and seek independence and privacy. While this can by a trying time, it is developmentally appropriate as teens practice the tasks of adulthood with their new cognitive and social skills.

One of the primary tasks of adolescence is the discovery of self. Self-esteem often changes in adolescence. Adolescents have generally high levels of self-esteem, but this varies from individual to individual. Children whose parents use an authoritative style of parenting have generally higher levels of self-esteem, because the parents foster their child's autonomy. Research also shows that both boys and girls who have an androgynous or masculine self-concept/identity have higher self-esteem (Burnett, Anderson, & Heppner, 1995), although cross-cultural research suggests that this may not be true for all cultures (Lobel, Slone, & Winch, 1997).

While peer relationships become important during middle childhood, they become even more so during adolescence. Friendships take on new functions. Intimacy and loyalty become important. Adolescents search for psychological closeness to their friends; they tend to feel that "nobody understands" them (see cognitive development, below), and their friends provide a forum to feel understood. Adolescence friendships are also characterized by loyalty where sticking up for one another becomes important in the cohesion of friendships.

Another aspect of friendship that emerges is self-disclosure, where teens tell each other personal things about themselves to be held in confidence among friends. Such intimacy among friends is not seen in middle school children, but it is an important part of adolescent friendships. Friends also provide social support to one another, and this helps ease coping with physical and emotional challenges that underlie puberty. Adolescents get to know their friends better as people rather than just as playmates. They learn about their friends' dreams and goals. They try to preserve friendships because of their shared intimacy and loyalty. They try to resolve conflicts with their close friends as opposed to ending the friendship when disagreements arise.

Peer groups and cliques also form among teen friends with similar characteristics. Peer groups become more prevalent and are more influential in adolescence than in previous developmental periods. Peer groups are formed based on similar interests and thinking. They are structured, often around shared family background, socioeconomic status, and attitudes. Peer pressure is often thought of as negative, but this is not always the case. Often peer groups pressure friends to abstain from drugs or smoking, and they can serve many positive functions. Special peer groups, often referred to as cliques, form, such as the "brains," "jocks," "druggies," and "popular kids." Cliques often have shared language (also seen in middle childhood), dress, and behaviors or activities. Association with peer groups and cliques, however, changes over time. Toward late adolescence teens are less concerned with cliques because, if they have acquired identity achievement, they have less need to have a crowd or peer define their identity. At any rate, peer groups help shape adolescent thinking and exploration of identities.

Friendship in middle childhood primarily occurs among same-sex friends, but adolescent friendships begin to include members of the opposite sex and romantic relationships emerge. Not all different-sex friendships evolve into romantic relationships, but most teens have a conceptual understanding of being "in love" with another. Similar to same-sex friendships, girls tend to seek psychological closeness with members of the opposite sex through self-disclosure, while boys seek this less. Romantic relationships tend to be intense but short-lived.

While romantic relationship development is important in adolescence, so is the decision about one's individual sexual development. By the time a teen completes high school, the majority of males and females are likely to have engaged in sexual intercourse (CDC, 2000). African Americans are the most likely to have had sexual intercourse (approximately 70%) and are more likely to have had sex before the age of 13 compared to other ethnic groups. However, African Americans are also the most likely ethnic group to use a condom (CDC, 2000). Approximately half of Hispanic Americans and whites have had sex by the time they complete high school, with a slightly higher percentage of Hispanic Americans than whites having done so. Sexually abused girls are also more likely to have had intercourse by age 15 than nonabused girls (Stock et al., 1997). Social factors are good predictors of the likelihood of sexual activity, including low self-esteem, social deviance, and child sexual abuse (Herrenkohl et al., 1998).

Much of our developmental theories focus on heterosexual development, but recent research has also looked at the unique challenges of gay and lesbian adolescents. Gay and lesbian adolescents face unique challenges compared to their heterosexual counterparts, including whether to "come out" and the response by peers and family. Gay and lesbian teens have a smaller dating pool since many teens are still discovering their sexuality. Many teens do not label themselves as gay or lesbian in adolescence, but rather as undecided while discovering their sexual and personal identities. Nonetheless, both heterosexual and gay and lesbian teens face many of the same insecurities and challenges. Both heterosexual and gay males are more likely to drink alcohol; heterosexual females and lesbians are more likely to diet; and both heterosexual and gay and lesbian teens are likely to fear rejection from their partners. However, many adolescent lesbians and gays feel "different" from their peers (Wormer, Wells, & Boes, 2000).

Some adolescents experience very difficult adjustments to their new physical, cognitive, and social changes. Some common manifestations of this transition include depression, suicide, and delinquent behavior. Each of these occurrences is correlated with a history of child maltreatment, but they can also occur in children who have not experienced maltreatment. A brief description of each is provided below, and they will be expanded upon as they relate to the manifestations of abuse or neglect.

Depression

Depression is the one of most common psychological problems of adolescence (Birmaker et al., 1996). It occurs more often in females than males and increases around the time of puberty. The symptoms of depression include feelings of sadness and hopelessness. Depression is also accompanied by behavioral changes. When adolescents are beginning to imagine the possibilities of their worlds, depressed teens feel hopeless about the future. Depressed teens may appear withdrawn, excessively worrisome, and even rebellious. Being depressed can make mastering developmental tasks more difficult for adolescents. Teen depression often goes overlooked and is characterized as teenage moodiness or a "phase," but it should be taken seriously and properly assessed.

Suicide

As you will see in the section on cognitive development, teenagers have the capacity for new thinking during adolescence. They can imagine a perfect world. They can cognitively explore solutions to problems and imagine an array of possibilities before them. This increase in cognitive sophistication is tremendous, and it opens up the door to thinking about various possibilities, including death for some teens. Coupled with new cognitive capabilities are the many stressors teens face. They have access to drugs and alcohol; guns are readily available in today's society; and they may have fewer social supports than before. Suicidal adolescents may give warning signs, have sleeping and eating changes, become agitated easily, and neglect their personal appearance. A suicidal adolescent may see death as one of many options toward ending her/his misery. Suicidal ideation (thinking about suicide) becomes a major threat when the person (1) has a plan for death; (2) has the means to accomplish the plan; and (3) lacks supervision so that a time for committing the plan is available. Two types of teens generally commit suicide. The first type includes intelligent and withdrawn teens who fail to meet their own standards, and the second is teens with delinquent and antisocial behaviors (Lehnert, Overholser, & Spirito, 1994). Suicide ideations among teens should always be taken seriously and assessed properly.

Delinquency

Juvenile delinquency is a social problem of great proportion. Maguire and Pastore (1997) report that almost half of all arrests for crime are of individuals between 10 and 20 years of age; and most arrests for juvenile delinquency occur among males rather than females. Therefore, while females may be more likely to internalize their anger and frustration, it seems that boys are more likely to act out behaviorally through delinquency. Juvenile delinquency will be discussed further in the section about the manifestations of child maltreatment.

Physical Development

The physical changes of puberty are the most obvious signs of adolescence. Within a few years, a child body is transformed into an adult body. The boy's testes release large quantities of testosterone, which result in facial and body hair, voice deepening, muscle growth, and overall growth in height and weight. The female ovaries release large quantities of estrogen and the adrenal gland releases hormones, which result in breast development, menstruation, body shape changes, and height growth. Both sexes undergo a growth spurt and a rapid gain in height, although girls encounter their growth spurt before boys because puberty generally starts earlier for girls than boys (Tanner, 1998). Eventually, however, boys catch up to girls and tend to be taller and heavier ultimately. Testosterone and estrogen are released in both boys and girls, but each sex receives a larger amount of one.

Sexual maturation is one of the most important aspects of puberty. The body becomes capable of human reproduction. The average age of menarche (first menstruation) for girls is 12.5, and the average age for spermarche (first ejaculation) is 13 for males. Although the physical signs of puberty seem quite sudden, the hormonal changes that underlie puberty begin much earlier. By the time the results of the hormonal changes are evident, they have been under way for some time.

In additional to sexual maturation, the skeletal system changes so that adolescents increase in height; their joints develop further, which allows better coordination. The muscular system continues to develop so that adolescents become stronger and have a high level of physical performance.

Cognitive Development

Adolescence is marked by changes in thinking and a shift from concrete to formal operational thought. Piaget named the time period from 11 or 12 to adulthood the Formal Operational Stage of Cognitive Development, which is the final stage of his developmental theory. The formal operational stage is characterized by increased cognition in many areas. Adolescents can think about possibilities rather than only concrete events, as during the previous stage (concrete operational stage). They can think abstractly and solve hypothetical problems. One consequence of this new thinking, however, is that teens may think they know the answers to complex and multidimensional problems. They sometimes become critical of their parents and their parents' choices. For example, a teen may think that she/he "knows" how to have a good marriage and critically tells her/his mother what she did wrong to ruin her own marriage. It is noteworthy that not all individuals reach the formal operational stage or all of the cognitive gains in it.

Adolescents are able to think about how things could be rather than merely how they are. Adolescent thinking is characterized by hypothetical thought. The teenager might think hypothetically about what her/his life will be like if she/he stays close to home for college or goes far away. Sometimes this new capacity for thinking frustrates parents since teens are constantly trying out their new ideas of politics, education, and relationships, among other things. They may make judgments about morality, and they often challenge traditional ideas.

Adolescents are also capable of deductive reasoning, and this is one of the primary reasons that courses like geometry are taught in high school rather than earlier. Teens are able to reason about "if-then" statements. They can systematically solve problems by starting with a premise and testing hypotheses. Adolescent science projects often reflect their deductive thinking capabilities.

Adolescent thinking is also characterized by egocentric thoughts. Teens tend to overestimate their significance among friends and groups and to feel that other people are keenly interested in them. They may feel that they have an imaginary audience, as if everyone is watching them. This helps explain why teens will spend a large amount of time getting ready, choosing an outfit, or fixing their hair. Or a teen may not want to go to a particular store for fear that someone might see her/him, in spite of the fact that the person seeing her/him would also be in the store. With this elevated sense of importance, teens may imagine their lives as ultimately being magical and heroic. For example, a teen may feel that all violence is wrong regardless of the reason because all individuals are created equal and deserve respect. She may feel that if she could only tell the Secretary of the Department of Health and Human Services this, the secretary would understand this wrongdoing and change policies regarding violence in our country.

In general, adolescents become more aware during adolescence—of themselves, others, and their place in the world. The combination of egocentrism and thinking about possibilities, rather than only realities, makes adolescence a time where teens feel they have explored all rational solutions to a problem but have rarely done so. The egocentrism in their thinking and their abilities to make personal decisions impacts their ability to consistently make well-informed decisions.

A unique aspect of the developmental manifestations of child maltreatment during adolescence is that the effects of maltreatment may be the culmination of years of abuse and neglect or the effects of recent maltreatment. In some circumstances, abuse has been occurring for many years, but the consequences may seem more apparent and troublesome during adolescence. The following sections will examine developmental consequences of physical abuse, sexual abuse, and neglect from ages 12 to 18.

DEVELOPMENTAL CONSEQUENCES OF CHILD MALTREATMENT AMONG ADOLESCENTS

Children who have been maltreated have been shown to have a range of problems in adolescence that span all areas of development. Physical abuse, neglect, and sexual abuse, although related, have developmentally different manifestations in adolescence. Although delinquency, sexual activity and depression are found among nonmaltreated adolescents, the degree and severity seen among maltreated children is greater. This section attempts to delineate the effects of three types of maltreatment, but they are a challenge to discretely categorize. Children who experience sexual abuse, for example, often experience violence or neglect to a certain degree. Similarly, neither physical abuse nor sexual abuse occurs without some component of neglect or emotional/psychological unavailability from a caregiver. As a result, the manifestations of maltreatment may overlap among the categories and types of maltreatment. This discussion is also confounded by the fact that maltreatment may continue into adolescence while some manifestations of maltreatment may be the effect of recent trauma.

Physical Abuse

Physical abuse affects not only young children, but also adolescents. It is often thought that once children become stronger, bigger, and more capable to fight back that physical abuse will stop. However, recent estimates suggest that 32% of all child physical abuse reports are for children between the ages of 11 and 17 (USDHHS, 1998), and the highest rate of physical abuse occurs in females in the 12–15 age group (USDHHS, 2002). This section will describe the developmental consequences of the physical abuse of adolescents. It is impossible, at this point, to differentiate between those whose physical abuse began during adolescence and those who have endured years of maltreatment. Therefore, some manifestations will overlap with previous developmental periods.

Cognitive-behavioral

Physically abused children have shown elevated levels of depression and suicidal behavior in adolescence (Brown et al., 1999). Male adolescents maltreated during their teen years also show increased anger and more deviant beliefs (Brezina, 1998). Physically abused teens tend to have particular problems with violence and aggression (Lewis, Mallough, & Webb, 1989). They lack the social controls and coping skills to effectively deal with their abuse, and thus they often externalize the problem through aggression and delinquency. However, Pelcovitz et al. (1994) found that adolescents had high levels of internalizing. Commonly, physically abused adolescents have little tolerance for their own frustrations and have an impaired ability to regulate their emotions. Physically abused adolescents appear to have large amounts of life stress, personal stress and distress, without appropriate ways to manage them.

Physically abused adolescents also show less commitment to school (Brezina, 1998), attention problems, and poor school performance (Williamson, Borduin, & Howe, 1991). Physically abused children are more likely to be suspended from school due to behavioral problems such as skipping classes or dropping out altogether, while neglected children are more often expelled due to academic problems (Egeland, 1997). What is evident from physically abused teens' school performance is that it is characterized by overt behavioral problems and drawing attention to oneself. While the neglected child may "blend in," the physically abused child is the leader of the pack with delinquency, externalizing behavioral problems and poor school performance. Nonetheless, adolescents who have been physically abused have been shown to have deficits in receptive and expressive language, as well as difficulty with self-related language (McFayden & Kitson, 1996), which may impact their ability to perform well in school.

During adolescence, teens have greater cognitive capacity. They begin to think hypothetically albeit egocentrically on many levels. Physically abused adolescents may have internalized that power. Their aggression may be a manner in which to control others or to have them control you. With a lifetime of maltreatment, adolescents may not reach the formal operational stage of Piaget's developmental theory, and therefore they may lack the ability to problem solve in such a way to imagine a better future and create a plan for achieving it.

Physical abuse has also been linked with various psychological diagnoses and problems. One of the potential consequences of physical abuse is post-traumatic stress disorder (Famularo, Kinscherff, & Fenton, 1990), which may involve recurrent memories, flashbacks, and fears associated with one's abuse. Physical abuse has also been associated with depression (Flisher et al., 1997; Pelcovitz et al., 1994) and borderline personality disorder (Famularo, Kinscherff, & Fenton, 1991) in adolescence. Other psychological correlates of physical abuse include conduct disorder, oppositional defiant disorder (Famularo et al., 1992), various anxiety disorders, and agoraphobia (Flisher et al., 1994). Adolescents may also experience suicidal ideations and attempt suicide (Riggs, Alario, & McHorney, 1990). These behaviors may extend into adulthood (Silverman, Reinherz, & Giaconia, 1996).

Socioemotional

Children who have been physically abused have been shown to use drugs and alcohol (Cavaiola & Schiff, 1988) and to get into trouble as result of their use (Egeland, 1997). Abused adolescents not only use drugs, drink alcohol, and smoke cigarettes (Kaplan et al., 1998), they also engage in antisocial and violent acts (Herrenkohl, Egolf, & Herrenkohl, 1997; Lewis et al., 1989), delinquency (Walker, Downey, & Bergman, 1989), and even risky sexual behavior (Herrenkohl et al., 1998). There seems to be an antisocial aspect of the physically abused child's substance use that is not seen among other maltreated children. For instance, neglected children also use drugs and alcohol, but they seem to abstain from the deviant and antisocial aspects of drinking and drugs that physically abused children engage in.

Adolescents who were maltreated as teens also exhibit low levels of parental attachment (Brezina, 1998). Attachment patterns are relatively stable over a lifetime, and therefore it is not surprising that maltreated teens report low attachment to parents.

Evidence also suggests that child physical abuse is associated with dating violence, both as a perpetrator and victim (Marshall & Rose, 1990). Research has shown a relationship among physical abuse and high coercive dating patterns (Wolfe et al., 1998). Dating and the development of romantic relationships is an integral part of adolescent development. When an individual has been physically abused and shown that physical power is a way to control another or to coerce compliance with individual goals, they may act out similar, aggressive roles in romantic relationships. Exploring dating patterns and behaviors of maltreated adolescents is of great importance because maltreated children are at increased risk of becoming victims or victimizers as intimate relationships develop (Wolfe, Wekerle, & Scott, 1997).

The use of physical punishment in childhood has been shown to be positively correlated with behavior problems and aggression (Egeland, 1997). Strauss (1995) found that physical punishment in childhood is related to aggression and other behavioral problems in adolescence, and Herrenkohl, Egolf, and Herrenkohl (1997) found that severe physical discipline in the preschool years was strongly related to assaultive behavior in adolescence. Specifically, the more severe the physical discipline in the preschool years, the higher the level of physical assault in adolescence. Males have been found to be more assaultive than females (Herrenkohl et al., 1997).

Children who have been physically abused also show high rates of delinquency in adolescence (Egeland, 1997; Brezina, 1998; Walker, Downey, & Bergman, 1989). Abused adolescents show higher rates of delinquency even when compared to teens in poverty and those in the general population (Kratcoski, 1984). Severe discipline and negative mother-child interaction are related to more aggressive behavior in adolescence (Herrenkohl, Egolf, & Herrenkohl, 1997). Adolescent aggression can be partially explained, by the internalization of physical punishment to meet personal needs.

Adolescents who have been physically abused also express anger toward themselves, but they often act on it in an external manner. They have difficulty expressing or feeling empathy and may attempt suicide (Riggs, Alario, & McHorney, 1990). One important aspect of socioemotional development in adolescence is identity; adolescents explore a variety of self-chosen identities before deciding on one. Adolescents who have been abused may try on the roles of perpetrator or perhaps have decided upon the role of victim after a lifetime of being abused.

Physical

Overall, adolescents who have been physically abused often complain of physical health problems. Abuse that occurs prior to adolescence may result in the early onset of puberty due to endocrine secretions (Finkelhor, 1995). On the other hand, evidence suggests that emotional and physical stress may result in delayed puberty (DeBellis & Putnam, 1995). As with other age groups who have been physically abused, abused adolescents may have burns, abdominal injuries, punching or kicking wounds, organ ruptures, and fractures, to name a few. They may not want to participate in sports or change in a locker room where their injuries will be apparent. In general, adolescents are physically capable of playing complex sports and activities, but physically abused children may have either new or old injuries that prevent them from performing at the level of their peers.

The decision to engage in sexual intercourse is both a social and physical decision among teenagers. Emotional aspects involve the evolution of romantic and intimate relationships, while physical consequences may include sexually transmitted diseases and pregnancy. Herrenkohl et al. (1998) found a strong relationship between a history of physical abuse and teenage parenthood. The strongest relationship between maltreatment and teenage parenthood exists among teens who were both neglected and physically abused during early childhood. Teenage parents who were abused in early childhood have also been shown to be less happy and have less self-respect (Herrenkohl et al., 1998).

Neglect

Neglect is most often identified among young children, but it occurs in adolescence as well. The most recent available data suggest that 4.9 males and 6.2 females between 12 and 15, and 2.3 males and 3.5 females between 16 and 17 were victims of neglect per 1,000 children in the population (USDHHS, 2002). Neglect is chronic rather than episodic; it also involves a lack of emotional care rather than mere physical care. As a result, neglect continues into adolescence and the consequences can be the culmination of years of emotional and physical deprivation.

Cognitive-Behavioral

Neglected children do poorer in school than either physically abused or sexually abused children (Egeland, 1997). Egeland also found that socioeconomic status was related to academic performance, and the relationship between neglect and SES has been noted. If neglect has been occurring for some time, the intellectual delays will be obvious as the child enters adolescence. The adolescent may be in special education courses. A neglected adolescent may also have lower overall intelligence levels, low achievement scores (Erickson & Egeland, 2002), and difficulty with problem solving. While problem solving is a critical task for each developmental period, the range of choices adolescents are faced with allows them to expand their critical thinking abilities, which becomes increasingly important as they enter adulthood.

In contrast to the behavioral problems seen in physically abused children, teens who have been neglected are more often expelled from school due to academic failure (Egeland, 1997; Erickson & Egeland, 2002). In general, children who have been neglected do less well academically than any other maltreatment group (Eckenrode, Laird, & Doris, 1993; Egeland, 1997). An impoverished environment that lacks social, cognitive, and physical stimulation paves the way for developmental delay. As a result academic failure is often seen among neglected teens; they drop out of school, are expelled, or lack the skill to complete school (Erickson & Egeland, 2002). Certainly this has long-term consequences for neglected adolescents as they enter adulthood and are given the responsibility of obtaining a job, raising a family, and positively contributing to society.

Adolescents who have been neglected may also lack coping and problem-solving skills. When confronted with a difficult situation or choice, the adolescent may appear confused. They may not have the coping skills to deal with issues that arise during adolescence or the forethought to plan for acceptable solutions. One characteristic of neglectful families is that they are often chaotic and lack family leadership and cohesion (Gaudin et al., 1996). Families help shape the way that we deal with problems and how we approach problem solving and planning. Children who have been neglected may have learned that not coping is an effective way to manage their life—for example ignoring the problem or failing to recognize the implications of compliance. One example applicable to a teenager is obtaining a job. In order to obtain a job, one must find a job opening, get an application, complete an application, return the application, interview, and follow- up. These several steps may be overwhelming because they require forethought and planning. Once an individual gets a job, she/he may have difficulty showing up for work on time and diligently working while there. Such issues seem mundane to many, but to a person with intellectual deficits and lack of adult direction, they seem tremendous. Similarly, the consequences of failing to do any of the aforementioned tasks is either not getting a job or getting fired for absences or poor work. As the adolescent ages and is faced with more adult decisions, such as paying bills and rent and buying food for one's family, the consequences become even more tremendous and add increasing amounts of stress to the family.

Socioemotional

Children who have been neglected show heavy alcohol (Erickson & Egeland, 2002) and drug use in adolescence (Egeland, 1997), but they rarely get in trouble for their substance use. This is interesting because physically abused children also use substances but get into more trouble and seem to exhibit antisocial behavior patterns in their use. Similar to physically abused and sexually abused children, neglected teens also have been shown to have social and emotional problems (Kempe & Kempe, 1978), including juvenile delinquency and arrest (Widom & Maxfield, 2001). In fact, Widom and Maxfield found that being abused or neglected as a child increased the likelihood of juvenile arrest by 59%.

Compared to other forms of maltreatment, teens whose parents psychologically neglected them were more likely to have attempted suicide (Erickson & Egeland, 2002; Egeland, 1997). Brown et al. (1999) found adolescent victims of neglect also had high rates of depression and suicidal behavior, although she found that sexually abused teens had the highest risk of depression and suicide.

The development of an identity is a primary task in adolescence. Neglected adolescents may appear apathetic and indifferent to this exploration. They may fail to explore alternative identities or settle on one quickly they often socially withdraw and isolate themselves (Hildyard & Wolfe, 2002). They may feel that they are worthless and have difficulty developing a plan for self-exploration or even the desire to do so.

Adolescents who have been neglected may have serious social and interpersonal difficulties. Neglected adolescents tend to engage in more antisocial behaviors and have low levels of social interaction. In social interactions the neglected adolescent may appear withdrawn and avoidant of peer interactions (Kaufman & Cicchetti, 1989). On the other hand, their behavior may be defiant and hostile and physically aggressive (Kempe & Kempe, 1978) in interpersonal relationships and in their own families.

Physical

Adolescents who have experienced neglect may continue to fall behind in physical development. The effects of neglect during adolescence are often the result of years of neglect. The adolescent may not have the coordination and skill to participate in sports as skillfully as other teens. Puberty may be delayed because of physical and emotional stress (DeBellis & Putnam, 1994). They may appear dirty and smell. The neglected adolescent may not have learned the self-care skills they are now expected to perform, which has implications for social relationships.

The decision to have a sexual relationship can also affect neglected teens. Experiencing neglect and both physical abuse and neglect together increases the risk of parenthood in both males and females in adolescence (Herrenkohl et al., 1998). Adolescent parents who have experienced only neglect in their childhood fail to show a decrease in happiness or self-respect, but teen parents who have experienced both abuse and neglect and physical abuse alone experience a decrease (Herrenkohl et al., 1998).

Sexual Abuse

The effects of the sexual abuse among teens are seen across developmental domains. Sexual abuse is different from physical abuse and neglect because more females are identified as victims of sexual abuse, whereas rates for physical abuse and neglect remain relatively similar (USDHHS, 2002). The median age of victimization for sexual abuse is 11 for girls and 8 for boys (USDHHS, 2002). Some sexual abuse victims manifest few consequences to their abuse, while for others their problems seem pervasive. Some victims need intensive treatment, while others need no treatment at all (Hecht et al., 2002).

What complicates the assessment of sexual abuse in adolescents is the tremendous sexual maturation that occurs during this time. It is often difficult to differentiate between normal sexual behavior and behavior that would indicate sexual victimization. Even though an adolescent may have consensual sexual contact with a peer, she/he may still experience sexual abuse at home. The difficulty lies in identifying the forensic evidence of sexual intercourse or contact, when the teen is both having consensual sex and also being forced into sex. Similarly, adolescents are sometimes blamed for their victimization by wearing provocative clothing or having consensual sexual relationships with multiple partners. What becomes complicated is not only assessment and understanding, but the adolescent's own understanding of her/his victimization. When a person has been repeatedly victimized by a supposedly trusted person, she/he may transfer that sense of powerlessness to peer and consensual relationships. On the other hand, sexually abused adolescents may learn to use sex as a bargaining tool, especially if they had engaged in forced prostitution or if their perpetrator would reward them with a gift or money after he/she had sexually abused them. At any rate, differences appear in the effects of sexual abuse of adolescents compared to younger children (Chaffin et al., 1996).

Cognitive-Behavioral

Teens who have been sexually abused may exhibit signs of anxiety, social withdrawal, poor attention (Egeland, 1997), aggressive behavior (Herrenkohl, Egolf, & Herrenkohl, 1997), and depression (Beitchman et al., 1992; Brown et al., 1999). They may have nightmares and obsessions; they may express frustration and hostility towards peer, themselves, and family members. Adolescents often disclose their abuse when they are angry, and do so intentionally as a result of their pent-up frustrations and hostility, rather than the accidental disclosure seen among younger children (Sorenson & Snow, 1991). The consequences of sexual abuse do not always manifest immediately, and often the onset of puberty may bring behavioral expressions of previous victimization.

Teens that have been sexually abused may also have a range of school problems (Runtz & Briere, 1986). Peer conflict, falling grades, poor concentration, and learning difficulties have been shown to be correlated with sexual abuse in adolescents (Miller-Perrin & Perrin, 1999). Truancy and delinquency have also been linked with previous sexual abuse (Browne & Finkelhor, 1986).

Adolescents who have been sexually abused may also self-mutilate. They might mutilate their bodies by cutting, carving, scratching, picking, or branding in an attempt to overcome the overwhelming feelings of being victimized. The purpose of self-mutilation is to reduce psychological and physiological pain; it allows a person to cope with her/his feelings, although the coping is maladaptive. Often, abused and neglected persons do not have appropriate ways to cope with the tremendous pain or guilt they feel from their victimization. One way to release the tension is to injure oneself, which provides immediate emotional relief to the unwanted emotion.

The behavior of sexually abused adolescents can also be overtly sexual, as is apparent across developmental stages (Mannarino & Cohen, 1996). In general, children and teens exhibit increased sexual behaviors, as well as more sexual problems, than nonabused children (Friedrich et al., 2001). While knowledge of sex is more acceptable in adolescence than in previous developmental stages, adolescents who have been sexually abused may be preoccupied with sex and have extensive sexual knowledge. Their language and behavior may be overtly sexual; and they may be promiscuous or engage in prostitution. An adolescent's promiscuity and possible prostitution are manifestations of their abuse, although many times such teens are interrogated as if their abuse and its consequences are their fault because of such behaviors.

It is important to differentiate between consensual intercourse and sexual abuse. Teens may be victimized by peers or engage in sexual relationships haphazardly. Consequences of promiscuous behavior include pregnancy and STD during adolescence. In the case of teen pregnancy, the child may also experience long-term consequences. Children of teen parents do less well than children born to older mothers, having low academic achievement and negative social behavior (Berk, 1999).

Adolescents who have been sexually abused may exhibit symptoms of posttraumatic stress disorder (PTSD), which is consistent with the symptoms and diagnoses of PSTD seen in younger children (Dubner & Motta, 1999; Ruggerio, McLeer, & Dixon, 2002). Common symptoms include reexperiencing the traumatic event with flashbacks, nightmares, and intrusive thoughts. They may appear to dissociate or disengage as a means of distancing themselves from the traumatic event. Dissociation allows an individual to become numb and to avoid the existence of sexual victimization. Sometimes dissociation can manifest in amnesia for the event where the individual cannot remember the traumatic event(s) at all, but this is most often with lengthy, chronic, violent, and earlyonset abuse (Briere & Conte, 1993). Individuals who cope in this way are often difficult in treatment. Adolescents and adults may cope with sexual abuse in both internal and external ways. For example, an adolescent may internalize her/his abuse with depressive symptoms and anxiety, and also externalize its aftermath through difficult interpersonal relationships, behavioral problems, academic problems, and promiscuity.

Socioemotional

Juvenile delinquency has been associated with prior sexual abuse (Egeland, 1997), including running away from home (Hibbard, Ingersoll, & Orr, 1990). Sexually abused adolescents also self-report more emotional and behavioral problems than nonabused teens (Hibbard, Ingersoll, & Orr, 1990). While all forms of maltreatment have been shown to be related to psychopathology in adolescence, anxiety and depression have been shown to be related to sexual abuse (Egeland, 1997).

Compared to teens who have been physically abused or neglected, sexually abused adolescents have the highest rates of depression (Gidyca & Koss, 1989) and suicide (Brown et al., 1999). The intent of the suicidal adolescent needs to be fully explored during assessment, because research has shown adolescents with a history of sexual abuse to be eight times more likely to repeat suicide attempts (ibid.). Like other aged victims, adolescent victims often have guilt around their victimization—feeling as if they were involved and in some way are responsible for their abuse.

Some children who have been sexually abused may become offenders in adolescence. However, in a review of sexual abuse histories of offenders, Hanson and Slater (1988) found that only 20–30% of offenders self-report being victimized as children themselves. There are several explanations for why a relationship exists between prior sexual abuse and the sexual abuse of others. One explanation is that individuals who have been sexually abused may regain their own powerlessness in their victimization by victimizing others. Social learning theory also provides another explanation, where the victim learns through her/his own experience to use others for their own gratification (Laws & Marshall, 1990). Other explanations include feelings of inadequacy that may lead to abusive behaviors (Chaffin, Letorneau, & Silovksy, 2002). Such explanations attempt to explain the cognitive processes that precede victimization and the lowering of inhibitions that make sexual victimization possible. It is important to reiterate, however, that not all victims become offenders; in fact, the overwhelming majority of persons who have been sexually abused fail to become sex offenders.

Adolescent girls who have been sexually abused also show increased risk of developing eating disorders, including bulimia, anorexia nervosa, and overeating, and are especially prone to develop bulimia (Hibbard, Ingersoll, & Orr, 1990). Sexual victimization takes away control for the victim; it makes them powerless in the sexually abusive situation. Some teens attempt to control their bodies through binging and purging; others through self-starvation. The ability to decide to eat or not allows one a tremendous amount of control, albeit unhealthy control. Others may overeat in response to the residual or current stress of the abuse. Some overeat in an attempt to make themselves appear less sexually attractive, hoping to deter the sexual advances of others.

Other adolescent victims may self-medicate through alcohol and drug use (Hibbard, Ingersoll, & Orr, 1990; Kelley, Thornberry, & Smith, 1997; Kilpatrick et al., 2000). The combination of alcohol or drugs and sexual promiscuity create a dangerous situation for adolescent victims of sexual abuse, and, in fact, for all teens. Research suggests that sexually abused adolescents perceive great benefits from substances which may lead to increased usage (Singer et al., 1994). An adolescent victim may use drugs/alcohol to feel numb and to feel like a "normal" teenager, and in such circumstances safe sex often goes wayward.

During adolescence, peer relationships take on important functions. Teens tend to spend more time with their peers than their parents, and the nature of their peer relationships change. Concepts such as loyalty become important; adolescents share personal feelings with one another to nurture a closeness and sense of commitment. Similarly, romantic relationships begin to develop. Thus, the onset of puberty, sexual maturation, and changes in friendships impact an individual's social and physical world. Adolescents who have been sexually victimized may have difficulty in friendships and relationships, because even as children they are often less trusting and perceive themselves as different than their peers (Mannarino, Cohen, & Berman, 1994). When a trusted person has victimized the individual, she/he may have great difficulty forming secure relationships. The presence of friendships generally helps mediate common adolescent problems (e.g., problems with friends, romantic partners, school), but adolescent victims may not have emotionally safe friendships to serve as a buffer for stress. On the other hand, the adolescent may use sex as a means of gaining access to a group of peers. Sometimes sexual promiscuity can further alienate the teen from a social group because she/he becomes labeled as a "slut" or "whore."

In addition, adolescents who have been sexually abused may prematurely adopt a sexual identity; an adolescent who is sexually abused may feel stigmatized from her/his sexual victimization and lack the energy to fully explore identity alternatives. Adolescents may perceive that they have limited identity options available to them, and their primary way of relating to individuals may be sexually.

Physical

Adolescents who have experienced sexual abuse may complain of a host of physical complaints, including stomachache and headache. They may have problems walking, sitting and sleeping; and they may have genital pain. With the onset of puberty, the adolescent may become pregnant; she may have chronic genital pain, itching, and odors. Other physical signs may include blood on hair or clothing, vaginal bleeding, and rectal bleeding. A parent may notice blood while doing laundry, the "disappearance" of clothing, or even excessive secrecy with respect to undergarments. Adolescents who have been sexually abused may experience painful urination or bowel movements. Other manifestations include swollen genitals, vaginal or penile discharge, and penile infection. An adolescent may develop sexually transmitted diseases (STDs) or have chronic STDs. Common STDs associated with sexual abuse include gonorrhea, syphilis, chlamydia, trachamatis, HIV infection, herpes, venereal warts, vaginitis, and pubic lice (Sattler, 1998); just as many are common with sexual activity alone. However, some children who have been sexually abused show no physical consequences.

One irrefutable consequence of sexual intercourse and sexual abuse is pregnancy. Children who have been maltreated are more likely to become pregnant in adolescence (Kelley, Thornberry, & Smith, 1997). Teen pregnancy has been found to delay vocational and educational goals on an average of three years (Klepinger et al., 1995). Pecora et al. (1992) report that the chances of an additional conception within the next two years ranges from 30 to 40%. The cognitive dissociation between sexual abuse and pregnancy can also be seen in circumstances where a girl is impregnated by her abuser. An adolescent, even faced with DNA results showing an abuser as the father, may insist that her boyfriend is the father. Similarly, if an adolescent becomes pregnant by an offender, she may deny that she is pregnant and fail to receive prenatal care. DNA evidence, however, can determine paternity in case of adolescent sexual abuse.

Pregnancy by a family member or offender has long-lasting effects on both the family and child. First, the family system is disrupted by irrefutable evidence of the child; if a family attempted to keep the abuse a secret, it is likely that other family members, friends, and neighbors will notice both the pregnancy and possible resemblance to the offender. The emotional consequences of unwanted pregnancy in adolescence, especially by an offender or family member, can be tremendous. Attachment can be impeded by a variety of factors, including the attributes of the child, parent, and conception. If the child resembles the offender, attachment can be negatively affected (see chapter 2). If the parent has dislike for the child before the child is born because of the circumstance of conception, attachment will be affected. Similarly, the adolescent mother has her own developmental issues and has experienced repeated sexual trauma, and this alone can affect her ability to parent her child. The consequences of an impaired attachment have already been discussed, and the long-term effects without intervention can be devastating. Additionally, even if the child is removed from the home and placed with a family member, the family member may experience similar feelings toward the child who was produced from incest or from sexual abuse.

CONCLUSION

This chapter has focused on the developmental consequences of physical abuse, neglect, and sexual abuse in adolescents from 12 to 18 years of age. However, many of the manifestations continue into adulthood, affecting adult relationships, work, and social circles. Adolescents are entering a period of their lives where they experience physical, mental, and sexual changes. They are capable of hypothetical and analytic thought; they are developing more intimate friendships and romantic and sexual relationships. The peer group becomes more important and teens spend more time away from their families with friends, while also gaining independence and self-understanding. As this chapter has demonstrated, adolescent victims of maltreatment have academic problems, experiencing both cognitive and intellectual deficits. Adolescent victims of maltreatment also have difficult interpersonal relationships, which may affect their ability to nurture romantic relationship with peers. Delinquent acts are often seen among maltreated adolescents, as well as increased likelihood of alcohol or drug use. Long-term consequences of victimization may result in pregnancy, STDs, or revictimization. The effects are tremendous to a development period that is the entryway into adulthood.

10

ADOLESCENCE

Ecological and Developmental Assessment of Maltreatment and Intervention

In this chapter we will focus on the assessment of child maltreatment and intervention needs for children 12 to 18 years of age. Youth today must master a complexity of skills and confront such a diverse group of choices that adolescence lasts over a decade of their life. Families also experience different challenges during a child's adolescent development. They are faced with the child going through puberty to develop full-grown bodies and sexual maturity. Youth are confronted with developing more mature peer relationships of both genders and developing a construct of self. The end of adolescence is characterized as the attainment of emotional and economic independence. Children ages 12 to 18 are presented with many challenges and opportunities during this stage and often struggle in managing day-to-day life. Adolescence presents enough of a challenge in a person's life without the added implications of child maltreatment.

Although the risk of maltreatment declines as the child gets older, adolescents are still at risk. Adolescents represent about 1 in 5 victims of child maltreatment (Thomlison, 1997). The highest physical abuse rates for girls occur during this developmental period, between the ages of 12 and 15, with 32% of all physical abuse reports being for children between 11 and 17 (USDHHS, 2000). The greatest risk of sexual abuse occurs between the ages of 7 and 13 (Finkelhor, 1994), and the highest risk for first experience of sexual abuse peaks between 11 and 13 years of age (Bolen, 1998; Russell, 1983). Additionally, children who have been victims of child maltreatment are more likely to experience recurrence based on the type of maltreatment, services offered, age of occurrence, race/ethnicity, and the identity of the perpetrator (USDHHS, 2000).

Many adolescents may have experienced child maltreatment during early or middle childhood and have never come to the attention of child welfare. Others may be experiencing physical abuse, sexual abuse, or neglect for the first time. Given the tremendous developmental gains across all domains, the adolescent often is in a place where she/he finally feels safe in disclosing the occurrence of child maltreatment in their life.

It is often in adolescence that the effects of child maltreatment manifest in a way that puts the youth in peril, including depression, suicide, substance abuse, criminal acts, self-mutilation, and pregnancy. These manifestations may be a result of ongoing child maltreatment or the effects of early maltreatment on current development. The knowledge of understanding normal adolescent development presented in chapter 9 will assist the practitioner in making sound assessments of child maltreatment and in making critical intervention decisions. The array of ecological risk and protective factors associated with child maltreatment and adolescent development are presented as another means of supporting the assessment and intervention for youth and their caregivers.

RISK AND PROTECTIVE FACTORS

As a review, please see Tables 10.1 and 10.2 and keep in mind that the preceding discussions in chapter 4, 6, and 8 are relevant to the assessment of children ages 12 to 18. Many of the same considerations concerning risk and protective factors need to be incorporated into the assessment. Again, the child may be coming to the attention of a professional for the first time, and the assessment should rely on each system level and all the possible factors indicative of child maltreatment currently or in earlier stages of the child's life.

Ontogenic Level

Previously we indicated that parents who were physically abused, sexually abused, or neglected by their caregivers were identified as more likely to maltreat their own child (Boyer & Fine, 1992; Cantrell et al., 1990; Gelles & Straus; 1987; Haynes et al., 1984; Herrenkohl, Herrenkohl, & Toedter, 1983; Pianta, Egeland, & Erickson, 1989; Straus, 1983; 1994; Whipple & Webster-Stratton, 1991). The intergenerational cycle of child maltreatment is far from confirmed, but it is a contributing factor in the multifaceted assessment presented in this book given that 30% to 40% of parents who experience maltreatment as a child will maltreat their own child (Kaufman & Zigler, 1987; Pianta et al., 1989). Additionally, maltreatment of children is a major contributing factor of attachment disorder (Levy & Orlans, 1998). The caregiver's developmental and attachment history is a critical area for consideration. Prior discussion focused on the parent's own attachment experiences as a child, how they were reared, and the influence this has on their own parenting abilities, thoughts, values, and practices. When you are assessing an adolescent, the parent's early childhood attachment is an important area of evaluation, but in addition the assessment should focus on other historical components of the parent's life related to rearing an adolescent child.

A parent's perception of her/his own history of care and attachment is related to the increase or decrease in risk of the parent maltreating her/his child. Child physical abuse and neglect have been associated with a caregiver who has a distorted perception of her/his own care (Crittenden, 1988).

Table 10.1 Risk Factors

	Infant and Toddler	Early Childhood	Middle Childhood	Adolescence
Parental				
Ontogenic	• Parent experienced child maltreatment as a child	• Parent experienced poor parenting during early childhood • Attachment issues	• Poor adaptation to school • Lack of integration into peer group • Sexually abused as a child • Confused patterns of attachment with mother	• Parent's own perception of their history of care and attachment
Microsystem				
Child	• Age itself • Born prematurely • Physical or mental disability • Infant tests positive for AOD • Race	• Excessive health or medical problems • Developmental delays	• Age • Oppositional or problem behaviors • Inappropriate sexual behaviors • Gender • Low self-esteem • Depression • External locus of control • Introverted	• Gender • Age • Pregnancy • Aggressive/hostile behavior • Cruelty to animals • Runaway behavior • Withdrawal from social relationships • Truancy • Delinquent-type behaviors • Poor peer relationships • Fire setting • Eating disorders • Alcohol and other drug use • Depressive symptoms • Suicidal behavior • PTSD • Increased sexual behaviors

Parent	• Not satisfied with the child • Does not enjoy parenting • Young parent • Not understanding role as caregiver • Lack of knowledge of child development • Substance abuse	• Perceptions of child • Inappropriate child expectations around development • Lower educational level • Authoritarian • Substance abuse • Depression • Aggressive behavior	• Depression • Withdrawal • Anger • Aggression • Antisocial personality • Obsessive-compulsive disorder • Serious mental illness • Paternal psychopathology • Low self-esteem • Poor self-concept • Negative perception of own identity • Loneliness • Lack of impulse control • Cognitive deficits and distortions • Unemployed • Substance abuser	• Certain parenting styles • Cognitive distortions and misperception • Not the birth parent • Substance abuse • Father with record of arrest • Four factors associated with risk of sexual abuse
Family	• Poverty • Stress in family environment • Interpersonal conflict between partners • Single parent	• Coercive child-rearing practices • Little positive interactions • Family lacks leadership, closeness, and negotiation skills	• Poor communication • Lack of emotional closeness • Social isolation • Disorganized • Less cohesive • Stepfather in the home • Victim not close to mother • No physical affection from father • Low income • Family isolation	• Lack emotional closeness • Lack of supervision by nonoffending parent • Mother not physically or psychologically available • Father experiencing unemployment • Role-reversal behavior • Poor marital history • Separation or divorce • Family isolation

(continued)

Table 10.1 continued

	Infant and Toddler	Early Childhood	Middle Childhood	Adolescence
			• Patriarchal family • Unemployment • Hostility between partners • Father-only homes	• More children in the home • Violence between partners • Abuse of animals • Multiple stressful life events • Poor living conditions • Disorganized
Exosystem	• Lack of social support	• Caring individual in the child's life • Neighborhood lacks both informal and formal social supports • Living in a violent community • Lack connection with community	• Social supports • Neighborhood that lacks resources • Fathers who do not access family social supports	• Lack of social network • Lack of extended family • Fewer peer relationships • Communities with high levels of violence
Macrosystem	• Cultural values that support violence • Attitudes toward how mothers should behave as a parent	• Culturally promoted attitudes and behaviors about parental rights to physically punish	• Stereotype of male dominance in sexual relationships • Social tolerance for sexual interest in children • Barriers to women's equality • Denial by society that sexual abuse exists	• Patriarchal system • Male entitlement • Sex role stereotypes • Social tolerance for objectification of children • Religion and law sanctioning of sexual interaction

Table 10.2 Protective Factors

	Infant and Toddler	Early Childhood	Middle Childhood	Adolescence
Parental Ontogenic	• Parent experienced secure attachment	• Parent experienced appropriate parenting during their early childhood • Continued to be securely attached to caregiver	• Successful in school • Developed peer group • Secure attachment	• Loving, supportive person in childhood • Therapeutic intervention • Integration of maltreatment experience
Microsystem Child	• Temperament • Goodness of fit with the parent	• Competent behavior • Positive temperament • Child is perceived as affectionate • Child is perceived to have high cognitive ability	• Competent behavior • Competent social and cognitive abilities • Positive self-esteem • Easy temperament	• Did not experience maltreatment in earlier stages • Developmentally competent • Sense of belonging and attachment • Social and cognitive competency
Parent	• Secure attachment as a child	• Adequate knowledge of preschool child development • Adequate developmental expectation of the child • Quality child-rearing conditions	• Adequate knowledge of middle childhood development • Adequate knowledge around home management	• Normal range on measures of behavior, social competence, and self-esteem • Psychological well-being • Success in other areas of life
Family	• Supportive significant other in the home	• Mothers who are happy with their partner relationship • Structured, consistent daily routine • Presence of father or father figure	• Brothers and sisters • Caregivers are emotionally supportive	• Mother is emotional available • Mothers who do not work outside of the home • Brother and sisters in the home • Less stressful home environments • Economic security

(continued)

Table 10.2 continued

	Infant and Toddler	Early Childhood	Middle Childhood	Adolescence
Exosystem	• Adequate formal and informal social support	• Adequate formal and informal social support • Living in a nonviolent community • Connections with the community	• Strong social networks • Family social supports • Well-resourced neighbor-hoods • Family's perception of neighborhood is positive	• Social support • Nonviolent communities • Neighborhoods that have well-being • High level of employment • High levels of resources
Macrosystem	• Cultural value of protecting children	• Culture that promotes nonphysical forms of punishment	• Society that acknowledges the magnitude of sexual abuse • Value equality of the sexes • No tolerance for the exploitation of children	• Society that does not objectify children as sexual

Factors that may potentially contribute to risk of maltreatment or protection in relation to the early attachment and development of the parent may include relationship with her/his own parents, history of maltreatment, foster care or adoption history, relationship with siblings and peers, violence in her/his home or her/his environment, and history of adolescent pregnancy.

Erickson and Egeland (2002) assert that four factors have been found empirically to distinguish parents who have had a history of abuse but do not go on to maltreat their own child. As discussed earlier, this is what is known as resilience, or strengths found in the ecology contributing to adaptive outcomes for persons experiencing adversity. They are as follows:

1. During their childhood they had a loving, supportive person that gave them a different view of themselves and others.
2. When they had a child they also had a supportive partner.
3. They experienced a therapeutic intervention that enabled them to resolve earlier issues.
4. They achieved an integration of the maltreatment experience into a coherent view of self.

Microsystem Level

The child developing an identity separate from the family and moving toward independence defines adolescence. Parental and family factors, as well as the child's own characteristics, still have bearing on the potential for occurrence of maltreatment in a family. Risk and protective factors are related to how maltreatment manifests in an adolescent and factors relevant to the circumstances of maltreatment during this development period.

Parental (Caregiver) Characteristics

Thus far we have covered a multitude of parental risk and protective factors that are associated with the likelihood of child maltreatment occurring within a family. It is critical in the assessment of an adolescent suspected to have been maltreated by her/his caregiver that the practitioner take the culmination of factors across all systems into account when making a disposition. The following factors should be considered along with all others.

RISK FACTORS   The parent's own developmental level is an important factor in how the parent behaves toward his/her own adolescent (Aber & Zigler, 1981). In many ways this is related to the ontogenic level and the parent's own history of care. Parenting styles that are characterized by stress, anger, hostility, depression, and isolation are related to an increased risk of child maltreatment (Kinard, 1995; Pianta et al., 1989; Whipple & Webster-Stratton, 1991; Wolfe, 1994). An authoritarian parenting style taken to the extreme is related to abusive behavior (Wolfe, 1999). This style is distinguished by insensitivity to the adolescent's level of ability, interest, or needs. It relies heavily on coercion, and the parent sees her/his authority as paramount. Any attempt by the child to challenge this authority is suppressed, often through hostile punishment.

As discussed earlier, child maltreatment is associated with caregivers who present with a number of cognitive distortions and misperceptions. Particularly during adolescence, when the youth is trying to establish her/his own identity contrary to the parent's expectations, parental cognitive processes may be associated with maltreatment. Caregivers may perceive their adolescent's behavior in a negative light and may view any transgression by the child as wrong, which may increase the likelihood of maltreatment (Azar & Siegel, 1990; Caselles & Milner, 2000).

Caregivers who are not the birth parent and are younger are more likely to maltreat their child (Bolen, 2001; Milner, 1998).

Parental substance abuse remains a risk factor during adolescence, as it has been associated with the majority of reported maltreatment cases across all age groups (McAlphine, Marshall, & Doran, 2001; Rittner & Dozier, 2000; USDHHS, 2001). Alcohol use in the family was also found to be related to increased risk of sexual abuse for adolescents (Bolen, 2001). In earlier chapters we indicated that substance abuse placed the child at risk because of how the alcohol or other drugs compromised parenting. Earlier discussion focused on how substance abuse contributes to lower frustration tolerance, interferes with parental judgment, and makes the acquisition of drugs the sole objective of the parent, all of which may increase child maltreatment in early stages of development as well as during the teenage years (Kelley, 2002). During the adolescent years substance abuse may serve as a vehicle of disinhibition for either inappropriate sexual behavior toward the child or acting out violently.

Fathers with a history of alcohol and other drug abuse, along with a record of arrest or convictions for nondomestic violence–related offenses, were more likely to both physically abuse their children and engage in domestic violence (Hartley, 2002).

In chapter 8 we discussed four preconditions that Finkelhor (1986) proposed must be present for a perpetrator to sexually abuse a child. Araji & Finkelhor (1986) also developed a multifactor model for understanding the etiology of sexually abusive acts with children. A number of caregiver risk factors can be grouped within these four factors associated with an increased possibility of sexual abuse. They are:

1. Emotional congruence. A fit between the caregiver's emotional needs and the characteristics of the child. Risk factors associated with this are arrested psychosexual development, immaturity, low self-esteem, low self-efficacy in social relationships, and narcissistic identification with the child as the adult's self.
2. Sexual Arousal for Children. Risk factors associated with this are physiological arousal by child stimuli, early sexual experiences with children or child pornography, early sexual experiences with adults, and hormone levels or chromosomal makeup,

3. Blockage. Indicates caregiver's fixation at a particular developmental stage that leaves the caregiver incapable of progressing to mutually satisfying adult relationships (Ferrara, 2002). Risk factors associated with this are castration anxieties (access to adult sexual behavior is blocked), unassertive, inadequate social skills, timid, inhibited or moralistic, insecure, sexual anxiety, and problems relating to adult women.

4. Disinhibition. Caregiver is set free from any inhibitors against having sex with children. Risk factors related to this are poor impulse control, alcoholism and alcohol abuse, substance abuse, psychosis, unemployment, loss of love, death of a relative, step-parent role, and association with groups such as Men and Boys (NAMBLA).

PROTECTIVE FACTORS   Caregivers who function within normal ranges on measures of behavior, social competence, self-esteem, and self-efficacy serve as protective factors against child maltreatment (Thomlison, 1997). The higher the psychological well-being of the caregiver, the more protective processes are in place for the adolescent (Belsky & Vondra, 1989). Parental success in other areas of functioning, such as work and school, serves as a buffer to potential child maltreatment (Wolfe, 1999). Availability of cultural resources may also help protect.

Child Characteristics

RISK FACTORS   Exposure to child maltreatment has damaging consequences for many aspects of functioning in adolescence: physical, cognitive, social, emotional, behavioral, and academic (Kolko, 1996a). By this developmental period, youth may have experienced repeated exposure to maltreatment, which leads to more severe symptoms as children grow older (Crittenden, Claussen, & Sugarman, 1994; Levy & Orlans, 1998). These symptoms, along with the risk factors presented formerly and at the present, are the assessment areas requiring attention. Recall that there is great overlap in risk factors across types of abuse, and it is difficult to distinguish factors as related to specific forms of maltreatment.

Gender can be considered a risk factor for sexual abuse, girls being more likely to be sexually abused than boys (Bolen, 2001). This is increased in adolescence since the highest risk for being sexually abused peaks between ages 11 and 13 (Bolen, 1998; Russell, 1983). Older children also experience more negative outcomes from the sexual abuse experience (Berliner & Elliott, 2002). Both boys and girls are at increased risk of sexual abuse if at any time they have lived without one of their birth parents or have a mother who is unavailable (Finkelhor et al., 1990). Children with disabilities are much more likely to be sexually abused than children who do not have disabilities (NCCAN, 1993). Pregnancy, particularly for a child 15 years of age or younger, should be suspect for child sexual abuse (Boyer & Fine, 1992) as should a sexually transmitted disease. Other indications of an adolescent being maltreated can be derived from their behavior.

Behavioral deviance may place stressors on the parent-child relationship when the parent reacts aggressively to the child actions (Kolko, 2002), placing the child at increased risk of maltreatment. Youth who exhibit nervous, aggressive, hostile, or disruptive behavior toward adults, especially parents, may be experiencing maltreatment. Further behaviors that serve as indicators of abuse are cruelty to animals, self-injury, runaway behavior, withdrawal from social relationships, truancy, delinquent-type behaviors, poor peer relationships, fire setting, eating disorders, and alcohol and other drug abuse (AHA, 2002; Clark, Lesnick, & Hegedus, 1997; Cohen, Berliner, & March, 2000; Dembo et al., 1998; Faver & Strand, 2003; Grogan-Kaylor & Otis, 2003; Lynch & Cicchetti, 1998).

Based on both clinical and nonclinical samples of children who have been sexually abused, empirical data show that teenagers have higher rates of emotional and behavioral problems. These include depressive symptoms, more anxiety, lower self-esteem, suicidal behaviors, post-traumatic stress disorder symptoms, running away from home, drug use, bulimia, increased sexual behavior, less social competence, far less trusting of others, and cognitive impairment (Berliner & Elliott, 2002; Clark & Kirisci, 1996; Cohen, Berliner, & March, 2000; Lynch & Cicchetti, 1998).

PROTECTIVE FACTORS   Children who have not experienced child maltreatment in infancy, early, or middle childhood are at less risk of experiencing it in adolescence. The more developmentally competent the child is when first exposed to child maltreatment, the more likely he/she is to be able to cope with the stress (Garbarino et al., 1992).

Adolescents having a sense of belonging and attachment are known to function better across settings (Belsky & Vondra, 1989; Kolko, 2002), which may provide safety from the possibility of abuse. Social and cognitive competency also promotes a protective process (Kinard, 1995).

Family Characteristics

RISK FACTORS   In chapter 8, a number of family risk factors were presented related to the increased risk of child sexual abuse. There are additional family dynamics placing adolescents at risk. Lack of emotional closeness and problems of communication in the family are related to the increased risk of sexual abuse (Berliner & Elliott, 2002; Coohey, 1996). Mother not physically or psychologically available, lack of supervision by the nonoffending parent, children who sleep alone, and a father experiencing unemployment are all dynamics that may reduce the external inhibitors in a family allowing the perpetrator access to the child (Ferrara, 2002; Finkelhor, 1986).

Other strong predictors of sexual abuse in families are a role-reversal between the child and parent, poor marital history, separation or divorce, family isolation, low education status of mother, and father either unemployed or has a low job status (Pecora et al., 2000). The more children in the home, the more likely maltreatment will occur, especially physical and educational neglect (Wolfe, 1999).

Violence in the partner relationship is associated with child maltreatment (Hartley, 2002; Dubowitz, 1999; Edelson, 1999; Wolfe, 1999). If one type of violence is occurring, it is likely other forms of abuse are as well. This factor is of particular concern for children 12 to 18 years of age. A child in adolescence will be much more likely to intervene in a domestic violence situation than a younger, more vulnerable child. A teenager attempting to stop violence against her/his mother may be subject to injury.

Domestic violence presents additional risk for the family. Adolescent behavior problems and discipline disagreements between caregivers may escalate the cycle of violence in the home (Edelson et al., 1991). Partner violence adds additional stress and turmoil in the family and heightens the risk of continued abuse. Lack of marital satisfaction is associated with negativeness to children (Belsky & Vondra, 1989). Mothers who experience domestic violence are less likely to be able to meet their children's needs.

Another area of family behavior found to be directly related to the risk of child maltreatment and domestic violence is the abuse of animals (AHA, 2002; Ascione, 1998; Flynn, 2000). As reported by AHA (2002), a large percentage of families being treated for child maltreatment also abuse animals. Domestic violence shelters report a high percentage of women who indicate their batterer either threatened or harmed their animal, and/or their child abused an animal (Ascione, 1998; Flynn, 2000). Either the parent or the child may be the perpetrator of animal abuse. Parents use cruelty to animals as a means of controlling their child or partner. Children often act out their victimization and anger on the animal.

Families who are more likely to maltreat are characterized by more stressful life events, lack of parental involvement and responsivity to the child, and more disorganization (Pianta et al., 1989). Additionally, similar to our discussion of the impact poverty has on a family, experiencing poor living conditions such housing deficits has been identified as a risk factor for child maltreatment (Kotch et al., 1995; Pelton, 1994).

PROTECTIVE FACTORS   Mothers who are emotionally available to their children serve as a protective mechanism against child abuse and neglect (Cicchetti & Rogosch, 1997). Children whose mothers do not work outside of the home are less likely to be sexually abused, but mothers who work part-time increase the risk of sexual abuse more so than mothers who work full-time. Children who live with both natural parents are significantly less likely to be sexually abused (Bolen, 1998).

As in middle-childhood, brothers and sisters in the home provide support and help the adolescent cope with the stressors of maltreatment (Anthony & Cohler, 1987; Hegar, 1988). Additionally, less stressful home environments and economic security (i.e., having backup resources such as savings) is a protective factor for families (Kaufman & Zigler, 1992).

Exosystem Characteristic: Risk and Protective Factor

Evaluating the influence of the exosystem on the microsystem, in the context of the family culture, requires that the actual influence be explored. Much of the influence the exosystem has on the microsystem, as well as the ecological embeddedness, is the stress and pressure structures in the exosystem exerted on the family system, including family dysfunction (Cicchetti & Lynch, 1993). To the extent that

family stress is already high, parental developmental history can predispose negative parenting, especially when one couples those factors with exosystem influences
that increase the probability of child maltreatment (Cicchetti and Lynch, 1993).

Social isolation from other social networks and extended family is associated with
maltreatment (Corse, Schmid, & Trickett, 1990; Garbarino, 1982). Mothers who
commit physical abuse are shown to have fewer peer relationships, more difficulties with extended family, and less social contact within their community than
nonabusing mothers (Corse, Schmid, & Trickett, 1990). Less social contact results
in less conformity to social and community parenting standards (Garbarino, 1977).

Youth between the ages of 12 and 17 rely heavily on social support to meet
developmental needs, and social support has been found to directly affect both
mental health and academic outcomes (Colarossi & Eccles, 2003). Adolescents
who have a supportive, caring adult in their life are protected from a number of
risk factors (Kirby & Fraser, 1997). The adult does not have to be a relative but
may be a teacher, mentor, or social worker from their community. Through providing a model of prosocial behavior, emotional and instrumental assistance, and
access to knowledge and information, support leads to feelings of self-worth,
higher self-esteem, and protection from environmental trauma (Colarossi &
Eccles, 2003; Masten, 1994).

Families who live in communities that experience high levels of violence are
more likely to experience domestic violence (Lynch & Cicchetti, 1998). Given
the earlier discussion of partner abuse contributing to child maltreatment, one
can see that the transactions among system levels, exosystem and microsystem,
have great influence on the probability of abuse occurring. Adolescents growing
up in a context where violence is happening at multiple levels are at increased risk
for maltreatment.

On the contrary, neighborhoods and communities that have well-being serve
as a protective factor against child maltreatment (Thomlison, 1997). Neighborhoods with higher levels of employment and resources are found to be more
cohesive and stable and are associated with lower rates of child maltreatment
(Garbarino et al., 1992; Melton & Barry, 1994).

Strong and supportive religious affiliation (Kaufman & Zigler, 1992) serves as
a protective factor for families. Although there is limited empirical evidence, two
studies found that children are at increased risk of sexual abuse if they are not
brought up in an organized religion (Bolen, 2001).

Macrosystem Level

The cultural context in which the adolescent resides has tremendous influence
on her/his life events. Belsky (1980) indicates that society's values and attitudes
around violence and children is one of the most important factors in promoting
child maltreatment. The underlying cultural mechanism that allows child abuse
and neglect, partner abuse, and animal cruelty has been argued to be the patriarchal
system that bestows men with the power of control over children, women, and
animals and then does not take seriously male violence (Bolen, 2001; Finkelhor,
1984; Flynn, 2000; Pecora et al., 2000).

Sexual abuse of children in our society is fostered by similar cultural attitudes, but it is more complex and can be better understood in the context of additional macrosystem risk factors. Male entitlement that extends across many domains, family, work, and relationships also includes sex. Through the socialization process, men and women come to understand their roles within cultural norms, especially the norm that men are seen as the aggressors and women as the less powerful and more vulnerable. Bolen (2001, p. 147) states, "The combined influences of a social environment of male entitlement, gendered stereotypes, and hostile attitudes towards females decrease disinhibitors for sexual abuse."

Societal tolerance for objectifying children as sexual objects witnessed through erotic portrayals of children in advertising, television, movies, and child pornography places adolescents at risk of being sexually abused. Religion and the law have historically not condemned sexual interaction with children (Araji & Finkelhor, 1986) by often blaming the victim and not the perpetrator, which reinforces perpetrators' rationalizations.

MALTREATMENT ASSESSMENT OF FAMILIES WITH ADOLESCENTS

The risk of maltreatment decreases substantially as the child reaches adolescence, but there are still many 12- to 18-year-olds being abused or neglected. Children 12 to 18 represent approximately 25% of the maltreatment cases. Girls 12 to 15 have the highest physical abuse rate. Another issue is recurrence of child maltreatment. If a child previously experienced child abuse or neglect, they are three times more likely to experience recurrence than children who did not experience child maltreatment (USDHHS, 2000). Often it is not until adolescence that a child may disclose they have been abused, particularly sexually abused. Assessment of suspected child maltreatment should take into account all prior discussion of critical areas and questions to make a valid determination.

Children between the ages of 12 and 18 are experiencing many developmental challenges. Teenagers experiment with sexuality, alcohol, legal or illegal drugs, identity, and independence. Behaviors related to these normal developmental issues in adolescence might present challenges in conducting an ecological and developmental assessment of suspected maltreatment. In chapter 9 the normal feelings and behaviors of the middle school and high school adolescent were described. It is important in the assessment process to filter observations and information gained through the context of adolescent development.

Certain behaviors, when not embedded in the ecological framework, may be misinterpreted as indicators of child maltreatment. Adolescents might express their individuality through piercing or tattooing; this should not be mistaken as self-injury, which is an indication of child maltreatment. Another example is sexual experimentation. Normal behaviors related to adolescent sexuality should not be misinterpreted as indicators of sexual abuse. These behaviors must be assessed as they relate to all other dynamics occurring in the family's ecology. As stressed throughout this book, it is essential that all assessment and intervention be grounded in the ecological framework in order to obtain a comprehensive view of the family.

Ontogenic Level

The childhood history of parents of adolescent children is as important to the assessment of child maltreatment as for the parents of infants. There is a great deal of empirical support and professional agreement that a caregiver's developmental and attachment history is related to how they parent their own children. Questions again need to be focused on the caregivers' experience in childhood with physical abuse, neglect, and sexual abuse. Studies indicate that childhood maltreatment exerts significant influence on adult attachment relationships, which in turn influence subsequent parenting behavior (Cicchetti & Toth, 2000). Other questions that focus on the parent's perception of her/his care and attachment as a child are valuable.

Assessment of suspected maltreatment of an adolescent child in reference to the caregiver's ontogenic level should center on the following questions:

- Did the parent experience physical abuse, neglect, or sexual abuse at any time from infancy through adolescence?
- How does the caregiver perceive her/his care as a child?
- How does the caregiver perceive the discipline they received as a child?
- What was her/his relationship with her/his parents during adolescence?
- Did the caregiver experience foster care or adoption?
- Did the caregiver experience separation from parent (e.g., hospital, living with a relative)?
- During adolescence did they have a supportive person that gave them a different view of themselves and others?
- Did the parent have good peer and sibling relationships in childhood and adolescence?
- Did the caregiver experience violence in her/his home or her/his environment during childhood and adolescence?

Microsystem Level

Parent

Risk and protective factors related to caregiver characteristics have been presented throughout the book, and a complete list can be found in tables 10.1 and 10.2. During the adolescent years, particular factors are more applicable and related to the more prevalent types of abuse for children who are between the ages of 12 and 18; physical abuse and sexual abuse.

Assessment related to the parent or caregiver should include the following questions:

- What is the caregiver's developmental level?

    What is the parent's own history of care as a child?
    How does the parent perceive her/his care as a child?

- What is the caregiver's parenting style?

    Is it characterized by stress, anger, and hostility?
    Is the parent depressed and isolated?
    Is the parent sensitive to the adolescent's level of ability, interest, or needs?
    Does the parent use coercion?

- Are the parent's expectations for the adolescent realistic?
- Does the parent recognize the adolescent's right to autonomy and independence?
- Is the caregiver the adolescent's birth parent as opposed to step or adoptive parent?
- Is the parent using alcohol excessively?
- Is the parent abusing drugs?
- Does the father or father figure have a history of arrest or convictions for nondomestic violence–related offenses?
- Is the parent socially competent?
- Is the caregiver successful in other areas of her/his life—work, school, and relationships?

As discussed earlier in the chapter, certain caregiver risk factors are associated with an increased possibility of sexual abuse. These factors in the context of the overall ecological and developmental assessment may help in determining the possibility or risk of sexual abuse. Questions to ask concerning these specific factors are:

- Does the caregiver appear immature?
- Does the caregiver have low self-esteem or low self-efficacy in social relationships?
- Does the parent have a narcissistic identification with the child?
- Did the caregiver have an early sexual experience with a child or child pornography (sexual abuse)?
- Did the caregiver have an early sexual experience with an adult (sexual abuse)?
- Does the caregiver have adult sexual relationships?
- Is the parent unassertive or does he/she have inadequate social skills?
- Does the caregiver have poor impulse control?
- Is the caregiver a step-parent?

Child

Youth between the ages of 12 and 18 recognized as suffering the effects of child maltreatment present new challenges to the professional. There are major differences between the school-aged child and the adolescent; adolescents have more autonomy, and greater verbal and cognitive skills; are forming more sophisticated relationships with peers; and are held responsible to greater expectations. In conducting an assessment with an adolescent child, the professional must recognize these differences and respect the child for where she/he is in the process of her/his development.

As previously discussed, normal adolescent behavior and feelings must be understood so the assessment of potential child maltreatment is a valid decision concerning the allegation. Child maltreatment occurs in the context of the family, but given the increased complexity of an adolescent life, the ecological framework for assessment is critical. It is essential to have a thorough understanding of the adolescent developmental history and symptomology as it is experienced in the context of the family and their environment. In this section, we will discuss child-related assessment areas to consider in the overall ecological assessment.

See Table 10.3 for questions that should be considered in assessing the developmental domains.

As is the case in school-aged children (see chapter 8), the assessment of an adolescent's attachment relationships move beyond observation of interaction with the caregiver to an assessment of the internalized representations of the caregiving relationship. Consequences of maltreatment are reflected in attachment relationships. Insecure attachment relationships in adolescents may be a result of prior or current maltreatment and is relevant across the lifespan.

Two scales discussed in chapter 8 may be appropriate, particularly for the younger adolescent. They are:

Relatedness scale (Wellborn & Connell, 1987). This scale has been used in studies with children in the school years and for a range of risk levels (Lynch & Cicchetti, 1992; 1997; Toth & Cicchetti, 1996). This seventeen-item child-report scale assesses two dimensions of children's relationship experience, emotional quality, and psychological proximity-seeking. "Emotional quality" refers to the range of emotions that a child experiences with the parent in an attempt to capture the overall emotional tone of the relationship from the child perspective. Specific emotions assessed include relaxed, ignored, happy, bored, mad, important, unimportant, scared, safe, and sad. Psychological proximity-seeking assesses the degree to which children desire to be psychologically closer to a caregiver. Items such as "I wish my Mom paid more attention to me" and "I wish my Dad knew me better" are included.

Projective storytelling task (McCrone et al., 1994). Fairly open measure that is qualitative in nature. The social worker would begin by asking the child to tell a story: "Once upon a time . . . can you finish the story?" Themes of attachment are interpreted from the story told by the child.

The Adult Attachment Interview (AAI) (Main & Goldwyn, 2000), with modifications, is another tool that has been used to study adolescents (Adam, Sheldon-Keller, & West, 1996). AAI asks the adolescent to describe her/his childhood attachment experiences and how they have impacted her/his development. This instrument measures attachment based on questions addressing her/his attachment experience, her/his current state of mind concerning the parent, and the overall state of mind. Although the practitioner may not use the scale in assessment, the areas of measurement are relevant to themes that can be explored in the assessment process.

Table 10.3 Assessing Children Ages 12–18

Cognitive-Behavioral	Socioemotional	Physical
• Is the adolescent capable of thinking abstractly?	• Is the adolescent in search of an identity?	• Does the adolescent show secondary sex characteristics (deepening of the voice, pubic hair, breast development)?
• Is the adolescent capable of thinking about possibilities, rather than only concrete events?	• Does the adolescent have friendships characterized by intimacy, loyalty, and psychological closeness?	• Has the adolescent undergone a growth spurt?
• Can the adolescent mentally solve hypothetical problems?	• Does the adolescent self-disclose to friends?	• Is the adolescent bigger and stronger than before?
• Does the adolescent seem critical of her/his parents and others?	• Does the adolescent have a peer group?	• Has the adolescent engaged in sexual intercourse?
• Can the adolescent solve if-then statements?	• Does the adolescent appear interested in romantic relationships?	• Has the adolescent experienced menarche (for girls) or spermarche (for boys)?
• Is the adolescent egocentric, especially in terms of appearance and/or clothing?		
• Is the adolescent more interested in social and other issues than before?		

12–18 Years

Included in the scale are a number of domains for experiences and state of mind (Manassis et al., 1999). They are:

EXPERIENCE
- Loving vs. unloving parenting in childhood
- Rejection: aversion to and/or efforts to minimize the child's expression of attachment
- Involving/role-reversing: parent attempts to elicit the attention and involvement of the child and/or seeks parenting for the child
- Pressure to achieve during childhood
- Neglect: inaccessibility when physically available

STATE OF MIND IN RESPECT TO THE PARENTS
- Idealization of the parent
- Involved anger expressed toward the parent during the interview
- Active, dismissing derogation of the parent

OVERALL STATES OF MIND
- Active, dismissing derogation of attachment or relationship experiences
- Frequency and strength of insistence upon inability to recall childhood
- Passivity of discourse, thought relevant to attachment
- Fear of loss of the child through death
- Unresolved/disorganized mourning for attachment figures
- Unresolved trauma other than loss: abusive, threatening, or very frightening behavior of an attachment figure

Neglect

Adolescents represent the age group with the lowest neglect rate. Developmentally, the adolescent is able to care for her/himself, obtain food, work and buy clothes; he/she may have figured out other resources to meet her/his needs, so it is not surprising that the incidence of neglect is minimal for this age group.

Forms of neglect do occur in adolescence. In the following section applicable areas of assessment will be highlighted. Discussions of neglect in chapter 8 are also extremely pertinent and should be considered.

NEGLECTFUL SUPERVISION
- Parent/caregiver leaving a child 15 years or younger to live without any adult supervision
- Parent allowing an adolescent to use alcohol or other drugs in the home
- Caregiver giving drugs or other contraband to the adolescent
- Caregiver expels the adolescent child from the home

MEDICAL NEGLECT
- Lack of medical or psychological services that poses a substantial risk of harm, including not addressing suicidal ideation
- Adolescents who become pregnant and are not given adequate care

EMOTIONAL NEGLECT OR ABUSE
- Caregiver does not acknowledge adolescent child's move toward autonomy, independence, and self-determination; continues to treat the adolescent like a young child
- Parent does not allow the child normal and appropriate privacy
- Caregiver uses excessive threats and psychological punishment
- Caregiver praising the adolescent's antisocial/delinquent behavior
- Parent instructs the adolescent in illegal activity
- Caregiver punishes the adolescent for engaging in normal behaviors (e.g., social interaction with peers, school activities, or dating).

PHYSICAL NEGLECT
- Does not provide for the adolescent's basic needs, shelter, food, clothing, etc., or special needs, such as tampons

Again, it is important to note that the behavioral indicators discussed below are associated with all types of abuse, as well as other trauma-related experiences. These indicators, along with the comprehensive ecological and developmental assessment, may support the disposition that maltreatment has occurred.

Questions and behavioral indicators to consider when assessing child maltreatment of an adolescent includes:

- Has the adolescent engaged in severe self-injury or mutilation, such as carving, branding, or burning her/his skin?
- Has the adolescent ever harmed or injured an animal?
- Has the adolescent ever had oral or genital contact with an animal?
- Has the adolescent ever run away from home?
- Is the adolescent aggressive, hostile, or disruptive toward adults, especially toward the parent?
- Is the adolescent acting out aggression, which may include petty thefts, giving trinkets to other children to form friendships, and stealing merchandise or money?
- Is the adolescent engaged in social relationships?
- Is the adolescent truant from school?
- Does the adolescent have an alcohol or drug problem?
- Does the adolescent have an eating disorder?
- Has the adolescent demonstrated any fire-setting episodes or particular fascination with fires?
- Does the adolescent exhibit any suicidal behaviors?
- Does the adolescent have depressive symptoms?

- Is the adolescent acting out sexually (beyond the normal expected experimentation in this age group)?
- Does the adolescent have excessive and obsessive sexual behaviors?
- Is the adolescent engaging in sex with children of unequal power or abilities?

Physical Indicators of Child Maltreatment

As indicated, adolescent girls between the ages of 12 and 15 have the highest physical abuse rate for females—3.1 victims for every 1,000 female children (USDHHS, 2000). (See chapters 4, 6, and 8 for physical indicators of abuse.) Because this is an important area of assessment for female adolescents, physical indicators related to the older child will be revisited. Recall that accidental injuries occur most commonly on the areas of bony prominence, such as knees, shins, elbows, forehead, hands, chin, and nose. Other areas that sustain an injury may be suspect for nonaccidental injury or abuse. These are:

- Distinctively shaped injuries such as a belt buckle or outline of an object like a paddle or belt.
- Switch marks produce red streaks that may resemble train tracks
- Loop marks as a result of a cord that is folded over and produces an elongated U shape.
- Circumferential tie marks around the ankles, wrists, or waist, suggesting that the child was restrained with a rope
- Mouth injuries that may indicate that the child was gagged, such as lacerations at the corner of the mouth
- Puncture wounds that resemble the end of a fork, comb, or other distinctive object
- Hair loss from parents pulling out clumps of a child's hair, resulting in bald patches on the scalp; often accompanied by surface bleeding
- Pressure bruises on the neck that resemble fingers or whole hands, suggesting the child was strangled or choked
- Slap marks that frequently leave linear, parallel bruises similar to the outline of fingers and can cause loose teeth, abrasions to inside of mouth, ruptured ear drums, and eye injuries
- Thick and thin marks in a looping fashion because of centrifugal force that are left from a belt
- Areas of mass bruising that occur when both flexible and fixed objects are used; caused when several blows land in the same approximate area
- Two black eyes without accompanying injury to the nose
- Rib fractures, especially if accompanied by pressure bruises on the ribcage that resemble fingers on hands
- Physical signs of sexual abuse are rare, but any injury in the genital region or other areas of the body that may be involved in sexual activity, such as the buttock or mouth, should be suspect for sexual abuse
- Specific physical indications of sexual abuse have been presented in chapters 6 and 8

Sexual Abuse

In chapter 8 we focused our child assessment discussion of sexual abuse on Finkelhor's (1984) conceptual model of the four preconditions of sexual abuse. In this chapter we will concentrate on another model, developed by Finkelhor and Browne (1986), in which they synthesized the short- and long-term clinical issues common to sexually abused children into four clinical dynamics (traumatic sexualization, stigmatization, betrayal, and powerlessness) that can guide the evaluation of suspected sexual abuse.

Since the majority of adolescents do not present with physical or medical evidence of sexual abuse they may show behavioral, emotional, or social indicators reflective of the outcomes of being sexually abused. Although many youth who are victimized will present with abuse-related problems, in a review of empirical studies it was shown that up to 40% do not demonstrate any problems (Kendall-Tackett, Williams, & Finkelhor, 1993). Furthermore, long-term effects of sexual abuse may not solely be a function of the sexual abuse but of other negative childhood experiences that include pathological elements, such as psychological abuse, neglect, or household dysfunction (Dong et al., 2003; Finkelhor et al., 1986).

The degree of dysfunctional behavior, social incompetence, and cognitive-emotional distress associated with being sexually victimized varies because the definition of sexual abuse, as discussed in chapter 1, ranges from noncontact abuse to penetration. Although the degree of contact is not proportional to the consequences to the child, one child may be extremely traumatized by fondling while another may not. Consequences are also mediated by resiliency, which includes a number of factors. Mediating factors include incident-related circumstances, family dynamics, and professional intervention. The factors that influence the effects of sexual abuse are:

Age of the child. The younger the child, the more vulnerable.

Preabuse state of functioning. How the child is functioning cognitively, socially, emotionally, and behaviorally (e.g., greater distress is associated with higher cognitive ability because the adolescent is aware of the implications).

Nature and extent of abuse. Negative effects are associated with greater violence, penetration, multiple offenders, closeness to offender, and longer duration and frequency.

Reaction of significant other. Before, during, and after disclosure; the more supportive, the better the outcomes.

Intervention and quality of intervention. How skillful the clinical and legal intervention is for the child will impact the level of distress for the child and the family.

Finkelhor and Browne's (1986) traumagenic dynamics have been found to be strong indicators of symptomology in children who experience childhood sexual abuse (Mannarino & Cohen, 1996). The traumagenic dynamics are generalized and may be associated with other types of maltreatment, but the conjunction of the four dynamics in one set of circumstances are what make the trauma of sexual abuse unique (Finkelhor & Browne, 1986). Using the four dynamics and the associated symptoms, an assessment framework is suggested for evaluating suspected sexual victimization of an adolescent.

TRAUMATIC SEXUALIZATION

Dynamics
- Child rewarded for sexual behavior inappropriate to developmental level
- Offender exchanges attention and affection for sex
- Sexual parts of child fetishsized
- Offender transmits misconceptions about sexual behavior and sexual morality
- Conditioning of sexual activity with negative emotions and memories

Assessment Questions
- Does the adolescent discuss confusion about sexual identity?
- Does the adolescent have confusion about sexual norms?
- Does the adolescent exhibit sexual preoccupations and compulsive sexual behaviors?
- Does the adolescent demonstrate precocious sexual activity?
- Does the adolescent display aggressive sexual behaviors?
- Is the adolescent promiscuous?
- Is the adolescent engaging in prostitution?

STIGMATIZATION

Dynamics
- Offender blames, denigrates victim
- Offender and others pressure child for secrecy
- Child infers attitudes of shame about activity
- Others have shocked reactions to disclosure
- Others blame child for events
- Victim is stereotyped as "damaged goods"

Assessment Questions
- Does the adolescent seem to be overly shameful or guilt-ridden?
- Does the adolescent have low self-esteem?
- Does the adolescent express a sense of differentness from others?
- Is the adolescent isolated from friends and/or family?
- Is the adolescent using drugs or alcohol?
- Is the adolescent involved in criminal activities?
- Is the adolescent self-mutilating?
- Is there any indication of suicide ideation?

BETRAYAL

Dynamics
- Trust and vulnerability manipulated
- Violation of expectation that others will provide care and protection

- Child's well-being disregarded
- Lack of support and protection from parent(s) and relatives

Assessment Questions
- Does the adolescent have a sense of grief, depression?
- Does the adolescent exhibit extreme dependency?
- Does the adolescent have ability to judge trustworthiness of others?
- Does the adolescent exhibit a mistrust, particularly of men?
- Does the adolescent display a lot of anger, hostility?
- Does the adolescent display clinging behaviors?
- Is there vulnerability to subsequent abuse and exploitation?
- Allowing own children to be victimized?
- Is the adolescent isolated?
- Is the adolescent uncomfortable in intimate relationships?
- Does the adolescent exhibit aggressive behaviors?
- Does the adolescent show delinquency behaviors?

POWERLESSNESS

Dynamics
- Body territory invaded against child's wishes
- Vulnerability to invasion continues over time
- Offender uses force or trickery to involve child
- Child feels unable to protect self and halt abuse
- Repeated experience of fear
- Child is unable to make others believe

Assessment Questions
- Does the adolescent express much anxiety, fear?
- Does the adolescent display a lowered sense of efficacy?
- Does the adolescent have a need to control; has the adolescent been cruel to animals?
- Is the adolescent identifying with the aggressor?
- Does the adolescent talk about having a lot of nightmares?
- Does the adolescent display phobias?
- Does the adolescent appear to have somatic complaints, eating, and/or sleeping disorders?
- Does the adolescent have depression?
- Does the adolescent have a dissociative disorder?
- Is the adolescent running away?
- Does the adolescent have school problems, truancy?
- Does the adolescent demonstrate aggressive behavior, such as bullying?

The four traumagenic dynamics are a mechanism for categorizing the trauma effects of sexual abuse and a way to support other indicators in confirming the occurrence of sexual abuse. In addition, taking the parental, familial, and exosystem characteristics into account will help accomplish a complete ecological and developmental assessment.

Family

Family or household functioning is related to the probability of whether an adolescent will experience child maltreatment. In the prior chapters we presented many family structural and functional issues associated with a family who experiences child maltreatment. In this chapter, risk and protective factors most relevant to the adolescent are offered. Prior family-level factors should also be considered in the overall assessment.

The following questions may be most applicable to western cultural norms. Cultural guides should be referred to for others.

- Does the family encourage self-sufficiency?
- Does the family encourage decision making?
- Does the family encourage independence and assertiveness?
- Is the family characterized by conflictual interactions?
- Are anger and aggression expressed openly?

Additional evaluation questions to address are:

- Is there emotional closeness in the family?
- Does the family have good communication? Are family members encouraged to act openly and express their feelings?
- Is there adequate supervision in the home of the adolescent, as well the suspected perpetrator?
- Is the mother physically and psychologically available to her adolescent child?
- Is the father (male partner) unemployed?
- What is the marital history of the parents?
- Is the family isolated?
- What is the educational level of the mother, and job status of the father?
- How many children are in the home?
- How many adults are in the home?
- Is there partner violence?
- Is there any abuse to the animals in the home?
- Is the household organized and stable?
- Does the mother work outside of the home?
- Are both parents in the home?

Exosystem Level

Assessment of the family's social environment seeks to evaluate the level of connectedness the family has in their exosystem and the family's access to resources. Including the assessment of the family's environmental context will direct the practitioner in understanding the environmental processes facilitating child maltreatment and will guide the practitioner toward processes promoting healthy families.

Some of the questions assisting in information gathering are:

- What connections does the family have with their community?
- What cultural connections does the family have?

- What is the frequency of contact?
- Does the family have extended family in the area?
- Does the family have any religious affiliation?
- What is the frequency and quality of the contact they have with extended family?
- Does the mother have positive peer relationships?
- Does the adolescent have social support from extended family or a trusting adult?
- Does the adolescent have a supportive, caring adult in her/his life (teacher, coach, and mentor)?
- Does the community the family resides in have high rates of violence?
- Does the community the family resides in have a high sense of well-being (high employment, resources, and stability)?

CONCLUSIONS

Conducting an assessment of suspected child maltreatment of an adolescent might at first seem an easier task than assessing a young child, but challenges exist. Adolescent children may have experienced child maltreatment for years, and determination of specific type of abuse may be complicated by their clinical presentation. As we have repeated throughout the book, the ecological and developmental indicators can be generalized across types of maltreatment. Good interviewing along with collecting information concerning all levels of the adolescent's ecology is crucial.

Another challenge may be that often adolescents have a better comprehension of the consequences of disclosing sexual abuse or acknowledging they have been physically abused. Disruption to the family, possible placement into a foster home, and threats from the perpetrator may all be reasons deterring an adolescent child from disclosure. It will take building a trusting relationship with the youth and understanding the dynamics and indicators of child maltreatment on all ecological levels in order to make a sound decision.

INTERVENTION FOR MALTREATED ADOLESCENTS AND THEIR FAMILIES

Adolescence is normally a time characterized by developmental pressure, but for youth living in the midst of multiple stressors, such as child maltreatment, disorganized families, and disadvantaged communities, the challenges to adolescents are more complicated. Often the adolescents who come to the attention of the child welfare system or other related systems have experienced long histories of multiple episodes of maltreatment, related behavioral and emotional problems, and possible foster care placement. The practitioner faces multifaceted challenges in service planning with the adolescent and her/his family.

In this chapter we have focused on the prevalence of physical abuse, particularly for the adolescent girl, and sexual abuse for both genders, in the discussion of assessment. The basis for recommendations to treatment modality choices is grounded in the assessment. As previously discussed, not all adolescents will be impacted by child maltreatment in the same way or exhibit clinical profiles, and therefore not all adolescents will require similar, if any, treatment. An adequate ecological and developmental assessment, which has been outlined throughout this book, will provide information concerning the adolescent's presenting problem. The assessment is fundamental in guiding the type of interventions most appropriate for the adolescent child. Intervention strategies range from supportive, to cognitive-behavioral, to interpretative, all in the context of individual, group, or family approaches. Key is determining the adolescent's capacity for a therapeutic relationship and in what context it should take place, as well as determining family involvement. Guided by the ecological and developmental assessment, intervention strategies that address clinical issues relevant to the child age 12 to 18 and related to sexual and physical abuse will be presented.

Sexual Abuse Intervention

While the focus of the book is on mental health interventions with families and children who experience child maltreatment, it would be negligent not to briefly discuss the need for medical examination of a child who has been sexually abused. Medical exams of victims of child sexual abuse are usually normal or inconclusive (Berenson et al., 2000). As discussed in chapter 1, perpetrators known to a victim will pursue a pattern of escalating sexual behavior (fondling, penetration with object, penile penetration) that will reduce the chances of injury and nonaccidental disclosure. Pursuing this course of behavior usually results in a physical examination that reveals normal genital anatomy (Christian & Rubin, 2002).

Bolen (2001, p. 235) points out four reasons it is critical to get a medical examination for children who have been sexually abused. An adolescent would have to agree to the exam.

- It reassures the victim and parents that the child is normal and healthy.
- It detects, treats, or prevents medical conditions as a result of sexual contact.
- It provides evidence for the protection of the child.
- It provides evidence to prosecute the offender.

To reiterate the theme throughout the book, safety first is the underlying assumption in all intervention planning. Sexual abuse cannot be effectively treated if it is ongoing. Decisions concerning removal of the offender from the home, placement of the adolescent into out-of-home care, and the participation of the nonoffending parent all must be made to assure that the youth is protected from further trauma. Once the adolescent child is safe, preferably in her/his own home, if not in kinship or foster care, treatment strategies and modalities can be generalized across settings.

After reviewing sexual abuse treatment outcome research, Olafson & Boat (2000) outlined several guidelines and principles that should be considered in determining the best course of intervention for adolescents and their families. They are:

- Cognitive-behavioral treatment approaches have been shown to be effective in treating traumatized children.
- There is no agreement about the efficacy of individual versus group treatment for sexually abused children. Clinical wisdom indicates that group treatment is an effective modality for adolescents, but this has not been supported empirically to date.
- Gender plays a role in response to sexual abuse and treatment. Boys exhibit more externalizing behaviors and girls more internalizing behaviors. Although it is not clear why, girls respond better to treatment.
- Outcome studies for adolescent victims of sexual abuse who are not perpetrators are inadequate, and research is greatly needed.
- It is critical to involve nonoffending parents in treatment in order to provide emotional support and to break down any denial. Additionally, the nonoffending parent can be taught child behavioral management and emotional support strategies when the adolescent needs help with managing behaviors.

Sexual abuse sequelae has been found to be closely associated with post-traumatic stress disorder (PTSD), the disorder that occurs most in children who experience sexual abuse, with rates increasing for sexual abuse survivors who experience violence, penetration, and multiple episodes (Berliner & Elliott, 2002; Wolfe, 1998). These symptoms include, but are not limited to, efforts to avoid thoughts, feelings, activities; physiologic amnesia; diminished interest in significant activities; detachment/estrangement from others; diminished affect; sense of foreshortened future; dreams; difficulty falling/staying asleep; irritability; difficulty concentrating; hypervigilance; exaggerated startle response; physiologic reactivity to cues; and autonomic hyperarousal.

PTSD has been established as a framework from which to view trauma and for conceptualizing sexual abuse sequelae. PTSD not only defined a highly stressful event as something that could evoke traumatic stress in nearly anyone, but it also established standards for its identification. As defined in the DSM-IV (p. 424):

> The essential feature of post-traumatic stress disorder is the development of characteristic symptoms following exposure to an extreme traumatic stressor involving direct personal experiences of an event that involves threatened death, actual or threatened serious injury, or other threat to one's physical integrity; or witnessing an event that involves death, injury or a threat to the integrity of another person; or learning about unexpected or violent death, serious harm, or threat of death or injury experienced by a family member or other close associates.

Empirically based intervention approaches addressing sexual abuse sequelae are well described in the mental health literature (Corcoran, 2000; Olafson & Boat, 2000; Wolfe, 1998). Because of the variation of presenting symptoms, no single therapeutic approach will be effective with all adolescents and their families. Most sexual abuse treatment programs offer several therapeutic modalities since the trauma effects are witnessed on a number of ecological levels. Individual counseling, family counseling, dyad counseling (child and nonoffending parent), group therapy, and support groups are all frequently utilized in a comprehensive clinical program. The theoretical orientations of programs are diverse, but the ones with strong empirical support are based on the cognitive-behavioral approach (CBT) (Berliner & Elliott, 2002; Chaffin & Hanson, 2000).

Deblinger & Heflin (1996) suggest that cognitive behavioral interventions are particularly appropriate for addressing problems related to sexually abused children and their families for the following reasons:

- The wide range of interventions in this treatment approach matches the wide range of symptoms victims' experience.
- Approach allows for flexibility and can be individually tailored but still be grounded in the cognitive-behavioral theoretical model.
- CBT is a short-term approach, but the education and coping skills it teaches parents and adolescents can be applied throughout the lifespan.
- Because the approach is active, practical, directive, and structured, it appears to be preferred by minority groups (as cited in Olafson & Boat, 2000).

The goal of CBT is to target the physical, mental, and behavioral reactions to the sexual abuse and reduce the adolescent's symptoms. CBT helps improve the adolescent's mood and behavior by examining confused or distorted patterns of thinking. During CBT, the adolescent learns that thoughts cause feelings and moods can influence behavior. If an adolescent is experiencing unwanted feelings or has problematic behaviors, the therapist works to identify the underlying thinking that is causing them. The therapist then helps the adolescent replace this thinking with more thoughts, appropriate feelings, and behaviors.

In the treatment of sexual abuse for the adolescent, CBT is intended to alleviate PTSD symptoms, correct misperceptions or distortions the child has about the abuse, and ameliorate behavior problems, especially sexual behaviors, developed as a consequence of the sexual abuse and related stressors. The main components of the CBT approach are psychoeducation, anxiety management, exposure, and cognitive therapy (Cohen, Berliner, & Mannarino, 2000).

The decision to involve the nonoffending parent in CBT treatment is part of the assessment process. In the case of intrafamilial sexual abuse the support of the nonoffending parent is critical to the adolescent's recovery (Bolen, 2001). Nonoffending parents are included in most treatment protocols, and most outcome studies show that the nonoffending parent benefits from treatment (Stauffer & Deblinger, 1996; Cohen & Mannarino, 1998). The parent component requires a parent who is willing and able to participate and implement the recommended procedures. Goals of treatment for the nonoffending parent are primarily to strengthen her/his role in the protection of the adolescent and to address her/his own issues of trauma. Often, the nonoffending parent presents with her/his own issues, including anger and hostility, low self-esteem, lack of support, feelings of inadequacy, and strong dependency needs. Until the nonoffending parent's needs are met, they are often too overwhelmed to be available to her/his adolescent.

Major components of the nonoffending parent's CBT treatment focus on individual therapy that addresses abuse-specific elements similar to the child. Additional components include attributions of responsibility, emotional support, behavior management, legal issues, and coping with one's own past abuse (Wolfe, 1998).

Behavioral management is an important component of the nonoffender's treatment protocol and one that is directed at assisting the caregiver in reducing unwanted behaviors (emotional and behavioral sequelae) of the adolescent resulting from the abuse. As previously discussed, the sexually abused adolescent often presents with sexual problems that include sexually acting out with peers, promiscuous behaviors, and engaging younger children in sexual behavior. Deblinger and Heflin (1996) describe a behavioral management program focusing on sexual problems that has the following components:

- Assesses sexual attitudes and knowledge of childhood sexuality
- Provides education about normal sexuality
- Teaches parents how to respond to adolescent's questions about sexuality
- Demystifies inappropriate sexual behavior by discussing why that sexual behavior develops

Behavioral management strategies include:

- Open communication between parent and adolescent about sexuality
- Clear consequences for inappropriate sexual behavior
- Development of prosocial behaviors to replace sexual behavior

While there is a great deal of empirical support for CBT, some caution the general use of it across all situations (Berliner & Elliott, 2002; Chaffin & Champion, 1997; Tzeng, Jackson, & Karlson, 1991). The CBT approach may not be effective or sufficient for adolescents who are experiencing dissociative, psychotic symptoms or other clinically significant symptomatology (Berliner & Elliott, 2002; Chaffin & Champion, 1997). Some assert that the CBT approach is too narrow and negates important factors that impact child maltreatment, such as the role of extended family and socioeconomic status (Tzeng, Jackson, & Karlson, 1991).

Physical Abuse Intervention

Adolescents who come to the attention of the child welfare system because of a substantiated report of physical abuse may have different treatment needs. Whether the onset of physical abuse occurred in adolescence or has been a pattern of behavior since early childhood will direct the therapeutic approach. Additionally, as discussed throughout the book, physical abuse can occur independently, but cooccurrence with other forms of abuse is common. Outcomes associated with different forms of abuse overlap, and therefore the presenting problem(s) may be a result of cooccurrence with other forms of abuse, as well as with other stressors, such as disorganized or violent family, poverty, and isolation.

Consequences of child maltreatment are either exacerbated or mediated by several factors and impact the subsequent problems in adolescence and adulthood. Characteristics of the abuse that may add to the trauma value include:

- Age of onset of the abuse
- Frequency and duration of abuse
- Number and characteristics of perpetrators involved in the abuse
- The relationship of the perpetrator to the adolescent
- The level of violence
- The family and institutional response to the abuse (Bagley, Wood, & Young, 1994; Browne & Finkelhor, 1986)

Beyond medical treatment for severe injuries to the adolescent, treatment of physical abuse usually focuses on the family, primarily the parent, and not on the adolescent unless she/he is displaying pathology. It is important to include the adolescent in the treatment process and to assess her/his needs. Once initial medical issues are resolved, the focus becomes one of protection, whether in the home or in an out-of-home placement. The primary treatment goal is for the physical abuse to stop. With the intervention of the child welfare agency this occurs immediately, but the concern then becomes future occurrence of maltreatment. Determining the safety of the adolescent is based on the ecological and developmental assessment of risk and protective factors aiding in predicting future abuse. Once safety is established, intervention is guided by the needs of the adolescent and her/his family.

The causes of physical abuse can best be understood in the context of the ecological model that provides a broad view and a focus on the interactional aspects of child maltreatment. Origins of physical abuse are entwined with the ontogenic level of the parent, early adult history, child-rearing practices, stressful environments, and social support. Given the complexity of physical abuse, treatment of families must be approached on the microsystem level, with the adolescent and the parent, and the exosystem level, with social support networks. Physical abuse sequelae vary greatly from family to family; therefore intervention is likely to vary. However, a review of the empirical and clinical findings has found common areas of impairment that should be considered for treatment and takes into consideration the need for a multistage approach.

As cited in Azar & Wolfe (1998), Wolfe and Wekerle (1993) summarized treatment needs for physically abused and neglected families as:

CHILD INTERVENTION NEEDS
- Problems in social relationship development, including problems with attachment formation, development of empathy, interpersonal trust, and affective expression.
- Problems in cognitive, language, and moral development that include poor social judgment, communication skills, and school performance
- Problems with self-control and aggression
- Concerns about future maltreatment

PARENT INTERVENTION NEEDS

- Emotional distress, learning impairments, and personality deficits that limit adult functioning
- Poor control of anger and hostility
- Inadequate and inappropriate methods of teaching, discipline, and child stimulation
- Inappropriate and nonrealistic perceptions and expectations of the child
- Problems with the use of alcohol or drugs, involvement with prostitution that interferes with parenting, and poor problem-solving skills

FAMILY/SITUATIONAL INTERVENTION NEEDS

- Partner discord and/or coercive family interactions and a history of domestic violence
- Chronic economic problems
- Social isolation and the inability to establish social supports

Many of these treatment needs can be effectively addressed through CBT approaches, but not all. Recall, coming from an ecological framework, that basic needs of the family must be taken care of before the family can invest energy into correcting cognitive and behavioral distortions. Housing, employment, and environmental and educational stressors may be as strong a contributing factor as the parental behavior, and this necessitates simultaneous interventions strategies on all levels.

Cognitive-behavioral treatment has not been empirically tested as extensively with families and adolescents who experience symptoms as a result of physical abuse as it has with sexual abuse. Given the earlier discussion of the overlap of symptomology among abuse types, it is suggested that CBT is an efficacious treatment approach for physically abusive families. Similar components of the CBT approach are applicable to work with families who physically abuse, including psychoeducation, anxiety management, exposure, and cognitive therapy (Cohen, Berliner, & Mannarino, 2000).

As suggested by Swenson & Kolko (2000), psychoeducation may include activities such as addressing the views of the family on violence and discipline, identifying attributes about the physical abuse, and safety planning and risk reduction. Anger and self-control management strategies using cognitive behavioral approaches have been found to be effective for both the adolescent and the parent in reducing anger and aggression (Action & During, 1992; Dangel, Deschner, & Rapp, 1989; Feindler et al., 1986; Kolko, 1996a; Whiteman, Fanshel, & Grundy, 1987; Wolfe et al., 1988). CBT techniques used in anger management programs include relaxation, assessment of cognitive and physiological anger cues, development of coping statements, substitution of anger-producing thoughts with relaxation and coping statement responses, and self-evaluation (Feindler et al., 1986).

Some physically abused adolescents present an opposite reaction to the maltreatment; they avoid overt expressions of anger. The adolescent child may be internalizing anger or showing other covert forms of anger, such as self-mutilation and eating disorders. The similar CBT strategies discussed are helpful in teaching adolescents appropriate ways to express their anger, especially relaxation and cognitive substitution (Swenson & Kolko, 2000).

Other CBT strategies helpful in reducing the potential for future physical abuse and reducing the adolescent's symptomology are child behavior management training programs that teach nonphysical discipline and developmentally appropriate expectations for children, and cognitive-behavioral techniques that address behavior. Methods commonly applied are:

Modeling and behavioral rehearsals. Behavioral rehearsal involves the use of role playing or simulating social exchanges. In this method, specific verbal and nonverbal behaviors to be changed are identified. The caregiver might practice newly acquired child management behaviors or the adolescent might practice social skills.

Feedback. Feedback is a method providing sensory or verbal information in response to certain behavioral processes. In the context of the role-play the practitioner gives positive feedback to the adolescent or the parent, emphasizing what they are doing correctly.

Cognitive restructuring. Cognitive restructuring is a method in which dysfunctional thinking patterns are identified as being illogical and/or as producing undesirable consequences. The adolescent and parent are trained to monitor faulty thinking and track the consequences of that thinking. Once distortions are identified, the adolescent or parent is guided to modify the faulty thinking and replace it with an alternative thought.

Skill training. Skill training involves parent training, anger control, and stress management. Skill training focuses on the acquisition of a set of skills that can be used to address a wide range of problems related to physical abuse. This training can be done in a group setting but may also involve some individualized training through specific feedback to parents about applying the skills to a particular problem. Training in the home may also be a crucial factor in the success of these programs. However, the main focus of this method is on mastery of skills rather than on solutions to a particular problem.

It is important to note that combinations of these techniques are required. It is not enough to provide anger and self control techniques, which may or may not be sufficient to change the parent or adolescent behavior. Additionally, family-based treatment, along with CBT treatment of the adolescent and the caregiver, is important for changing the relationships and structure of the family perpetuating the violence. Family-based treatment alone is not as effective as CBT (Kolko, 1996a; 1996b), but in order to meet treatment goals the practitioner will have to employ both approaches.

Treatment Across Abuse Type

Adolescents constitute a major group of children in the foster care system in the United States (USDHHS, 2000), and it is estimated that 20,000 adolescents are emancipated and leave foster care to assume independence every year (Scannapieco, 2000). Many of these young persons, because of emotional and social problems stemming from child maltreatment and the temporary life of foster care, are not prepared for self-sufficiency. Many adolescents in their biological or kin home also do not possess these skills for the same reasons.

The child welfare and related systems are responsible for ensuring that adolescents who have experienced child maltreatment be given opportunities to develop human and life skills training. Helping adolescents prepare for adult life without requiring total dependency on their family or the welfare system requires a range of services, strategies, and skills. In 1985, the Independent Living Initiative contained in Public Law 99-272 was adopted as part of the Comprehensive Omnibus Budget Reconciliation Act. The purpose was to appropriate funds to help adolescents make the transition from foster care to independence or interdependence (see Pecora et al., 2000). Many programs developed as a result of this initiative and are broadly called Independent Living Programs (ILP). These services are offered to the adolescent in a group setting or are integrated on an individual basis.

The ILPs focus on preparation for self-sufficiency by integrating services that prepare the adolescent for employment and provide life skills training to enhance the adolescent child's ability to manage daily living. There are six general areas; for further discussion of each, see Scannapieco, 2000.

> *Case management services.* Many of the program areas stem from the management of the case. The practitioners' goal is to offer intensive, relationship-based services using a task-centered and goal-oriented service model. Capitalizing on identified strengths, planning for independence is negotiated between the youth and the practitioner.
>
> *Educational services.* Education is significantly related to independent living outcomes for youth. Whether college preparatory or vocational courses, programs must support youth in identifying the importance of education.
>
> *Employment-readiness programs.* Using both individual and group methods, these programs focus on the skills youth need to obtain jobs. Skills focus on resume writing, completing job applications, interviewing techniques, and decorum. Effective strategies are modeling, role-playing, and "dress rehearsals."
>
> *Life skills training.* The emphasis of life skills programs is on education and training and not on counseling. Life skills training may encompass several components, but the most important are:
>
> - Interpersonal communication skills. Important to focus on verbal and nonverbal skills.
> - Problem solving and decision-making. Work on improving the ability of youth to make and select from alternative solutions through the development of problem-solving and decision-making skills.
> - Self-management and control. Self-assessment (evaluating one's own behavior to determine if it is adequate), self-monitoring (being able to monitor and be aware of current functioning), and self-reinforcement (providing one's own consequence for conduct).

- Strategies for coping with stress. Some of the more beneficial methods are relaxation techniques, imagery training, and cognitive restructuring of negative beliefs.
- Housing and financial skills. Locating an apartment, negotiating a rental agreement, performing housekeeping chores, purchasing bargains, preparing nutritious meals, and maintaining a savings or checking account.

Mentoring programs. The essential component in all programs is the use of an adult volunteer who is matched with an adolescent and whose task is to help the youth make a successful transition to early adult living. The mentor also provides a lifelong connection for the youth.

Social support networks. Supportive connections to family, extended family, previous foster parents, mentors, teachers, and others are important to subsequent well-being and self-sufficiency. Integral to an overall case plan is the linking of youth, who are working toward emancipation, to formal and informal social support networks.

CONCLUSION

Adolescence is the bridge between childhood and adulthood. Although maltreatment declines during adolescence, children are still at risk for all forms of maltreatment, especially sexual abuse among girls. The consequences of abuse and neglect in adolescence also become evident in ways that place youths in peril, such as depression, suicide, delinquency, and pregnancy. Maltreatment in childhood and adolescence can make a youth vulnerable to negative experiences in adulthood, such as criminal activity and future victimization. If assessed and treated properly and early enough, the cycle of maltreatment can be stopped. An ecological and developmental perspective can lead to the proper assessment of the developmental consequences of maltreatment and ecologically based interventions that will reduce both the immediate and long-term impact of youth maltreatment.

CASE: MATHIS FAMILY

Identifying Information

Rachel Thomas (15 years old), female victim

Mark Thomas (33 years old), biological father of Rachel

Carrie Mathis (32 years old), mother

Judy Mathis (50 years old), grandmother

Sarah Mathis (30 years old), aunt

Summary

A referral was received on Carrie Mathis for the physical abuse and neglectful supervision of Rachel Thomas. Carrie is nowhere to be found. Rachel awoke one day and her mother was gone. She has not returned for 10 days. Her aunt and grandmother live next door, so she went to their house and has been there ever since. Sarah Mathis, Rachel's maternal aunt, called CPS because she no longer wants the responsibility for taking care of Rachel. She has contacted her biological father, but he will not take care of Rachel unless "someone gives him custody."

Rachel told her aunt that her mother strips her naked, makes her lay spread eagled on the bed, and then whips her with a switch. According to the aunt, Rachel has some scars on her back. The CPS worker found the scars consistent with whippings. In addition, she found scars from cigarette burns and bruises in various stages of healing.

History of Referrals

Carrie Mathis was investigated and confirmed for physical abuse of Rachel when Rachel was 8 years old. At the time of this report, Carrie was on probation for injury to a child because of severe physical abuse of Rachel when she was 7. Substance use was a concern of the worker at the time of this investigation. The biological father was contacted to take the child. He agreed but never followed through. Rachel was then placed with Judy Mathis, her maternal grandmother, who lived next door. However, her grandmother promptly returned Rachel to her mother.

Level of Functioning

Carrie has a history of substance abuse. She has left Rachel before to go on drug binges. Her only friends are those who also do drugs, and Sarah Mathis reports that Carrie sells drugs and engages in prostitution for money. Carrie does not have a job and relies on her sister and mother (Judy and Sarah Mathis) to provide for Rachel's basic needs. When Carrie became pregnant, Judy Mathis wanted Carrie to have an abortion but she refused. However, when Mark left Carrie when she was 6 months pregnant, Carrie considered giving Rachel up for adoption. Judy and Sarah Mathis report that they are tired of taking care of Rachel and that she is "just like her no-good father."

The school has spoken to Carrie about Rachel's pervasive academic and behavioral problems. She is behind academically in school and is failing three courses. The school reported that she might be placed in special education courses. She has also recently been involved in several fights with other girls around boyfriend issues. In one she seriously injured another student and was suspended. She has been seen using marijuana and drinking beer on school grounds. She has recently made friends with some kids at school who also use drugs. Rachel has also been arrested for smoking marijuana and driving without a license. Neither Rachel nor her mother seems concerned about Rachel being placed in special education or her involvement with the law.

Case Exercise

1. What are the normal developmental expectations for the adolescent?
2. Consider the child's developmental level. What developmental manifestations can you identify that may be an indication of child maltreatment in the following domains?

   - Physical development
   - Cognitive-behavioral
   - Socioemotional

3. What role does culture play in the child's development?
4. Expand your assessment of the child's developmental level to the overall ecological model. Assess the family's risk and protective factors in the context of the ecological model.

   - Ontogenic Level
   - Microsystem
   - Exosystem
   - Macrosystem

5. What intervention strategies might you employ to facilitate development of the child?
6. What intervention strategies might you employ with the caregiver?
7. What cultural aspects of the family are important to consider for both assessment and intervention?

APPENDIX
CULTURAL RESPONSIVENESS
GUIDE REFERENCES

Cohen, N. A. (Ed.). (1992). *Child welfare: A multicultural focus.* Needham Heights: Allyn and Bacon.

Depoy, E., & Gilson, S. F. (2004). *Rethinking disability: Principles for professional and social change.* Belmount: Brooks/Cole-Thompson Learning.

Devore, W., & Schlesinger, E. G. (1996). *Ethic-sensitive social work practice.* (5th ed.). Needham Heights: Allyn and Bacon.

Everett, J. E., Chipungu, S. S., & Leashore, B. R. (Eds.). (1991). *Child welfare: An Africentric perspective.* New Brunswick, NJ: Rutgers University Press.

Hogan-Garcia, M. (2003). *The four skills of cultural diversity competence: A process for understanding and practice.* (2nd ed). Pacific Grove, CA: Brooks/Cole-Thompson Learning.

Lum, D. (2004). *Social work practice and people of color: A process-stage approach.* (5th ed.). Belmount: Brooks/Cole-Thompson Learning.

Ricketts, W. (1991). *Lesbians and gay men as foster parents.* Portland: University of Southern Maine.

Rothman, J. C. (1999). *The self-awareness workbook for social workers.* Needham Heights: Allyn and Bacon.

Samantrai, K. (2004). *Culturally competent public child welfare practice.* Pacific Grove, CA: Brooks/Cole-Thompson Learning.

Smith, T. B. (Ed.) (2004). *Practicing multiculturalism: Affirming diversity in counseling and psychology.* Boston: Pearson Allyn and Bacon.

Woodman, N. J. (Ed.). (1992). *Lesbian and gay lifestyles: A guide for counseling and education.* New York: Irvington.

REFERENCES

CHAPTER 1

Ammerman, R. (1990). Etiological models of child maltreatment. *Behavior Modification*, *14*(3), 230–254.

APSAC. (1995). *Psychological maltreatment of children: Practice guidelines*. American Professional Society on the Abuse of Children.

Berliner, L., & Elliott, D. M. (2002). Sexual abuse of children. In J. E. Myers, L. Berliner, J. Briere, C. T. Hendrix, C. Jenny, & T. A. Reid (Eds.), *The APSAC handbook on child maltreatment* (*2nd ed.*). Thousand Oaks, CA: Sage.

Berrick, J. D. (1997). Child neglect: Definition, incidence, and outcomes. In J. D. Berrick, R. Barth, & N. Gilbert (Eds.), *Child welfare research review*, *2*, 1–12. New York: Columbia University Press.

Besharov, D. J. (1990). *Recognizing child abuse: A guide for the concerned*. New York: Free Press.

Brooks, D., Barth, R. P., Bussiere, A., & Patterson, G. (1999). Adoption and race: Implementing the Multiethnic Placement Act and the Interethnic Adoption Provisions. *Social Work*, *44*(2), 167–178.

Costin, L. (1985). The historical context of child welfare. In J. Laird & A. Hartman (Eds.), *A handbook of child welfare: Context, knowledge, and practice*. New York: Free Press.

Costin, L., Karger, H., & Stoesz, D. (1996). *The politics of child abuse in America*. New York: Oxford University Press.

Dubowitz, H. (1999). Neglect of children's health care. In H. Dubowitz (Ed.), *Neglected children: Research, practice, and policy* (pp. 109–131). Thousand Oaks, CA: Sage.

Erickson, M. F., & Egeland, B. (2002). Child neglect. In J. E. Myers, L. Berliner, J. Briere, C. T. Hendrix, C. Jenny, & T. A. Reid (Eds.), *The APSAC handbook on child maltreatment* (*2nd ed.*). Thousand Oaks, CA: Sage.

Ferrara, F. F. (2002). *Childhood sexual abuse: Developmental effects across the lifespan*. Pacific Grove, CA: Brooks/Cole.

Garbarino, J., Guttman, E., & Seeley, J. W. (1986). *The psychologically battered child: Strategies for identification, assessment, and intervention*. San Francisco: Jossey-Bass.

Giovannoni, J. (1989). Definitional issues in child maltreatment. In D. Cicchetti & V. Carlson (Eds.), *Child maltreatment: Theory and research on the consequences and causes of abuse and neglect* (pp. 3–37). Cambridge, MA: Cambridge University Press.

Gustavsson, N., & Segal, E. (1994). *Critical issues in child welfare*. Thousand Oaks, CA: Sage.

Hall, G. S. (1904). *Adolescence: Its psychology and its relation to physiology, anthropology, sociology, sex, crime, religion, and education*. New York: Appleton.

Hart, S. N., Brassard, M. R., Binggeli, N. J., & Davidson, H. A. (2002). Psychological maltreatment. In J. E. Myers, L. Berliner, J. Briere, C. T. Hendrix, C. Jenny, & T. A. Reid (Eds.), *The APSAC handbook on child maltreatment (2nd ed.)*. Thousand Oaks, CA: Sage.

James, A., & Prout, A. (1997). *Constructing and reconstructing childhood*. London: Routledge Falmer.

Karger, H. J., & Stoesz, D. (1998). *American social welfare policy: A pluralist approach (3rd ed.)*. New York: Longman.

Katz, M. B. (1986). *In the shadow of the poorhouse: A social history of welfare in America*. New York: Basic Books, Inc.

Kempe, C. H., Silvermann, F. N., Steele, B. F., Droegemueller, W., & Silver, H. K. (1962). The battered child syndrome. *Journal of the American Medical Association, 181*(1), 17–24.

Kolko, D. J. (2002). Child physical abuse. In J. E. Myers, L. Berliner, J. Briere, C. T. Hendrix, C. Jenny, & T. A. Reid, *The APSAC handbook on child maltreatment (2nd ed.)*. Thousand Oaks, CA: Sage.

Lazoritz, S. (1990). Whatever happened to Mary Ellen. *Child Abuse and Neglect, 14*, 143–149.

McDaniel, N., & Lescher, N. C. (2004). The history of child protective services. In C. Brittain, & D. E. Hunt (Eds.), *Helping in child protective services: A competency-based casework handbook*. New York: Oxford University Press.

Miller, A. (1983). *For your own good: Hidden cruelty in child-rearing and the roots of violence*. New York: Farrar, Straus, Giroux.

Myers, J. E., Berliner, L., Briere, J., Hendrix, C. T., Jenny, C., & Reid, T. A. (2002). *The APSAC handbook on child maltreatment (2nd ed.)*. Thousand Oaks, CA: Sage.

O'Hagan, K. (1993). *Emotional and psychological abuse of children*. Toronto: University of Toronto Press.

Pecora, P. J., Whittaker, J. K., Maluccio, A. N., & Barth, R. P. (2000). *The child welfare challenge: Policy, practice, and research (2nd ed.)*. New York: Aldine De Gruyter.

Pfohl, S. J. (1977). The discovery of child abuse. *Social Problems, 24*(9), 310–323.

Radbill, S. X. (1968). A history of child abuse and infanticide. In R. E. Helfer & H. C. Kempe (Eds.), *The battered child* (pp. 3–17). Chicago: University of Chicago Press.

Sedlak, A. J., & Broadhurst, D. D. (1996). *Executive summary of the Third National Incidence Study of Child Abuse and Neglect*. Washington, DC: National Clearinghouse on Child Abuse and Neglect, USDHHS.

Sgroi, S. M., Blick, L. C., & Porter, F. S. (1982). A conceptual framework for child sexual abuse. In S. Sgroi (Ed.), *Handbook of clinical intervention in child sexual abuse*. Lexington, MA: Lexington Books.

Shepard, R. E. (1965). The abused child and the law. *Washington and Lee Law Review, 22*, 182–195.

Trattner, W. I. (1984). *From poor law to welfare state: A history of social welfare in America*. New York: Free Press.

U.S. Department of Health and Human Services, Administration for Children and Families. (2001). *A guide to the Multiethnic Placement Act of 1994 as amended by the Interethnic Adoption Provisions of 1996*. http://www.acf.hhs.gov/programs/cb/publications/mepa94/mepachp1.htm.

U.S. Department of Health and Human Services, Administration for Children and Families, Administration for Children, Youth and Families, Children's Bureau. (2002). *Child maltreatment 2002*. Washington, DC: U.S. Government Printing Office.

Watkins, S. A. (1990). The Mary Ellen myth: Correcting child welfare history. *Social Work*, 35(6), 500–503.

Wiehe, V. R. (1990). *Sibling abuse: Hidden physical, emotional, and sexual trauma*. Lexington, MA: Lexington Books.

Zuravin, S. (1991). Research definitions of child abuse and neglect: Current problems. In R. Starr, Jr. & D. Wolfe (Eds.), *The effects of child abuse and neglect* (pp. 100–127). New York: Gulliford.

Zuravin, S. (1999). Child neglect: A review of definitions and measurement research. In H. Dubowitz (Ed.), *Neglected children: Research, practice, and policy* (pp. 24–47). Thousand Oaks, CA: Sage.

CHAPTER 2

Aber, J. L., & Allen, J. P. (1987). Effects of maltreatment on young children's socioemotional development: An attachment theory perspective. *Developmental Psychology*, 23, 406–414.

Ainsworth, M. (1973). The development of mother-infant attachment. In B. Caldwell & H. Ricciuti, *Review of Child Development Research*, 3 (1–94). Chicago: University of Chicago Press.

Ainsworth, M., Blehar, M., Waters, E., & Wall, S. (1978). *Patterns of attachment*. Hillsdale, NJ: Lawrence Erlbaum Associates.

American Psychiatric Association. (1994). *The diagnostic and statistical manual of mental disorders, Fourth Edition (DSM-IV)*. Washington, DC: American Psychiatric Association.

Ammerman, R. (1990). Etiological models of child maltreatment. *Behavior Modification*, 14(3), 230–254.

Bandura, A. (1977). *Social learning theory*. Englewood Cliffs, NJ: Prentice-Hall.

Beckwith, L. (1990). Adaptive and maladaptive parenting: Implications for intervention. In S. Meisels and J. Shonkoff (Eds). *Handbook of early childhood interventions* (pp. 53–77). New York: Cambridge University Press.

Belsky, J. (1978). Three theoretical models of child abuse. *Child Abuse and Neglect*, 2(1), 37–49.

Belsky, J. (1980). Child maltreatment: An ecological integration. *American Psychologist*, 35(4), 320–335.

Belsky, J., Rovine, M., & Taylor, D. G. (1984). The Pennsylvania infant and family development project, III: The origins of individual differences in infant-mother attachment: maternal and infant contributions. *Child Development*, 55, 718–728.

Bolen, B. (1999). *Development of an ecological/transactional model of sexual abuse victimization and analysis of its nomological classification system*. Dissertation, University of Texas at Arlington.

Bowlby, J. (1982). Attachment and loss: Retrospect and prospect. *Annual Progress in Child Psychiatry and Child Development*, 52(4), 29–47.

Brazelton, T. D. (1988). Importance of early intervention. In E. Hibbs (Ed.), *Children and families: Studies in prevention and interventions* (pp. 107–120). Madison, CT: International Universities Press.

Bretherton, I., Ridgeway, D., & Cassidy, J. (1990). Assessing internal working models of the attachment relationship: An attachment story completion task for 3-year-olds. In M. Greenberg, D. Cicchetti, & E. Cummings (Eds.) *Attachment in the preschool years* (pp. 273–308). Chicago: University of Chicago Press.

Bronfenbrenner, U. (1979). *The ecology of human development: Experiments by nature and design*. Cambridge, MA: Harvard University Press.

Buchanan, A. (1996). *Cycles of child maltreatment: Facts, fallacies and interventions*. West Sussex, England: John Wiley and Sons, Ltd.

Burgess, R., & Conger, R. (1977). Differentiating abusing and neglecting parents by direct observation of parent-child interaction. In M. Lauderdale, R. Anderson, & S. Cramer (Eds.), *Child, abuse and neglect: Issues on innovation and implementation proceedings of the Second National Conference on Child Abuse and Neglect, April 17–20, 1977* (Volume II). National Center on Child Abuse and Neglect, Washington, DC (OHDS) 78-30248.

Carlson, E. (1998). A prospective longitudinal study of attachment disorganization/disorientation. *Child Development, 69*, 1107–1128.

Carlson, V., Cicchetti, D., Barnett, D., & Braunwald, K. G. (1989). Finding order in disorganization: Lessons from research on maltreated infants; attachments to their caregivers. In D. Cicchetti & V. Carlson (Eds.), *Child maltreatment: Theory and research on the causes and consequences of child abuse and neglect* (pp. 494–528). Cambridge: Cambridge University Press.

Cavaiola, A., & Schiff, M. (1988). Self-esteem in abused chemically dependent children. *Child Abuse and Neglect, 1*, 327–334.

Chess, S., & Thomas, A. (1982). Infant bonding: Mystique and reality. *American Journal of Orthopsychiatry, 52*, 213–222.

Christoffel, K. (1990). Violent death and injury in U.S. children and adolescents. *American Journal of Disease Control, 111*, 697–706.

Chun, B. (1989). Child abuse in Korea. *Child Welfare, 68*, 154–158.

Cicchetti, D., and Barnett, D. (1991). Attachment organization in maltreated preschoolers. *Development and Psychopathology, 3*, 397–411.

Cicchetti, D., and Carlson, V. (1991). *Child maltreatment: Theory and research on the causes and consequences of child abuse and neglect*. New York: Cambridge University Press.

Cicchetti, D., and Lynch, M. (1993). Toward and ecological/transactional model of community violence and child maltreatment. *Psychiatry, 56*, 96–118.

Cicchetti, D., & Rizley, R. (1981). *Developmental perspective on child maltreatment: New directions for child development*. San Francisco, CA: Jossey-Bass.

Cicchetti, D., & Toth, S. (1995). Child maltreatment and attachment organization: Implication for intervention. In S. Goldberg, R. Muir, & J. Kerr (Eds.), *Attachment theory: Social, developmental, and clinical perspectives* (pp. 279–308). Hillsdale, NJ: Analytic Press.

Coates, D., & Lewis, M. (1984). Early mother-infant interaction and infant cognitive predictors of school performance and cognitive behavior in six-year-olds. *Child Development, 55*, 1219–1230.

Corse, S., Schmid, K., & Trickett, K. (1990). Social network characteristics of mothers in abusing and nonabusing families and their relationships to parenting beliefs. *Journal of Community Psychology, 18*, 44–59.

Crittenden, P. (1985). Social networks, quality of parenting, and child development. *Child Development, 56*, 1299–1313.

Crittenden, P. (1988). Distorted patterns of relationships in maltreating families: The role of internal representation models. *Journal of Reproductive and Infant Psychology, 6*, 183–199.

Crittenden, P. (1992). Quality of attachment in the preschool years. *Developmental Psychopathology, 4*, 209–241.

Daro, D. (1988). *Confronting child abuse*. New York: Free Press.

DePanfilis, D. (1999). Intervening with families when children are neglected. In

H. Dubowitz (Ed.), *Neglected children: Research, practice, and policy*. Thousand Oaks, CA: Sage.

Dodge, K., Bates, J., & Petit, G. (1990). Mechanisms in the cycle of violence. *Science, 2*, 1678–1683.

Egeland, B., & Sroufe, L. (1981). Developmental sequelae of maltreatment in infancy. *New Directions for Child Development, 11*, 77–92.

Erickson, M., Sroufe, A., & Egeland, B. (1985). The relationship between quality of attachment and behavior problems in preschool in a high-risk sample. In I. Bretherton and E. Waters (Eds.), *Growing points of attachment theory and research. Monographs of the Society for Research in Child Development*, 50, 147–166.

Fontana, V. (1971). Which parents abuse. *Medical Insight, 3*(10), 16–21.

Fraser, M. (Ed.) (1997). *Risk and resilience in childhood: An ecological perspective*. Washington, DC: NASW Press.

Frodi, A., & Lamb, M. (1980). Infants at risk for child abuse. *Infant Mental Health Journal, 1*(4), 240–247.

Garbarino, J. (1977). The human ecology of child maltreatment: A conceptual model for research. *Journal of Marriage and the Family, 39*, 721–735.

Garbarino, J., and Gilliam, G. (1980). *Understanding abusive families*. Lexington, MA: Lexington Press.

Garbarino, J., & Sherman, D. (1980). High-risk neighborhoods and high-risk families: The human ecology of child maltreatment. *Child Development, 51*(1), 188–198.

Gaudin, J. M. (1993). Effective intervention with neglectful families. *Criminal Justice and Behavior, 20*, 69–89.

Gelles, R., & Strauss, M. (1988). Is violence toward children increasing? A comparison of 1975 and 1985 national survey rates. *Journal of Interpersonal Violence, 2*, 212–222.

Gil, D. (1970). *Violence against children: Physical child abuse in the U.S.* Cambridge, MA: Harvard University Press.

Giovannoni, J. (1970). Parental mistreatment: Perpetrators and victims. *Journal of Marriage and the Family, 33*, 649–657.

Goldberg, S. (1995). Introduction. In S. Goldberg, R. Muir, & J. Kerr (Eds.), *Attachment theory: Social, developmental, and clinical perspectives* (pp. 1–18). Hillsdale, NJ: Analytic Press.

Green, A. (1968). Self-destruction in physically abused schizophrenic children: Report of cases. *Archives of General Psychiatry, 19*, 171–197.

Harrison, P., Hoffmann, N., & Edwall, G. (1989). Differential drug use patterns among sexually abused adolescent girls in treatment for chemical dependency. *International Journal of Addictions, 24*, 499–514.

Harrison, P., Hoffmann, N., & Edwall, G. (1989). Sexual abuse correlates: Similarities between male and female adolescents in chemically dependent treatment. *Journal of Adolescent Research, 4*, 385–399.

Harwood, R. (1992). The influence of culturally derived values on Anglo and Puerto Rican mothers' perceptions of attachment behavior. *Child Development, 63*, 822–839.

Hepworth, D. H., Rooney, R. H., & Larsen, J. (2002). *Direct social work practice: Theory and skills*. Pacific Grove: Brooks/Cole Publishing Company.

Jackson, J. (1993). Multiple caregiving among African Americans and infant attachment: The need for an emic approach. *Human Development, 36*, 87–102.

Kaufman, J., & Zigler, E. (1989). The intergenerational transmission of child abuse. In D. Cicchetti and V. Carlson (Eds.), *Child maltreatment. Theory and research on the causes and consequences of child abuse and neglect* (pp. 129–150). New York: Cambridge University Press.

Kazdin, A., Moser, J., Colbus, D., et al. (1985). Depressive symptoms among physically abused and psychiatrically disturbed children. *Journal of Abnormal Psychology, 94*, 298–307.

Kempe, C., Silverman, F., Steele, B., Droegemueller, W., & Silver, H. (1962). The battered-child syndrome. *The Journal of the American Medical Association, 18*, 117–124.

Kempe, R., & Kempe, C. (1978). *Child abuse.* Cambridge: Harvard University Press.

Klein, M., & Stern, L. (1971). Low birth weight and the battered-child syndrome. *American Journal of Diseases of Children, 12*(2), 15–18.

Lamb, M., Gaensbauer, T., Malkin, C., & Schultz, L. (1985). The effects of child maltreatment on security of infant-adult attachment. *Infant Behavioral Development, 8*, 35–45.

Light, R. (1973). Abused and neglected children in America: A study of alternative policies. *Harvard Educational Review, 43*(4), 556–589.

Lum, D. (1999). *Culturally competent practice: A framework for growth and action.* Pacific Grove: Brooks/Cole Publishing Company.

Main, M., & Cassidy, J. (1988). Categories of response to reunion with the parent at age 6: Predicted from attachment classifications over a 1-month period. *Developmental Psychopathology, 24*, 415–426.

Main, M., Kaplan, N., & Cassidy, J. (1985). Security in infancy, childhood and adulthood: A move to the level of representation. In I. Bretherton & E. Waters, *Growing points in attachment theory and research in monographs for the Society for Research in Child Development, 209*, 50(1/2), 66–104.

Main, M., & Solomon, J. (1986). Discovery of a disorganized/disoriented attachment pattern. In T. B. Brazelton and M. W. Yogman (Eds.), *Affective development in infancy.* Westport, CT: Ablex.

Main, M., & Solomon, J. (1990). Procedures for identifying infants and disorganized/disoriented during the Ainsworth Strange Situation. In M. Greenberg, D. Cicchetti, & E. Cummings (Eds.). *Attachment in preschool years* (pp. 121–160). Chicago: University of Chicago Press.

Nash, M., Hulsey, T., Sexton, M., Harralson, T., & Lambert, W. (1993). Long-term sequelae of childhood sexual abuse: Perceived family environment, psychopathology, and dissociations. *Journal of Consulting and Clinical Psychology, 61*(2), 276–283.

Ousted, C., Oppenheimer, R., & Lindsay, J. (1974). Aspects of bonding failure: The psychopathology and psychotherapeutic treatment of families of battered children. *Developmental Medicine in Child Neurology, 16*, 447–457.

Park, M. (2001). The factors of child physical abuse in Korean immigrant families. *Child Abuse and Neglect, 25*, 945–958.

Payne, M. (1997). *Modern social work theory (2nd ed.).* Chicago, IL: Lyceum Books Inc.

Pecora, P., Whittaker, J., Maluccio, A., Barth, R., & Plotnik, R. (2000). *The child welfare challenge: Practice, policy, and research.* Hawthorne, NY: Aldine de Gruyter.

Perry, B. D. (1994). Neurobiological sequelae of childhood trauma: PTSD in children. In M. M. Murburg (Ed.), *Catecholamine function in posttraumatic stress disorder: Emerging concepts* (pp. 233–255). Washington, DC: American Psychiatric Press, Inc.

Perry, B. D. (1999). Incubated in terror: Neurodevelopmental factors in the "cycle of violence." In J. D. Osofsky (Ed.), *Children, youth, and violence: Searching for violence.* NY: Guilford Press.

Perry, B. (2000). The early years last forever: The importance of brain development. Lectureship materials. Corpus Christi, TX.

Peterson, P. (2000). *A handbook for developing multicultural awareness (3rd ed.).* Alexandria, VA: American Counseling Association.

Rumm, P., Cummings, P., Krauss, M., Bell, M., & Rivara, F. (2000). Identified spouse abuse as a risk factor for child abuse. *Child Abuse and Neglect, 24*(11), 1375–1381.

Saleebey, D. (1992). *The strengths perspective in social work practice.* New York: Longman.

Scannapieco, M., & Connell-Carrick, K. (2002). Focus on the first years: An eco-developmental assessment of child neglect for children 0 to 3 years of age. *Children and Youth Services Review, 24*(1/2), 1–14.

Schneider-Rosen, K., Braunwald, K., Carlson, V., & Cicchetti, D. (1985). Current perspectives in attachment theory: Illustration from the study of maltreated infants. In E. Bretherton & E. Waters (Eds.), *Growing points in attachment theory and research.* Monographs of the Society for Research in Child Development, *209, 50*(1/2), 194–210.

Spinetta, J., and Rigler, D. (1972). The child-abusing parent: A psychological review. *Psychological Bulletin, 77,* 296–304.

Sroufe, L. (1985). Attachment classification from the perspective of infant-caregiver relationships and infant temperament. *Child Development, 56,* 1–14.

Steinberg, L., Catalano, R., & Dooley, D. (1981). Economic antecedents of child abuse and neglect. *Child Development, 52*(3), 975–985.

Sweet, J., and Resick, P. (1979). The maltreatment of children: A review of theories and research. *Journal of Social Issues, 35*(2), 40–59.

Trickett, P., Aber, J., Carlson, V., & Cicchetti, D. (1991). The relationship of socioeconomic status to the etiology and developmental sequaelae of physical child abuse. *Developmental Psychology, 27,* 148–158.

Trickett, P., & Susman, E. (1988). Parental perceptions of child-rearing practices in physically abusive and nonabusive families. *Developmental Psychology, 24*(2), 270–276.

Tzeng, O., and Jackson, J. (1990). Common methodological framework for theory construction and evaluation in the social and behavioral sciences. *Genetic, Social, and General Psychology Monographs, 117*(1), 49–76.

Tzeng, O., Jackson, J., & Karlson, H. (1991). *Theories of child abuse and neglect: Differential perspectives, summaries, and evaluations.* New York: Prager.

UNICEF. (September 2003). A league table of child maltreatment deaths in rich nations. *Innocenti report card, no. 5.* Florence, Italy: Innocenti Research Centre.

U.S. Department of Health and Human Services, Administration on Children, Youth, and Families. (2002). *Child maltreatment 2000: Reports from the states to the National Child Abuse and Neglect Data Systems.* Washington, DC: U.S. Government Printing Office.

Wachs, T. D., & Green, G. E. (1982). *Early experience and human development.* New York: Plenum.

Waters, E., & Deane, K. (1985). Defining and assessing individual differences in attachment relationships: Q-methodology and the organization of behavior in infancy and early childhood. In I. Bretherton & E. Waters (Eds.), *Growing points in attachment theory and research.* Monographs of the Society for Research in Child Development, *209, 50* (1/2), 41–65.

Werner-Wilson, R., & Davenport, B. (2003). Distinguishing between conceptualizations of attachment: Clinical implications in marriage and family therapy. *Contemporary Family Therapy, 25*(5), 179–193.

Widom, C. (1989). The cycle of violence. *Science, 244,* 160–166.

Widom, C. (2000). Understanding the consequences of childhood victimization. In R. M. Reece (Ed.), *Treatment of child abuse: Common mental health, medical, and legal practitioners* (pp. 339–361). Baltimore, MD: Johns Hopkins University Press.

Wolkind, S., & Rutter, M. (1985). *Sociocultural factors in child and adolescent psychiatry.* Boston: Blackwell Scientific.

Wolock, I., & Horowitz, B. (1984). Child maltreatment as a social problem: The neglect of neglect. *American Journal of Orthopsychiatry, 54*(4), 530–543.

Wolfner, G., & Gelles, R. (1993). A profile of violence toward children: A national study. *Child Abuse and Neglect, 17,* 197–212.

Woody, D. (2003). Infancy and toddlerhood. In E. Hutchinson (Ed.), *Dimensions of human behavior: The changing life course (2nd ed.)* (pp. 113–158). Thousand Oaks, CA: Sage.

Yamaguchi, K., & Kandel, D. (1984). Patterns of drug use from adolescence to early childhood: Predictors of progression. *American Journal of Public Health, 74,* 673–681.

CHAPTER 3

Ainsworth, M., Blehar, M., Waters, E., & Wall, S. (1978). *Patterns of attachment.* Hillsdale, NJ: Lawrence Erlbaum.

Albus, K., & Dozier, M. (1999). Indiscriminate friendliness and terror of strangers in infancy: Contributions from the study of infants in foster care. *Infant Mental Health Journal, 20*(1), 30–41.

Alessandri, S. (1992). Mother-child interactional correlates of maltreated and nonmaltreated children's play behavior. *Development and Psychopathology 4*(2), 257–270.

Bartz, M., & Levine, E. (1978). Childrearing by black parents: A description and comparison to Anglo and Chicano parents. *Journal of Marriage and Family Therapy, 40,* 709–719.

Behrman, R. (1992). *Nelson textbook of pediatrics.* Philadelphia, PA: W.B. Saunders.

Belsky, J., & Vondra, J. (1989). Lessons from child abuse: The determinants of parenting. In D. Cicchetti & V. Carlson (Eds.), *Child maltreatment: Theory and research on the causes and consequences of child abuse and neglect* (pp. 153–202). New York: Cambridge University Press.

Berger, K. (2001). *The developing person through the lifespan (5th ed.).* New York: Worth Publishers.

Berk, L. (2001). *Development through the lifespan (2nd ed.).* Boston: Allyn and Bacon.

Bowlby, J. (1983). Attachment and loss: Retrospect and prospect. *Annual Progress in Child Psychiatry and Child Development, 52*(4), 29–47.

Bruce, D. (1992). Neurosurgical aspects of child abuse. In S. Ludwig & A. Kornberg (Eds.), *Child abuse: A medical reference (2nd ed.)* (pp. 117–130). New York: Churchill Livingston.

Casey, P., Bradley, R., & Wortham, B. (1984). Social and nonsocial home environments of infants with nonorganic failure-to-thrive. *Pediatrics, 73,* 348–353.

Chisholm, K., Carter, M., Ames, E., & Morison, S. (1995). Attachment security and indiscriminately friendly behavior in children adopted from Romanian orphanages. *Development and Psychopathology, 7,* 283–294.

Cicchetti, D., & Lynch, M. (1993). Toward an ecological/transactional model of community violence and child maltreatment: Consequences for child's development. *Psychiatry: Interpersonal and Biological Processes, 56*(1), 96–118.

Culp, R., Watkins, R., Lawrence, H., Letts, D., Kelly, D., & Rice, M. (1991). Maltreated children's language and speech development: Abused, neglected, and abused and neglected. *First Language, 11,* 377–389.

Dale, G., Kendall, J. C., & Humber, K. I. (1996). Mental health screening in foster care: A model for community-based service delivery and research in baltimore. Proceedings from The Eighth Annual Research and Training Center Conference, University of South Florida, Tampa. http://rtckids.fmhi.usf.edu/proceeding8th/chap5.htm.

Delambre, J., & Wood, M. (1997). *Epidemiological study of child abuse and neglect related fatalities: FY 1991–1995.* Kentucky Cabinet for Families and Children.

Egeland, B., Sroufe, L., & Erickson, M. (1983). The developmental consequences of different patterns of maltreatment. *Child Abuse and Neglect, 7,* 459–469.

Erickson, M., & Egeland, B. (2002). Child neglect. In J. Myers, L. Berliner, J. Briere, C. Hendrix, C. Jenny, & T. Reid (Eds.)., *The APSAC handbook on child maltreatment* (2nd ed.) (pp. 3–29). Thousand Oaks, CA: Sage Publications.

Gaensbauer, T., & Siegel, C. (1995). Therapeutic approaches to posttraumatic stress disorder in infants and toddlers. *Infant Mental Health, 16*(4), 292–305.

George, C., & Main, M. (1979). Social interactions of young abused children: Approach, avoidance, and aggression. *Child Development, 50,* 306–318.

Gowen, J. (1993). Study of the effects of neglect on the early development of the symbolic function (conference proceedings). In *Chronic Neglect Symposium proceedings, National Center on Child Abuse and Neglect.* Washington, DC: Government Printing Office.

Greenough, W., Black, J., & Wallace, C. (1987). Experience and brain development. *Child Development, 58,* 539–559.

Harwood, R. (1992). The influence of culturally derived values on Anglo and Puerto Rican mothers' perceptions of attachment behavior. *Child Development, 63,* 822–839.

Houck, G., & King, M. (1989). Child maltreatment: Family characteristics and developmental consequences. *Issues in Mental Health Nursing, 10,* 193–208.

Howes, C., & Eldredge, R. (1985). Responses of abused, neglected, and non-maltreated children to the behavior of peers. *Journal of Applied Developmental Psychology, 6,* 261–270.

Jackson, J. (1993). Multiple caregiving among African Americans and infant attachment: The need for an emic approach. *Human Development, 36,* 87–102.

Kendall, K., Williams, L., & Finkelhor, D. (1993). Impact of sexual abuse on children: A review and synthesis of recent empirical studies. *Psychological Bulletin, 113,* 164–180.

Kristiansson, B., & Fallstrom, S. (1987). Growth at the age of 4 years subsequent to early failure to thrive. *Child Abuse and Neglect, 11,* 35–40.

Mackner, L., Starr, R., & Black, M. (1997). The cumulative effects of neglect and failure to thrive on cognitive functioning. *Child Abuse and Neglect, 21*(7), 691–700.

Moore, K., & Persaud, T. (1998). *Before we are born (5th ed.).* Philadelphia: Saunders.

National Clearinghouse on Child Abuse and Neglect. (October 2001). *In focus: Understanding the effects of maltreatment on early brain development.* Washington, DC: Author.

Nowakowski, R. (1987). Basic concepts of CNS development. *Child Development, 58,* 598–595.

Oates, R., Peacock, A., & Forrest, D. (1984). Development in children following abuse and nonorganic failure to thrive. *American Journal of Diseases of Children, 138*(8), 764–767.

Okun, A., Parker, J., & Levendosky, A. (1994). Distinct and interactive contributions to physical abuse, socioeconomic disadvantage, and negative life events of children's social, cognitive, and affective adjustments. *Development and Psychopathology, 6,* 77–98.

Perry, B. (1994). Neurobiological sequelae of childhood trauma: Post-traumatic stress disorders in children. In M. Murberg (Ed.), *Catecholamines in post-traumatic stress disorder: Emerging concepts* (pp. 124–149). Washington, DC: American Psychiatric Press.

Perry, B. (1996). Neurodevelopmental adaptations to violence: How children survive the intragenerational vortex of violence [online]. Retrieved 5/4/04 from http://www.childtrauma.org/ctamaterials/vortex_violence.asp.

Perry, B. (1997). Incubated in terror: Neurodevelopmental factors in the "cycle of violence." In J. Osofsky (Ed.), *Children, youth, and violence: A search for solutions* (pp. 124–148). New York: Guilford Press.

Perry, B. (2003). Sexual abuse of infants: A five-part question focusing on sexual abuse during infancy. http://www.childtrauma.org/CTAMATERIALS/infant_abuse.asp.

Perry, B., & Pollard, R. (1998). Homeostasis, trauma, and adaptations: A neurodevelopmental view of childhood trauma. *Child and Adolescent Psychiatric Clinics of North America, 7*(1), 33–51.

Perry, B., Mann, D., Palker-Corell, A., Ludy-Dobson, C., & Schick, S. (2002). Child physical abuse. In D. Levinson (Ed.), *Encyclopedia of crime and punishment*, vol. 1 (pp. 197–202). Thousand Oaks, CA: Sage.

Reams, R. (1999). Children birth to three entering the state's custody. *Infant Mental Health Journal, 20*(7), 166–174.

Ricci, L. (2000). Initial medical treatment of the physically abused child. In R. Reece (Ed.), *Treatment of child abuse: Common ground for mental health, medical, and legal practitioners* (pp. 81–94). Baltimore, MD: John Hopkins University Press.

Rutter, M., Andersen-Wood, L., Beckett, C., Bredenkamp, D., Castle, J., Keppner, J., Keaveny, L., Lord, C., O'Connor, T., & English and Romanian Adoptees study team. (1999). Quasi-autistic patterns following severe global early privation. *Journal of Child Psychology and Psychiatry, 39*, 465–476.

Scannapieco, M., & Connell-Carrick, K. (2002). Focusing on the first years: An eco-developmental assessment of child neglect for children 0 to 3 years of age. *Child and Youth Services Review, 24*(8), 601–621.

Scheeringa, M., & Zeanah, C. (1995). Symptom expression and trauma variables in children under 48 months of age. *Infant Mental Health Journal, 16*(4), 259–269.

Shore, R. (1997). *Rethinking the brain*. New York: Families and Work Institute.

Singer, L. (1986). Long-term hospitalization of nonorganic failure to thrive infants: Developmental outcomes at 3 years. *Child Abuse and Neglect, 10*, 479–486.

Straker, G., & Jacobson, R. (1981). Aggression, emotional maladjustment, and empathy in abused children. *Developmental Psychology, 17*, 762–765.

Urquiza, A., Wirtz, S., Peterson, M., & Singer, V. (1994). Screening and evaluating abused and neglected children entering protective custody. *Child Welfare 73*(2), 155–171.

U.S. Department of Health and Human Services, Administration on Children, Youth, and Families. (2002). *Child maltreatment 2000: Reports from the states to the National Child Abuse and Neglect Data Systems*. Washington, DC: U.S. Government Printing Office.

Wang, C., and Daro, D. (1998). *Current trends in child abuse reporting and fatalities: The results of the 1997 Annual Fifty State Survey*. Chicago, IL: Prevent Child Abuse America.

Whipple, E., & Webster-Stratton, C. (1991). The role of parental stress in physically abusive family interactions. *Journal of Clinical Child Psychology, 19*, 302–312.

Woody, D. (2003). Infancy and toddlerhood. In E. Huchinson (Ed.), *Dimensions of human behavior: The changing life course* (pp. 113–158). Thousand Oaks, CA: Sage.

CHAPTER 4

American Academy of Pediatrics. (1993). Committee on child abuse and neglect. Shaken baby syndrome: Inflicted cerebral trauma. *Pediatrics, 92*, 872–875.

Appel, A. E., & Holden, G. W. (1998). The occurrence of spouse and physical child abuse: A review and appraisal. *Journal of Family Psychology, 12*, 578–599.

Ards, S., & Harrell, A. (1993). Reporting of child maltreatment: A secondary analysis of the national incidence surveys. *Child Abuse and Neglect, 17,* 337–344.

Azar, S. T., Breton, S. J., & Miller, L. R. (1998). Cognitive-behavioral group work and physical child abuse: Intervention and prevention. In K. C. Stoiber & T. R. Kratochwill (Eds.), *Handbook of group intervention for children and families.* Boston: Allyn and Bacon.

Barth, R. (1991). An experimental evaluation of in-home child abuse prevention services. *Child Abuse and Neglect, 15,* 363–375.

Belsky, J. (1980). Child maltreatment: An ecological integration. *American Psychologist, 35*(4), 320–335.

Belsky, J., Lerner, R. M., & Spanier, G. B. (1984). *The child in the family.* Reading, MA: Addison-Wesley.

Belsky, J., & Vondra, J. (1989). Lessons from child abuse: The determinants of parenting. In D. Cicchetti & V. Carlson (Eds.), *Child maltreatment: Theory and research on the causes and consequences of child abuse and neglect* (pp. 152–202). New York: Cambridge University Press.

Berrick, J. D., Needell, B., Barth, R. P., & Jonson-Reid, M. (1998). *The tender years: Toward developmentally sensitive child welfare services for very young children.* New York: Oxford University Press.

Besharov, D. J. (1990). *Recognizing child abuse: A guide for the concerned.* New York: Free Press.

Bowlby, J. (1969). *Attachment.* New York: Basic Books.

Boyer, D., & Fine, D. (1992). Sexual abuse as a factor in adolescent pregnancy and child maltreatment. *Family Planning Perspectives, 24,* 4–11.

Brayden, R., Atlemeier, W., Tucker, D., Dietrich, M., & Vietze, P. (1992). Antecedents of child neglect in the first 2 years of life. *Journal of Pediatrics, 120,* 426–429.

Bronfenbrenner, U. (1979). *The ecology of human development: Experiments by nature and design.* Cambridge, MA: Harvard University Press.

Brooks, W., & Weathers, L. (2001). Overview of shaken baby syndrome. In S. Lazoritz & V. J. Palusci (Eds.), *The shaken baby syndrome: A multidisciplinary approach.* New York: Haworth Maltreatment & Trauma Press.

Brown, J., Cohen, P., Johnson, J., & Salzinger, S. (1998). A longitudinal analysis of risk factors for child maltreatment: Findings of a 17-year prospective study of officially recorded and self-reported child abuse and neglect. *Child Abuse and Neglect, 22*(11), 1065–1078.

Cadzow, S. P., Armstrong, K. L., & Fraser, J. A. (1999). Stressed parents with infants: Reassessing physical abuse risk factors. *Child Abuse and Neglect, 23*(9), 845–853.

Caniano, D. A., Beaver, B. L., & Boles, E. T. (1986). An update on surgical management in 256 cases. *American Surgery, 203,* 219–224.

Cantrell, P. J., Carrico, M. F., Franklin, J. N., & Grubb, H. J. (1990). Violent tactics in family conflicts relative to familial and economic factors. *Psychological Reports, 66,* 823–828.

Chaffin, M., Kelleher, K., & Hollenberg, J. (1996). Onset of physical abuse and neglect: Psychiatric, substance abuse, and social risk factors from prospective community data. *Child Abuse and Neglect, 20*(3), 191–203.

Chance, T., & Scannapieco, M. (2002). Ecological correlates of child maltreatment: Similarities and differences between child fatality and nonfatality cases. *Child and Adolescent Social Work Journal, 19*(2), 139–161.

Cicchetti, D., & Lynch, M. (1993). Toward an ecological/transactional model of community violence and child maltreatment: Consequences for children's development. *Psychiatry: Interpersonal & Biological Processes, 56*(1), 96–118.

Cicchetti, D., & Toth, S. L. (1995). Child maltreatment and attachment organization: Implications and intervention. In S. Goldberg, R. Muir, & J. Kerr (Eds.), *Attachment theory: Social development and clinical perspectives* (pp. 279–308). Hillside, NJ: Analytic Press.

Colletta, N. D. (1983). At-risk for depression: A study of young mothers. *Journal of Genetic Psychology, 142*, 301–310.

Colletta, N. D., & Gregg, C. H. (1981). Adolescent mothers' vulnerability to stress. *Journal of Nervous and Mental Disease, 169*, 50–54.

Conger, R., Burgess, R., & Barrett, C. (1979). Child abuse related to life changes and perceptions of illness: Some preliminary findings. *Family Coordinator, 28*(1), 73–78.

Coohey, C. (1996). Child maltreatment: Testing the social isolation hypothesis. *Child Abuse and Neglect, 29*(3), 241–254.

Coohey, C. (1998). Home alone and other inadequately supervised children. *Child Welfare, 77*(3), 291–301.

Coulton, C., Korbin, J., Su, M., & Chow, J. (1995). Community level factors and child maltreatment rates. *Child Development, 66*, 1262–1276.

Delambre, J. W., & Wood, M. (1997). *Epidemiological study of abuse and neglect related child fatalities: FY 1991–1995.* Kentucky Cabinet for Families and Children.

Drake, B., & Pandey, S. (1996). Understanding the relationship between neighborhood poverty and specific types of child maltreatment. *Child Abuse and Neglect, 20*(11), 1003–1018.

Dubowitz, H. (Ed.). (1999). *Neglected children: Research, practice, and policy.* Thousand Oaks, CA: Sage.

Dutton, D. G. (1998). *The abusive personality: Violence and control in intimate relationships.* New York: Guilford.

Egeland, B., & Erickson, M. F. (1990). Rising above the past: Strategies for helping new mothers break the cycle of abuse and neglect, *Zero to Three, 11*, 29–35.

Emery, R. E., & Forehand, R. (1994). Parental divorce and children's well-being: A focus on resilience. In R. J. Haggerty, L. R. Sherrod, N. Garmezy, & M. Rutter (Eds.), *Stress, risk, and resilience in children and adolescents: Processes, mechanisms, and interventions* (pp. 64–99). New York: Cambridge University Press.

Erickson, M. F., & Egeland, B. (2002). Child neglect. In J. E. Myers, L. Berliner, J. Briere, C. T. Hendrix, C. Jenny, & T. A. Reid (Eds.), *The APSAC handbook on child maltreatment (2nd ed.).* Thousand Oaks, CA: Sage.

Erickson, M. F., & Kurz-Riemer, K. (1999). *Infants, toddlers, and families: A framework for support and intervention.* New York: Guilford.

Farber, E. A., & Egeland, B. (1987). Invulnerability among abused and neglected children. In E. J. Anthony & B. Cohler (Eds.), *The invulnerable child* (pp. 253–288). New York: Guilford.

Ferrara, F. F. (2002). *Childhood sexual abuse: Developmental effects across the lifespan.* Pacific Grove, CA: Brooks/Cole.

Finkelhor, D. (1986). Prevention: A review of programs and research. In D. Finkelhor & Associates (Eds.), *A sourcebook on child sexual abuse* (pp. 224–254). Beverly Hills, CA: Sage.

Fontana, V. (1971). Which parents abuse. *Medical Insight, 3*(10), 16–21.

Fraiberg, W. N., Adelson, E., & Sharpiro, V. (1975). Ghosts in the nursery: A psychoanalytic approach to impaired infant-mother relationships. *Journal of American Academy of Child Psychiatry, 14*, 387–421.

Frank, D. A., Augustyn, M., Knight, W. G., Pell, T., & Zuckerman, B. (2001). Growth, development, and behavior in early childhood following prenatal cocaine exposure: A systematic review. *Journal of the American Medical Association, 285*, 1613–1625.

Gaudin, J., Polansky, N., Kilpatrick, A., & Shilton, P. (1993). Loneliness, depression, stress, and social supports in neglectful families. *American Journal of Orthopsychiatry*, *63*(4), 597–605.

Gelles, R. J. (1992). Poverty and violence toward children. *American Behavioral Scientist*, *35*(3), 258–274.

Giardino, A. P., & Giardino, E. R. (2002). *Recognition of child abuse for the mandated reporter*. St. Louis, MO: G.W. Medical Publishing, Inc.

Gil, D. (1970). *Violence against children: Physical child abuse in the U.S.* Cambridge, MA: Harvard University Press.

Goerge, R. M., & Lee, B. G. (1999). Poverty, early childbearing, and child maltreatment: A multinomial analysis. *Children and Youth Services Review*, *21*(9/10), 755–780.

Hampton, R. L., & Newberger, E. H. (1985). Child abuse incidence and reporting by hospitals: Significance of severity, class, and race. *American Journal of Public Health*, *75*(1), 56–60.

Haynes, C. F., Cutler, C., Gray, J., & Kempe, R. S. (1984). Hospitalized cases of non-organic failure to thrive: The scope of the problem and short-term lay health visitors interventions. *Child Abuse and Neglect*, *8*, 229–242.

Herrenkohl, E. D., Herrenkohl, R. C., & Toedter, L. J. (1983). Perspectives on the intergenerational transmission of abuse. In D. Finkelhor, R. J. Gelles, G. T. Hotaling, & M. A. Straus (Eds.), *The dark side of families: Current family violence research*. Beverly Hills, CA: Sage.

Joffe, M. D. (2002). Child neglect and abandonment. In A. P. Giardino & E. R. Giardino (Eds.), *Recognition of child abuse for the mandated reporter* (pp. 39–52). St. Louis, MO: G.W. Medical Publishing.

Jones, E., & McCurdy, K. (1992). The links between types of maltreatment and demographic characteristics of children. *Child Abuse and Neglect*, *16*, 201–215.

Kaufman, J., & Zigler, E. (1989). The intergenerational transmission of child abuse. In D. Cicchetti and V. Carlson (Eds.), *Child maltreatment: Theory and research on the causes and consequences of child abuse and neglect*. New York: Cambridge University Press.

Kelley, S. J. (2002). Child maltreatment in the context of substance abuse. In J. E. Myers, L. Berliner, J. Briere, C. T. Hendrix, C. Jenny, & T. A. Reid (Eds.), *The APSAC handbook on child maltreatment* (*2nd ed.*). Thousand Oaks: Sage.

Kempe, C. H., Silvermann, F. N., Steele, B. F., Droegemueller, W., & Silver, H. K. (1962). The battered child syndrome. *Journal of the American Medical Association*, *181*(1), 17–24.

Klein, M., & Stern, L. (1971). Low birth weight and the battered child syndrome. *American Journal of Diseases of Children* (July), 12215–12218.

Kolko, D. J. (2002). Child physical abuse. In J. E. Myers, L. Berliner, J. Briere, C. T. Hendrix, C. Jenny, & T. A. Reid (Eds.), *The APSAC handbook on child maltreatment* (*2nd ed.*). Thousand Oaks, CA: Sage.

Lieberman, A. F., & Pawl, J. H. (1988). Clinical applications of attachment theory. In J. Belsky & T. Nezworski (Eds.), *Clinical implications of attachment* (pp. 325–351). Hillsdale, NJ: Lawrence Eribaum.

Lindsey, D. (2004). *The welfare of children*. New York: Oxford University Press.

Loiselle, J. (2002). Physical abuse. In A. P. Giardino & E. R. Giardino (Eds.), *Recognition of child abuse for the mandated reporter* (pp. 1–21). St Louis, MO: G.W. Medical Publishing.

Maluccio, A. N., Warsh, R., & Pine, B. A. (1993). Family reunification: An overview. In B. A. Pine, R. Warsh, & A. N. Maluccio (Eds.), *Together again: Family reunification in foster care* (pp. 3–19). Washington, DC: Child Welfare League of America.

McClain, P. W., Sacks, J. J., Froehlke, R. G., & Ewigman, B. G. (1993). Estimates of fatal child abuse and neglect, United States, 1979 through 1988. *Pediatrics, 91*(2), 338–343.

National Center on Child Abuse and Neglect (1994). *Protecting children in substance-abusing families: The user manual series.* Washington, DC: U.S. Department of Health and Human Services.

National Center on Child Abuse and Neglect. (1997). *National incidence and prevalence of child abuse and neglect (NIS-3).* Washington, DC: U.S. Department of Health and Human Services.

Osborne, Y., Hinz, L., Rappaport, N., Williams, H., & Tuma, J. (1988). Parent social attractiveness, parent sex, child temperament, and socioeconomic status as predictors of tendency to report child abuse. *Journal of Social and Clinical Psychology, 6*(1), 69–76.

Ounsted, C., Oppenheimer, R., & Lindsay, J. (1974). Aspects of bonding failure: The psychopathology and psychotherapeutic treatment of families of battered children. *Developmental Medicine and Child Neurology, 16,* 447–457.

Pelton, L. H. (1989). *For reasons of poverty.* New York: Praeger.

Pianta, R., Egeland, B., & Erickson, M. F. (1989). The antecedents of maltreatment: Results of the mother-child interaction research project. In D. Cicchetti & V. Carlson (Eds.), *Child maltreatment: Theory and research on the causes and consequences of child abuse and neglect* (pp. 152–202). New York: Cambridge University Press.

Reid, J., Maccheto, P., & Foster, S. (1999). *No safe haven: Children of substance-abusing parents.* National Center on Addiction and Substance Abuse at Columbia University. New York. 1–180.

Scannapieco, M., & Connell-Carrick, K. (2003). Families in poverty: Those who maltreat their infants and toddlers and those who do not. *Journal of Family Social Work, 7*(3), 49–70.

Scannapieco, M., & Connell-Carrick, K. (Under review). Focus on the first years: Ecological correlates of child maltreatment for families with children 0 to 4. *Child Maltreatment.*

Sedlak, A. (1997). Risk factors for the occurrence of child abuse and neglect. *Journal of Aggression, Maltreatment and Trauma, 1*(1), 149–187.

Sedlak, A., & Broadhurst, D. (1996). *The third national incidence study of child abuse and neglect: Final report.* Rockville, MD: Westat, Inc.

Seifer, R., & Schiller, M. (1995). The role of parenting sensitivity, infant temperament, and dyadic interaction in attachment theory and assessment. In E. Waters, B. E. Vaughn, G. Posada, & K. Kondo-Ikemura (Eds.), *Caregiving, cultural, and cognitive perspectives on secure-base behavior and working models: New growing pointes of attachment theory and research.* Monographs of the Society for Research in Child Development, *60,* 2–3.

Seifer, R. Schiller, M., Sameroff, A. J., Resnick, S., & Riordan, K. (1996). Attachment, maternal sensitivity, and infant temperament during the first year of life. *Developmental Psychology, 32,* 12–25.

Sroufe, L. A. (1985). Attachment classification from the perspective of infant-caregiver relationships and infant temperament. *Child Development, 56,* 1–14.

Straus, M. (1983). Ordinary violence, child abuse, and wife beating: What do they have in common? In D. Finkelhor, R. J. Gelles, G. T. Hotaling, & M. A. Straus (Eds.), *The dark side of families: Current family violence research* (pp. 213–234). Beverly Hills, CA: Sage.

Straus, M. (1994). Beating the devil out of them: Corporal punishment in American families. New Hampshire University, Family Research Lab.

Straus, M. A., Gelles, R. J., & Steinmetz, S. K. (1980). *Behind closed doors: Violence in the American family*. New York: Anchor.

Sullivan, P. M., & Knutson, J. F. (1998). The association between child maltreatment and disabilities in a hospital-based epidemiological study. *Child Abuse and Neglect*, *22*(4), 271–288.

Swetnam, L., Peterson, C. R., & Clark, H. B. (1983). Social skills development in young children: Preventive and therapeutic approaches. *Child and Youth Services*, *5*, 5–27.

Thomas, A., & Chess, S. (1977). *Temperament and development*. New York: Brunner/Mazel.

Trickett, P., Aber, J., Carlson, V., & Cicchetti, D. (1991). The relationship of socioeconomic status to the etiology and developmental sequelae of physical child abuse. *Developmental Psychology*, *27*, 148–158.

U.S. Census Bureau. (2003). Table C4: Children with grandparents by presence of parents, gender, race and Hispanic origin for selected characteristics: March 2002. Retrieved 7/22/03 from http://www.census.gov/population/socdemo/hh-fam/cps2002.

U.S. Department of Health and Human Services, Administration for Children and Families, Administration for Children, Youth, and Families, National Center on Child Abuse and Neglect. (1996). *Executive summary of the third national incidence study of child abuse and neglect*. Retrieved from http://www.calib.com/nccanch/pubs/statinfo/nis3.cfm.

Widom, C. S. (1989). Does violence beget violence? A critical examination of the literature. *Psychological Bulletin*, *106*, 3–28.

Wolfe, D. A. (1999). *Child abuse: Implications for child development and psychopathology*. Thousand Oaks, CA: Sage.

Zellman, G. (1992). The impact of case characteristics on child abuse reporting decisions. *Child Abuse and Neglect*, *16*, 57–74.

CHAPTER 5

Aber, J., & Alle, J. (1987). Effects of maltreatment on young children's socioemotional development: An attachment theory perspective. *Developmental Psychology*, *23*(3), 406–414.

Alessandri, S. (1991). Play and social behavior is maltreated preschoolers. *Development and Psychopathology*, *27*(3), 191–205.

Allen, D., & Tarnowski, K. (1989). Depressive characteristics of physically abused children. *Journal of Abnormal Child Psychology*, *17*, 1–11.

Ammerman, R. (1989). Child abuse and neglect. In M. Hersen (Ed.), *Innovations in child behavior therapy* (pp. 353–394). New York: Springer.

Anglin, J. (1993). *Vocabulary development: A morphological analysis*. Monographs of the Society for Research in Child Development, 58 (Serial no. 238), 10.

Azar. S. T., Robinson, D., Hekimian, E., & Twentyman, C. T. (1984). Unrealistic expectations and problem-solving ability in maltreating and comparison mothers. *Journal of Consulting and Clinical Psychology*, *52*, 687–691.

Basta, S., & Peterson, R. (1990). Perpetrator status and the personality characteristics of molested children. *Child Abuse and Neglect*, *14*, 555–566.

Beeghly, M., & Cicchetti, D. (1994). Child maltreatment, attachment and the self-esteem: Emergence of an internal state of lexicon in toddlers at high social risk. *Development and Psychopathology*, *6*, 5–30.

Beitchman, J., Zucker, K., Hood, J., DaCosta, G., Akman, D., & Cassavia, E. (1992). A review of the long-term effects of child sexual abuse. *Child Abuse and Neglect*, *16*(1), 101–118.

Berliner, L. (1991). Effects of sexual abuse on children. *Violence Update*, *1*(10), 1, 8, 10–11.

Berlinger, L., & Elliott, D. (1996). Sexual abuse of children. In J. Briere, L. Berliner, J. Bulkley, C. Jenny, & T. Reid (Eds.), *The APSAC handbook on child maltreatment* (pp. 51–71). Thousand Oaks, CA: Sage.

Berlinger, L., & Elliott, D. (2002). Sexual abuse of children. In J. Briere, L. Berliner, J. Bulkley, C. Jenny, & T. Reid (Eds.). *The APSAC handbook on child maltreatment* (*2nd ed.*) (pp. 55–78). Thousand Oaks, CA: Sage.

Burgess, R., & Youngblade, L. (1989). Social incompetence and the intergenerational transmission of abusive parental-behavior. In R. Gelles, G. Hotaling, D. Finkelhor, & M. Straus (Eds.), *New directions in family violence research* (pp. 38–60). Newbury Park, CA: Sage.

Briere, J. (1989). *Therapy for adults molested as children: Beyond survival*. New York: Springer.

Brown, E., & Kolko, D. (1999). Child victims' attributions about being physically abused: An examination of factors associated with symptom severity. *Journal of Abnormal Child Psychology*, *27*(4), 311–322.

Byram, V., Wagner, H., & Waller, G. (1995). Sexual abuse and body image distortions. *Child Abuse and Neglect*, *19*, 507–510.

Camara, L., Grow, J., & Ribordy, S. (1983). Recognition of emotional expression by abused children. *Journal of Clinical Child Psychology*, *12*, 325–328.

Carlson, B. (1991). Emotionally disturbed children's beliefs and punishment. *Child Abuse and Neglect*, *15*, 19–28.

Chaffin, M., Letourneau, E., & Silovsky, J. (2002). Adults, adolescents, and children who sexually abuse children. In J. Myers, L. Berliner, J. Briere, C. Hendrix, C. Jenny, & T. Reid (Eds.), *The APSAC handbook of child maltreatment* (*2nd ed.*) (pp. 205–232). Thousand Oaks, CA: Sage Publications.

Cole, P., & Putnam, F. (1992). Effects of incest on self and social functioning: A developmental psychopathology perspective. *Journal of Consulting and Clinical Psychology*, *60*, 174–184.

Costeff, H., Grosswasser, Z., & Goldstein, R. (1990). Long-term follow-up review of 31 children with severe closed head trauma. *Journal of Neurosurgery*, *73*, 684–687.

Crittenden, P., & Ainsworth, M. (1989). Child maltreatment and attachment theory. In D. Cicchetti & V. Carslon (Eds.), *Child maltreatment: Theory and research on the causes and consequences of child abuse and neglect* (pp. 432–463). New York: Cambridge University Press.

Crittenden, P. (1992). Treatment of anxious attachment in infancy and early childhood. *Developmental Psychopathology*, *4*, 575–602.

Dodge, K., Pettit, G., & Bates, J. (1994). Effects of physical maltreatment on the development of peer relations. *Development and Psychopathology*, *6*, 43–55.

Dodge, K., Pettit, G., & Bates, J. (1997). How the experience of early physical abuse leads children to become chronically aggressive. *In Developmental perspectives on trauma: Theory, research, and intervention* (Vol. 8, pp. 263–288). Rochester, NY: University of Rochester Press.

Drossman, D., Leserman, J., Nachman, G., Li, Z., et al. (1990). Sexual and physical abuse in women with functional or organic gastrointestinal disorders. *Annals of Internal Medicine*, *113*(11), 828–833.

Dubowitz, H., Davidson, N., Fiegelman, S., et al. (1992). The physical health of children in kinship care. *American Journal of Disabled Children*, *146*, 603–610.

Egeland, B., Sroufe, L., & Erickson, M. (1983). The developmental consequences of different patterns of maltreatment. *Child Abuse and Neglect*, *7*, 459–469.

Einbender, A., & Friedrich, W. (1989). Psychological functioning and behavior of sexually abused girls. *Journal of Consulting and Clinical Psychology, 57*, 155–157.

Eisenberg, N., Fabes, R., Shepart, S., Murphy, B., Guthrie, I., Jones, S., Friedman, J., Poulin, R., & Maszk, P. (1997). Contemporaneous and longitudinal prediction of children's social functioning from regulation to emotionality. *Child Development, 68*, 642–664.

Elliott, D., & Briere, J. (1994). Forensic sexual abuse evaluations of older children: Disclosures and symptomatology. *Behavioral Sciences and the Law, 12*, 261–277.

Erickson, M., & Egeland, B. (1996). Child neglect. In J. Briere, L. Berliner, J. Bulkey, C. Jenny, & T. Reid (Eds.). *The APSAC handbook on child maltreatment* (pp. 4–20). Thousand Oaks, CA: Sage Publications.

Erickson, M., & Egeland, B. (2002). Child neglect. In J. Myers, L. Berliner, J. Briere, C. Hendrix, C. Jenny, & T. Reid (Eds.). *The APSAC handbook on child maltreatment (2nd ed.)* (pp. 3–29). Thousand Oaks, CA: Sage Publications.

Erickson, M., Egeland, B., & Pianta, R. (1989). The effects of maltreatment on the development of young children. In D. Cicchetti & V. Carlson (Eds.), *Child maltreatment: Theory and research on the causes and consequences of child abuse and neglect* (pp. 647–684). New York: Cambridge University Press.

Everson, M., & Boat, B. (1990). Sexualized doll play among young children: Implications for the use of anatomical dolls in sexual abuse evaluations. *Journal of the American Academy of Child and Adolescent Psychiatry, 29*(5), 736–742.

Fantuzzo, J., delGaudio, W., Atkins, M, Meyers, R., & Noone, M. (1998). A contextually relevant assessment of the impact of child maltreatment on the social competencies of low-income urban children. *Journal of American Academy of Child and Adolescent Psychiatry, 37*(11), 1201–1208.

Fiering, C., Taska, L., & Lewis, M. (1998). The role of shame and attributional style on children's and adolescents' adaptation to sexual abuse. *Child Maltreatment, 3*, 129–142.

Finkel, M. (2000). Initial medical management of the sexually abused child. In R. Reece (Ed.), *Treatment of child abuse*. Baltimore, MD: John Hopkins University Press.

Flaherty, E., & Weiss, H. (1990). Medical evaluation of abused and neglected chidren. *American Journal of Disabled Children, 144*, 330–334.

Friedrich, W. (1993). Sexual victimization and sexual behavior in children: A review of recent literature. *Child Abuse and Neglect, 17*, 59–66.

Friedrich, W., Beilke, R., & Urquiza, A. (1987). Children from sexually abusive families: A behavioral comparison. *Journal of Interpersonal Violence, 2*, 391–402.

Friedrich, W., Dittner, C., Action, R., Berliner, L., Butler, J., Damon, L., Davies, W., Gray, A., & Wright, J. (2001). Child sexual behavior inventory: Normative, psychiatric, and sexual abuse comparisons. *Child Maltreatment, 6*, 37–49.

Frodi, A., & Smetana, J. (1984). Abused, neglected, and nonmaltreated preschoolers' ability to discriminate emotions in others: The effects of IP. *Child Abuse and Neglect, 8*, 459–465.

Gale, J., Thompson, R., Moran, T., & Sack, W. (1988). Sexual abuse in young children: Its clinical presentation and characteristic patterns. *Child Abuse and Neglect, 12*, 163–171.

Goerge, C., & Main, M. (1979). Social interactions of young abused children: Approach, avoidance, and aggression. *Child Development, 50*, 306–318.

Halfon, N., Mendoca, A., & Berkowitz, G. (1995). Health status of children in foster care. *Archives of Pediatric and Adolescent Medicine, 149*, 386–392.

Haskett, M., & Kistner, J. (1991). Social interactions and peer perceptions of young physically abused children. *Child Development, 62*, 979–990.

Herrenkohl, E., Herrenkohl, R., Toedter, L., & Yanushefski, A. (1984). Parent-child interactions in abusive and nonabusive families. *Journal of the American Academy of Child Psychiatry, 23*, 641–648.

Hibbard, R., Roghmann, K., & Hoekelman, R. (1987). Genitalia in children's drawings: An association with sexual abuse. *Pediatrics, 79*, 129–137.

Hochstadt, N., Jaudes, P., Zimo, D., & Schacter, J. (1987). The medical and psychosocial needs of children entering foster care. *Child Abuse and Neglect, 11*, 53–62.

Hoffman-Plotnik, D., & Twentyman, C. (1984). A multimodal assessment of behavioral and cognitive deficits in abused and neglected preschoolers. *Child Development, 55*, 794–802.

Howes C., & Eldredge, R. (1985). Responses of abused, neglected, and nonmaltreated children to the behavior of their peers. *Journal of Applied Developmental Psychology, 6*, 261–270.

Howes, C., & Espinosa, M. (1985). The consequences of child abuse for the formation of relationships with peers. *Child Abuse and Neglect, 9*, 397–404.

Hunter, J., Goodwin, D., & Wilson, R. (1992). Attributions of blame in child sexual abuse victims: An analysis of age and gender influences. *Journal of Child Sexual Abuse, 1*, 75–90.

Katz, K. (1992). Communication problems in maltreated children: A tutorial. *Journal of Childhood Communication Disorders, 14*(2), 147–163.

Kaufman, J., & Cicchetti, D. (1989). The effects of maltreatment on school-aged children's socioemotional development: Assessments in a day-care setting. *Developmental Psychology, 25*, 516–524.

Kavanaugh, K., Youngblade, L., Reid, J., & Fagot, B. (1988). Interactions between children and abusive versus control parents. *Journal of Clinical Child Psychology, 17*, 137–142.

Klimes-Dougan, B., & Kistner, J. (1990). Physically abused preschoolers' response to peers' distress. *Developmental Psychology, 26*, 599–602.

Kolko, D. (1992). Characteristics of child victims of physical violence. *Journal of Interpersonal Violence, 7*(2), 244–276.

Kolko, D. (2002). Child physical abuse. In J. Myers, L. Berliner, J. Briere, C. Hendrix, C. Jenny, & T. Reid (Eds.), *The APSAC handbook on child maltreatment* (2nd ed.) (pp. 21–54). Thousand Oaks, CA: Sage Publications.

Kolko, D., Moser, J., & Weldy, S. (1988). Behavioral/emotional indicators of sexual abuse in psychiatric inpatients: A controlled comparison with physical abuse. *Child Abuse & Neglect, 12*(4), 529–541.

Kolko, D., Moser, J., & Weldy, S. (1990). Medical/health histories and physical evaluation of physically and sexually abused child psychiatric patients: A controlled study. *Journal of Family Violence, 5*(4), 249–267.

Kress, F., & Vandenberg, B. (1998). Depression and attribution in abused children and their nonoffending caregivers. *Psychological Reports, 83*, 1285–1286.

Kriel, R., Krach, L., & Panser, L. (1989). Closed head injury: Comparison of children younger and older than 6 years of age. *Pediatric Neurology, 5*, 296–300.

Kunin, C. (1978). Sexual intercourse and urinary tract infections. *New England Journal of Medicine, 298*, 336–337.

MacLennan, B. (1994). Groups for poorly socialized children in elementary school. *Journal of Child and Adolescent Group Therapy, 4*, 243–250.

Mannarino, A., & Cohen, J. (1996). A follow-up study of factors that mediate the development of psychological symptomatology in sexually abused girls. *Child Maltreatment, 1*, 246–260.

Mannarino, A., Cohen, J., & Berman, S. (1994). The Children's Attributions and Perceptions Scale: A new measure of sexual abuse-related factors. *Journal of Clinical Child Psychology, 23*, 204–211.

McLeer, S., Debliner, E., Henry, D., & Orvaschel, H. (1992). Sexually abused children at high risk for posttraumatic stress disorder. *Journal of the American Academy of Child and Adolescent Psychiatry, 31*, 875–879.

Moffatt, M., Peddie, M., Stulginskas, J., et al. (1985). Health care delivery to foster children: A study. *Health Social Work, 9*, 71–96.

Olafson, E., & Boat, B. (2000). Long-term management of the sexually abused child: Considerations and challenges. In R. Reece (Ed.), *Treatment of child abuse.* Baltimore, MD: John Hopkins University Press.

Perez, C., & Widom, C. (1994). Childhood victimization and long-term intellectual and academic outcome. *Child Abuse and Neglect, 18*, 617–633.

Reidy, T. (1977). Aggressive characteristics of abused and neglected children. *Journal of Clinical Psychology, 33*, 1140–1145.

Ruggerio, K., McLeer, S., & Dixon, J. (2000). Sexual abuse characteristics associated with survivor psychopathology. *Child Abuse and Neglect, 24*, 951–964.

Salzinger, S., Samit, C., Kreiger, R., Kaplan, S., & Kaplan, T. (1986). A controlled study of the life events of mothers and maltreated children in suburban families. *Journal of the American Academy of Child Psychiatry, 25*, 419–426.

Sandnabba, N., Santtila, P., Wannas, M., & Krook, K. (2003). Age and gender specific sexual behaviors in children. *Child Abuse and Neglect, 27*, 579–605.

Schneider-Rosen, K., & Cicchetti, D. (1984). The relationship between affect and cognition in maltreated infants: Quality of attachment and the development of visual self-recognition. *Child Development, 55*, 648–658.

Shapiro, J., Leifer, M., Martone, M., & Kasem, L. (1992). Cognitive functioning and social competence as predictors of maladjustment in sexually abused girls. *Journal of Interpersonal Violence, 7*, 156–164.

Shonk, S., & Cicchetti, D. (2001). Maltreatment, competency deficits, and risk for academic and behavioral adjustment. *Developmental Psychology, 37*(1), 3–17.

Sroufe, L. (1996). *Emotional development: The organization of emotional lie in the early years.* Cambridge: Cambridge University Press.

U.S. Department of Health and Human Services, Administration on Children, Youth, and Families. (2000). Child maltreatment 1998: Reports from the states to the *National Child Abuse and Neglect Data Systems.* Washington, DC: U.S. Government Printing Office.

U.S. Department of Health and Human Services, Administration on Children, Youth, and Families. (2002). Child maltreatment 2000: Reports from the states to the *National Child Abuse and Neglect Data Systems.* Washington, DC: U.S. Government Printing Office.

Volbert, R., & van der Zanden, R. (1992). Sexual knowledge and behavior of children up to 12 years—what is age-appropriate? In G. Davies, S. Lloyd-Bostock, M. McMurran, & C. Wilson (Eds.), *Psychology, law, and criminal justice* (pp. 198–215). Portland: Walter Gruyter.

Walker, E., Gelfand, A., & Katon, W. (1995). Psychiatric diagnoses, sexual and physical victimization, and disability in patients with irritable bowel syndrome or inflammatory bowel disease. *Psychological Medicine, 25*, 1259–1267.

Walker, E., Katon, W., Roy-Byrne, P., Jemelka, R., & Russon, J. (1993). Histories of sexual victimization in patients with irritable bowel syndrome or inflammatory bowel disease. *American Journal of Psychiatry, 150*, 1502–1506.

Wodarski, J., Kurtz, P., Gaudin, J., et al. (1990). Maltreatment and the school-aged child: Major academic, socioemotional, and adaptive outcomes. *Social Work Research Abstracts*, *35*, 506–513.

Yates, A., Beutler, L., & Crago, M. (1985). Drawings by child victims of incest. *Child Abuse and Neglect*, *9*, 183–189.

CHAPTER 6

Adams, J. A., Harper, K., & Revilla, J. (1994). Examination findings in legally confirmed sexual abuse: It's normal to be normal. *Pediatrics*, *94*, 310–317.

American Psychiatric Association. (2000). *Diagnostic and statistical manual of mental disorders, DSM-IV-TR*. Washington, DC: Author.

Ammerman, R. T., Kolko, D. J., Kirisci, L., Blackson, T. C., & Dawes, M. A. (1999). Child abuse potential in parents with histories of substance abuse disorder. *Child Abuse and Neglect*, *23*, 1225–1238.

Azar, S. T. (1997). A cognitive-behavioral approach to understanding and treating parents who physically abuse their children. In D. A. Wolfe, R. J. McMahon, & R. Peters (Eds.), *Child abuse: New directions in prevention and treatment across the lifespan* (pp. 78–100). Thousand Oaks, CA: Sage.

Azar, S. T., Barnes, K. T., & Twentyman, C. T. (1988). Developmental outcomes in abused children: Consequences of parental abuse or a more general breakdown in caregiver behavior? *Behavior Therapist*, *11*(2), 27–32.

Azar, S. T., & Siegel, B. R. (1990). Behavioral treatment of child abuse: A developmental perspective. *Behavior Modification*, *14*, 279–300.

Azar, S. T., & Wolfe, D. A. (1998). Child physical abuse and neglect. In E. J. Mash & R. A. Barkley (Eds.), *Treatment of childhood disorders* (2nd ed.). New York: Guilford.

Baker, B. L., Brightman, A. J., Heifetz, L. J., & Murphy, D. M. (1976). *Behavior problems: A skills training series for children with special needs*. Champaign, IL: Research Press.

Bauer, W. D., & Twentyman, C. T. (1985). Abusing, neglecting and comparison mothers' responses to child-related and nonchild-related stressors. *Journal of Consulting and Clinical Psychology*, *53*, 335–343.

Belsky, J. (1980). Child maltreatment: An ecological integration. *American Psychologist*, *35*(4), 320–335.

Belsky, J., & Vondra, J. (1989). Lessons from child abuse: The determinants of parenting. In C. D. Carlson & V. Carlson (Eds.), *Child maltreatment: Theory and research on the causes and consequences of child abuse and neglect* (pp. 153–202). New York: Cambridge University Press.

Berliner, L., & Elliott, D. M. (2002). Sexual abuse of children. In J. E. Myers, L. Berliner, J. Briere, C. T. Hendrix, C. Jenny, & T. A. Reid (Eds.), *The APSAC handbook on child maltreatment* (2nd ed.). Thousand Oaks, CA: Sage.

Berrick, J. D., & Duerr, M. (1997). Preventing child neglect: A study of an in-home program for children and families. In J. D. Berrick, R. P. Barth, & N. Gilbert (Eds.), *Child welfare research review* (pp. 2, 63–83). New York: Columbia University Press.

Berrick, J. D., Needell, B., Barth, R. P., & Jonson-Reid, M. (1998). *The tender years: Toward developmentally sensitive child welfare services for very young children*. New York: Oxford University Press.

Brayden, R., Atlemeier, W., Tucker, D., Dietrich, M., & Vietze, P. (1992). Antecedents of child neglect in the first 2 years of life. *Journal of Pediatrics*, *120*, 426–429.

Brazelton, T. B. (1997). *Toilet training your child*. New York: Consumer Visions.

Cadzow, S. P., Armstrong, K. L., & Frazer, J. A. (1999). Stressed parents with infants: Reassessing physical abuse risk factors. *Child Abuse and Neglect, 23*(9), 845–853.

Chance, T., & Scannapieco, M. (2002). Ecological correlates of child maltreatment: Similarities and differences between child fatality and non-fatality cases. *Child and Adolescent Social Work Journal, 19*(2), 139–161.

Cicchetti, D., & Barnett, D. (1991). Attachment organization in maltreated preschoolers. *Development and Psychopathology, 3*, 397–411.

Cicchetti, D., & Lynch, M. (1993). Toward an ecological/transactional model of community violence and child maltreatment: Consequences for children's development. *Psychiatry, 56*, 96–118.

Cicchetti, D., & Lynch, M. (1995). Failures in the expectable environment and their impact on individual development: The case of child maltreatment. In D. Cicchetti & D. J. Cohen (Eds.), *Developmental psychopathology: Vol. 2. Risk, disorder, and adaptation* (pp. 261–279). New York: John Wiley.

Cicchetti, D., & Toth, S. L. (2000). Child maltreatment and attachment organization: Implications for intervention. In S. Goldberg, R. Muir, & J. Kerr (Eds.), *Attachment theory: Social, developmental, and clinical perspectives*. Hillsdale, NJ: Analytic Press.

Coohey, C. (1996). Child maltreatment: Testing the social isolation hypothesis. *Child Abuse and Neglect, 20*, 241–254.

Coohey, C. (2000). The role of friends, in-laws, and other kin in father-penetrated child physical abuse. *Child Welfare, 79*(4), 373–402.

Crittenden, P. M. (1988). Relationships at risk. In J. Belsky & T. Nezworski (Eds.), *Clinical implications of attachment theory* (pp. 136–174). Hillsdale, NJ: Lawrence Erlbaum.

Crittenden, P. M. (1993). An information-processing perspective on the behavior of neglectful parents. *Criminal Justice and Behavior, 20*, 27–48.

Daro, D. (1988). *Confronting child abuse: Research for effective program design*. New York: Free Press.

Dawson, B., DeArmas, A., McGrath, M. L., & Kelly, J. A. (1986). Cognitive problem-solving training to improve the child-care judgment of child neglectful parents. *Journal of Family Violence, 1*, 209–221.

DePanfilis, D. (1996). Social isolation of neglectful families: A review of social support assessment and intervention models. *Child Maltreatment, 1*(1), 37–52.

Dolz, L., Cerezo, M. A., & Milner, J. S. (1997). Mother-child interactional patterns in high- and low-risk mothers. *Child Abuse and Neglect, 21*(2), 1149–1158.

Dore, M. M., Doris, J. M., & Wright, P. (1995). Identifying substance abuse in maltreating families: A child welfare challenge. *Child Abuse and Neglect, 19*, 531–543.

Drach, K. M., & Devoe, L. (2000). Initial psychosocial treatment of the physically abused child: The issue of removal. In R. M. Reece (Ed.), *Treatment of child abuse: Common ground for mental health, medical, and legal practitioners*. Baltimore, MD: Johns Hopkins University Press.

Dubowitz, H., Black, M., Kerr, M., Starr, R., & Harrington, D. (2000). Fathers and neglect. *Archives of Pediatric and Adolescent Medicine, 154*, 135–141.

Dunst, C. J., Trivette, C. M., & Deal, A. G. (Eds.). (1994). *Supporting and strengthening families: Vol. 1. Methods, strategies, and practices*. Cambridge, MA: Brookline Books.

Ferrara, F. F. (2002). *Childhood sexual abuse: Developmental effects across the lifespan*. Pacific Grove, CA: Brooks/Cole.

Finkelhor, D., & Berliner, L. (1995). Research on the treatment of sexually abused children: Reviewed recommendations. *Journal of the American Academy of Child and Adolescent Psychiatry, 34*, 1–5.

Finkelhor, D., Williams, L. M., & Burns, N. (1988). *Nursery crimes: Sexual abuse in day care*. Newbury Park, CA: Sage.

Friedrich, W. N., Dittner, C. A., Action, R., Berliner, L., Butler, J., Damon, L., Davies, W. H., Gray, A., & Wright, J. (2001). Child sexual behavior inventory: Normative, psychiatric and sexual abuse comparisons. *Child Maltreatment, 6*, 37–49.

Garbarino, J., & Kostelny, K. (1992). Child maltreatment as a community problem. *Child Abuse and Neglect, 16*, 455–464.

Garbarino, J., & Sherman, D. (1980). High-risk neighborhoods and high-risk families: The human ecology of child maltreatment. *Child Development, 51*(1), 188–198.

Garbarino, J., Dubrow, N., Kostelny, K., & Pardo, C. (1992). *Children in danger: Coping with the consequences of community violence*. San Francisco: Jossey-Bass.

Gaudin, J. M., Jr., Wodarski, J. S., Atkinson, M. K., & Avery, L. S. (1990). Remedying child neglect: Effectiveness of social network interventions. *Journal of Applied Social Sciences, 15*, 97–123.

Gaudin, J., Polansky, N., Kilpatrick, A., & Shilton, P. (1993). Loneliness, depression, stress and social supports in neglectful families. *American Journal of Orthopsychiatry, 63*(4), 597–605.

Gaudin, J., Polansky, N., Kilpatrick, A., & Shilton, P. (1996). Family functioning in neglectful families. *Child Abuse and Neglect, 4*, 363–377.

Giardino, A. P., & Giardino, E. R. (2002). *Recognition of child abuse for the mandated reporter*. St. Louis, MO: G. W. Medical Publishing.

Granvold, D. K. (Ed.). (1994). *Cognitive and behavioral treatment: Methods and applications*. Pacific Grove, CA: Brooks/Cole.

Handen, B. L. (1998). Mental retardation. In E. J. Mash & R. A. Barkley (Eds.), *Treatment of childhood disorders* (2nd ed.). New York: Guilford.

Hobbs, T., & Peck, C. (1985). Toilet training people with profound mental retardation: A cost-effective procedure for large residential settings. *Behavioral Engineering, 9*, 50–57.

Kendall-Tackett, K. A., Williams, L. M., & Finkelhor, D. (1993). Impact of sexual abuse on children: A review and synthesis of recent empirical studies. *Psychology Bulletin, 113*, 164–180.

Kirby, L. D., & Fraser, M. W. (1997). Risk and resilience in childhood. In M. W. Fraser (Ed.), *Risk and resilience in childhood: An ecological perspective* (pp. 10–33). Washington, DC: NASW Press.

Lahey, B., Conger, R., Atkenson, B., & Treiber, F. (1984). Parenting behavior and emotional status of physically abusive mothers. *Journal of Consulting and Clinical Psychology, 52*, 1062–1071.

Larrance, D. T., & Twentyman, C. T. (1983). Maternal attributions and child abuse. *Journal of Abnormal Psychology, 92*, 449–457.

Liebert, R. M., & Fischel, J. E. (1990). The elimination disorders: Enuresis and encopresis. In M. Lewis & S. M. Miller (Eds.), *Handbook of developmental pathology*. New York: Plenum.

Lutzker, S. Z., Lutzker, J. R., Braunling-McMorrow, D., & Eddleman, J. (1987). Prompting to increase mother-baby stimulation with single mothers. *Journal of Child and Adolescent Psychotherapy, 4*, 3–2.

Maluccio, A. M., Abramczyk, L., & Thomlison, B. (1996). Family reunification of children in out-of-home care: Research perspectives. *Children and Youth Services Review, 18*, 4–5.

Masten, A. (1994). Resilience in individual development: Successful adaptation despite risk and adversity. In M. C. Wang & E. W. Gordon (Eds.), *Educational resilience in inner-city America: Challenges and prospects* (pp. 3–26). Hillsdale, NJ: Lawrence Erlbaum.

Miller-Perrin, C. L., & Perrin, R. D. (1999). *Child maltreatment: An introduction*. Thousand Oaks, CA: Sage.

National Center on Child Abuse and Neglect. (1993). *A report on the maltreatment of children with disabilities*. Washington, DC: U.S. Department of Health and Human Services.

Oldershaw, L., Walters, G. C., & Hall, D. K. (1986). Control strategies and noncompliance in abusive mother-child dyads: An observational study. *Child Development, 57,* 722–732.

Osofsky, J. D. (1999). The impact of violence on children. In *Domestic Violence and Children: The Future of Children, 9*(3), 33–49. Los Altos, CA: David and Lucille Packard Foundation.

Pecora, P. J., Whittaker, J. K., Maluccio, A. N., & Barth, R. P. (2000). *The child welfare challenge: Policy, practice, and research (2nd ed.)*. New York: Aldine De Gruyter.

Pelton, L. H. (1994). The role of material factors in child abuse and neglect. In G. B. Melton & F. D. Barry (Eds.), *Protecting children from abuse and neglect: Foundations for a new strategy* (pp. 131–181). New York: Guilford.

Radke-Yarrow, M., & Sherman, T. (1990). Hard growing: Children who survive. In J. Rolf, A. S. Masten, D. Cicchetti, K. H. Nuechterlein, & S. Weintraub (Eds.), *Risk and protective factors in the development of psychopathology* (pp. 97–119). Cambridge: Cambridge University Press.

Rathus, S. (2003). History, theories, and methods. In S. Rathus, *Voyages: Childhood and adolescence* (pp. 1–53). Belmont, CA: Wadsworth/Thomson Learning.

Reece, R. M. (2000). *Treatment of child abuse: Common ground for mental health, medical, and legal practitioners*. Baltimore, MD: Johns Hopkins University Press.

Reid, J., Macchetto, P., & Foster, S. (1999). *No safe haven: Children of substance-abusing parents*. New York: National Center on Addiction and Substance Abuse at Columbia University.

Richmond, G. (1983). Shaping bowel and bladder continence in developmentally retarded preschool children. *Journal of Autism and Developmental Disabilities, 13,* 197–204.

Richters, J. E., & Martinez, P. E. (1993). Violent communities, family choices, and children's changes: An algorithm for improving the odds. *Development and Psychopathology, 5,* 609–627.

Scannapieco, M., & Connell-Carrick, K. (In press). Families in poverty: Those who maltreat their infants and toddlers and those who do not. *Journal of Family Social Work*.

Scannapieco, M., & Connell-Carrick, K. (Under review). Focus on the first years: Ecological correlates of child maltreatment for families with children 0 to 4. *Child Maltreatment*.

Simons, R. L., Whitbeck, L. B., Conger, R. D., & Chyi-In, W. (1991). Intergenerational transmission of harsh parenting. *Developmental Psychology, 27,* 159–171.

Straus, M. A., & Smith, C. (1990). Family patterns and child abuse. In M. A. Straus & R. J. Gelles (Eds.), *Physical violence in American families: Risk factors and adaptations to violence in 8,145 families* (pp. 258–259). New Brunswick, NJ: Transaction.

Sullivan, P. M., & Knutson, J. F. (1998). The association between child maltreatment and disabilities in a hospital-based epidemiological study. *Child Abuse and Neglect, 22*(4), 271–188.

Trickett, P., & Susman, E. (1989). Perceived similarities and disagreements about child-rearing practices in abusive and nonabusive families: Intergenerational and concurrent family processes. In D. Cicchetti & V. Carlson (Eds.), *Child maltreatment: Theory and research on the causes and consequences of child abuse and neglect* (pp. 280–301). New York: Cambridge University Press.

U.S. Department of Health and Human Services, Administration for Children and

Families, Administration for Children, Youth, and Families, National Center on Child Abuse and Neglect. (1996). *Executive summary of the third national incidence study of child abuse and neglect*. Retrieved from www.calib.com/nccanch/pubs/statinfo/nis3.cfm.

U.S. Department of Health and Human Services, Administration for Children and Families, Administration for Children, Youth, and Families, Children's Bureau (2000). *Child maltreatment 2000*. Washington, DC: Author.

Werner, E. E. (1993). Risk, resilience, and recovery: Perspectives from the Kauai longitudinal study. *Development and Psychopathology, 5*, 503–515.

Whitman, B. (2002). Psychological and psychiatric issues. In A. P. Giardino & E. R. Giardino (Eds.), *Recognition of child abuse for the mandated reporter (3rd ed.)*. St. Louis, MO: G.W. Medical Publishing.

Wolfe, D. (1985). Child-abusive parents: An empirical review and analysis. *Psychological Bulletin, 97*, 462–482.

Wolfe, D. (1994). The role of intervention and treatment services in the prevention of child abuse and neglect. In G. B. Melton & F. D. Barry (Eds.), *Protecting children from abuse and neglect: Foundations for a new national strategy* (pp. 224–304). New York: Guilford.

Wolfe, D., & Wekerle, C. (1993). Treatment strategies for child physical abuse and neglect: A critical progress report. *Clinical Psychology Review, 13*, 473–500.

CHAPTER 7

Alessandri, S. (1991). Play and social behavior in maltreated preschoolers. *Development and Psychopathology, 3*, 191–205.

Allen, D., & Tarnowski, K. (1989). Depressive characteristics of physically abused children. *Journal of Abnormal Child Psychology, 17*, 1–11.

Ammerman, R. (1989). Child abuse and neglect. In M. Hersen (Ed.), *Innovations in Child Behavior Therapy*, 353–394. New York: Springer.

Azar, S. & Wolfe, D. (1989). Child physical abuse and neglect. In E. Mash and R. Barkley (Eds), *Treatment of childhood disorders (2nd ed.)* (pp. 501–544).

Berk, L. (1999). *Infants, children, and adolescents (3rd ed.)*. Boston: Allyn Bacon.

Berliner, L., & Elliott, D. (2002). Sexual abuse of children. In J. Myers, L. Berliner, J. Briere, C. Hendrix, C. Jenny, & T. Reid (Eds.). *The APSAC handbook of child maltreatment (2nd ed.)*, (pp. 55–78). Thousand Oaks, CA: Sage Publications.

Briere, J. (1989). *Therapy for adults molested as children*. New York: Springer Publishing.

Cavaiola, A., & Schiff, M. (1988). Behavioral sequalae of physical and/or sexual abuse in adolescents. *Child Abuse and Neglect, 12*, 181–188.

Cratty, B. (1986). Perceptual *and motor development in infants and children (3rd ed.)*. Englewood Cliffs, NJ: Prentice-Hall.

Crittenden, P., & Ainsworth, M. (1989). Child maltreatment and attachment theory. In D. Cicchett and V. Carlson (Eds.). *Child maltreatment: Theory and research on the causes and consequences of child abuse and neglect* (pp. 432–463). New York: Cambridge University Press.

Dean, A., Malik, M., Richards, W., & Stringer, S. (1986). Effects of parental maltreatment of children's conceptions of interpersonal relationships. *Developmental Psychology, 22*, 617–626.

Deblinger, E., McLeer, S., Atkins, M., Ralphe, D., & Foa, E. (1989). Posttraumatic stress in sexually abused, physically abused and nonabused children. *Child Abuse and Neglect, 13*, 403–408.

Dubner, A., & Motta, R. (1999). Sexually and physically abused foster care children and post-traumatic stress disorder. *Journal of Consulting and Clinical Psychology*, 67, 367–373.

Dubowitz, H., Davidson, N., Feigelman, S., et al. (1992). The physical health of children in kinship care. *American Journal of Disabled Children*, 146, 603–610.

Eckenrode, J., Laird, M., & Doris, J. (1993). School performance and disciplinary problems among abused and neglected children. *Developmental Psychology*, 29, 53–63.

Einbender, A., & Friedrich, W. (1989). Psychological functioning and behavior of sexually abused girls. *Journal of Consulting and Clinical Psychology*, 57, 155–157.

Erickson, M., & Egeland, B. (1996). Child neglect. In J. Briere, L. Berliner, J. Bulkey, C. Jenny, & T. Reid (Eds.), *The APSAC handbook on child maltreatment* (pp. 4–20). Thousand Oaks, CA: Sage Publications.

Erickson, M., & Egeland, B. (2002). Child neglect. In J. Myers, L. Berliner, J. Briere, C. Hendrix, C. Jenny, & T. Reid (Eds.), *The APSAC handbook on child maltreatment* (*2nd ed.*) (pp. 3–29). Thousand Oaks, CA: Sage Publications.

Erickson, M., Egeland, B., & Pianta, R. (1989). The effects of maltreatment on the development of young children. In D. Cicchetti & V. Carlson (Eds.), *Child maltreatment: Theory and research on the causes and consequences of child abuse and neglect* (pp. 647–684). New York: Cambridge University Press.

Famularo, R., Kinscherff, R., & Fenton, T. (1992). Psychiatric diagnoses of abusive mothers: A preliminary report. *Journal of Nervous and Mental Diseases*, 180, 658–661.

Fantuzzo, J. (1990). Behavioral treatment of the victims of child abuse and neglect. *Behavior Modification*, 14, 316–339.

Felitti, V. (1991). Long-term medical consequences of incest, rape, and molestation. *Southern Medical Journal*, 84, 328–331.

Fiering, C., Taska, L., & Lewis, M. (1998). The role of shame and attributional style on children's and adolescents' adaptation to sexual abuse. *Child Maltreatment*, 3, 129–142.

Finkel, M. (2000). Initial medical management of the sexually abused child. In R. Reece (Ed), *Treatment of child abuse: Common ground for mental health, medical, and legal practitioners* (pp. 3–13). Baltimore, MD: John Hopkins University Press.

Finkelhor, D. (1990). Early and long-term effects of child sexual abuse. *Professional Psychology: Research and Practice*, 21(5), 325–330.

Flaherty, E., & Weiss, H. (1990). Medical evaluation of abused and neglected children. *American Journal of Disabled Children*, 144, 330–334.

Friedrich, W. (1993). Sexual victimization and sexual behavior in children: A review of recent literature. *Child Abuse and Neglect*, 17, 59–66.

Friedrich, W., Beilke, R., & Urquiza, A. (1987). Children from sexually abusive families: A behavioral comparison. *Journal of Interpersonal Violence*, 2(4), 391–402.

Friedrich, W., Enbender, A., & Luecke, W. (1983). Cognitive and behavioral characteristics of physically abused children. *Journal of Consulting and Clinical Psychology*, 51, 313–314.

Friedrich, W., Fisher, J., Dittner, C., Acton, R., et al. (2001). Sexual behavior inventory: Normative, psychiatric, and sexual abuse comparisons. *Child Maltreatment*, 6(1), 37–49.

Friedrich, W., Jaworski, T., Huxasahl, J., & Bengtson, B. (1997). Dissociative and sexual behavior in children and adolescents with sexual abuse and psychiatric histories. *Journal of Interpersonal Violence*, 12, 155–171.

Gale, J., Thompson, R., Moran, T., & Sack, W. (1988). Sexual abuse in young children: Its clinical presentation and characteristic patterns. *Child Abuse and Neglect*, 12, 163–171.

Gelles, R., & Straus, M. (1990). The medical and psychological costs of family violence. In M. Straus & R. Gelles (Eds.), *Physical violence in American families: Risk factors and adaptations to violence in 8,145 families* (pp. 425–430). New Brunswick, NJ: Transaction Books.

Haskett, M. (1990). Social problem-solving skills of young physically abused children. *Child Psychiatry and Human Development, 21,* 109–118.

Hochstadt, N., Jaudes, P., Zimo, D., & Schacter, J. (1987). The medical and psychosocial needs of children entering foster care. *Child Abuse and Neglect, 11,* 53–62.

Hoffman-Plotkin, D., & Twentyman, C. (1984). A multimodal assessment of behavioral and cognitive deficits in abused and neglected preschoolers. *Child Development, 55,* 794–802.

Hotte, J., & Rafman, S. (1992). The specific effects of incest on prepubertal girls from dysfunctional families. *Child Abuse and Neglect, 16,* 273–283.

Howe, T., Tepper, F., & Parke, R. (1998). The emotional understanding of peer relations of abused children in residential treatment. *Residential Treatment for Children and Youth, 15*(3), 69–82.

Howing, P., Wodarski, J., Kurtz, P., & Gaudin, J. (1993). *Maltreatment and the school-aged child.* NY: Hawthorn Press.

Hufton, I., & Oates, R. (1977). Non-organic failure to thrive: A long-term follow-up. *Pediatrics, 59,* 73–77.

Hunter, J., Goodwin, D., & Wilson, R. (1992). Attributions of blame in child sexual abuse victims: An analysis of age and gender influences. *Journal of Child Sexual Abuse, 1,* 75–90.

Katz, K. (1992). Communication problems in maltreated children: A tutorial. *Journal of Childhood Communication Disorders, 14*(2), 147–163.

Kaufman, J., & Cicchetti, D. (1989). The effects of maltreatment on school-aged children's socioemotional development: Assessments in a day-care setting. *Developmental Psychology, 25,* 516–524.

Kolko, D., Moser, J., & Weldy, S. R. (1988). Behavioral/emotional indicators of sexual abuse in psychiatric inpatients: A controlled comparison with physical abuse. *Child Abuse and Neglect, 12,* 529–541.

Koverola, C., Pound, J., Heger, A., & Lytle, C. (1993). Relationship of child sexual abuse to depression. *Child Abuse and Neglect, 17,* 393–400.

Kress, F., & Vandenberg, B. (1998). Depression and attribution in abused children and their nonoffending caregivers. *Psychological Reports, 83,* 1285–1286.

Lanktree, C., & Briere, J. (1995). Outcomes of therapy for sexually abused children: A repeated measures study. *Child Abuse and Neglect, 19,* 1145–1156.

Lanktree, L., Briere, J., & Zaidi, L. (1991). Incidence and impact of sexual abuse in a child outpatient sample: The role of direct inquiry. *Child Abuse and Neglect, 15,* 447–453.

Levendosky, A., Okun, A., & Parker, J. (1995). Depression and maltreatment as predictors of social competence and social problem-solving skills in school-age children. *Child Abuse and Neglect, 19*(10), 1183–1195.

Mannarino, A., & Cohen, J. (1996). Abuse-related attributions and perceptions, general attributions and locus of control in sexually abused girls. *Journal of Interpersonal Violence, 11,* 162–180.

Mannarino, A., Cohen, J., & Berman, S. (1994). The Children's Attributions and Perceptions Scale: A new measure of sexual-abuse related factors. *Journal of Clinical Child Psychology, 23,* 203–211.

McLeer, S., Debliner, E., Henry, D., & Orvaschel, H. (1992). Sexually abused children at high risk for posttraumatic stress disorder. *Journal of the American Academy of Child and Adolescent Psychiatry, 31,* 875–879.

Miller-Perrin, C., Wurtele, S., & Kondrick, P. (1990). Sexually abused and nonabused children's conceptions of personal body safety. *Child Abuse and Neglect, 14,* 99–112.

Moffatt, M., Peddie, M., Stulginskas, J., et al. (1985). Health care delivery to foster children: A study. *Health Social Work,* 129–137.

Reid, J., Kavanagh, K., & Baldwin, D. (1987). Abusive parents' perceptions of child problem behaviors: An example of parental bias. *Journal of Abnormal Child Psychology, 15*, 457–466.

Reyome, N. (1993). A comparison of the school performance of sexually abused, neglected, and non-maltreated Children. *Child Study Journal, 23*(1), 17–38.

Roesler, T. (2000). Discovery of childhood sexual abuse in adults. In R. Reece (Ed.), *Treatment of child abuse*. Baltimore, MD: John Hopkins University Press.

Rogosch, F., Cicchetti, D., & Abre, J. (1995). The role of child maltreatment in early deviations in cognitive and affective processing abilities and later peer relationship problems. *Development and Psychopathology, 7*(4), 591–609.

Rust, J., & Troupe, P. (1991). Relationships of treatment of child sexual abuse with school achievement and self-concept. *Journal of Early Adolescence, 11*, 420–429.

Salzinger, S., Feldman, R., Hammer, M., & Rosario, M. (1993). The effects of physical abuse on children's social relationships. *Child Development, 64*, 169–187.

Salzinger, S., Kaplan, S., Pelcovitz, D., Samit, C., & Krieger, R. (1984). Parent and teacher assessment of children's behavior in child maltreating families. *Journal of the American Academy of Child Psychiatry, 23*, 458–464.

Saunders, B., Kilpatrick, D., Hanson, R., Resnick, H., & Walker, M. (1999). Prevalence, case characteristics, and long-term psychological correlates of child rape among women: A national survey. *Child Maltreatment, 4*, 187–200.

Tarter, R., Hegedus, A., Winsten, N., & Alterman, A. (1984). Neuropsychological, personality and familial characteristics of physically abused delinquents. *Journal of the American Academy of Child and Adolescent Psychiatry, 23*, 668–674.

Trickett, P., McBride-Chang, C., & Putnam, F. (1994). The classroom performance and behavior of sexually abused females. *Development and Psychopathology, 6*, 183–194.

Vondra, J., Barnett, D., & Cicchetti, D. (1989). Perceived and actual competence among maltreated and comparison school children. *Development and Psychopathology, 1*, 237–255.

Wang, C., & Daro, D. (1989). *Current trends in child abuse reporting and fatalities: The results of the 1997 annual fifty state survey*. Chicago: National Center on Child Abuse Prevention Research.

Wing, T., & Silvern, L. (1992). Type and extent of child abuse as predictors of adult functioning. *Journal of Family Violence, 7*, 261–281.

Wodarski, J., Kurtz, P., Gaudin, J., & Howing, P. (1990). Maltreatment and the school-aged child: Major academic, socioemotional, and adaptive outcomes. *Social Work, 35*, 506–513.

CHAPTER 8

Adams, J. A. (2001). Evolution of classification scale: Medical evaluation of suspected child sexual abuse. *Child Maltreatment, 6*(1), 31–36.

Ammerman, R. T., Kolko, D. J., Kirisci, L., Blackson, T. C., & Dawes, M. A. (1999). Child abuse potential in parents with histories of substance abuse disorder. *Child Abuse and Neglect, 23*, 1225–1238.

Anthony, E. J., & Cohler, B. (1987). *The invulnerable child*. New York: Guilford.

Azar, S. T. (1997). A cognitive-behavioral approach to understanding and treating parents who physically abuse their children. In D. A. Wolfe, R. J. McMahon, & R. Peters (Eds.), *Child abuse: New directions in prevention and treatment across the lifespan* (pp. 78–100). Thousand Oaks, CA: Sage.

Azar, S. T., Breton, S. J., & Miller, L. R. (1998). Cognitive-behavioral group work and physical child abuse: Intervention and prevention. In K. C. Stoiber & T. R. Kratochwill (Eds.), *Handbook of group intervention for children and families* (pp. 376–400). Needham Heights, MA: Allyn & Bacon.

Bagley, C., Wood, M., & Young, L. (1994). Victim to abuser: Mental health and behavioral sequels of child sexual abuse in a community survey of young adult males. *Child Abuse and Neglect, 8*, 683–697.

Belsky, J., & Vondra, J. (1989). Lessons from child abuse: The determinants of parenting. In C. D. Carlson & V. Carlson (Eds.), *Child maltreatment: Theory and research on the causes and consequences of child abuse and neglect* (pp.153–202). New York: Cambridge University Press.

Berliner, L., & Elliott, D. M. (2002). Sexual abuse of children. In J. E. Myers, L. Berliner, J. Briere, C. T. Hendrix, C. Jenny, & T. A. Reid (Eds.), *The APSAC handbook on child maltreatment (2nd ed.).* Thousand Oaks, CA: Sage.

Bolen, R. M. (2001). Risk factors for child sexual abuse victimization. In *Child sexual abuse: Its scope and our future* (pp. 135–161). New York: Kluwer Academic/Plenum Publishers.

Bolen, R. M., & Scannapieco, M. (1999). Prevalence of child sexual abuse: A corrective metanalysis. *Social Service Review, 73*(3), 281–313.

Brown, J., Cohen, P., Johnson, J., & Salzinger, S. (1998). A longitudinal analysis of risk factors for child maltreatment: Findings of a 17-year prospective study of officially recorded and self-reported child abuse and neglect. *Child Abuse and Neglect, 22* (11), 1065–1078.

Burgess, R. L., & Conger, R. D. (1978). Family interaction in abusive, neglectful, and normal families. *Child Development, 49*(4), 1163–1173.

Chaffin, M., Kelleher, K., & Hollenberg, J. (1996). Onset of physical abuse and neglect: Psychiatric, substance abuse, and social risk factors from prospective community data. *Child Abuse and Neglect, 20*(3), 191–203.

Chandy, J. M., Blum, R. W., & Resnick, M. D. (1996). Gender-specific outcomes for sexually abused adolescents. *Child Abuse and Neglect, 20*, 1219–231.

Christensen, M., Brayeden, R., Dietrich, M., McLaughlin, F., & Sherrod, K. (1994). The prospective assessment of self-concept in neglectful and physically abusive low income mothers. *Child Abuse and Neglect, 18*(3), 225–232.

Cicchetti, D., & Lynch, M. (1993). Toward an ecological/transactional model of community violence and child maltreatment: Consequences for children's development. *Psychiatry, 56*, 96–118.

Cicchetti, D., & Lynch, M. (1995). Failures in the expectable environment and their impact on individual development: The case of child maltreatment. In D. Cicchetti & D. J. Cohen (Eds.), *Developmental psychopathology: Vol. 2. Risk, disorder, and adaptation* (pp. 261–279). New York: John Wiley.

Cicchetti, D., & Rizley, R. (1981). Developmental perspective on the etiology, intergenerational transmission and sequelae of child maltreatment. *New Directions for Child Development, 11*, 31–55.

Cicchetti, D., & Toth, S. L. (2000). Child maltreatment and attachment organization: Implications for intervention. In S. Goldberg, R. Muir, & J. Kerr, *Attachment theory: Social developmental and clinical perspectives.* Hillsdale, NJ: Analytic Press.

Cicchetti, D., Toth, S. L., & Hennessy, K. (1993). Child maltreatment and school adaptation: Problems and promises. In D. Cicchetti & S. L. Toth (Eds.), *Child abuse, child development, and social policy* (pp. 301–330). Norwood, NJ: Ablex.

Cohen, J. A., & Mannarino, A. P. (1993). A treatment model for sexually abused preschoolers. *Journal of Interpersonal Violence, 8*, 115–131.

Cohen, J. A., & Mannarino, A. P. (2000). Predictors of treatment outcome in sexually abused children. *Child Abuse and Neglect, 24,* 983–994.

Cohen, J. A., Berliner, L., & Mannarino, A. P. (2000). Treating traumatized children: A research review and synthesis. *Trauma, Violence, and Abuse, 1,* 29–46.

Cohen, J. A., Berliner, L., & March, J. S. (2000). Treatment of children and adolescents. In E. B. Foa, T. M. Keane, & M. J. Friedman (Eds.), *Effective treatments for PTSD: Practice guidelines from the International Society for Traumatic Stress Studies* (pp. 106–138). New York: Guilford.

Coohey, C. (1996). Child maltreatment: Testing the social isolation hypothesis. *Child Abuse and Neglect, 20,* 241–254.

Coohey, C. (2000). The role of friends, in-laws, and other kin in father-penetrated child physical abuse. *Child Welfare, 79*(4), 373–402.

Corse, S., Schmid, K., & Trickett, P. (1990). Social network characteristics of mothers in abusing and nonabusing families and their relationships to parenting beliefs: *Journal of Community Psychology, 18,* 44–59.

Crittenden, P. M. (1988). Relationships at risk. In J. Belsky & T. Nezworski (Eds.), *Clinical implications of attachment* (pp. 136–174). Hillsdale, NJ: Lawrence Erlbaum.

Crosson-Tower, C. (2002). *Understanding child abuse and neglect.* Boston: Allyn and Bacon.

Daro, D. (1988). *Confronting child abuse: Research for effective program design.* New York: Free Press.

Deblinger, E. D., & Heflin, A. H. (1996). *Treating sexually abused children and their non-offending parents: A cognitive behavioral approach.* Thousand Oaks, CA: Sage.

DePanfilis, D. (1996). Social isolation of neglectful families: A review of social support assessment and intervention models. *Child Maltreatment, 1*(1), 37–52.

Dore, M. M., Doris, J. M., & Wright, P. (1995). Identifying substance abuse in maltreating families: A child welfare challenge. *Child Abuse and Neglect, 19,* 531–543.

Eckenrode, J., Laird, M., & Doris, J. (1993). School performance and disciplinary problems among abused and neglected children. *Developmental Psychology, 29*(1), 53–62.

Elliott, D. M., & Briere, J. (1994). Forensic sexual abuse evaluation of older children: Disclosures and symptomology. *Behavioral Sciences and the Law, 12,* 261–277.

Faust, J., Runyon, M., & Kenny, M. (1995). Family variables associated with the onset and impact of intrafamilial childhood sexual abuse. *Clinical Psychology Review, 15,* 443–456.

Ferrara, F. F. (2002). *Childhood sexual abuse: Developmental effects across the lifespan.* Pacific Grove, CA: Brooks/Cole.

Finkelhor, D. (1984). *Child Sexual Abuse: New theory and research.* New York: Free Press.

Finkelhor, D. (Ed.) (1986). *A sourcebook on child sexual abuse.* Beverly Hills, CA: Sage.

Finkelhor, D. (1994). Current information on the scope and nature of child sexual abuse. In *Future of Children: Sexual Abuse of Children, 4,* 31–53. Los Altos, CA: David and Lucile Packard Foundation.

Finkelhor, D., & Baron, L. (1986). High-risk children. In D. Finkelhor (Ed.), *A sourcebook on child sexual abuse.* Beverly Hills, CA: Sage.

Finkelhor, D., & Berliner, L. (1995). Research on the treatment of sexually abused children: A review and recommendations. *Journal of American Academy of Child and Adolescent Psychiatry, 34,* 1408–1423.

Finkelhor, D., & Browne, A. (1986). Initial and long-term effects: A conceptual framework. In D. Finkelhor (Ed.), *A sourcebook on child sexual abuse.* Beverly Hills, CA: Sage.

Finkelhor, D., Hotaling, G., Lewis, I. A., & Smith, C. (1990). Sexual abuse in a national survey of adult men and women: Prevalence, characteristics, and risk factors. *Child Abuse and Neglect, 14,* 19–28.

Ford, J. D., Racusin, R., Davis, W. B., Ellis, C., Thomas, J., Rogers, K., Reiser, J., Schiffman, J., & Sengupta, A. (1999). Trauma exposure among children with attention deficit hyperactivity disorder and oppositional defiant disorder. *Journal of Consulting and Clinical Psychology, 67,* 786–789.

Friedrich, W. N. (1995). *Psychotherapy with sexually abused boys: An integrated approach.* Thousand Oaks, CA: Sage.

Friedrich, W. N., Dittner, C. A., Action, R., Berliner, L., Butler, J., Damon, L., Davies, W. H., Gray, A., & Wright, J. (2001). Child sexual behavior inventory: Normative, psychiatric and sexual abuse comparisons. *Child Maltreatment, 6,* 37–49.

Garbarino, J. (1977). The human ecology of child maltreatment: A conceptual model for research. *Journal of Marriage and the Family, 39,* 721–736.

Garbarino, J. (1982). *Children and families in the social environment.* New York: Aldine.

Garbarino, J., Dubrow, N., Kostelny, K., & Pardo, C. (1992). *Children in danger: Coping with the consequences of community violence.* San Francisco: Jossey-Bass.

Garbarino, J., & Sherman, D. (1980). High-risk neighborhoods and high-risk families: The human ecology of child maltreatment. *Child Development, 51*(1), 188–198.

Garmezy, N. (1983). Stressors of childhood. In N. Garmezy & M. Rutter (Eds.), *Stress, coping, and development in children* (pp. 43–84). New York: McGraw-Hill.

Gaudin, J., Polansky, N., Kilpatrick, A., & Shilton, P. (1993). Loneliness, depression, stress and social supports in neglectful families. *American Journal of Orthopsychiatry, 63*(4), 597–605.

Gelles, R. (1975). The social construction of child abuse. *American Journal of Orthopsychiatry, 45*(5), 363–371.

Gil, D. (1970). *Violence against children: Physical child abuse in the U.S.* Cambridge, MA: Harvard University Press.

Gil, E. (1993). Individual therapy. In E. Gill & T. C. Johnson (Eds.), *Sexualized children* (pp. 179–210). Rockville, MD: Launch Press.

Gil, E. (1996). *Systematic treatment of families who abuse.* San Francisco, CA: Jossey-Bass.

Greenfield, L. A. (1996). *Child victimizer's: Violent offenders and their victims.* Washington, DC: U.S. Department of Justice.

Gutierres, S. E., & Todd, M. (1997). The impact of childhood abuse on treatment outcomes of substance abusers. *Professional Psychology Research and Practice, 28,* 348–354.

Hay, T., & Jones, L. (1994). Societal interventions to prevent child abuse and neglect. *Child Welfare, 73,* 379–405.

Hegar, R. L. (1988). Legal and social work approaches to sibling separation in foster care. *Child Welfare, 57,* 113–121.

Howing, P. T., Wodarski, J. S., Kurtz, P. D., & Gaudin, J. M. (1993). *Maltreatment and the school-aged child: Developmental outcomes and system issues.* New York, Haworth Press.

Jones, E., & McCurdy, K. (1992). The links between types of maltreatment and demographic characteristics of children. *Child Abuse and Neglect, 16,* 201–215.

Kelly, S. J. (1984). The use of art therapy with sexually abused children. *Journal of Psychological Nursing, 22,* 12–18.

Kendall-Tackett, K. A., Williams, L. M., & Finkelhor, D. (1993). Impact of sexual abuse on children: A review and synthesis of recent empirical studies. *Psychology Bulletin, 113,* 164–180.

Kinard, E. M. (1995). Assessing resilience in abused children. Paper presented at the Fourth International Family Violence Research Conference, Durham, NH.

Kinard, E. M. (1996). Social support, self-worth, and depression in offending and non-offending mothers of maltreated children. *Child Maltreatment, 1*(3), 272–283.

Lanktree, C. B. (1994). Treating child victims of sexual abuse. In J. Briere (Ed.), *Assessing and treating victims of violence* (pp. 55–66). San Francisco, CA: Jossey Bass.

Levy, T. M., & Orlans, M. (1998). *Attachment, trauma, and healing: Understanding and treating attachment disorder in children and families*. Washington, DC: Child Welfare League of America.

Light, R. (1973). Abused and neglected children in America: A study of alternative policies. *Harvard Educational Review, 43*(4), 556–598.

Lipovsky, J. A. (1992). Assessment and treatment of post-traumatic stress disorder in child survivors of sexual assault. In D. W. Foy (Ed.), *Treating PTSD: Cognitive-behavioral strategies* (pp. 127–159). New York: Guilford.

Lynch, M., & Cicchetti, D. (1991). Patterns of relatedness in maltreated and nonmaltreated children: Connections among multiple representational models. *Development and Psychopathology, 3*, 207–226.

Lynch, M., & Cicchetti, D. (1992). Maltreated children's reports of relatedness to their teachers. In R. C. Pianta (Ed.), *Relationships between children and non-parental adults: New directions in child development* (pp. 81–108). San Francisco: Jossey-Bass.

Lynch, M., & Cicchetti, D. (1997). Children's relationships with adults and peers: An examination of elementary and junior high school students. *Journal of School Psychology, 35*, 81–100.

Maccoby, E. E., & Martin, J. A. (1983). Socialization in the context of the family: Parent-child interaction. In P. H. Mussen (Ed.), *Handbook of child psychology* (pp. 1–101). New York: John Wiley.

Margolin, G., & Gordis, E. B. (2000). The effects of family and community violence on children. *Annual Review of Psychology, 51*, 445–479.

Mayer, A. (1991). *Sexual abuse: Causes, consequences, and treatment of incestuous and pedophilic acts*. Holmes Beach, FL: Learning Publications.

McCrone, E., Egeland, B., Kalkoske, M., & Carlson, E. (1994). Relations between early maltreatment and mental representations of relationships assessed with projective storytelling in middle childhood. *Developmental Psychopathology, 6*, 99–120.

Milner, J. S. (1993). Social information processing and physical child abuse. *Clinical Psychology Review, 13*, 275–294.

Mullen, P. E., Martin, J. L., Anderson, J. C., Romans, S. E., & Herbison, G. P. (1993). Childhood sexual abuse and mental health in adult life. *British Journal of Psychiatry, 163*, 721–732.

Nelson, S. (2000). Confronting sexual abuse: Challenges for the future. In C. Itzin (Ed.), *Some truths about child sexual abuse: Influencing policy and practice*. London/New York: Routledge.

Oates, R. K., O'Toole, B. I., Lynch, D. L., Stern, A., & Cooney, G. (1994). Stability and change in outcomes for sexually abused children. *Journal of the American Academy of Child and Adolescent Psychiatry, 33*, 945–953.

Olafson, E., & Boat, B. (2000). Long-term management of the sexually abused child. In R. M. Reece (Ed.), *Treatment of child abuse: Common ground for mental health, medical, and legal practitioners*. Baltimore, MD: Johns Hopkins University Press.

Olafson, E., Corwin, D., & Summit, R. (1996). Cycles of discovery and suppression. In *Texas Family Violence and Sexual Assault Institute. Trauma, amnesia and denial*. Austin: University of Texas.

Paniagua, F. (1994). *Assessing and treating culturally diverse clients: A practical guide*. Thousand Oaks, CA: Sage.

Pecora, P. J., Whittaker, J. K., Maluccio, A.N., & Barth, R. P. (2000). *The child welfare challenge: Policy, practice, and research* (2nd ed.). New York: Aldine De Gruyter.

Porter, F. S., Blick, L. C., & Sgroi, S. M. (1982). Treatment of the sexually abused child. In S. M. Sgroi (Ed.), *Handbook of clinical intervention in child sexual abuse*. Lexington, MA: Lexington Books.

Raiha, N., & Soma, D. (1997). Victims of child abuse and neglect in the U.S. Army. *Child Abuse and Neglect, 21*(8), 759–768.

Russell, D. E. H. (1986). *The secret trauma: Incest in the lives of girls and women*. New York: Basic Books.

Russell, D. E. H., & Bolen, R. L. (2000). *The epidemic of rape and child sexual abuse in the United States*. Thousand Oaks, CA: Sage.

Rutter, M. (1987). Psychosocial resilience and protective mechanisms. *American Journal of Orthopsychiatry, 57,* 316–330.

Saunders, B. E., Kilpatrick, D. G., Hanson, R. F., Resnick, H. S., & Walker, M. E. (1999). Prevalence, case characteristics, and long-term psychological correlates of child rape among women: A national survey. *Child Maltreatment, 4,* 187–200.

Scannapieco, M., & Connell-Carrick, K. (In press). Assessment of families who have substance abuse issues: Those who maltreat their infants and toddlers and those who do not. *Journal of Evidence-Based Social Work*.

Scannapieco, M., & Connell-Carrick, K. (In press). Families in Poverty: Those who maltreat their infants and toddlers and those who do not. *Journal of Family Social Work*.

Scannapieco, M., & Connell-Carrick, K. (Under review). Focus on the first years: Ecological correlates of child maltreatment for families with children 0 to 4. *Child Maltreatment*.

Sedlack, A. J., & Broadhurst, D. D. (1996). *Executive summary of the third national incidence study of child abuse and neglect*. Washington, DC: National Clearinghouse on Child Abuse and Neglect, USDHHS.

Sgroi, S. M. (1988). *Vulnerable populations*: Vol. 1. *Evaluation and treatment of sexually abused children and adult survivors*. Lexington, MA: Lexington Books.

Sgroi, S. M. (1989). *Vulnerable populations*: Vol. 2. *Sexual abuse treatment for children, adult survivors, offenders, and persons with mental retardation*. Lexington, MA: Lexington Books.

Steinberg, L., Catalano, R., & Dooley, D. (1981). Economic antecedents of child abuse and neglect. *Child Development, 52*(3), 975–985.

Swetnam, L., Peterson, C. R., & Clark, H. B. (1983). *Social skills development in young children: Preventive and therapeutic approaches. Child & Youth Services, 5,* 5–27.

Thomlison, B. (1997). Risk and protective factors in child maltreatment. In M. Fraser (Ed.), *Risk and resilience in childhood: An ecological perspective*. Washington, DC: National Association of Social Workers Press.

Toth, S., & Cicchetti, D. (1996). The impact of relatedness with mother on school functioning. *Journal of School Psychology, 34,* 247–266.

Trickett, P., & Susman, E. (1989). Perceived similarities and disagreements about child-rearing practices in abusive and nonabusive families: Intergenerational and concurrent family processes. In D. Cicchetti & V. Carlson (Eds.), *Child Maltreatment: Theory and research on the causes and consequences of child abuse and neglect* (pp. 280–301). New York: Cambridge University Press.

U.S. Department of Health and Human Services, Administration for Children and Families, Administration for Children, Youth, and Families, Children's Bureau (2000). *Child maltreatment 2000*. Washington, DC: Author.

U.S. Department of Health and Human Services, Children's Bureau (1996). *Third National Incidence Study of Child Abuse and Neglect*. Washington, DC: U.S. Government Printing Office.

Urquiza, A. J., & Winn, C. (1993). *Treatment for abused and neglected children: Infancy to age 18*. Washington, DC: National Center on Child Abuse and Neglect.

Veltman, M. W. M., & Browne, K. D. (2001). Three decades of child maltreatment research: Implications for the school years. *Trauma, Violence, and Abuse, 2*(3), 215–239.

Wellborn, J. G., & Connell, J. P. (1987). *Rochester Assessment Package for Children*. University of Rochester Children's Institute.

Wolfe, D. A. (1985). Child-abusive parents: An empirical review and analysis. *Psychological Bulletin, 97*, 462–482.

Wolfe, D. A. (1999). *Child Abuse: Implications for child development and psychopathology*. Thousand Oaks, CA: Sage.

Wolfner, G., & Gelles, R. (1993). A profile of violence toward children: A national study. *Child Abuse and Neglect, 17*, 197–212.

CHAPTER 9

Beitchman, J., Zucker, K., Hood, J., daCosta, G., Akman, D., & Cassavia, E. (1992). A review of the long-term effects of child sexual abuse. *Child Abuse and Neglect, 16*, 101–118.

Berk, L. (1999). *Infants, children, and adolescents*. Needham Heights, MA: Allyn Bacon.

Birmaker, B., Ryan, N., Williamson, D., Bret, D., & Kaufman, J. (1996). Childhood and adolescent depression: A review of the past 10 years. *Journal of the American Academy of Child and Adolescent Psychiatry, 35*, 1575–1583.

Black, K., & McCartney, K. (1998). Adolescent females' security with parents predicts the quality of peer interactions. *Social Development, 6*, 91–110.

Brezina, T. (1998). Adolescent maltreatment and delinquency: The question of intervening processes. *Journal of Research in Crime and Delinquency, 35*(1), 71–99.

Briere, J., & Conte, J. (1993). Self-reported amnesia for abuse in adults molested as children. *Journal of Traumatic Stress, 6*, 21–32.

Brook, J., Whiteman, M., Finch, S., & Cohen, P. (2000). Longitudinally foretelling drug use in the late twenties: Adolescent personality and social-environmental influences. *Journal of Genetic Psychology, 161*, 37–51.

Brown, C., & Finkelhor, D. (1986). Initial and long-term effects: A research review. In D. Finkelhor (Ed.), *A sourcebook on child sexual abuse* (pp. 143–179). Thousand Oaks, CA: Sage Publications.

Brown, J., Cohen, P., Johnson, J., & Smailes, E. (1999). Childhood abuse and neglect: Specificity on effects on adolescent and young adult depression and suicide. *Journal of the American Academy of Child and Adolescent and Psychiatry, 38*(12), 1490–1495.

Browne, A., & Finkelhor, D. (1986). Impact of child sexual abuse: A review of the research. *Psychological Bulletin, 99*(1), 66–77.

Burnett, J., Anderson, W., & Heppner, P. (1995). Gender roles and self-esteem: A consideration of environmental factors. *Journal of Counseling and Development, 73*, 323–326.

Cavaiola, A., & Schiff, M. (1988). Behavioral sequalae of physical and/or sexual abuse in adolescents. *Child Abuse and Neglect, 12*, 181–188.

Center for Disease Control. (2000). Youth risk behavior surveillance—United States, 1999. *Morbidity and Mortality Weekly Report, 49*, 1–96.

Chaffin, M., Bonner, B., Worley, K., & Lawson, L. (1996). Treating abused adolescents. In J. Briere, L. Berliner, J. Bulkley, C. Jenny, & T. Reid (Eds.), *The APSAC handbook on child maltreatment* (pp. 119–139). Thousand Oaks, CA: Sage.

Chaffin, M., Letourneau, E., & Silovsky, J. (2002). Adults, adolescents, and children who sexually abuse children: A developmental perspective. In J. Myers, J. L. Berliner,

J. Briere, C. Hendrix, et al. (Eds.), *The APSAC Handbook on Child Maltreatment, Second Edition* (pp. 205–232). Thousand Oaks, CA: Sage.

DeBellis, M., & Putnam, F. (1994). The psychobiology of child maltreatment: *Child and Adolescent Psychiatric Clinics in North America, 3*, 663–678.

Dubner, A., & Motta, R. (1999). Sexually and physically abused foster care children and post-traumatic stress disorder. *Journal of Consulting and Clinical Psychology, 67*, 367–373.

Eckenrode, J., Laird, M., and Doris, J. (1993). School performance and disciplinary problems among abused and neglected children. *Developmental Psychology, 29*, 33–56.

Egeland, B. (1997). Mediators of the effects of child maltreatment on developmental adaptation in adolescence. In *Developmental perspectives on trauma: Theory, research, and intervention*. Rochester, NY: University of Rochester Press.

Erickson, M., & Egeland, B. (2002). Child neglect. In J. Myers, L. Berliner, J. Briere, C. Hendrix, C. Jenny, & T. Reid (Eds.), *The APSAC handbook on child maltreatment* (2nd ed.) (pp. 3–29). Thousand Oaks, CA: Sage Publications.

Famularo, R., Kinscherff, R., & Fenton, T. (1990). Symptom differences in acute and chronic presentation of childhood posttraumatic stress disorder. *Child Abuse and Neglect, 14*, 439–444.

Famularo, R., Kinscherff, R., & Fenton, T. (1991). Posttraumatic stress disorder among children clinically diagnosed as borderline personality disorder. *Journal of Nervous and Mental Diseases, 179*, 428–431.

Famularo, R., Kinscherff, R., & Fenton, T. (1992). Psychiatric diagnoses of maltreated children: Preliminary findings. *Journal of the American Academy of Child and Adolescent Psychiatry, 31*(5), 863–867.

Finkelhor, D. (1995). The victimization of children: A developmental perspective. *American Journal of Orthopsychiatry, 65*, 177–193.

Flisher, A., Kramer, R., Hoven, C., Greenwald, S., Alegria, M., Bird, H., Canino, G., Connell, R., & Moore, R. (1997). Psychosocial characteristics of physically abused children and adolescents. *Journal of the American Academy of Child and Adolescent Psychiatry, 36*(1), 123–131.

Friedrich, W., Dittner, C., Action, R., Berliner, L., Butler, J., Damon, L., Davies, W., Gray, A., & Wright, J. (2001). Child Sexual Behavior Inventory: Normative, psychiatric, and sexual abuse comparisons. *Child Maltreatment, 6*, 37–49.

Gaudin, J., Polansky, N., Kilpatrick, A., and Shilton, P. (1996). Family functioning in neglectful families. *Child Abuse and Neglect, 20*(4), 363–377.

Gidyca, C., & Koss, M. (1989). The impact of adolescent sexual victimization: Standardized measures of anxiety, depression and behavioral deviancy. *Violence and Victims, 4*(2), 139–149.

Grotevant, H. (1996). Adolescent development in family contexts. In N. Eisenberg (Ed)., *Handbook of child psychology: Volume 3. Social, emotional, and personality development* (5th ed.) (pp. 1097–1149). New York: Wiley.

Hanson, R., & Slater, S. (1988). Sexual victimization in the history of sexual abusers: A review. *Annals of Sex Research, 1*(4), 485–499.

Hecht, D., Chaffin, M., Bonner, B., Worley, K., & Lawson, L. (2002). Treating sexually abused adolescents. In J. Myers, L. Berliner, J. Briere, C. Hendrix, C. Jenny, and T. Reid (Eds.). *The APSAC handbook on child maltreatment* (2nd ed.) (pp. 159–175). Thousand Oaks, CA: Sage Publications.

Herrenkohl, E., Herrenkohl, R., Egolf, B., & Russo, M. (1998). The relationship between early maltreatment and teenage parenthood. *Journal of Adolescence, 21*, 291–303.

Herrenkohl, R., Egolf, B., & Herrenkohl, E. (1997). Preschool antecedents of adolescent assaultive behavior: A longitudinal study. *American Journal of Orthopsychiatry, 6*(3), 422–431.

Hibbard, R., Ingersoll, G., & Orr, D. (1990). Behavior risk, emotional risk, and child abuse among adolescents in a nonclinical setting. *Pediatrics, 86,* 896–901.

Hildyard, K., & Wolfe, D. (2002). Child neglect: Developmental issues and outcomes. *Child Abuse and Neglect, 26*(6/7), 679–695.

Kandel, D., & Lesser, G. (1972). *Youth in two worlds.* San Francisco: Jossey-Bass.

Kaplan, S., Pelcovitz, D., Salzinger, S., Mandel, F., & Weiner, M. (1998). Adolescent physical abuse and suicide attempts. *Journal of American Academy of Child and Adolescent Psychiatry, 16*(6), 516–524.

Kaufman, J., & Cicchetti, D. (1989). Effects of maltreatment on school age children's socioemotional development: Assessments in a day-camp setting. *Developmental Psychology, 25*(4), 516–524.

Kelley, B., Thornberry, T., & Smith, C. (1997). *In the wake of child maltreatment.* Washington, DC: Department of Justice, Office of Juvenile Justice and Delinquency Prevention.

Kempe, R., & Kempe, C. (1978). *Child abuse.* Cambridge, MA: Harvard University Press.

Klepinger, D., Lundberg, S., & Plotnick, R. (1995). Adolescent fertility and the educational attainment of young women. *Family Practice Perspectives, 23,* 23–28.

Kilpatrick, D., Acierno, R., Saunders, B., Resnick, H., Best, C., & Schnurr, P. (2000). Risk factors for adolescent substance abuse and dependence: Data from a national sample. *Journal of Consulting and Clinical Psychology, 68,* 19–30.

Kratcoski, P. (1984). Perspectives on intrafamily violence. *Human Relations, 37,* 443–453.

Laws, D., & Marshall, W. (1990). A conditioning theory of the etiology and maintenance of deviant sexual preferences and behavior. In W. Marshall, D. Laws, & H. Barbaree (Eds), *Handbook of sexual assault: Issues, theories and treatment of the offender* (pp. 209–229). New York: Plenum.

Lehnert, K., Overholser, J., & Spirito, A. (1994). Internalized and externalized anger in adolescent suicide attempters. *Journal of Adolescent Research, 9,* 105–119.

Lewis, D., Lovely, R., Yeager, C., & Femina, D. (1989). Toward a theory of the genesis of violence: A follow-up study of delinquents. *Journal of the American Academy of Child and Adolescent Psychiatry, 28,* 431–436.

Lewis, D., Mallough, C., & Webb, V. (1989). Child abuse, delinquency, and violent criminality. In D. Cicchetti & V. Carlson (Eds.), *Child maltreatment: Theory and research on the causes and consequences of child abuse and neglect* (pp. 707–721). New York: Cambridge University Press.

Lobel, T., Slone, M., & Winch, G. (1997). Masculinity, popularity, and self-esteem among Israeli preadolescent girls. *Sex Roles, 36,* 385–408.

Maguire, K., & Pastore, A. L. (Eds). (1997). *Sourcebook of criminal justice statistics—1996.* Washington, DC: U.S. Department of Justice, Bureau of Justice Statistics.

Mannarino, A., & Cohen, J. (1996). Abuse-related attributions and perceptions, general attributions, and locus of control of sexually abused girls. *Journal of Interpersonal Violence, 11,* 162–180.

Mannarino, A., Cohen, J., & Berman, S. (1994). The Children's Attributions and Perceptions Scale: A new measure of sexual abuse-related factors. *Journal of Clinical Child Psychology, 23,* 204–211.

Marcia, J. (1966). Development and validation of ego identity status. *Journal of Personality and Social Psychology, 3,* 551–558.

Marshall, L., & Rose, P. (1990). Premarital violence: The impact of family origin violence, stress, and reciprocity. *Violence and Victims, 5,* 51–64.

McFayden, R., & Kitson, W. (1996). Language comprehension and expression among adolescents who have experienced childhood physical abuse. *Journal of Child Psychology and Psychiatry*, *37*(5), 551–562.

Miller-Perrin, C., & Perrin, R. (1999). *Child maltreatment: An introduction*. Thousand Oaks, CA: Sage.

Pecora, P., Whittaker, J., Maluccio, A., Barth, R., & Plotnick, R. (1992). *The child welfare challenge: Policy, practice, and research*. New York: Aldine de Gruyter.

Pelcovitz, D., Kaplan, S., Goldenberg, B., & Mandel, F. (1994). Posttraumatic stress disorder in physically abused adolescents. *Journal of American Academy of Child and Adolescent Psychiatry*, *32*(6), 1025–1038.

Riggs, S., Alario, A., & McHorney, C. (1990). Health risk behaviors and attempted suicide in adolescents who report prior maltreatment. *Journal of Pediatrics*, *118*, 815–821.

Ruggerio, K., McLeer, S., & Dixon, J. (2000). Sexual abuse characteristics associated with survivor psychopathology. *Child Abuse and Neglect*, *18*, 51–61.

Runtz, M., & Briere, J. (1986). Adolescent "acting-out" and childhood history of sexual abuse. *Journal of Interpersonal Violence*, *1*, 326–334.

Sattler, J. (1998). *Clinical and forensic interviewing of children and families: Guidelines for mental health, education, pediatric and child maltreatment fields*. San Diego, CA: Jerome M. Sattler.

Singer, M., Song, L., & Ochberg, B. (1994). Sexual victimization and substance abuse in psychiatrically hospitalized adolescents. *Social Work Research*, *18*, 68–74.

Silverman, A., Reinherz, H., & Giaconia, R. (1996). The long-term sequalae of child and adolescent abuse: A longitudinal community analysis. *Child Abuse and Neglect*, *8*(8), 709–723.

Sorenson, T., & Snow, B. (1991). How children tell: The process of disclosure in child sexual abuse. *Child Welfare*, *70*, 3–15.

Stock, J., Bell, M., Boyer, D., & Connell, F. (1997). Adolescent pregnancy and sexual risk-taking among sexually abused girls. *Family Planning Perspectives*, *29*(5), 200–205.

Strauss, M. (1995). *Beating the devil out of them: Corporal punishment by parents and its effects on children*. Boston: Lexington/MacMillan.

Tanner, J. (1998). Sequence, tempo, and individual variation in growth and development of boys and girls aged twelve to sixteen. In R. E. Muus and D. H. Porton (Eds.), *Adolescent behavior and society: A book of readings (5th ed.)* (pp. 34–46). New York: McGraw-Hill.

U.S. Department of Health and Human Servcies. (2002). *Child maltreatment 2000: Reports from the states to the National Abuse and Neglect Data System*. Washington, DC: U.S. Government Printing Office.

U.S. Department of Health and Human Services. (1988). Study findings: Study of national incidence and prevalence of child abuse and neglect (DHHS Publication No. ADM 20–01099). Washington, DC: Government Printing Office.

Walker, E., Downey, G., & Bergman, A. (1989). The effects of parental psychopathology and maltreatment on child behavior: A test of the diathesis-stress model. *Child Development*, *60*, 15–24.

Widom, C., & Maxfield, M. (2001). *An update on the "cycle of violence."* NIJ Research Brief. Washington, DC: National Institute of Justice.

Williamson, J., Borduin, C., and Howe, B. (1991). The ecology of adolescent maltreatment: A multilevel examination of adolescent physical abuse, sexual abuse, and neglect. *Journal of Consulting and Clinical Psychology*, *59*, 449–457.

Wolfe, D., Wekerle, C., & Scott, K. (1997). *Empowering youth to promote nonviolence: Issues and solutions*. Thousand Oaks, CA: Sage.

Wolfe, D., Werkele, C., Reitzel-Jaffe, D., & Lefebvre, L. (1998). Factors associated with abusive relationships among maltreated and nonmaltreated youth. *Development and Psychopathology, 10,* 61–85.

Wormer, K., Wells, J., & Boes, M. (2000). *Social work with lesbians, gays, and bisexuals: A strengths perspective.* Boston, MA: Allyn Bacon.

CHAPTER 10

Aber, J. L., & Zigler, D. (1981). Developmental consideration in the definition of child maltreatment. In R. Rizley & D. Cicchetti (Eds.), *New direction in child development: Developmental perspectives in child maltreatment* (pp. 1–29). San Francisco: Jossey-Bass.

Action, R. G., & During, S. M. (1992). Preliminary results of aggression management training for aggressive parents. *Journal of Interpersonal Violence, 7,* 410–417.

Adam, K. S. Sheldon-Keller, A. E., & West, M. (1996). Attachment organization and history of suicidal behavior in adolescents. *Journal of Consulting and Clinical Psychology, 64,* 264–292.

American Humane Association. (2002). The next step: Exploring the link between violence to people and animals. In *AHA, protecting children and animals: Celebrating 125 years* (pp. 60–64). Edgewood, CO: Author.

Anthony, E. J., & Cohler, B. (1987). *The invulnerable child.* New York: Guilford.

Araji, S., & Finkelhor, D. (1986). Abusers: A review of the research. In D. Finkelhor et al. (Eds.), *A sourcebook on child sexual abuse* (pp. 89–118). Beverly Hills, CA: Sage.

Ascione, F. R. (1998). Battered women's reports of their partners' and their children's cruelty to animals. *Journal of Emotional Abuse, 6,* 226–247.

Azar, S. T., & Siegel, B. R. (1990). Behavioral treatment of child abuse: A developmental perspective. *Behavior Modification, 14,* 279–300.

Azar, S. T., & Wolfe, D. A. (1998). Child physical abuse and neglect. In E. J. Mash & R. A. Barkley (Eds.), *Treatment of childhood disorders* (2nd ed.). New York: Guilford.

Bagley, C., Wood, M., & Young, L. (1994). Victim to abuser: Mental health and behavioral sequalae of child sexual abuse in a community survey of young adult males. *Child Abuse and Neglect, 18,* 683–697.

Belsky, J. (1980). Child maltreatment: An ecological integration. *American Psychologist, 35*(4), 320–335.

Belsky, J., & Vondra, J. (1989). Lessons from child abuse: The determinants of parenting. In C. D. Carlson & V. Carlson (Eds.), *Child maltreatment: Theory and research on the causes and consequences of child abuse and neglect* (pp. 153–202). New York: Cambridge University Press.

Berenson, A. B., Chacko, M. R., Wiemann, C. M., Mishaw, C. O., Friedrich, W. N., & Grady, J. J. (2000). A case-control study of anatomic changes resulting from sexual abuse. *American Journal of Obstetrics and Gynecology, 182,* 82–934.

Berliner, L., & Elliott, D. M. (2002). Sexual abuse of children. In J. E. Myers, L. Berliner, J. Briere, C. T. Hendrix, C. Jenny, & T. A. Reid (Eds.), *The APSAC handbook on child maltreatment (2nd ed.).* Thousand Oaks, CA: Sage.

Bolen, R. M. (1998). Predicting risk to be sexually abused: A comparison of logistic regression to even history analysis. *Child Maltreatment, 3*(2) 157–170.

Bolen, R. M. (2001). Risk factors for child sexual abuse victimization. In R. M. Bolen, *Child sexual abuse: Its scope and our future* (pp. 135–161). Norwell, MA: Kluwer Academic/Plenum.

Boyer, D., & Fine, D. (1992). Sexual abuse as a factor in adolescent pregnancy and child maltreatment. *Family Planning Perspectives, 24,* 4–11.

Browne, A., & Finkelhor, D. (1986). Initial and long-term effects: A review of the research. In D. Finkelhor (Ed.), *A sourcebook on child sexual abuse.* Beverly Hills, CA: Sage.

Cantrell, P. J., Carrico, M. F., Franklin, J. N., & Grubb, H. J. (1990). Violent tactics in family conflicts relative to familial and economic factors. *Psychological Reports, 66,* 823–828.

Caselles, C. E., & Milner, J. S. (2000). Evaluation of child transgressions, disciplinary choices, and expected child compliance in a no-cry and crying infant condition in physically abusive and comparison mothers. *Child Abuse and Neglect, 24,* 477–491.

Chaffin, M., & Champion, K. (1997). Treating sexually abused children and their non-offending parents: A cognitive behavioral approach. *Child Maltreatment, 2,* 81–83.

Chaffin, M., & Hanson, R. F. (2000). Treatment of multiply traumatized abused children. In R. M. Reece (Ed.), *Treatment of child abuse: Common ground for mental health, medical, and legal practitioners* (pp. 271–288). Baltimore, MD: Johns Hopkins University Press.

Christian, C. W., & Rubin, D. M. (2002). Sexual Abuse. In A. P. Giardino & E. R. Giardino (Eds.), *Recognition of child abuse for the mandated reporter.* St. Louis, MO: G.W. Medical Publishing.

Cicchetti, D., & Lynch, M. (1993). Toward an ecological/transactional model of community violence and child maltreatment: Consequences for children's development. *Psychiatry, 56,* 96–118.

Cicchetti, D., & Rogosch, F. A. (1997). The role of self-organization in the promotion of resilience in maltreated children. *Development and Psychopathology, 9,* 797–815.

Cicchetti, D., & Toth, S. L. (2000). Child maltreatment and attachment organization: Implications for intervention. In S. Goldberg, R. Muir, & J. Kerr. *Attachment theory: Social, developmental, and clinical perspectives.* Hillsdale, NJ: Analytic Press.

Clark, D. B., & Kirisci, L. (1996). Posttraumatic stress disorder, depression, alcohol use disorders and quality of life in adolescents. *Anxiety, 2,* 226–233.

Clark, D. B., Lesnick, L. A., & Hegedus, A. M. (1997). Traumas and other adverse life events in adolescents with alcohol abuse and dependence. *Journal of the American Academy of Child and Adolescent Psychiatry, 36,* 1744–1751.

Cohen, J. A., Berliner, L., & Mannarino, A. P. (2000). Treating traumatized children: A research review and synthesis. *Trauma, Violence, and Abuse, 1,* 29–46.

Cohen, J. A., Berliner, L., & March, J. S. (2000). Treatment of children and adolescents. In E. B. Foa, T. M. Keane, & M. J. Friedman (Eds.), *Effective treatments of PTSD: Practice guidelines from the International Society for Traumatic Stress Studies* (pp. 106–138). New York: Guilford.

Cohen, J. A., & Mannarino, A. P. (1998). A treatment study for sexually abused preschool children: Outcome during a one-year follow-up. *Journal of the American Academy of Child and Adolescent Psychiatry, 36,* 1228–1235.

Colarossi, L. G., & Eccles, J. S. (2003). Differential effects of support providers on adolescents' mental health. *Social Work Research, 27*(1), 19–30.

Coohey, C. (1996). Child maltreatment: Testing the social isolation hypothesis. *Child Abuse and Neglect, 20,* 241–254.

Corcoran, J. (2000). *Evidence-based social work practice with families: A lifespan approach.* New York: Springer.

Corse, S., Schmid, K., & Trickett, P. (1990). Social network characteristics of mothers in abusing and non-abusing families and their relationships to parenting beliefs. *Journal of Community Psychology, 18,* 44–59.

Crittenden, P. M. (1988). Relationship at risk. In J. Belsky & T. Nezworski (Eds.), *Clinical implications of attachment* (pp. 136–174). Hillsdale, NJ: Lawrence Erlbaum.

Crittenden, P. M., Claussen, A. H., & Sugarman, D. B. (1994). Physical and psychological maltreatment in middle childhood and adolescence. *Development and Psychopathology, 6*, 145–164.

Dangel, R. F., Deschner, J. P., & Rapp, R. R. (1989). Anger control training for adolescents in residential treatment. *Behavior Modification, 13*, 447–458.

Deblinger, E. D., & Heflin, A. H. (1996). *Treating sexually abused children and their nonoffending parents: A cognitive behavioral approach.* Thousand Oaks, CA: Sage.

Dembo, R., Williams, L., Berry, E., Getreu, A., Washburn, M., Wish, E., et al. (1988). The relationship between physical and sexual abuse and illicit drug use: A replication among a new sample of youths entering a juvenile detention center. *International Journal of the Addictions, 23*, 1101–1125.

Dong, M., Anda, R. F., Dube, S. R., Giles, W. H., & Felitti, V. J. (2003). The relationship of exposure to childhood sexual abuse to other forms of abuse, neglect, and household dysfunction during childhood. *Child Abuse and Neglect, 27*(6), 625–639.

Dubowitz, H. (Ed.). (1999). *Neglected children: Research, practice, and policy.* Thousand Oaks, CA: Sage.

Edelson, J. (1999). The overlap between child maltreatment and woman battering. *Violence Against Women, 5*, 134–154.

Edelson, J., Eisikovts, Z. C., Guttmann, E., & Sela-Amit, M. (1991). Cognitive and interpersonal factors in woman abuse. *Journal of Family Violence, 6*, 167–182.

Erickson, M. F., & Egeland, B. (2002). Child neglect. In J. E. Myers, L. Berliner, J. Briere, C. T. Hendrix, C. Jenny, & T. A. Reid (Eds.), *The APSAC handbook on child maltreatment (2nd ed.).* Thousand Oaks, CA: Sage.

Faver, C. A., & Strand, E. B. (2003). Domestic violence and animal cruelty: Untangling the web of abuse. *Journal of Social Work Education, 39*, 237–253.

Feindler, E. L., Ecton, R. B., Kingsley, D., & Dubey, D. R. (1986). Group anger-control training for institutionalized psychiatric male adolescents. *Behavior Therapy, 17*, 109–123.

Ferrara, F. F. (2002). *Childhood sexual abuse: Developmental effects across the lifespan.* Pacific Grove, CA: Brooks/Cole.

Finkelhor, D. (1984). *Child sexual abuse: New theory and research.* New York: Free Press.

Finkelhor, D. (1986). Abusers: Special topics. In D. Finkelhor (Ed.), *A sourcebook on child sexual abuse* (pp. 119–142). Beverly Hills, CA: Sage.

Finkelhor, D. (1994). Current information on the scope and nature of child sexual abuse. *Future of Children, 4*, 31–53.

Finkelhor, D., Araji, S., Baron, L., Peter, S. D., & Wyatt, G. E. (1986). *A sourcebook on child sexual abuse.* Thousand Oaks, CA: Sage.

Finkelhor, D., & Browne, A. (1986). Initial and long-term effects: A conceptual framework. In D. Finkelhor (Ed.), *A sourcebook on child sexual abuse.* Beverly Hills, CA: Sage.

Finkelhor, D., Hotaling, G., Lewis, I. A., & Smith, C. (1990). Sexual abuse in a national survey of adult men and women: Prevalence, characteristics, and risk factors. *Child Abuse and Neglect, 14*, 19–28.

Flynn, C. P. (2000). Woman's best friend: Pet abuse and the role of companion animals in the lives of battered women. *Violence Against Women, 6*(2), 162–177.

Garbarino, J. (1977). The human ecology of child maltreatment: A conceptual model for research. *Journal of Marriage and the Family, 39*, 721–732.

Garbarino, J. (1982). *Children and families in the social environment.* New York: Aldine De Gruyter.

Garbarino, J., Dubrow, N., Kostelny, K., & Pardo, C. (1992). *Children in danger: Coping with the consequences of community violence.* San Francisco: Jossey-Bass.

Gelles, R. J., & Straus, M. (1987). Is violence toward children increasing? *Journal of Interpersonal Violence, 2,* 212–222.

Grogan-Kaylor, A., & Otis, M. D. (2003). The effect of childhood maltreatment on adult criminality: A tobit regression analysis. *Child Maltreatment, 8,* 129–137.

Hartley Copps, C. (2002). The co-occurrence of child maltreatment and domestic violence: Examining both neglect and child physical abuse. *Child Maltreatment, 7,* 349–358.

Haynes, C. F., Cutler, C., Gray, J., & Kempe, R. S. (1984). Hospitalized cases of nonorganic failure to thrive: The scope of the problem and short-term lay health visitors interventions. *Child Abuse and Neglect, 8,* 229–242.

Hegar, R. L. (1988). Legal and social work approaches to sibling separation in foster care. *Child Welfare, 57,* 113–121.

Herrenkohl, E. D., Herrenkohl, R. C., & Toedter, L. J. (1983). Perspectives on the intergenerational transmission of abuse. In D. Finkelhor, R. J. Gelles, G. T. Hotaling, & M. A. Straus (Eds.), *The dark side of families: Current family violence research.* Beverly Hills, CA: Sage.

Kaufman, J., & Zigler, E. (1987). Do abused children become abusive parents? *American Journal of Orthopsychiatry, 57,* 186–192.

Kaufman, J., & Zigler, E. (1992). The prevention of child maltreatment: Programming, research, and policy. In D. J. Willis & E. W. Holden (Eds.), *Prevention of child maltreatment: Developmental and ecological perspectives* (pp. 269–295). Oxford, England: John Wiley & Sons.

Kendall-Tackett, K. A., Williams, L. M., & Finkelhor, D. (1993). Impact of sexual abuse on children: A review and synthesis of recent empirical studies. *Psychological Bulletin, 113,* 164–180.

Kelley, S. J. (2002). Child maltreatment in the context of substance abuse. In J. E. Myers, L. Berliner, J. Briere, C. T. Hendrix, C. Jenny, & T. A. Reid (Eds.), *The APSAC handbook on child maltreatment* (2nd ed.). Thousand Oaks, CA: Sage.

Kinard, E. M. (1995). Assessing resilience in abused children. Paper presented at the Fourth International Family Violence Research Conference, Durham, NH.

Kirby, L., & Fraser, M. (1997). Risk and resilience in childhood. In M. Fraser (Ed.), *Risk and Resilience in Childhood: An Ecological Perspective* (pp. 10–33). Washington, DC: NASW Press.

Kolko, D. J. (1996a). Clinical monitoring of treatment course in child physical abuse: Psychometric characteristics and treatment comparisons. *Child Abuse and Neglect, 20,* 23–43.

Kolko, D. J. (1996b). Individual cognitive behavioral treatment and family therapy for physically abused children and their offending parents: A comparison of clinical outcomes. *Child Maltreatment, 1*(4), 322–342.

Kolko, D. J. (2002). Child physical abuse. In J. E. Myers, L. Berliner, J. Briere, C. T. Hendrix, C. Jenny, & T. A. Reid (Eds.), *The APSAC handbook on child maltreatment* (2nd ed.) (pp. 21–54). Thousand Oaks, CA: Sage.

Kotch, J., Browne, D., Ringwalt, C., Stewart, P., Ruina, E., Holt, K., Lowman, B., & Jung, J. (1995). Risk of abuse or neglect in a cohort of low-income children. *Child Abuse and Neglect, 19,* 1115–1130.

Levy, T. M., & Orlans, M. (1998). *Attachment, trauma, and healing: Understanding and treating attachment disorder in children and families.* Washington, DC: Child Welfare League of America Press.

Lynch, M., & Cicchetti, D. (1991). Patterns of relatedness in maltreated and nonmaltreated children: Connections among multiple representational models. *Developmental Psychopathology, 3,* 207–226.

Lynch, M., & Cicchetti, D. (1992). Maltreated children's reports of relatedness to their teachers. In R. C. Pianta (Ed.), *Relationships between children and non-parental adults: New directions in child development* (pp. 81–108). San Francisco: Jossey-Bass.

Lynch, M., & Cicchetti, D. (1997). Children's relationships with adults and peers: An examination of elementary and junior high school students. *Journal of School Psychology, 35,* 81–100.

Lynch, M., & Cicchetti, D. (1998). An ecological-transactional analysis of children and contexts: The longitudinal interplay among child maltreatment, community violence, and child's symptomatology. *Development and Psychopathology, 10,* 235–257.

Main, M., & Goldwyn, R. (2000). Adult attachment scoring and classification system. In M. Main (Ed.), *Systems for assessing attachment organization through discourse, behavior and drawings.* Cambridge: Cambridge University Press.

Manassis, K., Owens, M., Adam, K. S., West, M., & Sheldon-Keller, A. E. (1999). Assessing attachment: Convergent validity of the adult attachment interview and the parental bonding instrument. *Australian and New Zealand Journal of Psychiatry, 33,* 559–567.

Mannarino, A. P., & Cohen, J. A. (1996). A follow-up study of factors which mediate the development of psychological symptoms in sexually abused girls. *Child Maltreatment, 1*(3), 246–260.

Masten, A. (1994). Resilience in individual development: Successful adaptation despite risk and adversity. In M. C. Wang & E. W. Gordon (Eds.), *Educational resilience in inner-city America: Challenges and prospects* (pp. 3–26). Hillsdale, NJ: Lawrence Erlbaum.

McAlphine, C., Marshall, C., & Doran, N. (2001). Combining child welfare and substance abuse services: A blended model of intervention. *Child Welfare, 80*(2), 29–50.

McCrone, E. Egeland, B. Kalkoske, M., & Carlson, E. (1994). Relations between early maltreatment and mental representations of relationships assessed with protective storytelling in middle childhood. *Developmental Psychopathology, 6,* 99–120.

Melton, G. B., & Barry, F. D. (1994). Neighbors helping neighbors: The vision of the U.S. Advisory Board on Child Abuse and Neglect. In G. B. Melton & F. D. Barry (Eds.), *Protecting children from abuse and neglect: Foundations for a new national strategy* (pp. 1–14). New York: Guilford.

Milner, J. S. (1998). Individual and family characteristics associated with intrafamilial child physical and sexual abuse. In P. K. Trickett & C. J. Schellenback (Eds.), *Violence against children in the family and community* (pp. 141–170). Washington, DC: American Psychological Association.

National Center for Child Abuse and Neglect. (1993). *A report on the maltreatment of children with disabilities.* Washington, DC: U.S. Department of Health and Human Services.

Olafson, E., & Boat, B. W. (2000). Long-term management of the sexually abused child: Considerations and challenges. In R. M. Reece (Ed.), *Treatment of child abuse: Common ground for mental health, medical, and legal practitioners.* Baltimore, MD: Johns Hopkins University Press.

Pecora, P. J., Whittaker, J. K., Maluccio, A. N., & Barth, R. P. (2000). *The child welfare challenge: Policy, practice, and research* (2nd ed.). New York: Aldine De Gruyter.

Pelton, L. (1994). The role of material factors in child abuse and neglect. In G. B. Melton & F. D. Barry (Eds.), *Protecting children from abuse and neglect: Foundations for a new national strategy* (pp. 131–181). New York: Guilford.

Pianta, R., Egeland, B., & Erickson, M. F. (1989). The antecedents of maltreatment: Results of the Mother-Child Interaction Research Project. In D. Cicchetti & V. Carlson (Eds.), *Child maltreatment: Theory and research on the causes and consequences of child abuse and neglect* (pp. 203–253). Cambridge: Cambridge University Press.

Rittner, B., & Dozier, C. D. (2000). Effects of court-ordered substance-abuse treatment in child protective services cases. *Social Work, 45*(2), 131–142.

Russell, D. E. H. (1983). The incidence and prevalence of intrafamilial and extrafamilial sexual abuse of female children. *Child Abuse and Neglect, 7*, 133–146.

Scannapieco, M. (2000). Preparing youth for independent living: What are the best methods for reaching self-sufficiency? In H. Dubowitz & D. DePanfilis (Eds.), *Handbook for child protection practice*. Thousand Oaks, CA: Sage.

Scannapieco, M., & Connell-Carrick, K. (In press). Families in poverty: Those who maltreat their infants and toddlers and those who do not. *Journal of Family Social Work.*

Scannapieco, M., & Connell-Carrick, K. (Under review). Focus on the first years: Ecological correlates of child maltreatment for families with children 0 to 4. *Child Maltreatment.*

Stauffer, L. B., & Deblinger, E. (1996). Cognitive behavioral groups for nonoffending mothers and their young sexually abused children: A preliminary treatment outcome study. *Child Maltreatment, 1*, 65–76.

Straus, M. A. (1983). Ordinary violence, child abuse and wife beating: What do they have in common? In D. Finkelhor, R. J. Gelles, G. T. Hotaling, & M. A. Straus (Eds.), *The dark side of families: Current family violence research*. Beverly Hills, CA: Sage.

Straus, M. A. (1994). *Beating the devil out of them: Corporal punishment in American families*. Lexington, MA: Lexington Books.

Swenson, C. C., & Kolko, D. J. (2000). Long-term management of the developmental consequences of child physical abuse. In R. M. Reece (Ed.), *Treatment of child abuse: Common ground for mental health, medical, and legal practitioners* (pp. 271–288). Baltimore, MD: Johns Hopkins University Press.

Thomlison, B. (1997). Risk and protective factors in child maltreatment. In M. Fraser (Ed.), *Risk and resilience in childhood: An ecological perspective*. Washington, DC: National Association of Social Workers Press.

Toth, S., & Cicchetti, D. (1996). The impact of relatedness with mother on school functioning. *Journal of School Psychology, 34*, 247–266.

Tzeng, O. C. S., Jackson, J. W., & Karlson, H. C. (1991). *Theories of child abuse and neglect*. New York: Praeger.

U.S. Department of Health and Human Services, Administration for Children and Families, Administration for Children, Youth, and Families, Children's Bureau (2000). *Child maltreatment 2000*. Washington, DC: Author.

U.S. Department of Health and Human Services, Substance Abuse and Mental Health Services Administration. (2001). *Blending perspectives and building common ground. A report to Congress on substance abuse and child protection*. Washington, DC: Author.

Wellborn, J. G., & Connell, J. P. (1987). *Rochester Assessment Package for Children*. University of Rochester Children's Institute.

Whipple, E. E., & Webster-Stratton, C. (1991). The role of parental stress in physically abusive families. *Child Abuse and Neglect, 15*, 279–191.

Whiteman, M., Fanshel, D., & Grundy, J. F. (1987). Cognitive-behavioral interventions aimed at anger of parents at risk of child abuse. *Social Work, 32*, 469–474.

Wolfe, D. A. (1994). The role of intervention and treatment services in the prevention of child abuse and neglect. In G. B. Melton & F. D. Barry (Eds.), *Protecting children from abuse and neglect: Foundations for a new national strategy* (pp. 224–304). New York: Guilford.

Wolfe, D. A. (1999). *Child abuse: Implications for child development and psychopathology.* Thousand Oaks, CA: Sage.

Wolfe, D. A., Edwards, B., Manion, I., & Koverola, C. (1988). Early intervention for parents at risk of child abuse and neglect. *Journal of Consulting and Clinical Psychology, 56*, 40–47.

Wolfe, D. A., & Wekerle, C. (1993). Treatment strategies for child physical abuse and neglect: A critical progress report. *Clinical Psychology Review, 13*, 473–500.

Wolfe, V. V. (1998). Child sexual abuse. In E. J. Mash & R. A. Barkley (Eds.), *Treatment of childhood disorders.* New York: Guilford.

Zuravin, S., & DiBlasio, F. (1996). The correlates of child physical abuse and neglect by adolescent mothers. *Journal of Family Violence, 11*(2), 149–166.

INDEX

Page numbers in italics refer to tables in the text.

291